Parent – Infant Relationships

Monographs in Neonatology

Thomas K. Oliver, Jr., M.D.
Series Editor

Parent – Infant Relationships

Edited by

Paul M. Taylor, M.D.

Division of Neonatology
Magee-Women's Hospital
Department of Pediatrics
University of Pittsburgh School of Medicine
Pittsburgh, Pennsylvania

GRUNE & STRATTON

A Subsidiary of Harcourt Brace Jovanovich, Publishers

NEW YORK   LONDON   TORONTO   SYDNEY   SAN FRANCISCO

Grune & Stratton, Inc.
111 Fifth Avenue
New York, New York 10003

Distributed in the United Kingdom by
Academic Press, Inc. (London) Ltd.
24/28 Oval Road, London NW 1

Library of Congress Catalog Number 80-83727
International Standard Book Number 0-8089-1289-5
Printed in the United States of America

Contents

Foreword

I have long been interested in (and envious of) people who have made successful mid-career changes in their scientific lives. Paul Taylor, the editor of *Parent-Infant Relationships*, is such a person. For nearly two decades, Taylor devoted his attention to oxygen dissociation, pulmonary physiology and pathophysiology of the neonate, and to issues relating to intensive care of the prematurely born newborn. In these endeavors he brought distinction to himself, including elected membership in the Society for Pediatric Research and the American Physiological Society.

Then just a few years ago he decided to shift ground in a major way—to look critically at a number of issues relating to parent–infant relationships. By the time he decided to enter the field, both the scientific and lay community had been bombarded with the concepts of bonding and attachment. Although these were—and are—important concepts, the scientific rigor with which conclusions were reached was clearly open to some question. Taylor's entry into this field of inquiry, with his solid scientific background, has been a needed development.

In this book, Taylor presents some of his work, but in addition has successfully recruited a number of other leaders in the field to record their experiences. The volume is divided into three sections: Basic Developmental Processes; Influences of Professional Practices; and Relationships at Risk: Approaches to Intervention.

I believe this volume will be a vital text for investigators as well as practitioners in the field. It is indeed a welcome addition to the series, Monographs in Neonatology.

Thomas K. Oliver, Jr., M.D.
Series Editor

Preface

The essays presented here consider the general premise that practices and attitudes of providers of perinatal care influence the quality of the early parent–infant relationship and therefore, arguably, the developmental outcome of the child. Invited authorities from many of the disciplines concerned with child development and behavioral, psychological, and emotional aspects of child bearing and child rearing have addressed this premise from their particular points of view. I thank them for their cooperation and excellent contributions.

Effects of perinatal care practices on the parent–infant relationship are difficult to demonstrate with certainty. The several reviews in this volume face this issue squarely and emphasize the problem of assessing the impact of specific perinatal experiences on subsequent complex and multidetermined behaviors and relationships. Thus experimental studies cited in these reviews have yielded data that usually suggest, but rarely prove, effects of perinatal practices on the behaviors and relationships of parents and infants. When these studies are taken together, however, the strong sense emerges that how we care for families-to-be and new families does influence the quality of parent–infant relationships.

It is hardly visionary to maintain that parents are best prepared to establish a healthy relationship with their new baby if they are knowledgeable about infant behavior and child rearing; feel in control during labor, delivery, and the early postpartum period; have ready access to their infant and to each other during the postpartum hospital stay; and have had the benefits of screening of (and, if necessary, help with) their adaptations to pregnancy and early parenthood. Several of the essays detail practical approaches to achieving these ideal circumstances.

I hope this volume will prove of interest and value to students of infant and child development, and to those who both provide perinatal care and plan to improve practices and systems for its delivery in the future. And I trust that this work will stimulate further investigation of the development of parent–infant relationships, and of how perinatal caregivers can best facilitate these relationships to achieve their full potential for the development of both children and parents.

Contributors

William A. Altemeier, III, M.D.

Professor of Pediatrics
Vanderbilt University Medical School
Chief, Department of Pediatrics
Nashville General Hospital
Nashville, Tennessee

Roberta A. Ballard, M.D.

Chief, Department of Pediatrics
Mount Zion Hospital and Medical
    Center
San Francisco, California

Lee W. Bass, M.D.

Clinical Professor of Pediatrics
Department of Pediatrics
University of Pittsburgh School of
    Medicine
Pittsburgh, Pennsylvania

T. Berry Brazelton, M.D.

Associate Professor of Pediatrics
Harvard Medical School
Chief, Child Development Unit
The Children's Hospital Medical
    Center
Boston, Massachusetts

Elsie R. Broussard, M.D., De.P.H.

Professor of Public Health Psychiatry
Department of Health Services
    Administration
Graduate School of Public Health
University of Pittsburgh
Pittsburgh, Pennsylvania

Susan B. G. Campbell, Ph.D.

Associate Professor
Department of Psychology
University of Pittsburgh
Pittsburgh, Pennsylvania

Richard L. Cohen, M.D.

Professor and Chief of Child Psychiatry
Department of Psychiatry
University of Pittsburgh School of
    Medicine
Western Psychiatric Institute and Clinic
Pittsburgh, Pennsylvania

Christy A. Cutler, M.A.

Research Associate
The National Center for the
    Prevention and
    Treatment of Child Abuse
    and Neglect
Department of Pediatrics
University of Colorado Medical Center
Denver, Colorado

**Sheena Davidson, B.A., R.N., B.Sc.N.,
M.S.N.**

Assistant Professor
School of Nursing
University of British Columbia
Vancouver, Canada

Martha F. Davison, M.D.

Fellow, Child Guidance Center
Children's Hospital
University of Pennsylvania
Philadelphia, Pennsylvania

Janet G. Dean, B.A.

The National Center for the
    Prevention and
    Treatment of Child Abuse
    and Neglect
Department of Pediatrics
University of Colorado Medical Center
Denver, Colorado

Peter DeChateau, M.D.

Associate Professor
Department of Pediatrics
Karolinska Institute
Karolinska Hospital
Fack
Stockholm, Sweden

Robert N. Emde, M.D.

Professor of Psychiatry
Department of Psychiatry
University of Colorado Medical School
Adjunct Professor of Psychology
University of Denver
Denver, Colorado

Carolyn B. Ferris, R.N.

Coordinator, Alternative Birth
    Center
Department of Pediatrics
Mount Zion Hospital and Medical
    Center
San Francisco, California

Peter A. Gorski, M.D.

Director of Developmental and
    Behavioral Pediatrics
Department of Pediatrics
Mount Zion Hospital and Medical
    Center
Assistant Clinical Professor of
    Pediatrics
University of California, San Francisco
San Francisco, California

Jane D. Gray, M.D.

The National Center for the
    Prevention and
    Treatment of Child Abuse
    and Neglect
Department of Pediatrics
University of Colorado Medical Center
Denver, Colorado

Barbara Lee Hall, M.S.W., A.C.S.W.

Assistant Director, Department of
    Medical Social Work
Magee-Women's Hospital
Pittsburgh, Pennsylvania

Shelley Hymel, M.A.

Department of Psychology
University of Illinois at
    Champaign-Urbana
Champaign, Illinois

Nancy A. Irvin, M.S.S.A.

Research Social Worker
Department of Pediatrics
Mount Zion Hospital and Medical
    Center
San Francisco, California

Lesley A. Joy, B.Sc., M.A.

Department of Psychology
Simon Fraser University
Burnaby, B.C., Canada

C. Henry Kempe, M.D.

Director, The National Center for the
    Prevention and
    Treatment of Child Abuse
    and Neglect
Department of Pediatrics
University of Colorado Medical Center
Denver, Colorado

Carol H. Leonard, Ph.D.

Research Psychologist
Department of Pediatrics
Mount Zion Hospital and Medical
    Center
San Francisco, California

Klaus K. Minde, M.D., F.R.C.P. (C)

Professor of Psychiatry and Pediatrics
University of Toronto
The Hospital for Sick Children
Toronto, Ontario
Canada

Susan O'Connor, M.D.

Assistant Professor of Pediatrics
Vanderbilt University Medical School
Assistant Chief
Department of Pediatrics
Nashville General Hospital
Nashville, Tennessee

Howard J. Osofsky, M.D., Ph.D.

Staff and Research Psychiatrist
Menninger Foundation
Clinical Professor of Gynecology and
    Obstetrics
University of Kansas Medical School
Topeka, Kansas

Joy D. Osofsky, Ph.D.

Staff and Research Psychologist
Menninger Foundation
Adjunct Associate Professor
Department of Human Development
University of Kansas
Topeka, Kansas

Susan Lee Painter, B.A., M.A.

Department of Psychology
University of British Columbia
Vancouver, Canada

Ross D. Parke, Ph.D.

Professor of Psychology
Department of Psychology
University of Illinois at
    Champaign-Urbana
Champaign, Illinois

Thomas G. Power, M.A.

Department of Psychology
University of Illinois at
    Champaign-Urbana
Champaign, Illinois

Howard M. Sandler, Ph.D.

Associate Professor
Department of Psychology
Peabody College of Vanderbilt
    University
Nashville, Tennessee

Kathryn B. Sherrod, Ph.D.

Assistant Professor
Department of Psychology
Peabody College of Vanderbilt
    University
Nashville, Tennessee

Paul M. Taylor, M.D.

Professor of Pediatrics, and Obstetrics
    and Gynecology
University of Pittsburgh School of
    Medicine
Director, Division of Neonatology
Magee-Women's Hospital
Pittsburgh, Pennsylvania

Barbara R. Tinsley, M.A.

Department of Psychology
University of Illinois at
    Champaign-Urbana
Champaign, Illinois

Peter M. Vietze, Ph.D.

Senior Staff Fellow and Research
    Psychologist
Child and Family Research Branch
National Institute of Child Health and
    Human Development
Bethesda, Maryland

Tannis MacBeth Williams, B.A., M.S.,
    Ph.D.

Associate Professor
Department of Psychology
University of British Columbia
Vancouver, Canada

Jerome H. Wolfson, M.D.

Clinical Professor of Pediatrics
Department of Pediatrics
University of Pittsburgh School of
    Medicine
Pittsburgh, Pennsylvania

PART I

Basic Developmental Processes

Susan B. G. Campbell
and Paul M. Taylor

1

Bonding and Attachment: Theoretical Issues

It is an accepted principle of child development that a warm, nurturing, and consistent relationship between infant and parents is essential for healthy psychological development. Recent observations have increased our understanding of important aspects of early parent–infant relationships, yet a tendency to confuse the related concepts of attachment and bonding and to move well beyond the data has led to conclusions with complex and far-reaching implications for hospital care of newborns. The notions of bonding and attachment have a bearing on obstetric and pediatric hospital care practices, especially in view of the recent American Medical Association guidelines to promote "attachment and bonding of mothers and their infants." It is the goal of this paper to examine the concepts of parent–infant bonding[1] and parent–infant attachment,[2] both central constructs with profound implications for an understanding of normal social-emotional and cognitive development.

The term 'bonding' is used most often to refer to a rapid process, occurring immediately after birth, that reflects mother-to-infant attachment. Bonding is seen as being facilitated by physical contact between a mother and her newborn through skin-to-skin contact, suckling, mutual visual regard, and fondling. The quality of bonding is studied by observing affectionate behaviors that the mother shows toward her infant, primarily touching, eye contact, holding, and caressing, which are assumed to reflect that "bond." Research and theory on bonding are particularly associated with the work of Klaus

and Kennell,[1] who used the terms bonding and attachment inter-
changeably.

Most students of parent–infant interaction use the term attachment somewhat differently. Introduced by Bowlby,[2,3] the term attachment has come to refer to a hypothetical construct reflecting the
quality of the affectional tie between infant and parents, especially
mother, that develops gradually during the first year of life.

Thus, both bonding and attachment refer to aspects of the affectional relationship between parents and infants. Bonding is primarily
unidirectional (parent→infant), rapid (within the first hours or days
after birth), and facilitated or optimized by physical contact. Attachment, on the other hand, is reciprocal (mother⇌infant), develops
gradually during the first year of life, and is influenced by psychological variables such as the quality, timing, and pacing of adult-child
encounters.

It can be argued that the establishment of a strong mother-to-
infant bond immediately post-partum should facilitate the development of mother–infant attachment during the first year by sensitizing
mothers to their infants' cues, thereby enhancing the quality of the
mother–infant interaction. This is a theoretical possibility as yet
unsupported by data.

Theories of bonding and attachment are predicated on the ethol-
ogic observations that particular species–specific behavior patterns
are highly predictable and are regularly elicited by certain stimulus
configurations, especially when the organism is in a state of biologic
readiness.[1,2,4] Thus subhuman mammalian mothers and newborn
infants instinctively behave, from the time of the infant's birth, in
ways that promote proximity between mother and infant and thereby
facilitate caretaking behavior. Species-specific behavior patterns of
the infant seem to release maternal behaviors at a time when mothers
appear to be particularly sensitive to such cues. Such behaviors have
survival value for both the individual infant and the species. Observations of disrupted or disturbed maternal caretaking behavior following brief experimental separation of newborn rats,[5] goats,[6] and monkeys[7] from their mothers have led to the speculation that in the
human, too, there may exist an especially sensitive period for the
development of optimal mother–infant bonding.[1,8,9]

Species-specific maternal and infant behavior patterns of animals
are stereotyped in contrast to the wider range of behavior observed in
human mothers and infants that serves the goal of species survival.[2,10]
There are both invariant and variant features to this behavior.
Invariant features transcend cultural, geographic, and personality
differences. For instance, infant cries alert the caretaker, who will

then usually approach the infant and engage in some behavior such as soothing, feeding, or changing the infant's diaper. These caretaking behaviors in turn will usually quiet the infant, who will then engage in behaviors such as rooting, sucking, eye contact, or cuddling. Individual differences in mothers and infants as well as variations in cultural practices will influence the specifics of the maternal response as well as its timing and effect.

BONDING

Klaus and Kennell[1] suggested that there exists a sensitive period immediately after birth during which the human mother is most likely to develop strong affectional bonds with her infant, and further suggested that the traditional separation of mothers and infants at birth following hospital delivery may impair the establishment of an optimal mothering relationship and later psychologic adjustment: "It is our hypothesis that this entire range of problems [from mild maternal anxiety to child abuse] may result largely from separation and other unusual circumstances which occur in the early newborn period as a consequence of present hospital care policies." It is in response to this conviction that the AMA underlined the importance of facilitating bonding by permitting mothers and infants to remain together in the period immediately after birth.

The initial formulation by Klaus and Kennell of a maternal sensitive period was based on studies that indicated that separation of infant from mother immediately after birth could lead to a disruption of mothering in certain animal species.[1,9,11] Observations of interactional problems in some mothers separated from newborn infants because of illness or prematurity strengthened their analogy between the animal data and deviant maternal behavior in humans.[9,12] Further analysis of hospital care practices in which even healthy newborns are separated from their mothers at birth prompted these pediatricians to postulate an adverse effect of immediate postpartum separation of mothers and infants and to suggest that immediate contact between mother and newborn might facilitate mother-to-infant bonding.[1,11]

Evidence for the existence of a sensitive period and the potentially damaging effects of separation have been drawn from retrospective studies of the epidemiology of parenting failures and from studies of the effects of early contact on breastfeeding and mother–infant interaction. Review of these studies indicates that the conclusions and statements they have generated go beyond what the data actually prove. Although Klaus and Kennell[1] suggested that a number of long-term negative consequences may result from mother–infant separation at birth, only four studies have actually observed mother–infant interaction beyond the hospital stay,[11,13–16] and systematic observations of infant behavior have rarely been included.[14,16,17] A number of studies have paired early contact with rooming-in or other modifications in routines that were not adequately controlled. Furthermore, the studies were based on small samples in which a number of potentially confounding variables were not considered. The possibility of a sensitive period shortly after birth during which separation may impede optimal mother–infant bonding has recently been picked up and oversimplified by the mass media and is being accepted with enthusiasm by a growing number of consumers. Analysis of the evidence on which the notion of a sensitive period is based seems in order.

Premature and sick infants are overrepresented among cases of child abuse and psychosocial failure to thrive.[18–20] It has been suggested that parenting failures associated with prematurity and other problems at birth may result from the early separation of mother and infant.[1,11,13] It must be kept in mind, however, that these studies were contaminated by a variety of uncontrolled variables, such as poverty, family disorganization, parental psychopathology, and poor prenatal care, all of which are associated with premature and other high-risk births as well as with distortions in parenting. If separation due to illness results in an impairment in the bonding process, this should be reflected in patterns of interaction, yet studies of mother–infant interaction in matched groups of mothers of full-term infants and those medically at risk have not unequivocally shown less affectionate or appropriate mothering among mothers of premature or sick infants.[21–25] Two studies specifically reported more protective and affectionate behavior from mothers of high-risk infants.[21,22]

The strongest support to date for the Klaus and Kennell position comes from a recent prospective study by O'Connor et al.,[26] who reported that rooming-in was associated with decreased incidence of parenting failure. Only one case of child abuse was reported for the 134 who roomed-in, as compared with 8 cases of battering, neglect, or failure to thrive among the 143 infants given traditional nursery care. Rooming-in infants and their mothers were not given early contact, but were brought together after the first seven hours.

Several studies from Sweden, Brazil, and Guatemala reviewed by Klaus and Kennell[1] and by Lozoff et al.[27] indicated that skin-to-skin contact and early suckling within the first hour after birth are associated with prolonged breastfeeding. So far, data on only one of these samples have been reported beyond the first three months.[14] Although the maintenance of breastfeeding is associated with fewer infections during infancy and with better nutrition among infants in developing countries,[1,2,4] it is not necessarily an index of mother-to-infant bonding. A host of factors other than maternal feelings will influence the decision to breastfeed, as well as how long it is continued.

The crucial test of the hypothesis that early contact will have a long-term influence on maternal behavior must come from studies that observe mother–infant interaction over time and find continuing differences between mother–infant dyads who did and did not experience close physical contact immediately postpartum. Six studies have actually addressed the issue of mother–infant interaction directly by making systematic observations of behavior.[11,13–16,28,29] Those studies that have followed their samples beyond the period of hospitalization yield equivocal results.

Klaus, Kennell, and associates were the first to attempt to assess the effects of extra, early contact on later mother–infant interaction.[11,13,30] Fourteen inner-city, bottle-feeding primigravidas, mainly poor, black, and unmarried, received their naked infants for one hour during the first three hours after birth, and for five hours each day for the next three days. Control mothers matched on demographic variables were treated in the standard manner: a glimpse of the baby after delivery, a brief contact at 12 hours, and then contact for scheduled feedings at four hour intervals. Data collected at one month[11] and at one year[13] indicated that mothers in the extra-contact group were more affectionate and expressed more positive attitudes toward their infants than control mothers. At one year, although extended-contact mothers were more responsive to their infants' distress during a physical examination, they did not differ from control mothers in their behavior during free play, during a structured interview, or during psychological testing of their infant. Assessment of maternal speech at two years[30] indicated that a better linguistic environment for their children's language learning was provided by a subsample of five extra-contact mothers than by a subsample of five regular-contact mothers.

De Chateau[14] also studied the effect of extra close physical contact on mothering behavior at 36 hours, 3 months, and 1 year in a sample of Swedish middle-class primigravidas. His experimental manipulation lasted a mere 15 minutes, beginning 20 minutes after delivery, during which a group of 22 women were permitted skin-to-skin contact with and suckling by their naked infant. A matched group of 20 women served as controls. Each group received identical modified rooming-in care. Early-contact mothers held their infants more at 36 hours. At a three month home visit, extended-contact mothers held their infants in the "en face" position more often and kissed their infants more, and their infants were likewise more responsive and alert. At one year, extra-contact mothers were more affectionate than control mothers with their children (see Chapter 7). These findings were accounted for by differences between extended-contact and regular-contact mothers of boys, but not of girls. Comparison of the extended-contact primiparous mothers with a sample of regular-contact multiparous mothers at 36 hours showed no differences.

A recent study by Carlsson et al.[28] noted more affectionate behavior during nursing at two and four days in Swedish women permitted skin-to-skin contact with their babies for the first one-to-two hours after delivery than in controls not given extra contact. Postpartum contact exerted this effect whether or not it was paired with a more flexible and supportive ward routine. When a home feeding was observed at six weeks postpartum, however, no differences were found between extra- and regular-contact groups on 18 maternal and infant behaviors,[16] nor did maternal interviews on early postpartum and caretaking experiences reveal differences. While Carlsson et al. did not examine their data for sex by contact interactions, their results are intriguing, particularly in view of our own similar findings.

We and Dr. Floyd Taylor are conducting a study at the University of Pittsburgh to test the hypotheses that one hour of extra contact postpartum will be associated with enhanced maternal affectionate behavior toward, and perception of, her infant, as well as increased attachment of infant-to-mother at one year and improved subsequent psychological, cognitive, and language development. We have overcome the sample-size problem by randomly assigning 100 white, middle-class primigravidas to extra-contact and control groups. The two groups are similar as to salient demographic factors and as to details of management of labor and delivery. Analgesics, which influence infant responsiveness following birth,[34] were administered similarly to experimental and control mothers.

Analysis of data on the first 50 dyads[15] indicates a more positive feeding interaction between extra-contact mothers and their male infants when observed in hospital at two days and at home at one month. Consistent with de Chateau,[14] however, no effects of extra-contact were found for female infant–mother dyads. Further, in line with Carlsson,[16] this effect had disappeared by one year when infants and mothers were assessed on a complex measure of attachment.[17] More detailed data analysis on 68 mother–infant dyads indicates virtually no differences between extra- and regular-contact pairs, examined separately by sex of infant, in the quality of attachment or the quantity of specific maternal or infant behaviors observed at one year postpartum. Further, no differences in cognitive functioning were found at one year.

When the early studies of bonding, which attempt to establish the existence of a sensitive period and to define its limits, are carefully scrutinized, their weaknesses become apparent. For example, Hales et al.[29] compared the effects of immediate and delayed skin-to-skin contact and routine hospital care. Twenty lower-class Guatemalan women were left with their nude firstborn infants immediately after birth, while an additional 20 women were first permitted contact with their firstborn nude infants 12 hours postpartum. A third group was presented with their infant wrapped in a blanket at 12 hours. Observations of feeding behavior were made at 36 hours. Affectionate behaviors were defined as eye contact with, looking at, talking to, kissing, smiling at, and fondling the baby. Intensity of affectionate behavior was greatest for the early nude-contact group, intermediate for the delayed nude-contact group, and lowest for the delayed wrapped-contact group. Analysis of the individual behaviors indicated that eye-to-eye contact or holding the infant in the "en face" position accounted for the aggregate differences and was the only variable significantly higher in the early-contact group. Although Hales et al. considered these to be results in support of a sensitive period and an early-contact effect, it is noteworthy that the groups of mothers did not differ significantly in the frequency of looking at, talking to, kissing, smiling at, or fondling their infants or in the amount of holding during nonfeeding times. These would certainly be considered attachment behaviors. Thus if a significant effect of early contact actually occurred, it was a weak one indeed.

In summary, extra physical contact between mother and infant shortly after delivery is associated with prolonged breastfeeding and increased maternal affectionate behavior during the lying-in period and, in three longer-term studies, at one month, three months, and one year. These findings have been interpreted as evidence for the existence of a sensitive period during which mothers are most likely to form a strong affectional tie to their infants.[1,27,29] The Klaus and Kennell study is widely quoted as supporting the concept of a sensitive period immediately after birth. That interpretation is difficult to accept, since their experimental design featured both one hour of relatively early contact (i.e., during the first three hours) and a total of 15 hours of rooming-in over the first three days. Moreover, the underprivileged women in that study were especially likely to benefit from the extra attention given them and their infants by the hospital staff. The striking findings by O'Connor et al.[26] that rooming-in alone was associated with virtual elimination of gross parenting breakdown in families at high psychosocial risk indicate that extra contact subsequent to the first hours of life may have explained much of the effect of Klaus and Kennell's experimental manipulation. De Chateau's provocative observations, on the other hand, provide support for the existence of a sensitive period within minutes of birth during which the firstborn infant's presence with or absence from his mother affects maternal behavior and possibly the infant's development through the first year of his life. The failure of Carlsson to find effects lasting beyond the hospital stay and our findings which also indicate that early contact effects dissipate over the first year of life suggest, however, that this phenomenon has been greatly overinterpreted in both the research and clinical literature.

The outcome variables in the studies by Klaus and Kennell and by de Chateau are complex and multidetermined behaviors. Even though both research groups studied relatively homogenous sets of mothers, their study populations were sufficiently small that it cannot be assumed that all or even most major variables that might potentially confound results were equally distributed between extra-contact and control groups. For this reason, these studies are compatible with, but do not conclusively prove, the existence of a postpartum sensitive period. Further, the nonconfirmatory findings of other studies, indicate that this issue is far from resolved.

Future studies should address the role of the infant in the reciprocal interactions involved in the development of bonding and subsequent attachment.[2] Recent observations of newborns indicate that they are wide-eyed and alert for about one hour after birth and then become drowsy and fall asleep.[31-33] The duration of this alert period appears to be influenced by the amount and type of medication administered during labor and delivery.[34] Prophylactic administration of silver nitrate solution, routinely given during the first few minutes of life, interferes with the newborn's tendency to visually scan the environment[35] and engage in brief, though intense, eye contact with mother or others in visual proximity. (Silver nitrate solution was deferred for hours in each of the extra-contact studies cited above.) Variations in obstetric and early neonatal care practices may thus influence both the infant's early stimulation and responsiveness. It follows that such care practices may well modify the effects of early contact and must be taken into account whenever the impact of early contact is assessed.

Individual differences present from birth in the infant's ability to elicit interaction and in such behaviors as the frequency and duration of crying, soothability, cuddliness, and visual alertness have been documented by Brazelton[36] and Korner.[37] The effect of these individual differences on the process of bonding, however, has not been systematically studied. It is logical to suppose that different infants will elicit different patterns of mothering and that these individual differences should begin to exert their influence from the first contact between infant and mother. The infant may be seen as an active partner in the establishment of reciprocal patterns of interaction. This has been discussed by several investigators who documented the mutual and reciprocal flow of interaction between mother and infant in the first weeks of life.[38-40] Observations of early feeding indicate that more alert and responsive infants elicit more stimulation,[40] and there is no reason to suppose that this process should not begin at birth and influence the development of bonding. To date, however, studies of bonding have looked primarily at maternal affectionate behavior with little emphasis on the infant's role in the process.

The importance of knowledge of the infant's behavior to a better understanding of the bonding process is illustrated by a closer examination of data from de Chateau's study. A number of infant and maternal behaviors were observed during home visits at three months. Early-contact infants were more visually alert, laughed more, and cried less. Early-contact mothers looked at their infants more "en face" and kissed them more. The reciprocal nature of these behaviors is obvious, but cause–effect relationships are difficult to disentangle. Mothers may more often look at and kiss infants who are more visually alert when held in the "en face" position. The observations of Stern and others[38-40] suggest that a mutually regulated sequence of interaction is being maintained by both partners regardless of who initiates a particular sequence. In the absence of longitudinal data on early infant characteristics such as visual alertness, cuddliness, and soothability, it is difficult to conclude that the 15 minutes of extra contact alone led to the differences in mothers that in turn influenced maternal and infant behavior at 3 months. It is possible that the extra-contact infants were more alert and positive in mood to begin with or became so as a result of the extra contact. In other words, it is conceivable that in small study samples a chance preponderance of alert, reactive infants in extra-contact groups could account for much of the effect attributed to early contact.

We feel that it is both humane and natural for the healthy baby to be together with mother and father shortly after birth. Most parents who have been with their newborn infant from birth describe becoming acquainted with the infant at that time to be an enriching and memorable experience. Whether or not early and extended contact leads to other than experiential benefits, we feel that it should be offered to all healthy mothers, fathers, and infants. The desirability of early contact stands quite independent of the idea that it is a facilitator of, much less a precondition for, subsequent optimal mother–infant interactions and relationships. Such a notion puts unnecessary constraints on human adaptability and resilience, and it fails to account for satisfactory attachments between most adults and their foster or adopted children[41] and satisfactory psychosocial development of most premature infants.[42]

The growing wave of enthusiasm for early mother–infant contact, generated partially by the hope (as yet unsupported by data) for long-lasting developmental benefits for the infant, contains significant potential dangers. We are concerned that early contact may come to be accepted by some physicians as a panacea for incipient psychosocial problems and that reliance on it may delay appropriate intervention. It is also troubling to contemplate that as the public may come to regard early contact as an important requirement for mental health, those mothers who must be separated from their infants for reasons beyond their control may be burdened by guilt and, furthermore, may initiate a self-fulfilling prophecy of negative interactions with the infant. We recommend that parents who wished but were unable to enjoy early contact with their infant be counseled that early contact, although pleasant and desirable, is in no way essential for optimal parent–infant bonding and subsequent interactions and relationships with the child. Such parents might benefit by being told of the usual good developmental outcome of premature and adopted infants, many of whom experience prolonged separation from their parents before initial contact.

ATTACHMENT

The complexity of affective development is well illustrated by a consideration of the work on mother–infant attachment. Attachment theory, first outlined by Bowlby[2,3] and elaborated by Ainsworth[10,43] and others,[44,45] is based on the concept that the affectional tie between mother and infant develops out of species-specific response patterns preprogrammed to ensure that infants will be cared for and, therefore, that the species will survive. A large body of evidence confirms many of Bowlby's ideas about the development of the attachment relationship during the first year of life. Findings relating the quality of attachment at one year to earlier mother–infant interaction and to later social and cognitive development are of particular theoretical and practical importance.

According to Bowlby,[2] the infant's crying, smiling, sucking, clinging, and, later, following serve the goal of initiating or maintaining proximity between mother and infant and qualify as attachment behaviors. Crying and smiling are considered social signaling systems that tend to bring the mother into contact with the infant. Once contact is achieved it can be maintained by clinging and sucking. Both the infant and the mother can initiate and maintain contact. Thus from the beginning both mother and infant are active partners in the development of a reciprocal system of interaction.

Attachment behaviors in early infancy are seen as species-specific social responses that can be elicited by any member of the species. With development of the infant's perceptual, cognitive, and affective systems these responses become more complex, are influenced by a greater range of stimuli, and are directed toward specific figures in the environment. At the time the infant is three months old any adult can elicit a social smile; by eight months it is likely that only parents or other familiar figures will elicit a smile immediately upon encounter. The rapid approach of an unfamiliar person may cause distress in some infants, while it is highly unlikely that rapid approach of the mother will lead to distress; it may, on the contrary, terminate crying. Similarly, being picked up by any adult is likely to terminate crying in the three-month-old, but not in the eight-month-old infant. Thus with development, attachment behaviors are directed differentially to various people in the infant's environment. Moreover, the same behavior may have different meanings depending on the context. For example, crying may be a signal to a stranger not to approach.

Others have increased the list of attachment behaviors to include other forms of social interaction such as looking at, vocalizing to, and engaging in play.[46,47] Since infants often look at, approach, and vocalize to adults to whom they are not attached, this highlights the distinction between attachment and attachment behavior. Attachment is a hypothetical construct indicating an enduring affectional relationship that organizes our explanations of behavior and exists independent of time and space, while attachment behaviors permit inferences about attachment only in particular circumstances.[43,44] No one behavior or constellation of behaviors in and of itself can be taken as evidence of attachment, since the expression of the affective tie between mother and infant varies with the developmental level of the child and the typical interaction patterns of individual mother–infant pairs.

A behavior indicating attachment in one situation may indicate something very different in another. Anyone who has interacted with a one-year-old child is aware that playful, affiliative, and exploratory behaviors may be directed at a friendly but nonintrusive stranger more often than toward a mother. Thus the one-year-old child in the pediatrician's office may be quite content to play with toys, talk to the doctor, and even examine the doctor's beard or glasses as long as mother is nearby and nothing remotely threatening is happening. Although some components of attachment behavior also may be directed toward the pediatrician in this example, namely looking at, vocalizing to, approaching, and even touching, these affiliative and exploratory behaviors cannot be construed as attachment behaviors, although they might be if directed at mother. Moreover, once the physical examination begins and the situation changes from pleasant social interaction to one that is potentially threatening or uncomfortable, thereby eliciting distress, it becomes obvious to any observer who the attachment figure is. The normally attached infant in this situation usually seeks comfort by approaching, clinging to, and crying for his mother. This is one example of what Ainsworth described as the balance between attachment and exploration.[43,48] In the initial stages of a novel but nonthreatening situation, the securely attached infant uses the mother as a secure base from which to explore things and people in the environment. Once the situation changes, however, and an element of threat appears, the balance shifts away from exploration to attachment and the mother becomes a source of protection and comfort.

This illustrates several main features of the attachment relationship. It is characterized by differential responsiveness, particularly when the infant is under stress. Furthermore, stress leads the infant to seek contact with the attachment figure, and the infant derives comfort from that contact. The mother or other attachment figure serves as a secure base from which the infant explores. Additional features of attachment include some protest at separation and greeting upon reunion. As Sroufe and Waters[44] pointed out, however, the quality of attachment cannot be inferred from the amount of clinging or the intensity of separation protest. Attachment is a qualitative, not quantitative, concept. The securely attached infant sure of mother's return may not protest at separation, but will acknowledge her return and then actively seek social interaction with her.

Studies that clarify the relationship between the quality of attachment and other features of the infant's social and cognitive development are of particular importance in understanding the nature of attachment. Early mother–infant interaction patterns are reflected in the quality of the attachment relationship at one year. A series of in-depth studies by Ainsworth and her colleagues have shown that early maternal behavior influences later attachment.[48–53] Of central importance is the responsiveness of the mother to the infant's signals, her ability to respond appropriately and sensitively to the infant's cues. Mothers who responded to their infants abruptly or who paced their behavior to their own needs or schedules rather than to the infant's differed from more sensitive mothers in their behaviors in a number of situations. Their infants, in turn, were found to be less securely attached when studied in a standardized laboratory situation, the Ainsworth Strange Situation, at one year of age.

Ainsworth and her coworkers found associations between mothers' responsiveness to crying, acceptance of the infant, flexibility of feeding schedules, and quality of their social interaction with the infant. Mothers responsive to infant cries also tend to engage their infants in more playful interactions and to feed them on demand schedules. These mothers were characterized by Ainsworth as correctly reading their infant's communications and responding to them promptly and appropriately, as accepting their infants along with the temporary restriction they placed on their activities, and as cooperating rather than interfering with their baby's ongoing activities. Mothers at the other extreme tend not to react quickly or at all to their infant's cries, spend more time engaged in caretaking than in playful face-to-face interaction, and tend to feed their infants on a rigid schedule whether or not the infant is hungry. These mothers tend to be relatively insensitive to their infant's communications and tend not to respond to them contingently. They may be rejecting and resentful of their infants and tend to be controlling with minimal concern for the infant's mood or wishes. Many mothers, of course, fall between these extremes on the continua Ainsworth called sensitivity–insensitivity, cooperation–interference, and acceptance–rejection.[49,51]

These patterns of maternal behavior are associated with a number of specific infant behaviors that have important implications for childrearing practices. Infants whose cries were ignored at three months tended to cry more during the last quarter of the first year than infants whose mothers were responsive to their cries.[52] Similarly, infants whose mothers were more responsive to their signals tended to be more compliant[51] and to become less upset by routine, everyday separations.[50] These patterns of maternal responses were also related in predictable ways to patterns of attachment in a standardized laboratory situation, suggesting that infants who learn that their needs will be met and their signals responded to develop certain expectations about the environment, as well as feelings of mastery and competence.[45,51] Out of this develops a sense of security akin to what Erickson called "basic trust."[54] Secure and content, these infants are free to contend with the developmental tasks of exploration and environmental mastery.

The Ainsworth Strange Situation[48] is frequently used to assess the attachment of mother and infant; it also provides an excellent illustration of what is meant by the quality of attachment. In a set sequence of brief episodes, the infant's reactions to a new environment, a strange adult, and separation from and reunion with mother are observed. This standardized laboratory situation permits comparability across subjects and also highlights separation and reunion behaviors more clearly than do naturalistic observations.[44] During an initial free play period with mother present, it is possible to assess the infant's use of the mother as a base for exploration of a new and interesting environment. The appearance of a friendly, nonintrusive stranger permits assessment of the infant's social interaction with a strange adult with mother present as well as the infant's reaction to the stranger when mother has left. The infant's behavior when left alone and upon reunion with mother is then observed.

Three general patterns of attachment have been described by Ainsworth and coworkers and replicated by others.[43,44,48–53] The securely attached infant tends to explore the environment and show interest in the stranger when mother is present. Her departure leads to a decrease in exploratory behavior and decreased interest in the stranger, who may or may not be some source of comfort. Securely attached infants show clearly differential behavior upon the mother's return, however. They greet her by some combination of running and clinging, holding out their arms, and smiling and vocalizing. They settle reasonably quickly once reunited and resume their play. Ambivalently attached infants may or may not explore the environment and show interest in the stranger. The main characteristic of their ambivalent behavior is seen during reunion with mother, when they show a mixture of seeking and resisting contact with her. Sroufe and Waters[44] noted the angry quality to this behavior. Mother-avoidant infants tend to resist contact on reunion and to be less distressed than other infants when left alone with the stranger. Behavior toward the stranger and mother is less differential than that shown by securely or ambivalently attached infants. These patterns of attachment appear to persist over time: Matas et al.[55] reported that 48 of 50 infants were classified similarly when assessed in the strange situation at 12 months and again at 18 months.

These patterns of attachment at one year appear to be related to the quality of mother–infant interaction throughout the first year of life.[48-53] Maternal responsiveness, acceptance, and cooperation are associated with secure patterns of attachment at one year. Similarly, ambivalent and avoidant behaviors are associated with a greater tendency for mother to be insensitive, less accepting, and more interfering. Main[56] reported that mothers of infants who avoided or ignored their mothers during reunion in the strange situation tended, during earlier home observations, to reject physical contact with their infants, to express anger toward them, and to be generally cold and unexpressive. Mothers of securely attached infants, on the other hand, usually engaged their infants in positive, playful, face-to-face inter-action at home during the first four months.[43] Unreplicated studies indicate that securely attached infants have more advanced cognitive development at one year[57] and are more competent in their approach to problem solving at two years.[55] Mothers of the securely attached group were more supportive of their infants during a problem-solving observation at two years.

The long-term stability of these qualitative aspects of the attach-ment relationship and their implications for later social, emotional, and cognitive development remain to be explored, yet there is a growing body of evidence relating positive mother–infant interaction to more competent cognitive functioning through the preschool years.[58] Furthermore, there is evidence that securely attached infants form more positive relationships with others.[59] It is reasonable to hypoth-esize that the quality of attachment will also influence the quality of relations with peers and that a secure attachment will be reflected in more positive peer interaction in preschool and school-age youngsters.

The relationship between bonding and attachment should by now be clear. If indeed early contact heightens maternal feelings of affection and sensitivity to the infant's individual response style, this should be reflected in the patterns of caretaking that have been shown to influence the quality of attachment at one year. Thus the increased mutual visual regard and holding reported in the early-contact studies should in fact be associated with subsequent increased maternal responsiveness to infant cries and social bids and not merely an increase in the frequency of these behaviors. If this is so, extra, early postpartum contact should lead to more secure mother–infant attach-ment at one year. We are currently testing the hypothesis that early contact will be associated with an increased number of infants classified as securely attached in the Ainsworth Strange Situation at one year. Preliminary analysis of the interactions of 68 mother–infant pairs does not support this hypothesis.

IMPLICATIONS

There is suggestive evidence that early mother–infant contact immediately postpartum may influence the quality of later mother–infant attachment. This area needs much further research, especially since the studies to date have been interpreted by some to suggest that early contact will prevent parenting failures and other forms of child psychopathology that stem from disturbed parent–child relationships. Studies published to date on the effects of early contact have been short-term observations of small numbers of mother–infant dyads with inadequate comparisons of the multiplicity of variables that may influence the quality of attachment. The contributions of the infants to the development of maternal–infant bonding remain to be studied.

The concept of attachment as outlined by Bowlby and Ainsworth highlights the complexity of human behavior by describing the reciprocal nature of the development of the attachment relationship and its changes over time[2–10] and underscores the importance of examining patterns of interaction rather than discrete behaviors and of examining them in context.[43,47] Data from a large number of studies suggest that the quality of mother–infant attachment influences later social, affective, and cognitive development.

This concept has several clinical implications. Until more data are in on the effects of early contact, intervention and prevention programs for mothers and infants must look beyond bonding to attachment. Enhancing maternal sensitivity through early mother–infant contact and more family-centered obstetric care are only steps in a process that should begin with parenting education during the first pregnancy, if not earlier.

Disturbances in the development of young children often result from parental mishandling that reflects either ignorance about the process of development or inappropriate childrearing practices. One cannot assume that all parents will accurately read their infant's signals and know how to respond appropriately or that they will have an adequate understanding of child development. For example, many parents think that very young infants need only milk, a dry diaper, and sleep. They are surprised to learn about the capacities of the newborn and that infants require physical contact and cognitive stimulation.

Understanding the meaning of behaviors at different ages is important as well. In the first few months of life, infant cries usually signal discomfort or distress. Often parents report that they ignore such cries for fear of "spoiling" the infant. Where immediate responses to all cries of the ten-month-old child, regardless of context, would indeed be inappropriate and likely to lead to problems, it is hardly likely that the cries of the six-week-old infant are manipulative attempts to control the parents. In view of the findings of Bell and Ainsworth[52] on maternal responsiveness to early crying and later crying and attachment, this may be an important pointer for some parents. Parent education programs, particularly for groups at risk for parenting problems, appear to be logical and necessary supplements to the humanization of hospital care practices.

In addition to parent education programs, which are preventive in nature, we must be more sensitive to early interactional problems between parent and infant, and prepared to intervene as early as possible in the developmental sequence. It is often clear when observing mother and infant during a routine physical exam or during free play in the waiting room that problems exist. Intervention strategies that focus on the quality of parent–child interaction and provide parents with alternative ways of relating to their infant are more likely to achieve results than nondirective counseling methods.[60] Moreover, intervention and prevention programs must be focused on both parents rather than available only to mothers. Infants seek comfort from and contact with fathers as well as mothers. Recent evidence supports the clinical awareness of the father's important contribution to the infant's later psychosocial development.[61] Despite the emphasis in the developmental literature on mother–infant interaction, Schaffer and Emerson,[59] in one of the early studies on attachment, noted that the father was the primary attachment figure in 27 percent of their sample, even though the mother was the primary caretaker. Particularly in families where there is a disturbance in the mother–infant relationship, the father may interact with the infant in ways that prevent later psychologic disturbance.

Research on bonding and attachment suggests that the development of a reciprocal, mutually regulated process of interaction between infant and caretaker begins in the moments immediately after birth. Our understanding of the long-term implications of these early interactions for later cognitive and social-emotional development and functioning is far from complete. Research efforts and theoretical formulations must continue to be directed toward a more complete understanding of early parent–infant relationships and their development over time. Specific important issues in need of more careful research include the effects of various modifications in hospital care practices, the contributions of infants to the development of patterns of interaction, the role of the father in early social development, and the relationship between parental and child personality styles and patterns of interaction, to mention a few.

At a practical level, it appears that primary prevention and early intervention programs must be multifaceted, focusing on a range of potential problem areas, including prenatal health care and nutrition, educational programs in child development and parenting, family-centered birth and hospital stay arrangements, and increased sensitivity of caregivers to aberrant patterns of early mother–infant and father–infant interaction. Given the present state of our knowledge, focus on only one or some of these areas will be inadequate.

We must resist the temptation to rely too securely on the hope that child development will be optimized by ideal care practices during brief episodes such as the lying-in period. It would be unfortunate if such a discrete segment in the life of a family were seen as having such overriding influence on the course of child development that other aspects of primary and secondary prevention of developmental disorders were overlooked.

REFERENCES

1. Klaus MH, Kennell JH: Maternal–Infant Bonding. St. Louis, Mosby, 1976
2. Bowlby, J: Attachment and Loss, vol I: Attachment. New York, Basic Books, 1969
3. Bowlby J: The nature of the child's tie to his mother. Int J Psychoanal 39:350–373, 1958
4. Hinde RA: Animal Behavior: A Synthesis of Ethology and Comparative Psychology. New York, McGraw-Hill, 1966
5. Rosenblatt JS: The basis of synchrony in the behavioral interaction between the mother and her offspring in the laboratory rat, in Foss BM (Ed): Determinants of Infant Behaviour, vol 3, London, Methuen, 1965
6. Hersher L, Moore AU, Richmond JB: Effect of postpartum separation of mother and kid on maternal care in the domestic goat. Science 128:1342–1343, 1958
7. Sackett G, Ruppenthal CG: Some factors influencing the attraction of adult female macaques to neonates, in Lewis M, Rosenblum LA (Eds): The Effect of the Infant on its Caregiver. New York, Wiley, 1974
8. Barnett CR, Leiderman PH, Grobstein R, et al: Neonatal separation: The maternal side of interactional deprivation. Pediatrics 45:197–205, 1970

9. Klaus MH, Kennell JH: Mothers separated from their newborn infants. Pediatr Clin North Am 17:1015–1037, 1970

10. Ainsworth MDS: Object relations, dependency, and attachment: A theoretical review of the infant–mother relationship. Child Dev 40:969–1025, 1969

11. Klaus MH, Jerauld R, Kreger N, et al: Maternal attachment: Importance of the first postpartum days. N Engl J Med 286:460–463, 1972

12. Klaus MH, Kennell JH, Plumb N, et al.: Human maternal behavior at first contact with her young. Pediatrics 46:186–192, 1970

13. Kennell JH, Jerauld R, Wolfe H, et al.: Maternal behavior one year after early and extended postpartum contact. Dev Med Child Neurol 16:172–179, 1974

14. de Chateau P: Neonatal care routines: Influences on maternal and infant behavior and on breast feeding. University Medical dissertations. Umeå, Sweden, 1976

15. Taylor PM, Taylor FH, Campbell SBG, et al.: Effects of extra contact on early maternal attitudes, perceptions, and behaviors. Presented at the Society for Research in Child Development, San Francisco, 1979 (unpublished)

16. Carlsson SG, Fagerberg H, Horneman G, et al.: Effects of various amounts of contact between mother and child on the mother's nursing behavior: A follow-up study. Infant Behav Develop 2:209–214, 1979

17. Ottaviano CM, Campbell SBG, Taylor PM: Early contact and infant–mother attachment at one-year. Presented at the Society for Research in Child Development, San Francisco, 1979 (unpublished)

18. Elmer G, Gregg GS: Developmental characteristics of abused children. Pediatrics 40:596–602, 1967

19. Klein M, Stern L: Low birth weight and the battered child syndrome. Am J Dis Child 122:15–18, 1971

20. Shaheen E, Alexander D, Truskowsky M, et al.: Failure to thrive—a retrospective profile. Clin Pediatr 7:255–261, 1968

21. Beckwith L, Cohen S, Parmelee AH: Risk, sex, and situational influences in social interaction with premature infants. Presented at the meeting of the American Psychological Association, Montreal, 1973 (unpublished)

22. Campbell SB: Maternal and infant behavior in normal, high risk, and difficult infants. Presented at the meeting of the Society for Research in Child Development, New Orleans, 1977 (unpublished)

23. Field TJ: Effects of early separation, interactive deficits, and experimental manipulations on infant–mother face-to-face interaction. Child Dev 48:763–771, 1977

24. Hock E, Coady S, Cordero L: Patterns of attachment to mother of one-year-old infants: A comparative study of full-term infants and prematurely born infants who were hospitalized throughout the neonatal period. Presented at the meeting of the Society for Research in Child Development, Philadelphia, 1973 (unpublished)

25. Leifer AD, Leiderman PH, Barnett C, et al.: Effects of mother–infant separation on maternal attachment behavior. Child Dev 43:1203–1218, 1972

26. O'Connor SM, Vietze PM, Sherrod KB, et al.: Reduced incidence of parenting disorders following rooming-in. Pediatrics (in press)

27. Lozoff B, Brittenham GM, Trause MA, et al.: The mother–newborn relationship: Limits of adaptability. J Pediatr 91:1–12, 1977

28. Carlsson SG, Fegerberg H, Horneman G, et al.: Effects of amount of contact between mother and child on the mother's nursing behavior. Dev Psychobiol 11:143–150, 1978

29. Hales DJ, Lozoff B, Sosa R, et al.: Defining the limits of the sensitive period. Dev Med Child Neurol 19:454–461, 1977

30. Ringler NM, Kennell JH, Jarvella R, et al.: Mother-to-child speech at 2 years—
    Effects of early postnatal contact. J Pediatr 86:141–144, 1975
31. Desmond MM, Franklin RR, Vallbona C, et al.: The clinical behavior of the newly
    born. J Pediatr 62:307–325, 1963
32. McLaughlin FJ, O'Connor SM, Deni R: Potential attachment behaviors in new-
    borns in the first hour postpartum. Presented at the International Conference on
    Infant Studies, Providence, 1978 (unpublished)
33. Emde RN, Swedberg J, Suzuki B: Human wakefulness and biological rhythms
    after birth. Arch Gen Psychiatr 32:780–783, 1975
34. Parke R, O'Leary S, West S: Mother–father–newborn interaction: Effects of
    maternal medication, labor, and sex of infant. Proc. Annual Convention Am.
    Psychol. Ass., 1972 (Abstr)
35. Butterfield PM, Emde RN, Platt BB: Effects of silver nitrate on initial visual
    behavior. Am J Dis Child 132:426, 1978
36. Brazelton TB: Neonatal Behavioral Assessment Scale. London, Spastics Interna-
    tional Medical, 1973
37. Korner A: Individual differences at birth: Implications for early experience and
    later development. Am J Orthopsychiatr 41:608–619, 1971
38. Brazelton TB, Koslowski B, Main M: The origins of reciprocity: The early
    mother–infant interaction, in Lewis M, Rosenblum LA (Eds): The Effect of the
    Infant on its Caregiver. New York, Wiley, 1974
39. Stern DN: A microanalysis of mother–infant interaction: Behavior regulating
    social contact between a mother and her 3½-month-old twins. J Am Acad Child
    Psychiatr 10:501–517, 1971
40. Condon WS, Sander LW: Neonate movement is synchronized with adult speech:
    Interactional participation and language acquisition. Science 183:99–101, 1974
41. Gardner DB, Hawkes GR, Burchinal LB: Noncontinuous mothering in infancy and
    development in later childhood. Child Dev 32:225–234, 1961
42. Werner EE, Bierman JM, French FE: The Children of Kauai. Honolulu, Univ of
    Hawaii Press, 1971
43. Ainsworth MDS: The development of infant–mother attachment, in Caldwell BM,
    Riccuiti HR (Eds): Review of Child Development Research, vol 3. Chicago, Univ
    of Chicago Press, 1973
44. Sroufe LA, Waters E: Attachment as an organizational construct. Child Dev
    48:1184–1199, 1977
45. Schaffer HR: The growth of sociability. London, Penguin, 1971
46. Lewis M, Goldberg S: Perceptual-cognitive development in infancy. Merrill-Palmer
    Q 15:81–100, 1969
47. Coates B, Anderson E, Hartup WW: Interrelations and stability in the attachment
    behavior of human infants. Dev Psychol 6:218–230, 1972
48. Ainsworth MDS, Bell SM: Attachment, exploration and separation: Illustrated by
    the behavior of one-year-olds in a strange situation. Child Dev 41:49–67, 1970
49. Ainsworth MDS, Bell SM: Some contemporary patterns of mother–infant inter-
    action in the feeding situation, in Ambrose JA (Ed): Stimulation in Early Infancy.
    London, Academic, 1969
50. Stayton DJ, Ainsworth MDS: Individual differences in infant responses to brief,
    everyday separations as related to other infant and maternal behaviors. Dev
    Psychol 9:226–235, 1973
51. Stayton DJ, Hogan R, Ainsworth MDS: Infant obedience and maternal behavior.
    The origins of socialization reconsidered. Child Dev 42:1057–1069, 1971

52. Bell SM, Ainsworth MDS: Infant crying and maternal responsiveness. Child Dev 43:1171–1190, 1972
53. Blehar MC, Lieberman A, Ainsworth MDS: Early face-to-face interaction and its relation to later infant–mother attachment. Child Dev 48:182–194, 1977
54. Erickson E: Childhood and Society. New York, Norton, 1950
55. Matas L, Arend RA, Sroufe LA: Continuity of adaptation in the second year: The relationship between quality of attachment and later competence. Child Dev 49:547–556, 1978
56. Main M: Mother-avoiding babies. Presented at the Society for Research in Child Development, Denver, 1975
57. Bell SM: The development of the concept of the object as related to infant–mother attachment. Child Dev 41:291–311, 1970
58. Clarke-Steward KA: Interactions between mothers and their young children: Characteristics and consequences. Monogr Soc Res Child Dev 38, No. 153, 1973
59. Schaffer HR, Emerson PE: The development of social attachment in infancy. Monogr Soc Res Child Dev 29, No. 3, 1964
60. Tavormina JB: Basic models of parent counseling: A critical review. Psychol Bull 81:827–835, 1974
61. Lynn DB: The Father: His Role in Child Development. Monterey, Brooks/Cole, 1974

Howard J. Osofsky

and Joy D. Osofsky

2

Normal Adaptation to Pregnancy and New Parenthood

In recent years there has been an increased recognition of the psychological adjustments which occur during pregnancy and new parenthood—with some awareness that at least to a considerable extent the success of these adjustments will relate to the outcome for each of the individual parents, their relationship as a couple, and the quality of parenting which they are able to offer to the infant. To date most of the studies have focused upon the woman and her adjustments to pregnancy and new parenthood. Far fewer have dealt with the male's coping processes; more frequently they have dealt with somewhat related areas such as the role of the father in child development.[1] Relatively little emphasis has been placed on the adjustments of the couple as a unit and the changes that occur in their relationship, their expectations of one another, and their overall marital contract. This chapter reviews the data that is currently available and presents information from our own clinical and research work to illustrate some of the issues that occur for couples and that may be expected to influence their adjustments to parenthood and their roles in parenting.

THE EXPECTANT MOTHER

General Concepts

Many investigators have viewed pregnancy as a period of considerable upheaval for a woman—a psychological stress, a normative crisis, or a developmental phase. In Benedek's view, pregnancy represents a developmental phase, extending the continuum of earlier developmental phases.[2] She describes factors that influence the continuation of personality development into adulthood and states that pregnancy brings up earlier conflictual feelings that need to be worked through by the individual. According to Benedek, the maturational potential and growth are influenced by the level of psychological development that the individual has achieved, psychobiological factors, and an interaction with the reality experiences during pregnancy and the adjustment to new parenthood.

Bibring and colleagues[3,4,5] described pregnancy, like puberty or menopause, as a period of crisis involving profound psychological as well as somatic changes. These crises represent important developmental steps and require significant adjustments for the individual. The outcome is influenced by current reality factors and by conflicts that have been unresolved earlier in life. On the basis of their work with women whom they followed longitudinally with psychoanalytically oriented interviews, social work interviews, and psychological testing, they postulated that the stresses that pregnant women normally experience may create a temporary picture resembling severe disintegration. They emphasize, however, the temporary nature of this picture and its response to support by the clinical staff working with a patient, and state that the outcome of the crisis more often leads to psychological health than to severe neurotic solutions. They feel that the more severe the psychological disturbance is before pregnancy, the more it can be anticipated that dramatic problems will emerge during this period. At times, depending on the inner conflicts of the woman, the pregnancy may relieve difficulties which she experienced clinically and promote the solutions of neurotic tensions.

Caplan[6] also described pregnancy as a 'crisis' for the woman (a term that he modified somewhat in subsequent writings).[7] The woman's emotional state varies at different stages during the pregnancy, depending on her capacity for adjustment to the psychological and physiological changes. Caplan postulated that two components contribute significantly to the woman's emotional status during pregnancy: (1) her reactions to the sexual aspects of the reproductive process that are associated with her personality structure and sexual development; and (2) the process whereby she develops psychologically into the role of mother during the course of pregnancy, a process influenced by her relationship with her own mother and women who have served as important role models.

Normative Psychological Adjustment for the Female

A number of studies have been carried out to improve our understanding of the normative psychological adjustment to pregnancy and the difficulties that contribute to emotional disturbance during the period of pregnancy and adjustment to motherhood. Some have focused upon the woman's relationship with her own mother and, to a lesser extent, upon her relationship with her husband. Some have looked at psychological factors that influence the outcome of pregnancy and long-term implications of psychological difficulty during pregnancy and following childbirth. Several investigators have applied the findings to clinical situations in an attempt to lessen patient risk and difficulty. For the sake of pertinence and brevity, we will focus upon a limited number of representative studies.

Shereshefsky and Yarrow[8] reviewed the findings of a study involving 62 predominantly middle-class families during pregnancy and early parenthood. The women had psychological testing and underwent repeated psychiatric interviews beginning at three-to-four months of pregnancy, and continuing until six months following delivery. Home visits and interviews with the husbands were carried out, but primary emphasis was on data obtained from the wife. Personality factors were related to maternal adaptation. In particular, women's perceptions of their mothers and their relationships to their mothers were related to their own capacities and their reactions to and fears of pregnancy. Fewer relationships were noted between the couples' patterns of mutual support and pregnancy outcome; however, limitations in the design of the study may have contributed to this finding. Serious marital disharmony was found in 21 percent of the families initially, and considerable individual disruptions, including occasional episodes of infidelity during the pregnancy, were noted. Families burdened with more stresses initially and those already involved in serious marital disharmony at the time of pregnancy tended to have more stresses than others in the sample. Considerable emotional shifts were noted in 40 percent of the women, supporting the notion of pregnancy as both a stressful time and a developmentally major one in the woman's life. Adaptive problems could be identified early in the pregnancy and maternal attitudes and acceptance were significantly related to several aspects of the infant's adaptation.

Leifer[9] studied 19 white, middle class primigravidas using extensive interviews and personality measures. She noted the degree of personality stability achieved in early pregnancy to be predictive of psychological growth experienced throughout pregnancy and early parenthood. In this study, most of the women also experienced the early phases of parenthood as a period of crisis, frequently exceeding that of pregnancy. Further, although most women experienced pregnancy and early parenthood as a period of psychological stress, only part of the sample concomitantly experienced a growing sense of adulthood and personality integration suggestive of a new developmental phase. The findings are consistent with those of Rossi,[10] and suggest that the emotional upheaval accompanying pregnancy is not a step towards maturation for all women. At the same time, and consistent with Bibring's position,[3-5] Leifer[9] found that the development of maternal feelings during pregnancy, and the resulting attachment to the fetus and new baby, is not a transient reaction. She noted a developmental quality and concluded that the reactions evolving during pregnancy are usually indicative of future mothering behaviors.

Weigert et al.[11] studied 52 predominantly middle class, well educated, white, Protestant women, usually from the beginning of the second trimester of pregnancy until three months after delivery. The women all underwent psychological testing and had repeated psychiatric and social work interviews. In addition, their husbands were interviewed once during the pregnancy and once following the delivery. Twenty-eight of the women developed a significant increase in emotional difficulties during the pregnancy. All women experienced an increase in their dependency needs. Two principal areas of marital conflict emerged related to patterns of dominance–submission and methods of meeting each other's needs. Especially important were struggles revolving around the woman's sense of femininity and her relationship with her mother. Women who were unable to use their mothers as models more frequently experienced emotionally difficult pregnancies.

Colman[12] studied six apparently normal primigravidas from the beginning of pregnancy for 15 months in group, hospital, and home settings. He focused on the overall psychological experience, medical symptoms and concerns, and approaches to labor and delivery. He found that in order to evaluate the prospective mother and make sense out of the form and quality of her postdelivery adjustment, the "total pregnancy system" rather than the "clinic visiting woman" must be studied. One of the key determinants in this system was the husband's reaction to the pregnancy.

Chertok et al.[13] reviewed and evaluated psychosomatic aspects of childbirth with special emphasis upon preparation for childbirth and pain during labor and delivery. Related to these interests, he studied 200 married, primiparous French women with semistructured interviews and psychological tests administered intermittently during the course of pregnancy and the hospital stay. Special emphasis was placed upon negative experiences and difficulties encountered during development and pregnancy. Significant relationships were found between patterns of difficulty and coping and the course of labor and delivery. These seemed related to the internal pulls that women experienced during pregnancy and the negative experiences that occurred during their childhood and development. Consistent with previously cited studies, Chertok concluded that pregnancy and childbirth optimally can be an integrative developmental process.

Emotional Disturbance and Pregnancy

Emotional disturbances during pregnancy seem to be related to psychological readiness for the process, emotional stability or instability at the time of pregnancy, early life experiences, overall social situation, and the very significant hormonal shifts that occur. Several investigations have focused on these relationships. For the sake of brevity and pertinence, emphasis will be placed on a limited number of the relevant studies with some focus on the question of postpartum depression.

Loesch and Greenberg[14] studied two very different groups of women through psychiatric interviews during pregnancy. Although both groups consisted mainly of primigravidas, one was composed of graduate student wives and the other of young women who were pregnant out-of-wedlock and residing in an institution. They found that in nearly all of the married women, a group not consciously seeking psychiatric aid, pregnancy represented a period of mixed feelings with underlying moods of anxiety and depression. In their interviews they saw little of the so-called "self-contained comfort" that has often been described by others. Rather, they were struck by the attitude of uncertainty and the generalized feelings of lack of confidence. It is of interest that the concerns were greatly diminished in many of the mothers during a second pregnancy and in mothers in the group who had undergone previous deliveries.

Paffenbarger and McCabe[15] reported a study of mental illness among women of childbearing age in Ohio during 1957–1958, comparing relative incidences of problems at various stages or conditions of womanhood. Age-adjusted rates of mental illness were substantially lower for pregnant women than for new mothers and nonpregnant women. An explosive peak in problems characterized the first month following delivery, but the rates then reverted to nonchildbearing levels. Recurrence of parapartum mental illness with subsequent pregnancies was common, with prepartum difficulties invariably recurring in the prepartum period and postpartum difficulties in the postpartum period. They concluded that problems that develop during pregnancy, if unresolved, are likely to recur in subsequent pregnancies; however, if they are dealt with in some kind of adaptive fashion during the course of pregnancy, a normal growth experience may result.

The question of the relationship between hormonal changes associated with pregnancy and the increased incidence of psychiatric disturbances during the postpartum period has received considerable focus. Although an in-depth review is not appropriate here, some representative studies are worthy of inclusion. Treadway et al.[16] performed simultaneous biochemical and psychological evaluations during pregnancy and following delivery. They found that the increased incidence of clinically significant disorders among women in the postpartum period may be due to the increased environmental stresses and maternal responsibilities in association with the lack of rebound from the biochemical changes in pregnancy.

Dalton[17] carried out a prospective study of mood changes during pregnancy and puerperium in 189 women. She found an evolution in mood changes in those who later developed puerperal depression that was characterized by anxiety at the first antenatal visit, elation during later pregnancy, and depression in the puerperium. Arguments are made in favor of a hormonal etiology of puerperal depression.

Asch and Rubin[18] described four postpartum syndromes that are not often recognized: infanticide and child battering, the grandmother reaction, the adoptive mother reaction, and the father reaction. It may be noted that these reactions are derived from experiences involving the person's mental representations of pregnancy, parturition, and motherhood and are not confined to the biological mother. The phenomena of successive generations of postpartum reactions in women is described and explained as being grandmother-oriented. They found that similar reactions occurred in successive generations of mothers — not through genetic transmission, but rather by relatively specific psychological stimuli in early life; this, however, did not exclude the possibility of constitutional predisposition as well. The presented case material from postpartum reactions consistent with the notion that the early mothering experience of the new parent, the vicissitudes of separation and individuation from her mother, her sibling experience, and the nature of the oedipal resolution are extremely important. Since they described reactions in subjects who were not parturients and who therefore did not have hormonal and physiological changes, they concluded that postpartum reactions are primarily psychogenic.

Uddenberg and Nilsson[19] reported a study of 95 nulliparious women who were interviewed during pregnancy and four months postpartum. They were interested in whether or not one could predict mental disturbance postpartum from symptoms during pregnancy. They found that women who were mentally disturbed during pregnancy had a better prognosis if the social situation was otherwise good. In women without emotional symptoms, denial of the pregnancy and sensations connected with it suggested poor adaptation postpartum; this is consistent with findings from studies on vomiting and nausea in pregnancy. The authors concluded that when a woman appears well adapted during her pregnancy it may be more difficult to predict mental adaptation postpartum. A tendency to keep the pregnancy experience out of the consciousness, however, should be regarded as a warning. A "totally healthy pregnancy" without any of the ailments typical for pregnant women, far from being a favorable prognostic sign, may indicate that the woman may have difficulties in adapting to motherhood.

THE EXPECTANT FATHER

General Concepts

As has been noted, in comparison to the literature on expectant motherhood, considerably less work has been carried out on the psychological aspects of expectant fatherhood. Of the limited number that have been done, few have focused on the process itself as a developmental phase.

Parens[20] suggested that significant developmental maturational factors influence the male and his role during his wife's pregnancy. Parens cites Benedek in stating that one can differentiate in the male that organization which, paralleling motherliness, directs the man's reproductive drive organization toward fatherliness. He states that fatherliness is a secondary developmental process compared with motherliness, in that a male's earliest security and his orientation to the world have been learned through identification with his mother and only eventually is that early identification surpassed by the need to identify with a male figure.

Benedek[2,21] reported about the adaptational situation of fatherhood, referring to normal maturational and developmental components of the processes, including the influences of early parent–child and sibling relationships and the resolution of early conflicts. She also stressed the wife's role in influencing the husband's emotional response to the pregnancy, suggesting that the father's attitude toward the child may be influenced by the communicative experience with his wife, and that the emotional course of pregnancy may stabilize or disrupt the marriage, thus becoming largely responsible for the psychological environment of the child.

Normative Psychological Adjustment for the Male

Gurwitt's well thought through report[22] of a male psychoanalytic patient's experiences and reactions before and during his wife's pregnancy—although it may have limitations in generalizability because it is a single case study of an individual in psychoanalysis—is useful in pointing out the depth of the father-to-be's pregnancy experience and the resultant alterations in the couple's relationship. During the pregnancy the couple underwent a remarkable sharing of psychological events, and through their new experiences and their reexperiences of old issues, their relationship altered, faltered, and was strengthened as they as individuals experienced growth. Although their marriage and heterosexual relationship began in young adulthood, the joint creation of a child introduced a new level of relatedness. The husband's major upheavals occurring around the conception and the unfolding stages of pregnancy in part were reactions to the events of the pregnancy and in part reflected significant events in his early life, including his mother's becoming pregnant again when he was quite young and his reactions to the explanations and birth of his sibling. During his wife's pregnancy, the patient underwent a reworking of relationships to parental figures, siblings, and his wife. On the basis of the material, Gurwitt has divided the experience beginning prior to conception and continuing through childbirth into periods involving the man's getting ready, entering into the process, and coming to terms with it.

In a recent study, Herzog[23] followed 103 men whose wives gave birth to apparently premature infants at 25–39 weeks of gestation. He utilized retrospective interviews for up to 24 months following the delivery. Although reporting marked individual differences in the men's experiences, he noted that 35 of the men were in touch with feelings and fantasies pertaining to the pregnancy. Among this group there appeared to be periods similar to those described by Gurwitt.[22] Herzog found considerable shifts in the men's sexual fantasies, a reworking of feelings about their fathers and, in some, a preoccupation with gastrointestinal symptoms. Especially after quickening, he has observed the appearance of aggressive fantasies, concerns about hurting the baby, and a sense of magic and mystery about the process of creation. Although the numbers of men reporting feelings may have been diminished because of the retrospective nature of the study, and the feelings described may have been influenced by the stresses of the baby's being born prematurely, there are suggestions of common themes and a reworking of earlier issues—at least for some of the men.

Emotional Disturbance

In the relatively small number of studies that have focused on emotional difficulties in expectant and new fathers, some findings have emerged which may be of pertinence to the more normative experience of men in general. Zilboorg,[24] as part of a more general paper, described three men with depressive reactions either to impending parenthood or to parenthood itself. On the basis of clinical information and theoretical concepts, he postulated that these individuals felt guilty about actual or threatened parenthood and that they were concerned about their unusually strong, angry, and hurtful thoughts and feelings. Such men may be able to function at least in a limited manner in the role of husband or lover, but are driven into conflict with the threat of parenthood, sometimes needing to deny that the child is theirs. Other conflicts that tend to emerge are an equation of the child with a sibling, with considerable rivalry resulting and an unconscious envy of their wives for their ability to be pregnant.

Because of his impression that pregnancy universally has psychological effects on the male and because of a wish to stimulate further work and discussions on the effects of pregnancy and childbirth on men, Jarvis[25] reported clinical descriptions of four men who became disturbed while their wives were pregnant or following the birth of their children. All of them reacted to the emergence of unconscious conflicts. The differences in outcome appeared to be related to differences in ego structure, early conflicts, and development. Based on the findings, Jarvis suggested that postpartum reactions in women, including postpartum depressions, should be reexamined taking into account the effect of the man's reactions to pregnancy and childbirth on the woman.

Ginath[26] reported reactions of the male to his wife's pregnancy and childbirth assuming that normally the process is an important step in a male's development. He surveyed reactions aroused in the male, such as envy of the woman for her capability to become pregnant and give birth, rivalry toward the fetus or the baby, and inclination toward regression. He described difficulties, including such severe psychopathological reactions as psychosis, that were generated by unsolved childhood conflicts. In men developing a psychosis during or after their wives' first pregnancy and delivery, the condition was reexacerbated after further pregnancies and childbirths.

Towne and Afterman[27] reported a temporal relationship and a pregnancy or birth of a child in the patient's family. All of the men had unfulfilled, demanding, dependency needs characteristic of the relationships with important people in their environment. The patients' wives were controlling, possessive, and unable to accept their excessive demands. The failure to meet their needs resulted in hostility and poorly suppressed aggression. Not infrequently, the aggression was selfdirected. Thus, there seemed to be a constellation of variables to explain the men's severe reactions to a woman's pregnancy.

Wainwright[28] indicated that psychopathological reactions to fatherhood probably appear with more frequency than is commonly recognized. Since the illness is usually attributed by the patient to other external stresses, the importance of the recent birth of a child may be overlooked by the therapist. Often both the treater and the patient are unaware of the intense reaction to fatherhood. He points out that the dynamic factors precipitating these reactions in men are not in themselves specific to people with mental illness; therefore it would be well for supportive personnel to ascertain the meanings that fatherhood has for the spouse of the pregnant patient, as well as for the woman herself.

CLINICAL PERSPECTIVES ON EXPECTANT AND NEW PARENTHOOD

The material to follow concerning the importance of expectant and new parenthood as a developmental phase is derived from three sources: (1) clinical experience of the first author in obstetrics and gynecology; (2) clinical experience, again by the first author, in psychiatry; and (3) the findings of studies involving coping of couples during pregnancy and new parenthood conducted by the two of us. These studies have been designed to develop measures to identify couples who are at risk for adjustment difficulties to pregnancy and/or new parenthood and to develop clinical tools which can be used by professionals or their assistants in helping such couples.

Brief Clinical Histories

It is worthwhile to summarize briefly the histories of four individuals who were participants in our research study in order to provide some additional information about the pregnancy experience. We would like to emphasize that these should be viewed not only as specific examples but as an introduction to the types of stressful experiences that women and men in general undergo in preparation for parenthood.

J.S. is a 27-year-old faculty member at a nearby university. She is the youngest of three children, having two older brothers. Her father died when she was a teenager and her mother remarried a successful, but distant, man. Mrs. S. describes her early upbringing with some difficulty. Her father, an apparently warm man, was very much involved with responsibility of his business and career and had little time for his children. Her mother, while at home as a housewife, was preoccupied with her husband's success and spent relatively little direct time caring for the children. Her oldest brother, age 41, was the product of a prior marriage, and during most of Mrs. S.'s childhood he lived with his father. Her other brother, age 29, was sent away to a boarding school when she was age 10. Mrs. S. describes her childhood as a somewhat lonely one. There were few children in the area where she grew up and, due to religious differences, she experienced discrimination in the school neighborhood. To her, a major factor that influenced her development was the sudden death of her father of a heart attack when she was 14 years old. This occurred at a time when she was struggling with the issues of growing up and wanting to relate meaningfully with her parents.

She married her husband, a faculty member in another department, while she was attending the university. Because of her wishes to complete her education and initiate her career and because of doubts that she experienced related to becoming a parent, they used birth control and deferred having a child for several years. When she tried to become pregnant, she then had difficulty, experiencing three questionable miscarriages. When she finally became pregnant, she had substantial bleeding from the 10th through the 14th weeks, requiring bedrest.

Initially she felt surprised and ecstatic about being pregnant. As the pregnancy went on, however, she felt progressively anxious and worried about the baby's normality and her ability to cope with the pregnancy, delivery, and motherhood. She feared the loss of her career that she had struggled so hard to achieve. She wanted to be able to nurse the baby and become the type of mother that she felt she had lacked during childhood and, at the same time, worried about the loss of professional identity and the other changes that parenthood might bring. She strongly wished for a girl in order to give her opportunities that she had felt to be missing in her own life. When the baby was born and turned out to be a girl, she was thrilled, but as she identified with the child she at times felt resentful of the good care which she in actuality was providing for her. She at times felt conflicted, envious, and resentful and experienced temporary difficulties in coping, requiring outside help.

M.L. is a 31-year-old social worker. She is the youngest of three children, having one brother and one sister. Her parents are alive and she describes them as having quite different interests, but as warm, supportive individuals. She described her rural background and her Protestant upbringing and added that she and her husband regularly attended church with a strong commitment to the ethics of religion. She met her husband, a psychologist, because of his work in a related agency. He had recently divorced and had two teenage children from his first marriage. They carefully planned and looked forward intensely to their first pregnancy. That pregnancy appeared free from complications until four hours before labor and delivery, when Mrs. L. noted the cessation of fetal movement. When she arrived in the hospital, she was told that no heartbeat could be detected and, after a lengthy labor, an eight-pound-three-ounce stillbirth female was delivered.

Mrs. L. became pregnant again approximately six months later. She and her husband found themselves to be very tense during this pregnancy, worrying as to whether anything that they might do would result in another stillbirth. When Mrs. L. had spotting at the end of her third month, she panicked and found it difficult to be reassured. Intercourse became especially anxiety provoking, with fears that the baby might be harmed or that labor might ensue prematurely. Although the couple remained close, they found it progressively difficult to communicate as the due date approached. Mrs. L. described a feeling of "walking on eggshells," as though superstitious that something might go wrong at any time. When she was feeling optimistic about the birth, she would also note feelings of guilt, as though she should not be happily anticipating the birth of a new baby out of respect for her dead baby. These feelings were especially pronounced at anniversary points that had a special meaning for her in relationship to her first pregnancy and to her plans for her first baby. She went into labor three weeks prior to her due date and gave birth to a six-pound-three-ounce boy. Although thrilled that she had a live baby, she also found herself irritated and disappointed with him. He seemed small and puny to her. He was not like and did not measure up to her first dead child. Although she felt that these feelings were irrational and inappropriate, she was aware of them and was concerned about her relationship with the baby. Although warm in her behavior, she inwardly felt intermittently distant and sad. Over a course of weeks she began to see more special traits in her son, becoming aware of his alertness and feeling that he was robust in spite of his size. Aided by her husband, some friends who had had similar experiences, and the child's own qualities, she found herself progressively more invested in and relaxed with her son. While the feelings of sadness about the first pregnancy loss have continued, they have seemed to become more tempered and less intense.

F.J. is a 34-year-old father of four, physician, specializing in internal medicine. He is the youngest of five children, having three sisters and one brother. His parents are alive and he described them as poor, but warm. He freely discussed his Italian background and his devout Roman Catholic upbringing, although adding that at present he attends church primarily because of the children. He met his wife while in medical school, at which time she was studying to be a nurse. Although also Catholic, she wanted to defer having children and wished to use appropriate birth control. He, however, felt uncomfortable using birth control, and she became pregnant during the initial month of their marriage. During the third month of pregnancy, career opportunities necessitated their moving to a new community 2000 miles away from her family. His wife felt especially pressured and trapped during this period of time, wanting the pregnancy and feeling close to her husband, and yet wishing she were not pregnant and feeling that she had few supports during this difficult time. Although he finds it hard to explain fully, Dr. J. noted that he began to feel more strongly attached to one of the women at work and shortly thereafter began to have an affair with her. He states that, "In some screwy sort of way I felt upset with my wife, angry toward her, and at times jealous of her. You may not believe it but I worried that in some ways I would be hurtful and that I was trying to protect her and the baby by having an affair." In addition to his anger at her, he strongly conveyed what felt to him to be an irrational concern that he might hurt the baby—with a flavor of being destructive to a new, younger sibling. The affair continued until the time of delivery, after which he abruptly terminated it. He remarked, "Once she had the baby, there was no longer any reason for the affair. It didn't make sense any more."

The pattern of feeling the need to have an affair and engaging in one recurred with each of his wife's pregnancies and ended each time with the birth of the baby. During the last pregnancy, his wife discovered his infidelity, became depressed, and began an affair herself following the birth of the baby. The couple sought professional help, have both been in therapy, and at present feel that they have resolved their difficulties and are closer than ever.

Of some note, this pattern of feeling attracted to other women, and to a lesser extent of having affairs for the first time during practice, is one which has been apparent in the course of the first author's obstetrical practice. It has been observed in a number of patients and colleagues, even those who planned their pregnancies carefully and who felt desirous of the coming child.

S.E. is a 33-year-old, twice-married, once-divorced business executive whom we interviewed with his wife during the course of the pilot investigations. He is the older of two children, having a 31-year-old sister. His mother is alive and in good health. His father died four years prior to the onset of the pregnancy as a result of a combination of a lymphoma and heart disease. Mr. E. described his family as a close one, with his mother being warm but somewhat pressuring in style. He described his father in very warm terms, at times tearfully, but also mentioned his father's strictness and tendency to temper outbursts. He had begun to establish a very successful career in another community but, following a large business deal, came home to find that his wife had left him for another man. He experienced acute emotional distress during the process of the marital breakup and underwent psychotherapy for the next two years.

His second marriage, to a nurse, was somewhat stormy with repeated episodes of fighting and breaking up. In part to cement the marriage and in part because of his strong desire to have children, he and his wife planned the present pregnancy. Initially all seemed to go well. As months went on, however, the couple found themselves becoming more distant and communicating less well with each other. The wife began to wonder whether he was strong enough and whether she could depend on him enough in his new role as father. She found her needs changing and questioned whether he could meet these needs. He in turn found himself angrier at her, less sexually excited and, against his will, reacting more the way his father had when he was a child. After the birth of the baby, he found himself picking on his wife, wanting her to stay at home more, feeling less attracted to her in general, and resenting and criticizing her for nursing their daughter—suggesting that it would be better for her to bottle-feed the baby. At the same time he felt devoted to his wife and extremely close to and protective of the baby. It was striking to observe his rivalry with his daughter and his feelings of being replaced, similar to those which he experienced with his sister. It was also striking to note his anger and his devotion to his wife, now mother. He was shocked when he returned home from a two-week trip during which he had his biggest business success to find that his wife had left, taking the child with her. At present both spouses are in psychotherapy and are attempting to work through their personal and marital difficulties.

CONCERNS OF EXPECTANT PARENTS

Mothers

Obstetrical experience and our pilot investigations have both contributed to the impression that women undergo considerable stresses and upheavals during the course of pregnancy and following birth of the baby, especially a first child. In spite of and perhaps related to their initial enthusiasm about being pregnant and a desire for the baby, many women experience fears and concerns about themselves and the unborn baby. A common worry is whether the baby will be normal. Women especially worry if there are realistic concerns; for example, women who are predisposed to major complications during the pregnancy have special concerns and women over the age of 35 worry about the increased risk of Mongolism. But even if there are no medical problems, women still worry. Perhaps they are afraid that they will be denied the opportunity to have a healthy baby and to experience the pleasures of motherhood. They worry about whether they can or have hurt their baby. With the issues raised by modern magazines, radio, and television, mothers are especially concerned about the effects of alcohol, smoking, pills, over- and undereating, using additives, consuming artificial sweeteners, and even worrying itself.

Women also worry about themselves. They wonder whether they will die or be injured during pregnancy or especially during childbirth. Quite frequently a woman may express concerns about how the infant will get out, will she be injured in the process, will her body be distorted or mutilated? Especially with a first pregnancy, the woman may wonder how she will know when labor has begun, will she get to the hospital on time, what will labor and delivery be like, how much will it hurt, and will she lose control?

All women have concerns about the changes in their bodies during pregnancy. These feelings vary considerably, depending on the woman, the support she receives from her husband, and the attitudes that she has picked up from her mother and other important people in her life. For most women, pregnancy and motherhood represent truly becoming a woman. Some women describe feeling like a woman for the first time after the onset of a pregnancy. Especially with the first pregnancy, women may enjoy the early signs of pregnancy and the beginnings of looking pregnant, anticipating wearing maternity clothes, and enjoying the stares and changed attitudes of people around them. Not all of the feelings about their looks are happy ones, however. Many women feel awkward and ugly—some from the beginning of the pregnancy. As the pregnancy goes on, women may describe themselves as fat, looking like balloons, or being distorted. Women who have prided themselves on being young, attractive, and slim may find it difficult to adjust to the changes in their weight and figures. Along with these concerns, women commonly express questions about whether they will regain their figures after the pregnancy is over.

Physical symptoms may be especially disconcerting to the woman. Increased breast fullness and sensitivity may cause discomfort and even pain. Women may worry about the frequency of urination, constipation, and periodic fatigue which frequently accompany pregnancy. Various smells may become offensive to them. They may have problems eating foods because of their odors, or difficulty engaging in intercourse because of problems resulting from normal body odors.

In addition, women become aware of psychological shifts which they are experiencing. Especially after they feel quickening, women frequently become more preoccupied with themselves and their coming babies. At times, it may seem as though a woman has room for no one else—including her husband. Women frequently experience mood swings that are dramatic and more extreme than they have experienced previously. For many women the changes in mood seem relatively unprovoked and difficult to control.

Women frequently describe changes in their relationships with their husbands. Although some of the changes relate to their growing concerns with themselves and the coming baby, some may also feel resentful. The mother-to-be may become progressively aware of the changes that are going to follow the birth of the baby. She may worry about the necessary adjustments in her career with increased responsibilities at home. No matter how egalitarian the couple, the mother usually shoulders more responsibility for child-rearing than the father. The woman may come to resent her husband because of the required changes in her life that he does not have to make. These feelings may alternate with warm desires for motherhood and the coming baby. At the same time the woman may be aware of a growing dependence upon her husband, including concerns about his job, his earning capacity, and his overall providing abilities. Some women express comfort over this growing sense of dependence; others feel resentful and wish to maintain their independence at all costs. Some women describe for the first time a growing concern about their marriage. Whereas their husbands may have been fine as lovers and spouses, they wonder whether this man has the capacity to be a good father and provide the emotional security that they now desire for themselves and their future children.

Women tend to note a number of sexual changes during pregnancy. Although there is considerable variability, in general, women feel less sexual desire at times during pregnancy. Some women report a gradual decline as pregnancy goes on. Most women experience a considerable decline in interest, frequency of intercourse, and sexual arousal and enjoyment in the last months of pregnancy. (Recent data reported by Naeye[29] suggest that intercourse, and especially orgasmic intercourse, may contribute to premature labor and to fatal fetal infection closer to term. This data, however, is based on peripherally collected material from the Collaborative Perinatal Project carried out 20 years ago, has inconsistencies, and is contrary to the clinical experience reported to us by many physicians. The work needs to be replicated, but in any case, the reports that we have received from patients antedated the publication of Naeye's study.) Factors that women have described to us include fatigue and increased breast tenderness early in pregnancy, contributing to a feeling of being less sexually aroused. As the pregnancy goes on, women have described feeling more embarrassed about their appearance; they may feel awkward, obese, bloated, and conscious of additional swelling around the vaginal and labial areas. They may not feel that they look particularly sexy or attractive. Late in the pregnancy some women have described a sense of embarrassment and modesty, feeling that their genital area is particularly engorged and open. Some women describe a preference for being held and cuddled, but being afraid of denying their husbands intercourse. Women frequently are aware of their preoccupation with a coming baby with resultant decreased spontaneity and interest in intercourse. Especially with a first pregnancy, women have described concerns about intercourse hurting the baby, about labor ensuing following intercourse, and about the Brakston-Hicks contractions that frequently accompany intercourse resulting in labor. It should be noted that not all women report a diminishing interest in sex during pregnancy. A fair number have an increased desire for sex. They feel warm, particularly feminine, and easily aroused. They sometimes find their orgasms more powerful and their sexual experiences more pleasurable. These feelings can fluctuate throughout pregnancy, but a considerable number of women feel an increased arousal especially during the first several months of pregnancy—and some throughout pregnancy. Some women with increased sexual desires have described worrying about whether their feelings are normal, wondering whether they will seem abnormal to their husbands, and whether their husbands will be upset and turned off by these feelings.

Following the birth of the baby, a new mother may experience confusing feelings. While in the hospital she may be especially aware of being alone and isolated and missing her husband. Some women have also described to us missing the feeling of being pregnant and of not having the baby still within the uterus. In addition, women describe an awareness of the very real changes that are going on in their lives. More than they had expected, they feel confronted with the responsibilities of parenthood. When they go home from the hospital and are confronted by fatigue and by the baby's demands, frequently they question when will this end? When will things be normal again? It takes a considerable time for people to realize that the old sense of what was normal will not return, but that a different kind of normalcy will occur.

Fathers

Men also undergo stresses, upheavals, and adjustments during their wives' pregnancies and following the birth of the baby. Initially most men experience a sense of excitement and pride when they find out that their wives are pregnant. There are obviously exceptions, for example, men who have been forced into a marriage because of the pregnancy or men who have felt tricked or pressured by their wives into the pregnancy. Even in this group, however, after the initial anger most of the men have become accepting of the pregnancy and have welcomed the forthcoming child. Frequently the pregnancy has made the men feel more manly, thus helping to settle doubts about their virility and potency and concerns about whether their wives might leave them for other men.

Following the initial sense of excitement and pride, other feelings frequently emerge. Husbands describe feeling strange, not totally themselves. Some have talked worriedly about the current and antic-ipated changes in their lives and in their relationships with their wives. A considerable number in various ways have spoken about their feelings of neediness and rivalry toward the baby. Most men have described a greater sense of responsibility which at times feels overwhelming. Because of their wives' preoccupation with the coming baby, men frequently feel alone and sense a loss of intimacy and difficulty in communicating. At times they are frightened by the changes that are occurring and are concerned that their wives may die during childbirth and leave them alone.

Some men have described feelings of envy of their wives' ability to reproduce and have a baby growing within their bodies. They feel like bystanders, unable to experience as directly the changes in fetal growth, the beginning feelings of life, and the patterns of fetal movement. In order to compensate for these feelings, a number of husbands have found themselves engaging in their own creative efforts during the pregnancy, including trying to improve their jobs, writing books, planting gardens, and raising litters of dogs.

At times men have expressed other worries about becoming fathers. They wonder generally what kind of fathers they will be. Will they be like their fathers or, as many men desire, be able to do things differently? Will they be adequate parents and role models for their children?

New feelings frequently emerge about their wives. Often men describe being more comfortable with their wives, feeling great warmth and tenderness, and seeing them as being more beautiful during the pregnancy. Yet at the same time, men at least intermittently may also experience their wives as ugly and clumsy. They may take the mood shifts and frustrations that their wives experience as a normal part of pregnancy as personal criticisms. Thus, men often find themselves reacting irritably toward their wives, with these mixed feelings evoking a sense of confusion and guilt.

Because of the husbands' conflicts about neediness and taking on the parental role, the pregnancy is a time when men frequently engage in fantasies about other women. A small number of men have affairs during this time. A larger number of men have described their intermittent wishes to be out of the marriage, with subsequent feelings of confusion and guilt. They may worry whether this woman, whom they have loved as a companion and a spouse, is the woman whom they wish to be the mother of their children—whether she will measure up to their own mothers. They may also experience a sense of panic, a feeling of being trapped, wondering whether they are ready to settle down, have children, and accept the responsibilities of parenthood.

Men frequently gain weight during the course of their wives' pregnancies. Some men at times feel physically ill, mimicking the symptoms of their wives. Although feeling guilty, a number of men have on occasion voiced the question, "Is the child really mine? You can be sure of the mother but not the father."[30]

Fathers-to-be are especially concerned if there has been a sterility problem or if their wives have had a miscarriage or a stillbirth with a preceding pregnancy. These fathers find themselves unusually worried, or as some have put it, "walking on eggshells" during the pregnancy. They are especially fearful about having intercourse, worrying that the sperm, the sexual excitement, or the uterine contractions will initiate bleeding or, later in pregnancy, begin labor. When there has been a problem with a previous pregnancy, the level of anxiety tends to be highest at about the same time during the current pregnancy, for example, during the first trimester when there has been an early miscarriage and late in the pregnancy when there has been a stillbirth. Where there has been a previous stillbirth, the husband may feel guilty about looking forward to the forthcoming baby. His complex emotions and his needs to be the supportive individual may contribute to his being overly stoical and not sharing his concerns with his wife. These may complicate and further lead to additional feelings of the couple's growing apart and having difficulty communicating during the pregnancy.

Sexual concerns are common during the pregnancy. With a heightened sense of virility and feelings of increased warmth toward their wives, some men have discussed feeling more sexually relaxed and more easily aroused during the pregnancy. Many men and even some of the same men on other occasions have discussed feeling less sexually relaxed and interested, however. They feel uncomfortable having intercourse with their pregnant wives, feeling afraid that they may hurt them or the baby, and that intercourse may initiate bleeding or labor. Although feeling irrational about their concerns, some have raised questions about whether the ejaculated semen can be hurtful to the baby, and some have discussed specific fantasies of causing anomalies or destroying part of the baby—often a portion of the head, such as the eye. Husbands have also described feelings that intercourse with a pregnant woman is wrong, as though it is defiling her body. Related to these concerns, not only may husbands feel less aroused, but some experience a loss of erections and a degree of impotence for the first time in their married lives. With the loss of erections and other anxieties accompanying intercourse, a smaller number of men have described panicky feelings about their own sexual adequacy and feelings of being attracted to other men, usually of a time-limited nature.

DISCUSSION AND CONCLUSION

Bibring,[3] in her theoretical paper about women's psychological processes in pregnancy stated,

> We believe it to be a more adequate, a more inclusive, assumption to consider pregnancy as a crisis that affects all expectant mothers, no matter what their state of psychic health. Crises, as we see it, are turning points in the life of the individual, leading to acute disequilibrium which under favorable conditions result in specific maturational steps toward new functions. We find them as developmental phenomena at points of no return between one phase and the next when decisive changes deprive former central needs and modes of living of their significance, forcing the acceptance of highly charged new goals and functions (Erikson[33]). Pregnancy as a major turning point in the life of the woman represents one of these normal crises, especially for the primigravida who faces the impact of this event for the first time.

In another paper[4] she and her colleagues state, "In pregnancy, as in puberty and menopause, new and increased libidinal and adjustive tasks confront the individual, leading to the revival and simultaneous emergence of unsettled conflicts from earlier developmental phases and to the loosening of partial or inadequate solutions of the past. . . . The outcome of this crisis is of the greatest significance for the mastery of the thus initiated phase." Although Bibring has written specifically about the woman and has focused on the biological as well as the psychological components that the woman experiences during pregnancy, it is likely that many of her assumptions have equal relevance for the expectant and new father as well.

Consistent with this broad definition, we hypothesize that for the wife and husband—as individuals and as a couple—expectant and new parenthood represents a crisis and a developmental opportunity for maturation and new growth. Their lives will change in meaningful and irreversible ways, and as with other major steps in growth, they may experience significant internal pain. Prior to the birth of a baby, even if a loving couple, the wife and husband, are relatively autonomous individuals. With the pregnancy both spouses are participating in the creation of another human being who will represent each of them, their relationship, and an individual in its own right. Through their participation in the creation and growth of another individual, they will experience important shifts in themselves and in their relationship with one another. Not all women and men may experience conscious severe upheavals. Yet it would appear, especially when they become parents for the first time, that all individuals on some level undergo considerable shifts and internal disequilibrium, and few if any are the same afterward as they were before the pregnancy.

Both our clinical and research findings have been striking in that women and men without overt psychiatric symptoms preceding the pregnancy have experienced considerable lability and feelings of being unsettled during the pregnancy and following the birth of the baby. They have demonstrated regressive pulls with conflictual themes similar to those described for more disturbed individuals, although their overt symptoms have been less intense, more transient, and more responsive to supportive intervention. As with more disturbed individuals, the choice and timing of their symptoms—and the degree of adequacy of solutions—appear related to unresolved conflicts and developmental difficulties. Life circumstances, including perinatal complications, degree of economic stability, religious background and patterns, family and community supports, and the strength of the marital relationship with the ability to make required maturational shifts in the relationship all appear to play important roles.

It is important, however, to see the increase in symptoms at this time as part of a normative process and not only as a reflection of psychopathology. Erikson[31,32] described major steps in human growth and stressed the reactions and upheavals that occur as part of the growth process. Considerable disequilibrium and crisis can herald the beginning of a new growth phase. The conflicts that have been observed in expectant and new parents would appear to be universal. The specific manifestations of the conflicts appear to depend on the individual's personality make-up and life circumstances at the beginning of and during the process. Under optimal circumstances, expectant and new parenthood would appear to offer the opportunity for better resolution of past conflicts and an enhancement of the maturational process. In the process of becoming parents, reworking the marital relationship, and establishing an interaction with their child, the wife and husband have the opportunity, albeit with pain, for greater fulfillment of age-appropriate tasks and enjoyments. The burden may be greater for individuals with more unresolved conflicts, but even in more difficult situations, better solutions are a likely possibility with appropriate support and intervention.

In summary, it has become accepted that women, even psychologically normal women, experience considerable psychological upheavals during pregnancy and the adjustment to a new baby. This upheaval has been referred to as a psychobiological stress, a normative crisis, or a developmental phase. In any case, it has been recognized that the time is one of considerable importance and that the process can result optimally in further maturational growth and, less optimally, in long-lasting difficulty or poor adjustment. Considerably less attention has been given to the male's psychological adjustments and less clear formulations have been made about his internal struggles. The limited data that are available have focused more upon grossly abnormal responses and severe psychopathology.

On the basis of our clinical experience and preliminary research data, it can be proposed that expectant and new parenthood represents an important developmental phase for both parents. Normal as well as disturbed women and men on some level will be affected by the process. They will experience an intensification of current conflicts, an emergence of unsettled solutions from the past, and a loosening of partial or inadequate solutions from the past. There will also be the opportunity for important developmental growth and mastery. It is recognized that more work is needed to be able to prognosticate psychological growth or various less successful solutions. Our current work is attempting to address these and related areas. It is hoped that it may assist in helping couples as individuals, as members of a marital dyad, and as prospective and new parents.

REFERENCES

1. Parke R: Perspectives on father–infant interaction, in Osofsky JD (Ed): Handbook of Infant Development. New York, Wiley, 1979
2. Benedek T: Parenthood as a developmental phase: A contribution to the libido theory. J Am Psychoanal Assoc 7: 389–417, 1959
3. Bibring GL: Some considerations of the psychological processes in pregnancy. Psychoanal Study Child 14: 113–121, 1959
4. Bibring GL, Dwyer TF, Huntington DS, et al.: A study of the psychological processes in pregnancy and of the earliest mother–child relationship. I. Some propositions and comments. Psychoanal Study Child 16: 9–24, 1961
5. Bibring GL, Dwyer TF, Huntington DS, et al.: A study of the psychological processes in pregnancy and of the earliest mother–child relationship. II. Methodological considerations. Psychoanal Study Child 16: 25–72, 1961
6. Caplan G: Psychological aspects of maternity care. Am J Public Health 47: 25–31, 1957
7. Caplan G: Emotional implications of pregnancy and influences on family relationships, in Stuart HC, Prugh DG (Eds): The Healthy Child: His Physical, Psychological and Social Development. Cambridge, Massachusetts, Howard University Press, 1960
8. Shereshefsky PM, Yarrow, LJ: Psychological Aspects of a First Pregnancy and Early Postnatal Adaptation. New York, Raven Press, 1973
9. Leifer M: Psychological changes accompanying pregnancy and motherhood. Genetic Psychol Monogr 95: 55–96, 1977
10. Rossi AS: Transition to parenthood. J Marriage and the Family 30: 26–39, 1968
11. Weigert EV, Wenner NK, Cohen MB, et al.: Emotional aspects of pregnancy in Wenner NK, Cohen MB (Eds): Final Report of Washington School of Psychiatry Project: Clinical Study of the Emotional Challenge of Pregnancy. 1968, manuscript
12. Colman AD: Psychological state during first pregnancy. Am J Orthopsychiatr 37: 788–797, 1969
13. Chertok L, Bonnaud M, Borelli M, et al.: Motherhood and Personality. London, Tavistock Publications, 1969
14. Loesch JG, Greenberg NH: Some specific areas of conflicts observed during pregnancy: A comparative study of married and unmarried pregnant women. Am J Orthopsychiatr 32: 624–636, 1962
15. Paffenbarger RS, McCabe LJ: The effect of obstetric and perinatal events on risk of mental illness in women of childbearing age. Am J Pub Health 56: 400–407, 1966
16. Treadway CR, Kane FJ, Jarrahi-Zadeh A, et al.: A psychoendocrine study of pregnancy and puerperium. Am J Psychiatr 10: 86–92, 1969
17. Dalton K: Prospective study into puerperal depression. Brit J Psychiatr 118: 689–692, 1971
18. Asch SS, Rubin LJ: Postpartum reactions: Some unrecognized variations. Am J Psychiatr 131: 870–874, 1974

19. Uddenberg N, Nilsson L: The longitudinal course of paranatal emotional disturbance. Acta Psychiatr Scand 52: 160–169, 1975
20. Parens H: Parenthood as a developmental phase. J Am Psychoanal Assoc 23: 154–165, 1975
21. Benedek T: The psychobiology of pregnancy, in Anthony EJ, Benedek T (Eds): Parenthood: Its Psychology and Psychopathology. Boston, Little, Brown, 1970
22. Gurwitt AR: Aspects of prospective fatherhood. Psychoanal Study Child 31: 237–270, 1976
23. Herzog JM: Patterns of expectant fatherhood. 1979 (Unpublished manuscript)
24. Zilboorg G: Depressive reactions related to parenthood. Am J Psychiatr 87: 927–963, 1931
25. Jarvis W: Some effects of pregnancy and childbirth on men. J Am Psychoanal Assoc 10: 689–700, 1962
26. Ginath Y: Psychoses in males in relation to their wives' pregnancy and childbirth. Israel Ann Psychiatr 12: 227–237, 1974
27. Towne RD, Afterman J: Psychosis in males related to parenthood. Bull Menninger Clin 19: 19–26, 1955
28. Wainwright WH: Fatherhood as a precipitant of mental illness. Am J Psychiatr 123: 40–44, 1966
29. Naeye RL: Coitus and associated amniotic-fluid infection. N Engl J Med 301: 1198–1200, 1979
30. Strinberg A: The Father. Boston, International Pocket Library, 1912
31. Erikson E: Childhood and Society. New York, W.W. Norton, 1950
32. Erikson E: Growth and crisis of the "healthy personality." In Kluckholm C, Murray H, Schneider D (Eds), Personality in Nature, Society and Culture (2nd ed) New York, Knopf, 1973

Richard L. Cohen

3
Maladaptation to Pregnancy

The relationship between a woman's experience during pregnancy, labor, delivery, and the neonatal period and the status of her infant has been well described in the literature[1-14] and in other contributions to this volume. It is therefore of critical importance for the obstetrician and perinatologist to become familiar with the signs of emotional disorder during pregnancy and the perinatal period; to become conversant with some of the most common syndromes and conditions that may surface during this time; and to be familiar with criteria for referral to and collaboration with mental health clinicians.

Our growing recognition of these states has resulted in the blossoming of the field of "psychologic obstetrics" or psychoobstetrics over the past ten or fifteen years. Entire volumes are now available that deal with the psychologic aspects of conception, pregnancy, labor, delivery, and modern obstetric care. For the reader interested in pursuing these subjects in more detail, there are several excellent review volumes and monographs that may be useful in fleshing out the necessarily brief treatment this area will receive in this chapter.[15-22]

The obstetrician and perinatologist may no longer view these subjects from afar. Modern, high-technology medical care is introducing its own set of problems and etiologic components. As maternal and fetal mortality rates decline, it is the author's clinical impression that morbidity rates are increasing for psychologically handicapping conditions in mother and child. Some of these conditions may be unavoidable at the present state of our scientific knowledge. Increased morbidity rates of psychologic disorders may have a strong iatrogenic component. There is a growing body of evidence that modern obstetric care may be a two-edged sword in the sense that procedures designed to protect mother and infant from major stressors may, when inappropriately applied, become a part of the problem instead of a part of the solution.[23-26]

In any case, it becomes important to understand those major factors that may interfere with a woman's capacity to adapt to the developmental tasks of pregnancy, to learn to recognize early cues of maladaptation, and to develop simple, teachable techniques for early intervention.

EMOTIONAL AND PSYCHIATRIC DISORDERS OF PREGNANCY

There is no satisfactory classification scheme for the emotional and psychiatric disorders of pregnancy. Part of the reason for this lack lies in the controversy over the nature of pregnancy itself. At the extremes, the proponents of the pure medical model view pregnancy as an illness and tend to classify all of the subsequent complications of pregnancy and the neonatal period as subsets of that illness state. At the other end of the spectrum are many clinicians and teachers who view pregnancy simply as a normal developmental progression (such as adolescence or middle age), although it may be a period of increased vulnerability to stress requiring more kinship and social and professional support.[27-31]

It is therefore easy to see why a satsifactory classification of disorders becomes difficult to formulate. On a practical, everyday basis, it is probably wisest to approach this problem in a broad-based manner. There *are* conditions that may be associated with pregnancy that assume unquestionable pathologic proportions. At the same time, behavior and/or emotional responses may appear that the clinician can safely view as exaggerations of the normal personality of the woman or, at worst, transient disturbances that will clear spontaneously as the woman's normal defense mechanisms come into play during pregnancy and subsequently.

The classification system in Table 3-1 is admittedly idiosyncratic. It attempts to straddle the question of pregnancy as an illness versus pregnancy as a developmental period. The author makes no claim concerning its scientific validity, but it is experience-based and does broadly represent the spectrum of behavioral disorders that may be encountered in a large obstetric practice.

Table 3-1
Partial Classification of Emotional and Psychiatric
Disorders That May Be Associated with Pregnancy and the
Postpartum Period

I. *Psychiatric syndromes*
    A. *Psychotic states*
        1. Schizophrenia or schizophreniform disorders
        2. Affective disorders
            a. Endogenous disorders
                Manic-depressive illness
                Unipolar states
            b. Exogenous disorders
                Reactive depressions
            c. Postpartum depression*
    B. *Psychoneurotic disorders*
        1. Acute and chronic anxiety states
        2. Phobias
        3. Neurotic depression
II. *Conditions in which psychologic forces may be a
     significant contributory factor*
    1. Functional sterility
    2. Habitual spontaneous abortion
    3. Hyperemesis gravidarum
    4. Preeclampsia
    5. Pseudocyesis
    6. Pathologic cravings and pica
    7. Prolonged and dystonic labor
III. *Failure to achieve "developmental milestones" of
      pregnancy and the neonatal period*
    1. Continued faulty or nonacceptance of pregnancy
        beyond quickening
    2. Inability to develop an emotional affiliation with
        the fetus
    3. Inability to perceive the neonate as a separate
        individual

*There is no consensus with respect to whether so-called post-partum depressions are primarily determined by endogenous (e.g., major shifts in hormone levels following parturition) or psychosocial (e.g., inability to adapt to a nonpregnancy state) factors. Hence it seems best to list it separately for the present.

It would serve no useful purpose to describe at length the clinical syndromes listed under the first categories in Table 3-1. Obviously, these are described at length in the current literature in clinical psychiatry and obstetrics. It is the author's intent to focus primarily on the third category in the classification, particularly because these factors have received the least attention in the literature and, even more importantly, because (1) they probably occur with the highest degree of frequency in obstetric practice and (2) they lend themselves to intervention by obstetricians, perinatologists, and allied health personnel without the necessary involvement of psychiatric consultants or collaborators.[32-34]

Conversely, the incidence of the first two categories is almost certainly lower. Also, intensive intervention for these syndromes almost always necessitates the involvement of psychiatric expertise, at least on a consultative if not collaborative level. In category I, recognition of a fullblown psychotic or psychoneurotic condition should be cause for psychiatric referral during pregnancy or the neonatal period. Although there is considerable evidence to suggest that schizophrenic states do not become worse during pregnancy (some investigators report that they even improve), their existence carries grave portent for the offspring. Similarly, the appearance of depression during pregnancy usually does not carry the same risk of suicide that it may at other times. The existence of this clinical state both for the course of labor and delivery and for the subsequent care of the child carries grave implications, however, and psychiatric intervention should always be considered seriously.[35-46]

The appearance of a category II syndrome may involve more elective types of referral for psychiatric consultation, depending upon the clinical persuasions of the obstetrician and the individual characteristics of each case. There are times when the emotional component of one of these category II states is so clearly evident and of such major proportions that psychiatric referral is definitely in the best interests of mother and offspring. At other times, physiologic factors may appear to far outweigh any emotional components, so that psychiatric referral may carry less potential for contributing to effective intervention.[47-56]

It is the conditions listed under category III that are most relevant for primary care identification and intervention. The remainder of our discussion will therefore be devoted to these phenomena.

It may be argued that the category III "conditions" do not represent clinical syndromes. This is indeed true and characterizes the paradoxic nature of pregnancy. These "states" or "conditions" actually represent developmental failures or arrests. A four-year-old child who has not yet learned how to play cooperatively with his age mates may not merit a clinical diagnosis. Nevertheless, his behavior does indicate the probability of a developmental lag in an important area of psychosocial development. The same generalization applies to category III states. These represent major milestones in the developmental course of pregnancy for a woman, and failure to attain any or all of them renders both the family and the child at risk for future development.[15-23]

SOME ETIOLOGIC FACTORS CONTRIBUTING TO MALADAPTATION TO PREGNANCY AND THE NEONATAL PERIOD

Both developmental and crisis theory teach us that adaptation and coping behavior in the face of novel situations evolve from an interaction between constitutional endowment in the individual and past and current environmental influences. Some of these influences may be perceived as noxious by the individual and others as facilitating or supportive. Nowhere in human development can one find a more clearcut paradigm that demonstrates the aptness of this theoretical construct than in pregnancy, and most characteristically in the first pregnancy.[15,57,58]

In the absence of mental retardation or other serious constitutional deficits that may limit a woman's capacity to solve problems and to cope with new situations, one may reasonably assume that her capacity to adapt to the demands and the tasks of pregnancy is generally related to the overall balance between stresses and supports, both past and present. It is not safe to assume that factors that may be perceived as stressful during other developmental periods are so perceived during pregnancy, or that those perceived as stressful by one woman may be seen similarly by the next. Several studies that have involved the interviewing of large numbers of apparently normal pregnant women have shown, however, that most stressful factors tend to fall into one of several identifiable categories. Although rank ordering of the importance of life experiences involves methodology fraught with pitfalls, there is some agreement[59] that these types of stresses are seen by women approximately in the following order of importance:

1. *Adverse prior experience in childbearing or childrearing:* Any event or experience during the current or other pregnancies that is perceived by the mother as having the possibility of either damaging the fetus now in utero or being predictive of future problems in the child-to-be. This category includes a seemingly endless list of possibilities for the woman. These may run the gamut from such specific events as falling down the steps or being

involved in an automobile accident during the pregnancy to such global and diffuse experiences as having been angry and upset at one's mate during the first trimester or having had great difficulty conceiving. Additional illustrations will be supplied below.

2. *Conflicts and/or defects in support systems:* Major conflict, whether past or present, between the woman and one of her major support systems. Although common sense might dictate that major marital conflict might be perceived as more stressful during pregnancy than other factors, it is not true with most women. Actually, significant, unresolved conflict with one's mother or other primary female caretaker seems to be more stressful than marital conflict. If the conflict has been lifelong and, characteristically, worsened around puberty, so that the woman feels unsure and uncertain of herself as a female and a mothering figure, the tension during pregnancy and the early months of life of the child may be quite burdensome.

3. *Inadequate preparation for childbearing or childrearing:* For primagravidas, particularly those with no younger siblings and little or no experience babysitting, their sense of having no analogous life to return to in order to help them prepare for childbearing and childrearing may be quite stressful.

4. *Maternal health concerns* may be present. If the woman perceives herself as having any condition that may be made worse by childbearing or childrearing, her capacity to emotionally accept the pregnancy and affiliate with the fetus may be seriously interfered with.

Obviously, the above categorization is incomplete, but it is surprising that the great majority of stressful factors can be fitted into one of the above areas. Even financial stress, when carefully discussed with the woman, usually turns out to be related to her perception of her support systems rather than a genuine concern about economics. Women who perceive themselves as closely affiliated with their families, strongly supported by their husbands emotionally, and well cared for by professionals do not appear to be overly distressed by poor finances or other environmental deprivations.

The same is true of geographic relocations. These may be reported as stressful by the woman, but on closer analysis it is the sudden change of support systems inevitably accompanying major relocations that is most troubling.

For emphasis, then, we might label the following hypothetical case as one in which maladaptation was very probable because of the presence of several of the highest-risk etiologic agents in the absence of adequate support systems.

Mrs. X is an 18-year-old, recently married woman who has come to live in a new community located 500 miles from her home of origin. She is the younger of two siblings, having an older brother who is severely retarded. Her own mother has been preoccupied with the care of the brother for many years, and there has been serious conflict between mother and daughter concerning both the latter's rights and privileges in the family and the fact that she has felt "cheated" because most of the family's resources have gone to the care of her disabled brother. Her physician has recently told her that she is suffering from incipient diabetes and will have to be most careful during her pregnancy. She has had no experience in taking care of infants or younger children, knows no one in her new community, and feels that her husband is becoming increasingly interested in sports and television as she progresses through her pregnancy and becomes less physically attractive to him.

The above case, although exaggerated for illustrative purposes, is by no means unusual. Although such instances do not arise on a daily basis in most offices, they are seen frequently enough in this or milder forms to raise the index of suspicion for the clinician that this young woman is developmentally at risk and may require some special attention during her pregnancy and thereafter.

IDENTIFICATION OF RISK FACTORS DURING PREGNANCY

We will continue to address ourselves here to the issues of maladaptive behavior during pregnancy and the most important contributory stresses to that behavior. The diagnosis and assessment of gross mental disorder during pregnancy is a broader (although perhaps simpler) subject that is treated systematically in many available texts in general psychiatry. In any event, the identification of gross psychiatric disease falls into the category of tertiary prevention. We are concerned here more with primary and secondary prevention.

In order to do effective *primary prevention,* the clinician must identify the number and severity of intercurrent stresses present together with the relative strength of various support systems in operation (marital, kinship, societal, and professional).

Primary Prevention Approaches

There is now a substantial body of literature that indicates that it is possible to perform a reasonably adequate preventive psychosocial screening during the prenatal period in approximately 15 minutes and without the use of highly sophisticated mental health personnel.[32,60] Under these circumstances, there is little excuse for any woman not to have the advantage of such clinical screening at some point during her pregnancy. Although, in general, the earlier such screening is performed the better, it is also true that if this is done during the first trimester, life situations may alter significantly and some of the screening may need to be repeated at a later date in order to remain valid.

There are several types of key questions that may be asked that will assist the woman in sharing information about which she may be anxious, depressed, or confused. These questions need not be leading ones, nor should they be threatening or confronting in nature. They should allow the woman room to respond if she wishes, or to give tangential answers if she is not yet ready to deal with material that is highly emotionally charged for her.

Basically, the questions are aimed at identifying the woman who has recently relocated or is inexperienced or alienated or seriously conflicted about her pregnancy or about childrearing. They should also identify the woman who is realistically fearful concerning the outcome of her pregnancy as it may impact on her own physical status or the immediate status of the infant and its long-term development. Her responses must be evaluated in the context of her overall parity formula, the trimester of her pregnancy, and her socioeconomic status.

Although any professional or paraprofessional person may be trained to administer such a technique, the responses should be reviewed and evaluated by the responsible physician. In doing so, heightened sensitivity to the apparently "illogical" or "irrelevant" response to a screening question is in order. Several illustrations may serve to underscore the fact that the manifest content of a response may in no way convey the actual impact of the question on the mother's thinking process.

During psychosocial screening, Mrs. B. was asked, "Has anything happened to you during your pregnancy that causes you concern about how the baby will be?" The mother, after a significant pause, said, "Yes, I had a very disturbing telephone call from my own mother a few weeks ago."

On the surface, such a response has a paralogical overtone to it that may lead the clinician to think that this mother may be either irrational or mentally ill. Follow-up inquiry of this mother once the screening had been evaluated led her to reveal information that she has not disclosed previously. She indicated that her own mother had told her that she had not been the firstborn child (as she had always believed) but that there had been an earlier pregnancy in which the offspring had been born with several severe congenital deformities and had died at three weeks of age. The mother had been "protected" from this information all of her 24 years, believing that she had been the firstborn child. The maternal grandmother had chosen this moment to reveal this "family secret." The patient was in a panic over this and yet had revealed nothing about the telephone call either to her husband or the obstetrician until the above question was asked of her. Her entire attitude about the pregnancy had changed following the telephone call, and she was now in a constant state of fearful apprehension about what would go wrong, whether or not the baby would be intact, and, even if it appeared to be so, whether or not it would harbor some secret defect that she would not be able to discern until it was older.

Mrs. G. was asked the same question as noted above and responded, "Yes, my husband is in jail on a drug charge."

Again, the manifest content is perplexing if taken only at face value, Mrs. G. was questioned in more depth at her next prenatal visit: Why indeed would this affect the baby? She explained at some length that she had read a newspaper article indicating that drugs and alcohol had an adverse effect both on the liver and brain. She had learned following conception of the extensive nature of her husband's proclivity for substance abuse. Would this not, she reasoned, be transmitted in some way to the baby, causing it to be "mentally ill" (her exact words)? She felt she would know immediately on looking at her newborn if it were mentally ill. Indeed, during a follow-up interview 48-hours postnatally she stated that the baby had "a bad disposition" and that it had "snapped back" when she had attempted her first breastfeeding.

Mrs. T. was asked, "Do you plan to raise your child any differently from the way you were raised?" Her unhesitating response was, "Yes. My mother worked all the time."

Here, perhaps the physician may safely assume that the answer means exactly what it seems to mean. Further questioning revealed, however, that Mrs. T.'s mother removed herself from the house for many reasons other than required working hours; that she had an unbridled temper and that the children had to tiptoe about the house when she was within earshot; and that she often lost control and abused the children, especially Mrs. T. Now, pregnant herself, Mrs. T. felt irritable, short tempered, and unready to accept responsibility for an infant. She feared that she would not know what the baby wanted and that the inevitable result would be explosive and abusive behavior on her own part.

Mrs. J. was asked the simple screening question, "What was your reaction when you found out that you were pregnant?" She answered, "Oh boy. You don't want to know. I'm going to sue the drug company that makes those birth control pills!" (Nervous laughter.)

Follow-up inquiry revealed that Mrs. J. had conceived when she believed herself to be "on the pill." She had been angry because the pregnancy was inconvenient and untimely. She was just beginning to accept the idea that she was pregnant when a neighbor in whom she had confided told her that if she had conceived while taking oral contraceptives that her child would be born sterile. Mrs. J. was now depressed but was masking her mood with a jocular, flippant approach to the whole matter.

Each of the above cases presents different problems both in assessment and management. Nevertheless, it must be evident that to have dismissed the initial responses to the screening questions as inconsequential would have represented serious errors in clinical judgment.

In summarized form in Table 3-2 is a series of suggested questions that often serve to elicit useful information concerning the presence of significant stress factors and/or the absence of adequate supports in crucial areas. In addition, some typical "at risk" responses are included for illustrative purposes. These are actual responses in every instance, elicited from a variety of pregnant women either in a university prenatal clinic or in a private obstetric office.

It should be evident from Table 3-2 and the cases above that simple, often "innocent" questions may trigger associative thinking in the woman that may assist her in verbalizing feelings of ideas that she has not been able to share previously and that may have a major impact on her ability to adjust to the pregnancy, to cope with labor and delivery, and to adapt to the new baby and its particular individual characteristics.

IDENTIFICATION OF MALADAPTIVE RESPONSES

Secondary prevention involves the identification of early decompensation in the face of stress and inadequate support, but prior to the time that serious clinical syndromes emerge.

Secondary Prevention Approaches

In general, when the stresses perceived by a woman tend to overwhelm her internal and environmental strengths, signs of decompensation begin to appear. During pregnancy, these most often take

Table 3-2
Sample Questions and Responses to Elicit "At Risk" Responses for Maladaptation to Pregnancy

Sample Questions	Illustrations of "At Risk" Responses
1. Identification of adverse previous experience in childbearing or childrearing	
"Has anything happened (to you) in the past (or during this pregnancy) that might affect the baby?"	1. "Mother died giving birth to me"
	2. "Sexual intercourse caused the baby to 'ball up'"
	3. "My sister had a retarded baby"
	4. "My last baby was born dead"
	5. "My husband's ex-wife called me and said she hopes the baby dies"
	6. "Watched a horror movie on TV. Think the baby might be deformed"
2. Major conflict with support system	
"Do you plan to raise your children any different from the way you were raised?"	1. "I won't send my kids away to school like I was"
	2. "My mother was always sick or tired"
	3. "Yes. My mother never approved of anything I did"
"Is your husband (father of the baby) much help to you?"	1. "Are you kidding? He's like another child to take care of"
	2. "He's angry because I got pregnant"
	3. "I'm beginning to wonder if I married the right man"

59

Table 3-2 (continued)

Sample Questions	Illustrations of "At Risk" Responses
3. Lack of prior experience in infant and child care (for primagravidas)	
"How much experience did you have as you were growing up in taking care of children?"	1. "None, I'm really terrified"
	2. "I guess I was sort of spoiled. My mother wouldn't ever let me help around the house"
	3. "I grew up in a house full of adults. There were never any kids around"
4. Maternal health concerns	
"Do you have any condition that you think might be made worse by being pregnant?"	1. "I had rheumatic heart disease when I was a teenager"
	2. "Not really. Just nerves, I guess"
	3. "I'm usually crippled up for months with my back after I have a baby"

the form (as outlined above) of inability to accept the pregnant state, faulty affiliation with the fetus, or problems in developing a reality-based perception of the neonate and the beginnings of an emotional bond with it.

Usually, the identification of these maladaptive behaviors requires less structured interviewing or questioning and is more recognizable by conventional clinical observation. Nevertheless, certain indicators or clues should be highlighted because these are particularly useful in sharpening the clinician's awareness that something may be seriously amiss and may require planned intervention.

REJECTION OF THE PREGNANCY

It is common knowledge that rejecting or at least ambivalent attitudes toward the news that one is pregnant are common and almost universal. Even in planned pregnancies, there may be inconveniences or life changes brought about by the conception that invoke afterthoughts or mixed feelings. In almost all instances, the strongly negative attitudes begin to dissolve around the time of quickening and are usually resolved by the third trimester. Continued overt and frank rejection of the pregnancy into the third trimester does not require clinical acumen to identify. Unfortunately, the rejection may be disguised both from the clinician and the gravid woman. Useful behavioral clues include the following: (1) mother denies or ignores body and appearance changes; (2) mother constantly overreacts to body and appearance changes; (3) mother is preoccupied with vague emotional and/or physical unremediable complaints; (4) at advanced stages of pregnancy, mother dresses and engages in activities that suggest she is not pregnant.

FAILURE TO DEVELOP EMOTIONAL AFFILIATION
WITH FETUS

For most women, the fetus does not become a real, growing human being until quickening occurs. Quickening usually stimulates a sense of positive anticipation in the mother, a growing acceptance of the pregnancy, and the beginnings of nesting behavior. This mounting awareness of a separate "person" who can move independently and who responds to sound, motion, and the maternal physiologic state all combine to help the mother begin to experience a sense of closeness to the fetus and a growing curiosity about what it will be like to live with and take care of it. These are healthy signs of affiliation. Clues that the mother may not be taking this next adaptive step in the pregnancy include the following: (1) absent or minimal response to quickening; (2) disturbed or distorted response to quickening (e.g.,

"He's like a wild man. He never gives me any rest"); (3) absent nesting behavior in the third trimeter, especially in primigravidas (no name selection, no living space planned for baby, etc.); (4) absence of any fantasies about what the fetus is like or what the baby will be like, or predominantly negative fantasies.

FAILURE TO SHOW A REALITY-BASED PERCEPTION OF AND TIE TO THE NEONATE

The mother must now make a transition from her fantasy-based perception of the fetus to the development of a perception of the real characteristics of the baby if she is to (1) care for it properly, (2) respond to its communications, and (3) develop a pleasurable relationship with it. With traditional hospital-based care, these phenomena are difficult to evaluate during the first 48 hours or so. However, following this typical "maternal lag" period, useful clues that this final step in the psychologic process of reproduction is not occurring include the following: (1) mother cannot describe any distinguishing physical or behavioral characteristics of her offspring; (2) mother attributes inappropriate characteristics to offspring ("He's mean and stubborn just like my father was"); (3) mother adultomorphizes child and cannot endow it with infant status (e.g., "He looks so intelligent. I just know he's going places").

DISCUSSION AND CONCLUSIONS

It is clearly impossible to catalogue all of the risk factors and indicators of maladaptive behavior that should alert the physician that the course of pregnancy and parturition may be in jeopardy. A substantial body of experience is now available to document the conclusions that any series of events or conditions that are perceived by the mother as threatening, depleting, or potentially harmful to either the child or herself (or both) may seriously compromise her capacity to make the several adaptive steps that characterize the modal pregnancy. Therefore a high index of suspicion is warranted. One must be particularly cautious about summarily dismissing responses that appear irrelevant, illogical, or without medical foundation.

Particular attention should be paid during any pregnancy where screening and observation reveals one or more of the following ten circumstances:

1. History of loss of the mother's mother before her own puberty and without adequate replacement by a substitute maternal figure.
2. Chronic conflict with or alienation from one's own mother and other female relatives.
3. Previous birth of a damaged child.
4. Mother reports older child to be emotionally disturbed or behaviorally disordered.
5. Chronic marital discord, especially if focus of conflict is around childbearing or childrearing.
6. Mother has had virtually no preparation for sexual experience, childbearing, or childrearing.
7. Mother reports experience she fears will damage baby (especially if she does not respond to simple, direct explanation and reassurance by physician).
8. Behavior indicating overt or disguised rejection of pregnant state as late as third trimester.
9. Absence of nesting behavior (especially in primigravidas) in third trimester.
10. Inability to show early signs of identifying baby's individual characteristics during early weeks of extrauterine life.

Admittedly, these ten indicators constitute a rather coarse net for identifying those pregnant women who may require more than "routine" explanation and professional support. Nevertheless, a surprising percentage of patients seriously at risk will be picked up using these criteria and the methods of screening described previously.

It cannot be emphasized too strongly that no firm diagnostic conclusions or treatment decisions should be made from the appearance of at-risk indicators or from the early signs of maladaptive behavior. These constitute only an early warning system; they permit the sorting out of that relative minority of patients who will require more intensive interviewing and observation in order to ascertain which of them may require additional intervention.

Some patients may require only more frequent but conservative monitoring. Others may require the marshalling of special community resources such as family or marital counseling agencies and child welfare services. Still others may warrant referral to mental health centers or psychiatrists.

Another source of support and early intervention available to obstetricians may be the pediatrician or pediatric service, if one has been identified by the family. Early involvement of the pediatrician during the pregnancy, as a child-oriented "expert" who may be available to the mother to respond to her questions and to perform anticipatory counseling, can prove indispensable. Also, the pediatrician who is more exposed to the "mythology" of child development that may be in vogue at the time may be more attuned to distortions of fact that may be identified through incisive questioning.

Some pediatricians even choose to conduct a semistructured type of family interview during the prenatal visit. This allows them to identify the assets and liabilities for child care in the family early on. They can then deal in a more proactive fashion with the family's concerns during the early months of the child's care instead of being compelled to react to crises as they arise.

Conversely, the importance of a searching interview by the obstetrician during the routine postnatal visit is often revealing for both mother and physician. This is an opportunity to settle any "unfinished business" the mother may be experiencing about the pregnancy and especially about her confinement. This is particularly indicated if there were complications surrounding the labor and delivery. The use of electronic or chemical monitors, special medications, or any special manipulative procedure often leaves the mother with troubling questions about her own or the baby's status. Even if adequate explanations were given in the hospital, these are often misunderstood or distorted under the stress of the moment. The physician should not assume that even the highly educated or intelligent mother understands what has happened to her and what the immediate and long-range effects, if any, may be. In fact, educated mothers may be too embarrassed to ask simple ("stupid") questions.

Finally, these activities may increase moderately the amount of time that must be spent with new patients during early contacts (and commensurately, the scope of clinical responsibility accepted). Many advantages are likely to accrue as a result, including (1) a smoother clinical course during pregnancy, labor, and delivery; (2) fewer "emergency" visits and phone calls and less "medical shopping" by the patient and her family; (3) fewer psychophysiologic reactions; (4) greater sense of reward from the practice of obstetrics or perinatal medicine; and (5) a less complicated and stressful start for mother and infant and a higher likelihood of subsequent healthy child development.

Although systematic studies are not available, this writer is convinced that the investment of time and energy required by the use of this approach to identification of paranatal maladaptive reactions is, in the long run, conserving of both time and energy. *Proactive* coping with problems arising in clinical practice is generally a much more economical manner of delivering quality care than the *reactive* or "putting-out-fires" style of practice.

REFERENCES

1. Flapan M: A paradigm for the analysis of childbearing motivations of married women prior to birth of the first child. Am J Orthopsychiatr 39:402–417, 1969
2. Colman AD: Psychological state during the first pregnancy. Am J Orthopsychiatr 39:788–797, 1969
3. Kazzaz DS: Attitude of expectant mothers in relation to onset of labor. Obstet Gynecol 26:585–591, 1965
4. Werner E, Bierman JM, French FE, et al.: Reproductive and environmental casualties: A report on the ten-year follow-up of the children of the Kauai pregnancy study. Pediatrics 42:112–127, 1968
5. Jessner L, Weigert E, Foy JL: The development of parental attitudes during pregnancy, in Anthony EJ, Benedek T (Eds): Parenthood. London, Churchill, 1970, pp 209–244
6. Engstrom L, Getterstam G, Holmberg NG, et al.: Psychosocial factors in pregnancy. J Psychosom Res 8:151–155, 1964
7. Gordon ER, Gordon AK: Social factors in the prediction and treatment of emotional disorders of pregnancy. Am J Obstet Gynecol 77:1074–1083, 1959
8. Cohen RL: Pregnancy stress and maternal perception of infant endowment. J Ment Subnorm, June 1966
9. Stott DH: Follow-up study from birth of the effects of prenatal stresses. Dev Med Child Neurol 15:770–787, 1973
10. Davids A, DeVault S, Talmadge M: Anxiety, pregnancy and childbirth abnormalities. J Consult Psychol 25:74–77, 1961
11. Davids A, Rosengren WR: Social stability and psychological adjustment during pregnancy. Psychosom Med 24:579–583, 1962
12. Davids A, DeVault S: Maternal anxiety during pregnancy and childbirth abnormalities. Psychosom Med 24:464–470, 1962
13. McDonald RL: Fantasy and the outcome of pregnancy. Arch Gen Psychiatr 12:602–606, 1965
14. Gillman RD: The dreams of pregnant women and maternal adaptation. Am J Orthopsychiatr 38:688–692, 1968
15. Caplan G: Emotional implications of pregnancy and influences on family relationships, in Stuart HC, Prugh DG (Eds): The Healthy Child. Cambridge, Mass., Harvard Univ, 1962, pp 72–82
16. McDonald RL: The role of emotional factors in obstetric complications: A review. Psychosom Med 30:222–237, 1968
17. Williams CC, Williams A, Griswold MS, et al.: Pregnancy and life change. J Psychosom Res 19:123–129, 1975
18. Werner E, Smith RS: Kauai's Children Come of Age. Honolulu, Univ Hawaii, 1977
19. Lerner B, Raskin R: Davis EB: On the need to be pregnant. Int J Psychoanal 48:288–297, 1967
20. Uddenberg N, Nilsson L: The longitudinal course of paranatal emotional disturbance. Acta Psychiatr Scand 52:160–169, 1975

21. Benedek T: The psychobiology of pregnancy, in Anthony EJ, Benedek T (Eds): Parenthood. London, Churchill, 1970, pp 137–151

22. Grimm E, Benet W: The relationship of emotional adjustment and attitudes to the course and outcome of pregnancy. Psychosom Med 28:34–49, 1966

23. Shugarman M: Paranatal influences on maternal-infant attachment. Am J Orthopsychiatr 47:407–421, 1977

24. Berg RB: Early discharge of low birthweight babies. Hosp Prac, October 1970, pp 149–154

25. Starkman MN: Psychological responses to the use of the fetal monitor during labor. Psychosom Med 38:269–277, 1976

26. Chard T, Richards M: Benefits and Hazards of the New Obstetrics. London, Heineman Medical, 1977

27. Treadway CR, Treadway CR, Kane FJ, et al.: A psychoendocrine study of pregnancy and the puerperium. Am J Psychiatry 125:1380–1386, 1969

28. Karacin I, Heine W, Agnew HW, et al.: Characteristics of sleep patterns during late pregnancy and the postpartum period. Am J Obstet Gynecol 101:579–586, 1968

29. Lynn DB: The Father: His Role in Child Development. Monterey, Brooks/Cole, 1974, pp 225–231

30. McNeil TF, Kauj L: Length of interbirth intervals in female psychiatric patients and controls. J Can Psychiatr Assoc 20:219–222, 1975

31. Hern WM: The illness parameters of pregnancy. Soc Sci Med 9:365–372, 1975

32. Horsley S: Psychological management of the prenatal period, in Howells JG (Ed): Modern Perspectives in Psycho-Obstetrics. Edinboro, Oliver & Boyd, 1972, pp 291–313

33. Cohen RL: Some maladaptive syndromes of pregnancy and the puerperium. Obstet Gynecol 27:562–570, 1966

34. Frommer EA, O'Shea G: Antenatal identification of women liable to have problems in managing their infants. Br J Psychiatr 123:149–156, 1973

35. Zax M, et al.: Birth outcomes in the offspring of mentally disordered women. Am J Orthopsychiatr 47:218–230, 1977

36. Wenner NK, Cohen MB, Weigert EV, et al.: Emotional problems in pregnancy. Psychiatry 32:389–410, 1969

37. Biele AM: Unwanted pregnancy: Symptom of depressive practice. Am J Psychiatr 128:754, 1971

38. Whitlock FA, Edwards JE: Pregnancy and attempted suicide. Compr Psychiatr 9:1–12, 1968

39. Bratfos O, Haug JO: Puerperal mental disorders in manic depressive females. Acta Psychiatr Scand 42:285–294, 1966

40. Pitt B: "Atypical" depression following childbirth. Br J Psychiatr 114:1325–1335, 1968

41. Yalom ID, Lunde DT, Moos RH, et al.: "Postpartum blues" syndrome. A description and related variables. Arch Gen Psychiatr 18:16–27, 1968

42. Melges FT: Postpartum psychiatric syndromes. Psychosom Med 30:95–108, 1968

43. Wilson JE, Barglow P, Shipman W: The prognosis of postpartum mental illness. Compr Psychiatr 13:305–316, 1972

44. Protheroe C: Puerperal psychosis: A long-term study 1927–1961. Br J Psychiatr 115:9–30, 1969

45. Dalton K: Prospective study into puerperal depression. Br J Psychiatr 118:689–692, 1971

46. Harder T: The psychopathology of infanticide. Acta Psychiatr Scand 43:196–245, 1967

47. Howells JG: Modern Perspectives in Psycho-Obstetrics. New York, Brunner/Mazel, 1972, pp 31–50, 53–65, 233–250, 269–282, 283–290

48. Lubin B, et al.: Mood and somatic symptoms during pregnancy. Psychosom Med 37:136–146. 1975

49. Glick ID, Salerno LJ, Royce JR: Psychophysiologic factors in the etiology of preeclampsia. Arch Gen Psychiatr 12:260–266, 1965

50. Malmquist A, Kaij L, Nilsson A: Psychiatric aspects of spontaneous abortion. I. A matched control study of women with living children. J Psychosom Res 13:45–51, 1969

51. Kaij L, Malmquist A, Nilsson A: Psychiatric aspects of spontaneous abortion: II. The importance of bereavement, attachment and neurosis in early life. J Psychosom Res 13:53–59, 1969

52. Majerus PW, Guze SB, Delong WB, et al.: Psychologic factors and psychiatric disease in hyperemesis gravidarum: A follow-up study of 69 vomiters and 66 controls. Am J Psychiatr 421–428, 1960

53. Guze SB, Delong WB, Majerus PW, et al.: Association of clinical psychiatric disease with hyperemesis gravidarum: A three-and-one-half year follow-up study of 48 patients and 45 controls. N Engl J Med 261:1363–1368, 1959

54. Grimm ER: Psychological investigation of habitual abortion. Psychosom Med 24:369–378, 1962

55. Gunter LM: Psychopathology and stress in the life experience of mothers and premature infants: A comparative study. Am J Obstet Gynecol 86:333–340, 1963

56. Kaplan DM, Mason EA: Maternal reactions to premature birth viewed as an acute emotional disorder. Am J Orthopsychiatr 30:539–552, 1960

57. Bibring G: Some consideration of the psychological processes in pregnancy. Psychoanal Study Child 14:113, 1959

58. Bibring G, Dwyer TF, Huntington DS: A study of the psychological processes in pregnancy and of the earliest mother–child relationship. II. Methodological considerations. Psychoanal Study Child 16:9, 1961

59. Halper MM, Cohen RL, Beitenman ET, et al.: Life events and acceptance of pregnancy. J Psychosom Res 12:183–188, 1968

60. Cohen RL: Experiences of pregnancy: Some relationships to the syndrome of mental retardation, in Menolascino F (Ed): Psychiatric Approaches to Mental Retardation. New York, Basic Books, 1970, pp 633–651

T. Berry Brazelton

4

Behavioral Competence of the Newborn Infant

In the past, the newborn infant has been thought of as helpless, insensitive, and ready to be entirely shaped by his environment. This model of helplessness and insensitivity served many purposes in the past. It allowed his caregivers to feel in control and to feel absolutely necessary to him. In the case of sick infants, it allowed medical personnel to feel that their interventions were not as painful as they might have been perceived by a thinking, feeling organism. Finally, in an era when many infants were to die, this contributed to a kind of depersonification that may have protected the infant's parents from investing too early in each infant. Many cultures in which the neonatal death rate is high still institutionalize such practices as not speaking of the newborn as a baby but as a phoenix[1] or of not naming him until he is three months old and more likely to survive.[2]

Our concepts of reinforcing parents for early attachment to neonates is a new one. At this time in history, we can afford to urge young parents to attach to a new baby, since very few will die. Even when infants do not survive, we have become convinced that grief reactions will be handled better by parents who have proceeded to attach to the infant than by those who are never allowed to touch or to see the dying infant.[3] If the infant does survive, we feel there is a kind of energy available to new parents to bond to the infant right

Supported in part by grants from Robert Wood Johnson Foundation, Carnegie Foundation, and William T. Grant Foundation.

around delivery and for the new adjustment to parenting.[4] In our society we have depersonalized the delivery process to such an extent that parents feel manipulated and out of control. Hence any effort to give them a feeling of importance around this event will reinforce them for competence and is likely to become a force for earlier and more sensitive attachment to the individual baby. Certainly their joy in achievement of a normal delivery is likely to feed their sense of fulfillment as parents and to reinforce their self-confidence in the adaptation necessary to each new infant. Klaus and Kennell and associates[5] have shown that attention to parents' needs for bonding to the new infant will result in expectable gains in cognitive, linguistic, and affective competence in the infant and child later in his development.

There are other potent and often destructive influences on parenting that make it important that we begin to value the neonate's contribution to his new environment. Since parents' inclination is to nurture the newborn, to value his reactions to their handling, to voice, to vision, it becomes a real putdown to these reactions if we as physicians do not value them in the neonate. If we do attend to them, change neonatal nurseries and lying-in arrangements to value and capture the neonate's best periods of alert responsiveness, we place a stamp of approval both on the parents' attention to the neonate and on the newborn as an important, interactive person from the start. We are providing new, confused parents with a way of communicating with their infants. We are showing them that the neonate can lead them when they are confused.

The demands of a complex, undirected society, coupled with the lack of support (often even negative input) that is provided new parents by our present nuclear family system, leave most parents insecure and at the mercy of tremendous internal and external pressures. They have been told that their infant's outcome is to be shaped by them and their parenting; at the same time there are few stable cultural values on which they can rely for guidance in setting their course as new parents. Most new parents are separated emotionally from their own parents' standards by the generation gap and all that it implies. Our present generation has actively separated itself from the beliefs and mores of the preceding generation. For example, we can cite the ambivalence with which the press and other media are treating Spock's previously accepted ideas.[6] I am not questioning the need for a change in childrearing practices—I certainly endorse many of the revisions—but I want to show how one more potential prop has been eliminated from the young parents' armamentarium for support. Physicians are not readily available to many young parents, and nurse-practitioners are not quite filling the gap yet, although I hope and believe that they will be doing so before long. Pediatricians and physicians in family medicine will be pressed toward a primary care paradigm lest they lose the most rewarding and precious asset a physician has: the feedback from maintaining a supportive, interactive relationship with parents as they foster the development of their children.

Our society's backup for parenting often is a negative one. There is virtually no opportunity for most children as they grow up in small, lonely nuclear family settings to experience how their own or other parents go about raising small brothers and sisters. As a result, they come to parenting with little experience of their own.

The childbirth education groups have shown the importance of preparation for childbirth itself. This preparation points up another missed but powerful potential—that of preparing young couples for their roles as parents.

An infant is not as helpless as he seems, however, and there are rewards as well as messages from an infant that can guide a new mother and new father as they confront their new roles. There are strengths inherent in the parent–infant system, including a reciprocal interactional system between a baby and its parents that can provide rewards for each of them, for the infant comes well equipped to signal his needs and his gratitude to his environment. In fact, he can even make choices about what he wants from his parents, and shut out what he doesn't want in such powerful ways that I no longer see him as a passive lump of clay but as a powerful force for stabilizing and influencing those around him. What I believe we must do is to uncover and expose these infant strengths to parents, to demonstrate the infant's behavior on which they can rely, and to support young parents in their own individualized endeavor to reach out for, attach to, and *enjoy* their new infants! But this is no mean task.

What is the adaptive purpose of prolonged infancy in the human? No other species has as long a period of relative dependency, and I believe that it is important to look for the adaptive advantages in rules of nature, selected over many generations for their survival value. Compared to that of any other species, the human neonate is relatively helpless in the motor sphere and relatively complex, even precocious, in the sensory sphere. This enforces a kind of motoric dependence and a freedom for acquisition of the many patterns of sensory and affective information that are necessary to the child and adult human for mastering and surviving in a complex world. In other words, the prolonged period of infancy allows for early and affective transmission of all the mores and instrumental techniques evolved by society—and a kind of individuality inherent in each culture.

As the potential for early intervention increases, it becomes more and more important that we be able to evaluate infants at risk as early as possible with an eye to more sophisticated preventive and therapeutic approaches. Early intervention may prevent a compounding of problems that occurs all too easily when the environment cannot adjust appropriately to the infant at risk. Premature and minimally brain-damaged infants seem to be less able to compensate in disorganized, depriving environments than are well-equipped neonates, and their problems or organization in development are compounded early.[7] Quiet, nondemanding infants do not elicit necessary mothering from already overstressed parents and are selected by their neonatal behavior for kwashiorkor and marasmus in poverty-ridden cultures such as are found in Guatemala and Mexico.[8,9] Hyperkinetic, hypersensitive neonates may press a mother and father into a kind of desperation that produces childrearing responses from them that reinforce the problems of the child so that he grows up in an overreactive, hostile environment.[10] Parents of children admitted to the wards of the Children's Hospital in Boston for clinical syndromes such as failure to thrive, child abuse, repeated accidents and poisonings, and infantile autism are often successful parents of other children. By history, they associate their failure with the one child to an inability to "understand" him from the neonatal period onward, and they claim a difference from the other children in his earliest reactions to them. If we are to improve the outcome for such children, assessment of the risk in early infancy could mobilize preventive efforts and programs for intervention before the neonate's problems are compounded by an environment that cannot understand him without such help.

We need more sophisticated methods of assessing neonates and for predicting their contribution to the likelihood of failure in the enivronment–infant interaction. We also need to be able to assess at-risk environments because the impracticality of spreading resources too thin points to the necessity of selecting target populations for our efforts at early intervention. With better techniques for assessing strengths and weaknesses in infants and the environments to which they will be exposed, we might come to better understand the mechanisms for failures in development that result in some of the above-mentioned syndromes. Even desperate socioeconomic conditions produce comparable stresses in many families whose children do not have to be salvaged from the clinical syndromes of child abuse, failure to thrive, and kwashiorkor. Minimally brain-damaged babies do make remarkable compensatory recoveries in a fostering environment. Understanding the infant and the problems he will present to his parents may enhance our value as supportive figures for them as they adjust to a difficult infant.

The Apgar score[11] is the traditional and most universal criterion for assessing the newborn's well-being in the delivery room. Its primary effect has been for the anesthetist and obstetrician to focus attention on the neonate. Its five categories —color, respiratory effect, cardiac effort, body tone, and responsiveness to aversive stimuli— measure the functions necessary to sustain life. The score reflects the neonate's capacity to respond to the stress of labor and delivery. The score is influenced to a certain extent by any perinatal event, such as moderate hypoxia, drugs or anesthesia given the mother, prolonged, labor, cesarean section, etc.; but since the score is done in the first five minutes after delivery only, it basically measures the immediate capacity of the neonate for an "alarm" reaction. The kind and depth of depression that may follow later and that represents the depleted resources of the baby is in no way predicted by the Apgar score. Subtle effects of insults such as hypoxia or drugs are easily overlooked by the Apgar score, since it is necessary to have a substantial insult to impair the gross functioning of neuromuscular, cardiac, or respiratory systems.

The limited predictive ability of the Apgar score has been a disappointment to pediatricians and pediatric neurologists. At an initial screening level, however, it is important. Drage et al.[12] reported a fourfold increase in neurologic abnormalities at one year in infants with low five minute Apgar scores compared to those with high scores. Only 4.3 percent of those with low five minute Apgar scores had gross neurologic abnormalities, however. More subtle effects at outcome were suggested by Lewis et al.,[13] who studied visual attentiveness at 3, 9, and 13 months of age in babies with normal Apgar scores at one minute. In this group, they differentiated between those with scores of 7–9 and those with scores of 10 in their capacity to respond to complex visual tasks. Their results suggest that the Apgar score in some way reflects a spectrum of behavior that may predict future functioning, if we use more sensitive tests along with it.

The concept that the newborn functions only at a brain-stem level of nervous organization[14] has led to rather stereotyped neurologic examinations that assess reflex behavior with an oversimplified positive–negative approach. Not until recently was it recognized that the higher brain centers serve to modify responses through partial inhibition or facilitation in the neonate and that the intact function of the CNS can be determined by a qualitative assessment of responses in the neonatal period. Brain-damaged infants may have reflex responses available but they may be distortedly exaggerated or partially suppressed, stereotyped, or obligatory; the quality of these responses is different from that of the graded ones seen in an intact baby. Hence the more recent neurologic examinations provide scoring systems for these qualitative differences, and the scores become more predictive of good function.

In order to record and evaluate some of the integrative processes evidenced in certain kinds of neonatal behavior, we have developed a behavioral evaluation scale that tests and documents the infant's use of state behavior (state of consciousness) and the response to various kinds of stimulation.[15]

Since the neonate's reactions to all stimuli are dependent on his ongoing "state," any interpretation of them must be made with this in mind. His use of state to maintain control of his reactions to environmental and internal stimuli is an important mechanism and reflects his potential for organization. State no longer need be treated as an error variable, but serves to set a dynamic pattern to allow for the full behavioral repertoire of the infant. Specifically, our examination tracks changes in state over the course of the exam, and its lability and direction. The variability of state indicates the infant's capacities for self-organization. His ability to quiet himself, as well as his need for stimulation, also measures this adequacy.

The behavior exam tests for neurologic adequacy with 20 reflex measures and for 26 behavioral responses to environmental stimuli, including the kind of interpersonal stimuli that mothers use in their handling of the infant as they attempt to help him adapt to the new world. Best performance is used to overcome variables. In the exam, there is a graded series of procedures—talking, hand on belly, restraint, holding, and rocking—designed to soothe and alert the infant. His responsiveness to animate stimuli (e.g., voice, face) and to inanimate stimuli (e.g., rattle, bell, red ball, white light, temperature change) is assessed. Estimates of vigor and attentional excitement are measured, and an assessment is made of motor activity and tone and autonomic responsiveness as he changes state. With this examination given on successive days we have been able to outline (1) the initial period of alertness immediately after delivery, presumably the result of stimulation of labor and the new environmental stimuli after delivery, (2) the period of depression and disorganization that follows and that lasts for 24–48 hours in infants with uncomplicated deliveries and no medication effects, but for longer periods of 3–4 days if the infants have been compromised from medication given their mothers during labor, and (3) the curve of recovery to "optimal" function after several days. This third period may be the best single predictor of individual potential function, and it seems to correlate well with the neonate's retest ability at 30 days.[16] The shape of the curve made by several examinations may be the most important assessment of the basic CNS intactness of the neonate's ability to integrate CNS and other physiologic recovery mechanisms and of the strength of his compensatory capacities when there have been compromising insults to him during labor and delivery. A condensed list of the behavioral items are indicated in Table 4-1.

In addition to the 26 items of behavior, assessed on a 9-point scale, there are 20 reflex responses that are also assessed.

We feel that the behavioral items elicit more important evidences of cortical control and responsiveness, even in the neonatal period. The neonate's capacity to manage and overcome the physiologic demands of this adjustment period in order to attend to, to differentiate, and to habituate to the complex stimuli of an examiner's maneuvers may be an important predictor of his future central

Table 4-1
Neonatal Behavioral Assessment

Behavioral Items
1. Response decrement to repeated visual stimuli
2. Response decrement to rattle
3. Response decrement to bell
4. Response decrement to pinprick
5. Orienting response to inanimate visual stimuli
6. Orienting response to inanimate auditory stimuli
7. Orienting response to animate visual—examiner's face
8. Orienting response to animate auditory—examiner's voice
9. Orienting response to animate visual and auditory stimuli
10. Quality and duration of alert periods
11. General muscle tone in resting and in response to being handled (passive and active)
12. Motor maturity
13. Traction responses as he is pulled to sit
14. Cuddliness—responses to being cuddled by the examiner
15. Defensive movements—reactions to a cloth over his face
16. Consolability with intervention by examiner
17. Peak of excitement and his capacity to control himself
18. Rapidity of buildup to crying state
19. Irritability during the exam
20. General assessment of kind and degree of activity
21. Tremulousness
22. Amount of startling
23. Lability of skin color (measuring autonomic lability)
24. Lability of states during entire exam
25. Self-quieting activity—attempts to console self and control state
26. Hand-to-mouth activity

nervous system organization. Certainly, the curve of recovery of these responses over the first neonatal week must be of more significance than the midbrain responses detectable in routine neurologic exams. Repeated behavioral exams on any two or three days in the first ten days after delivery might be expected to be sensitive predictors of future CNS function.

In this exam are couched behavioral tests of such important CNS mechanisms as (1) "habituation," or the neonate's capacity to shut out disturbing or overwhelming stimuli, (2) choices in attention to various objects or human stimuli (a neonate shows clear preferences for female versus male voices, and for human versus nonhuman visual stimuli), and (3) control of his state in order to attend to information from his environment (the effort to complete a hand-to-mouth cycle in order to attend to objects and people around him). These are all evidenced in the neonate and even in the premature infant, and seem to be more predictive of CNS intactness than are reflex responses.[17]

What are some of the built-in strengths of the human neonate? A few examples will demonstrate how powerful these are as economical determinants of how he will conserve himself in a new overwhelming world and how he can quickly acquire the information he needs to choose to make his caregivers familiar with him and responsive to him in a way that will latch them onto him at a critical period for them both. Right out of the uterus (1) he can and does turn his head to the human voice repeatedly, and his face alerts as he searches for its source; (2) he will attend to and choose a female vocal pitch over any other;[18] (3) humanoid sounds are not only preferred to pure tones in an equivalent range of pitch, but when he is tested with continuous sucking as a response system he stops sucking briefly after a pure tone then goes on sucking steadily, whereas after a human tone he stops sucking and then continues in a burst-pause pattern of sucking (as if he were expecting more important information to follow, and as if the pauses in the sucking were designed to allow for attention to this further information);[19] (4) he will attend to and follow with eyes and full 90-degree head-turning a picture of a human face, but will not follow a scrambled face, although he will look at it wide-eyed for a long period (in the delivery room and before any caretaking has been instituted);[20] (5) he will turn to and prefer milk smells above those of water or sugar water; and (6) he can taste and respond to with altered sucking patterns the difference between human milk and a cow's milk formula designed to exactly produce the contents of breast milk.[21]

There are two questions that might shed light on the potential for recovery and development of neonates. If these complex responses are present, does the neonate learn from experiencing them? If he can learn from the experience of controlling input, from his choices, from his efforts at state control, does his attempt to integrate his CNS in order to respond become an organizing influence? I have been impressed by the efforts to improve the environments for neonates and at-risk infants.

The studies of the effects of stimulation in the neonatal period on the recovery of premature and other high-risk neonates have been limited so far to groups of neonates who are in our present deprivation system, but there is increasing evidence that sensory input that is *appropriate* to the state of physiologic recovery of that neonate may act powerfully to further his weight gain, his sensory integrity, and even his outcome. For example, Pettigrew[22] found that for kittens specific visual input was necessary for the development of the specificity of initially undifferentiated cells, and Blakemore and Cooper[23] found that visual cortex neurons responded predominantly to stimuli that were equivalent to the environment in which the kittens were reared. In both cases, however, these effects were found only after a given level of CNS maturity had been achieved. Prior to that time, exposure had no effect because it did not appropriately fit the organism's level of development.

Most of the studies on early stimulation have not been individualized to the subjects. We have evidence that leads us to feel that each premature or recovering neonate *must* be examined for the possibility of sensory overloading. A premature infant will respond to a soft rattle with head turning away from the rattle (and other evidences of shutting it out), whereas a normal neonate will turn toward the rattle and search for it.[24] We feel that this crude example of the finely defined thresholds for appropriate sensory stimuli, as opposed to those that must be "coped with" or shut out, must be taken as seriously as whether we offer stimulation or not. In the recovery phase, a high-risk baby may be too easily overwhelmed, and "routine" stimulation may force him into an expensive coping model, whereas grading the stimuli to his particular sensory needs may further his recovery as well as his ultimate CNS outcome. How can we tell when he is being overloaded? We can tell by watching his color changes, his kind of respirations, and his state of alertness and accounting for evidences of fatigue. A stressed neonate must be observed for evidence of excessive physiologic demands as he responds to a stimulus for attention; investment in a learning paradigm has its own cost, and this cost must be balanced against his capacity to manage the cost at his stage of physiologic recovery. Using Kearsley's ideas[25] about the relative degree of attention to a stimulus as it is measured against the physiologic demands, we have a clearly defined area of "appropriate" versus "inappropriate" properties of all stimuli that can be applied to each neonate individually and the amount and the quality of stimulation that can be offered to every at-risk neonate without expense.

The studies by Sander et al.[26] show that the infant shapes his motility and his "state" behavior to the environment, *particularly* if it is sensitive to him and to his individual needs. Two models of regulation occurred with the neonates and caretakers they studied. The first related to basic regulation of endogenous biorhythmicity and was entrained by specific extrinsic cues in relation to the neonate's endogenous rhythm. Entrainment was most effective when the exogenous cue approximated the point in time at which a shift in the endogenous cycle was occurring. With the repeated establishment of contingent relationships between state changes in the infant and specific configurations in caretaking events, entrainment was favored. The second model depended on the caretaker and infant achieving a regulatory balance based on mutual readiness of states, and with this the stage was set to facilitate initial cognitive development. As the partners appreciated a mutual regulation of states of attention, they began to learn about and from each other, and a kind of reciprocity of affective interaction ensued.

We have shown that as early as three weeks there is a clear differentiation between the infant's kind of attention, as well as of all of his behaviors when he is attending to an object versus a person,[27] and now we know that he can further differentiate *between persons*—father, mother, and stranger—with a clearly different set of behaviors. If this behavioral attentional set can be shaped as early as this, it denotes a kind of "readiness" for learning that is inexpensive and adaptive for him. Of course, it leads to more and appropriate adult interaction for him. His responses become adaptive in providing him with a feedback source of appropriate stimuli from the adults around him, as well as a way of his demonstrating behaviorally to the sensitive adult that now he or she is on target with the infant.

In our laboratory at Children's Hospital Medical Center, we have been looking at this early reciprocal interaction between infants and their parents and, more recently, infants and strangers. We start at two weeks and continue with them until 24 weeks in a laboratory situation designed to film and analyze the ingredients of early reciprocity as it develops between infants and familiar adults (Fig. 4-1). We film the infants in a reclining chair (or baby seat) as the adult comes in to lean over him and enlist his attention in "games" or "play." We first found that as early as we could film it we saw

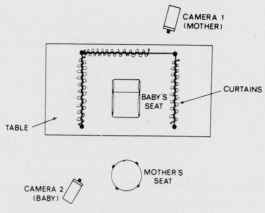

Fig. 4-1.   Laboratory setting.

completely different kinds of behavior and attention with a mother and with an attractive object (Fig. 4-2).[28]

With an attractive object, as it was brought into "reach" space (about 12 inches out in front of him), his attention and face became "hooked" as his extremities and even his fingers and toes pointed out toward it, making brief swipes out toward it, as he attended with a rapt, fixed expression on his face. When he was satiated, his attention broke off abruptly and he averted his eyes or turned his whole head and body away for a brief period before he came back for a further period of "hooked" attention. Thus he established a jagged homeostatic curve of attention, and his arms and legs displayed jerky components of reach behavior as they attended to the object—all at a time when a reach could not be achieved successfully.

With his mother, his attention and motor behavior were entirely different; movements of his eyes, his face, his mouth, and his extremities all became smooth and cyclic. As he attended, he moved out slightly toward the object with his head, his mouth, his eyes, and even with his legs, arms, fingers, and toes, but almost immediately the approach behavior was followed by smooth, cyclic withdrawal behavior, as if he expected his mother (or father) to come out to him. His attention was cyclic also, and he looked intently at her (his) face, lidded his eyes or turned them slightly to one side, or up and down, still keeping the parent in peripheral view, but alternating between attention and reduced attention, in average cycles of four per minute over a three minute observation period. This attention–withdrawal cycle within a period of reciprocal interaction looked as if it followed a homeostatic curve of involvement and recovery that was smooth and

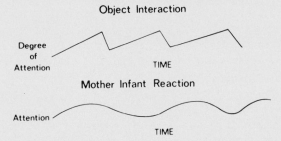

Fig. 4-2. Pattern of change in attention to attractive objects is abrupt and jagged; to mother, smooth and cyclic.

signaled a period of intense involvement between infant and parent. The parent cycled, too—playing a kind of swan's mating dance as he or she moved in to pass on information or behavior when the infant was looking and withdrew slightly to let up in intensity when the infant withdrew (Fig. 4-3).

We have been able to characterize the relative reciprocity and amount of affective, and even cognitive, information that a parent can transmit in such a period by the cyclic quality of the interaction. In parents who are too anxious and are insensitive to their infants' homeostatic needs (this parallels the demands of the physiologic systems of an immature organism such as the neonate), the infant necessarily turns off his attention and spends most of the period keeping the tense parent in his peripheral field, checking back from time to time. In failing interactions, the jagged attentional system of the infant resembles a very sparse period of object attention (Fig. 4-4). One can see from some of the failing interactions that the sparseness of message transmission is in direct contrast to a smooth homeostatic curve of attention in an optimal period of reciprocity. Not only

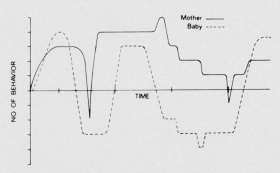

Fig. 4-3. Interaction in which mother is sensitive to baby's needs to look away and recover.

does such a cycle allow for long periods of attention without exhausting the immature physiologic systems of the infant, but it also provides a rich matrix for choices and change in attention at any moment. These cycles also provide a matrix for adaptability of a very sensitive kind to the few caregivers who must become important to the infants.

We think that we are seeing a reliable difference between mothers and fathers as they perform in this system. Mothers start out and remain smoother, more low-keyed, more cyclic themselves, using other behaviors such as touching, patting, vocalizing, and smiling to "contain" the baby and provide him with a gently containing matrix for early responses such as smiles, vocalizations, and reaches, but they don't seem to be in such a hurry for these to develop, and they are sensitive (often extremely so) to the competing physiologic demands of the infant.[29]

On the other hand, most fathers (and there are notable exceptions) seem to present a more playful, jazzing-up approach (Fig. 4-5). Their displays are rhythmic in timing and even in quality. As one watches this interaction, it seems that a father is expecting a more heightened, playful response from the baby. And he gets it! Amazingly enough, an infant by two or three weeks displays an entirely different attitude (more wide-eyed, playful, and bright-faced) toward his father than to his mother. The cycles might be characterized as higher, deeper, and even a bit more jagged. The total period of playful attention may be shorter if the small infant gets overloaded, but as he gets older the period of play is maintained for a longer time.[30]

What does this kind of reciprocal "set" mean to the infant? It certainly appears to be basic to the healthy development of infant–parent reciprocity. My own feeling is that we are tuning in on the basic homeostatic systems that govern the physiologic processes,

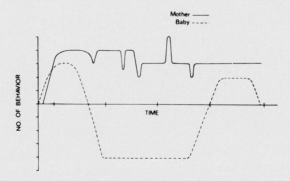

Fig. 4-4. Interaction in which mother is insensitive and baby spends most of time looking away.

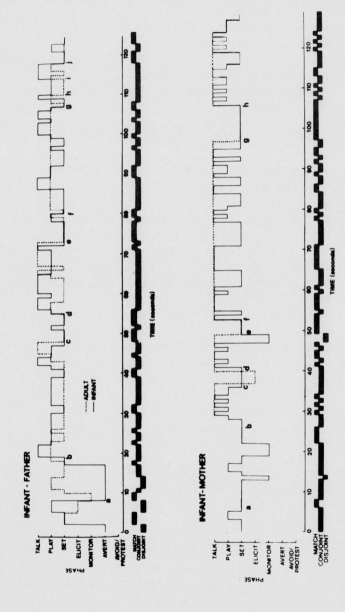

Fig. 4-5. Father keeps baby at higher level of intensity although communication rhythm is comparable to mother–infant rhythm.

as well as the attentional ones, in the developing infant. If these are "shaped" by his environment in one way, they may press him toward a psychophysiologic adjustment of one kind or another. Certainly when an environment can tune to the baby's needs for such elegant homeostatic controls, the attention *and* physiologic cycles can be smooth, rich, adjustable. I can easily jump to the kind of tuning up of the CNS cycles that must find regulation as well as input from the environment to proceed toward optional development of motor and cognitive skills. I think we are looking at the precursors of affective development that are so necessary to the child's total development. We have examples from Harlow's monkeys[31] and from Rene Spitz's and from Provence's later studies of institutionalized infants,[32,33] which show that development did not proceed when there was no such nurturing from the environment.

For the infant, such a reciprocal system, when it is going well, acts as fuel and information for his ongoing development, entertaining the fueling from within that he receives as feedback from learning each new developmental task. Robert White called this latter force a "sense of competence." Both an inner sense of competence and feeling from a gratifying reciprocity with his environment are necessary to the infant's optimal development.

For the parents, the feedback from such a reciprocal system is just as rewarding as it is to the infant, and fuels their energy for continuing in such a demanding ongoing relationship as "good" parenting requires. Their awareness of when they are successful must be felt unconsciously when things are going well, and we as supportive experts could and should point out such periods so that they can become consciously aware of their successes as guidelines to their parenting efforts.

For instance, the neonate's behavioral repertoire is eminently fitted for "capturing" a new parent. As he stops crying to turn his head toward her voice, as he "chooses" her voice over a competing male voice, as he turns to root at her breast when she cuddles him, as he nestles his soft head in the corner of her neck when he is placed at her shoulder, a new mother is captivated. We and others[34,35] have found that demonstrating this behavior to parents in the first few days after delivery does indeed alert them to the individual assets of their neonate, and they behave in a significantly more nurturant fashion thereafter.[36] With difficult infants it may be even more critical that we share their difficult behavior with new parents and set up an alliance with them to help them work it out with our supportive help. The behavior of the neonate is certainly designed to capture his parents, but when it is a disappointment to them or when they cannot find a "fit" with him it can turn them away from him. As many mothers of babies who have failed to thrive say when they are asked, "He never reached me," or, "I never could reach him." The behavior of the newborn can be assessed and captured by the professional to foster the parent–child relationship, and, where it predicts to stress in that relationship, as a communication system for professional intervention to alleviate that stress. Sharing the observable behavior and reactions of the neonate with his parents becomes a powerful technique for the professional toward establishing a working relationship with them from the very first.

REFERENCES

1. Blum R, Blum E: Health and Healing in Rural Greece. Palo Alto, Stanford Univ, 1965
2. LeVine RA, LeVine BB: Nyansongo: A Gusii community in Kenya, in Whiting B (Ed): Six Cultures: Studies of Child Rearing. New York, Wiley, 1963
3. Klaus MH, Kennell JH: Mothers separated from their newborn infants. Pediatr Clin North Am 17:1015–1037, 1970
4. Klaus MH, Kennell JH, Plumb N, et al.: Human maternal behavior at the first contact with her young. Pediatrics 46:187–192, 1970
5. Ringler NM, Kennell JH, Jarvella R, et al.: Mother to child speech at two years— Effects of early postnatal contact. J Pediatr 86:141–144, 1975
6. Spock B: The Common Sense of Baby and Child Care. New York, Duell, Sloan & Pearce, 1946
7. Greenberg NH: A comparison of infant–mother interactional behavior in infants with atypical behavior and normal infants, in Hellmuth J (Ed): Exceptional Infant, vol 2. New York, Brunner Mazel, 1971, p 390
8. Cravioto J, Delcardie ER, Birch HG: Nutrition, growth and neurointegrative development. Pediatrics 38:319–320, 1966
9. Klein RE, Lester BM, Yarbrough C, et al.: On malnutrition and mental development: Some preliminary findings, in Chaves A, Borges H, Basta S (Eds): Nutrition, vol 2. Basel, Karger, 1975, pp 315–321
10. Heider GM: Vulnerability in infants and young children. Genet Psychol Monogr 73:1–216, 1966
11. Apgar VA: A proposal for a new method of evaluation of the newborn infant. Anesth Analg 32:260–267, 1953
12. Drage JS, Kennedy C, Berendes H, et al.: The Apgar score as an index of infant morbidity: A report from the Collaborative Study of Cerebral Palsy. Dev Med Child Neurol 8:141–148, 1966
13. Lewis M, Bartels B, Campbell H, et al.: Individual differences in attention. Am J Dis Child 113:461–465, 1967
14. Peiper A: Cerebral Function in Infancy and Childhood. New York, Consultants Bureau, 1963
15. Brazelton TB: Neonatal Behavioral Assessment Scale. London, National Spastics Society, 1973
16. Horowitz FD, Self PA, Paden LN, et al.: Newborn and four week retest on a

normative population using the Brazelton newborn assessment procedure. Presented at the Annual Meeting of the Society for Research in Child Development, Minneapolis, 1971 (unpublished)

17. Tronick E, Brazelton TR: Clinical uses of the Brazelton Neonatal Behavioral Assessment, in Friedlander BZ, Sterritt GM, Kirk GE (Eds): Exceptional Infant, vol 3: Assessment and Intervention. New York, Brunner Mazel, 1975

18. Eisenberg RB, Griffin EJ, Coursin DB, et al.: Auditory behavior in the human neonate: A preliminary report. J Speech Hear Res 7:245–269, 1964

19. Eimas P, Siqueland E, Lipsitt L: Work in progress. Brown University, 1975 (unpublished)

20. Goren C: Form perception, innate form preferences, and visually mediated head-turning in the human neonate. Presented at the Annual Meeting of the Society for Research in Child Development, Denver, 1975 (unpublished)

21. MacFarlane A: Personal communication. Oxford University, England, 1975

22. Pettigrew JD: The effect of visual experience on the development of stimulus specificity by kitten cortical neurones. J Physiol 237:49–74, 1974

23. Blakemore C, Cooper GF: Development of the brain depends on the visual environment. Nature 228:477–478, 1970

24. Als H, Tronick E, Brazelton TB: Manual for the behavioral assessment of the premature and at-risk newborn (an extension of the Brazelton Neonatal Behavioral Assessment Scale). Presented at the Annual Meeting of the American Academy for Child Psychiatry, Toronto, 1976 (unpublished)

25. Kearsley RB: The newborn's response to auditory stimulation: A demonstration of orienting and defensive behavior. Child Dev 44:582–590, 1973

26. Sander LW, Chappell PF, Gould SB, et al.: An investigation of change in the infant–caretaker system over the first week of life. Presented at the Annual Meeting of the Society for Research in Child Development, Denver, 1975 (unpublished)

27. Brazelton TB, Koslowski B, Main M: The origin of reciprocity in the mother–infant interaction, in Lewis M, Rosenblum L (Eds): The Effect of the Infant on its Caregiver, vol 1. New York, Wiley, 1974

28. Tronick E, Adamson L, Wise S, et al.: Mother–infant face-to-face interaction, in Gosh S (Ed): Biology and Language. London, Academic, 1975

29. Brazelton TB, Tronick E, Adamson L, et al.: Early mother–infant reciprocity. Ciba Found Symp 33, 1975, pp 137–154

30. Yogman M, Dixon S, Adamson L, et al.: The development of infant interaction with fathers. Work in progress. Children's Hospital Medical Center, Boston, 1975 (unpublished)

31. Seay B, Hansen E, Harlow HF: Mother–infant separation in monkeys. J Child Psychol Psychiatr 3:123–132, 1962

32. Spitz R: Hospitalization: An inquiry into the genesis of psychiatric conditions in early childhood. Psychoanal Study Child 1:53–74, 1945

33. Provence S, Lipton RC: Infants in Institutions. New York, International Universities, 1962

34. Erickson ML: Assessment and Management of Developmental Changes in Children. St. Louis, Mosby, 1976, pp 67–70

35. Field TM, Dempsey JD, Hallock NH, et al.: The mother's assessment of the behavior of her infant. Inf Behav Dev 1:156–167, 1978

36. Parker WB, Als H, Brazelton TB: Neonatal behavior and the attachment process between a mother and her infant. Work in progress. Children's Hospital Medical Center, Boston, 1978 (unpublished)

Robert N. Emde

5

Emotional Availability: A Reciprocal Reward System for Infants and Parents with Implications for Prevention of Psychosocial Disorders

"Be there!" Although my teachers gave voice to this in medical school, and I listened, it was not until this phrase echoed in my psychiatric training that I understood it for what it is—the cardinal principle of therapy. I have since learned that this principle goes beyond psychiatrists and physicians; it engages all health care professionals. From the patient's side, a sense of the helper's ongoing availability is fundamental for progress—the basic stuff for building trust and a measure of equanimity in the midst of problems, perturbations, and illness. From the helper's side, a sense of the patient's accomplishment in the midst of therapeutic availability, without necessary therapeutic "intervention," is also fundamental for progress—the stuff which builds confidence in the seasoned therapist. Again and again we find that a patient is apt to discover options in an atmosphere of ongoing diagnosis where the helper is an available listener, where there is another human being who is interested in understanding what is meaningful and complex.

Dr. Emde is supported by Research Scientist Award #5 KO2 MH 36808 and NIMH Project Grant #2 RO1 MH 22803. This chapter is based on a keynote address originally given to a symposium "Intervention in Infancy", April 27, 1979, Pittsburgh, Pennsylvania.

Over the years I have learned still more about availability—that it is more effective if it is of a certain sort, if it includes an empathic sensitivity which allows for resonance with a variety of feelings; feelings that orient us in any given encounter to what is both uniquely individual and commonly human. This kind of availability, emotional availability, goes beyond a therapeutic principle; it is a developmental principle. The emotional availability of another serves to facilitate development by fostering security, exploration, and learning. In cognitive terms, it has the effect of encouraging movement through an expanding world of self and environment. Further, it can be thought of as operating through a reward system which, although biologically based, is realizable only in a social setting.

This essay will consider the beginnings of emotional availability in the infant–parent relationship and, in particular, it will consider those rewards that make development possible. Being there during pain and discomfort is certainly a part of emotional availability, but our psychology has tended to neglect rewards. But now, considering the widespread prevalence of child neglect and abuse, I think we would do well to ask about the rewards in parenting. There must be some. Parenting is time-consuming, demanding, and often requires the laying aside of other endeavors. Yet it is obviously essential for survival of our species.

Evolutionary biology has emphasized survival to reproductive age and the corresponding biological importance of pleasure in sexuality with its reciprocal social rewards for sexual activity. It is a fact that in our post-Freudian world, pleasures in this realm are now acknowledged as vitally important in their own right. But what about after conception? The altricial human must be cared for. Surely there must be a biology of pleasure in parenting to correspond to a biology of pleasure in sexuality. I propose that, if we look, we might identify such forms of pleasure; we might then understand their "vicissitudes"—distortions, deflections, and inhibitions. After all, developmental processes of parenting, like developmental processes of sexuality, may encounter conflict as well as satisfaction.

SOURCES OF REWARDS

My thesis is that there is a biologically-based reward system for infants and parents. Rewards exist for interaction whether we consider the infant, the parent, or their developing relationship. Learning theories have emphasized that rewards are features that shape behavior. For years, such theories described how mothers "shaped" babies, but we are now beginning to appreciate how much babies "shape" mothers—and other adults as well.[1-3] When researchers look at interactions between parent and young baby, the lion's share of shaping is being done by the baby. This makes sense: the parent is capable of accommodating and responding to the baby's activities, while the baby has a limited capacity to accomodate to the parent's activity. Then, as the baby develops, the situation changes. By the end of the first year, interactions between baby and parent are more nearly symmetrical, with openings and accommodations more equally distributed between partners.[4-6] Our longitudinal research[7] and that of others[2] leads to thinking about three "phases" of social interaction during the first postnatal year. Since these phases begin with and depend upon what the infant's unfolding biology brings to a reciprocal reward system, they will guide our discussion. The phases are (1) the newborn period (which we define as extending through the first two postnatal months); (2) the awakening of sociability (2–7 months); and (3) the onset of focused attachment (8 months through the end of the first year).

Rewards from Infants

THE NEWBORN PERIOD

There is something about the appearance of the very young infant that is intrinsically appealing. The head is disproportionately large, by adult standards, and contains particular characteristic features: a protruding, large forehead; large eyes set below the midline of the head; and round, protruding cheeks. In addition, the baby has thick, short extremities, a rounded body, and soft and elastic body surfaces. These are features which Lorenz[8] has referred to as "babyness."

This stimulus configuration of attractiveness has received experimental support in human studies.[9,10; see discussion 11] Of particular interest is a study by Chandler wherein attractive baby features were more compelling for adolescent girls who had passed through puberty than for age-matched adolescent girls who had not gone through puberty and adolescent boys. These results, along with the species-wide nature of the phenomenon itself, suggest that "babyness" may correspond to a physiologically-related incentive system in adults for nurturing the young baby.

The newborn's "thrashing of arms and legs"[2] has also been identified as an important stimulus for eliciting caring. Certainly a newborn's response capacity for being soothed from a thrashing-crying state to a quiescent one is experienced as rewarding; a parent is told in this way that she or he is needed and appreciated.

The cuddliness of a newborn is also an important source of reward. Parents feel good about a baby who snuggles, who conforms to a posture of being held, and who can responsively alter his state, not just by being smoothed (i.e., going from arousal to quiescence), but by becoming alert and looking into another's face when being held. A major longitudinal study[12] found that cuddliness was one of the few aspects of individual differences among infants that proved stable over time, suggesting that this sort of reward may have consistent biological variation important for parenting.

Other aspects of the young infant give appeal. John Benjamin used to speak of the aesthetic aspects of what he referred to as "kinesthetic unity" between mother and infant, that sense of harmonious molding of infant to mother which was often captured by the great painters. Rene Spitz emphasized the pleasing qualities of the breast-feeding infant who blissfully looks up into his mother's face. Winnicott,[13] Erikson,[14] and Solnit and Provence[15] have indicated that the newborn's appearance of helplessness is rewarding in another sense: it gives parents a sense of fulfillment by the developmental fact of the infant's becoming less helpless with time.

THE AWAKENING OF SOCIABILITY

One has to remember, as Robson[16] has emphasized, that the newborn period can often be trying. Appeal in the midst of crying and demandingness can sometimes be aversive. But, as Robson has put it: "In dealing with the human species, nature has been wise . . ." (1967, p. 15). Robson was referring to the developmental onset of increased eye-to-eye contact and social smiling. As will be seen below, there is much more in the developmental cluster that I refer to as "the awakening of sociability".

Around two months, what the infant brings to a social interaction takes a giant step forward. Parents often state that their baby is now more human and less of a doll-like creature to be cared for. A baby at this age brings pleasures in immediate face-to-face rewards, in rewards emanating from wakefulness and state development, and in rewards from a greatly enhanced learning capacity.

In an immediate sense, when one approaches a baby at two months there is a world of difference. A triad of developmental advances are apt to give pleasure and strong incentive for continuing to be with the baby; they tell us the baby is in a good mood and wants more of us. These rewarding features include (1) enhanced eye-to-eye contact, (2) social smiling, and (3) social vocalizing.

Enhanced eye-to-eye contact around two months has not only been described in the naturalistic setting,[7,17] but has also been documented experimentally. In an elegant program of perceptual studies, Haith and his colleagues[18,19] have shown that significant differential looking at the face has its developmental onset at seven weeks of age, when there is a prominent scanning of the eye region. The social smile, which so delights parents, also appears around two months. Although smiling has developmental antecedents, there is a shift from endogenous smiling (related to rhythmically-occurring states and not generally experienced as rewarding by parents) to exogenous smiling, which flowers in response to outside stimulation and becomes most prominent in social encounters.[20] Social vocalization, with cooing in response to the face of another, begins within one to two weeks after the flowering of the social smile and adds further joy to one's encounter with the baby. Altogether, parents find an irresistible delight in their beaming, cooing baby, who looks at them engagingly and shows what can only be interpreted as pleasurable excitement as baby's face lights up and there is a bicycling activity of arms and legs. Some parents now think of their baby as "playful"; there is a sense of back-and-forth smiling, vocalizing and looking; a kind of affirming, fun-filled encounter now seems a gratifying addition to caregiving.

An important background for these immediate social rewards is found in the development of infant wakefulness and state. A decrease in nonhunger fussiness occurs around two to three months of age.[7,21-24] Further, an increase in the amount of wakefulness occurs over the first two months.[7,25] The distribution of wakefulness also changes, with more of wakefulness during the day and less at night. What has been called "settling," with sleeping through the night and more available nonfussy wakefulness in daytime, must be rewarding for parents. But even more important for parental pleasure is the fact that wakefulness seems used "in a new way,"[23] with increased exploratory activity, whether with toys, mobiles or faces.

There thus seems to be an intricate orchestration involved in unfolding of infant rewards at this age. The interplay of smiling, cooing, and engaging-looking against a background of more nonfussy wakefulness and exploratory activity—all seem to act in concert to enhance the baby's social appeal. This interplay can be appreciated further by considering learning. Enhanced learning has been shown in its three experimental realms of operant conditioning, classical conditioning, and habituation. In one form or another, all of these are easily demonstrable after two months of age, but more difficult to demonstrate before then.[see reviews 26,27] After two months the infant can learn in a variety of ways, can accommodate and change its behavior in a social situation, and can adjust to what is familiar, thereby completing learned activities so that exploration of the new is possible. It is therefore not surprising that there is a surge of exploratory activity with new learning capacities. Piaget,[28] in his scheme of cognitive development, notes that the infant becomes increasingly involved in activities that are "designed to make interesting spectacles last." In the natural course of events, a delighted mother and father are often part of these "interesting spectacles." Aside from the inherent attractiveness of wanting to be involved in such activities, there is additional incentive for interaction when a parent sees that a baby's behavior is changing as a result of her or his input.

THE ONSET OF FOCUSED ATTACHMENT

We believe these phases of interaction are based on maturationally-timed developmental shifts in the infant's central nervous system organization. Elsewhere[7] we have referred to these shifts as "biobehavioral" and have also described their manifestations in state development, EEG changes, and autonomic nervous system reactivity. In addition to the shift that occurs at two months, another shift in wakefulness and sleep state organization takes place between seven and nine months. At this age there is also a change which has further emotional significance to parents. Up to this time, although their baby may have smiled or reacted more pleasantly to them as compared with strangers, showing off baby to a variety of people was easy and substitute caregiving was relatively uncomplicated. Now things are different. The baby may cry when mother or father leaves, and there is likely to be a display of fearfulness when a stranger approaches.[7,29] Although substitute caregiving is more difficult, parents feel needed and special. The developmental message from their baby is compelling: no one else will do. The mechanism of this commonplace observation has been elaborated in an ingenious operant learning experiment by Fouts and Atlas.[30] They showed that infants of six and nine months experience mother's face as rewarding; in contrast, a stranger's face is experienced as neutral at six months and has negative reinforcing value at nine months.

This is also a time when the infant sits up and begins to crawl. There is more mobility. In the realm of cognition the infant shows a beginning understanding of means–end relationships and of intentionality in the sense of anticipating an event independent of action. (This marks the onset of Piaget's stage IV of sensorimotor development.) Out of sight is not out of mind; the infant can remove a cloth covering a hidden object that he has seen disappear under it. Related to this advance in cognitive capacity is an advance in emotional capacity. Whereas before emotions were primarily social signals, anticipating and guiding behavior from others, now they are internal psychological signals as well. Now emotions anticipate and guide instrumental behaviors of the infant. From our point of view, an infant can now demonstrate fearfulness expressions in advance of avoidance, pleasure expressions in advance of approach.

There is now play in addition to playfulness. Simple games begin, with peek-a-boo social games and give-and-take games with balls or favorite toys. Freud[31] and Spitz[32] have discussed how these games seem to have a theme of withdrawal and return and may bear some fundamental relationship to the comings and goings of caregivers, as well as to the infant's beginning sense of mastery in coping with such experiences.

Rewards from Parents

How do parents reward infants? We begin with the obvious. Species-wide, there is high readiness for parental tuning-in to infants' needs. Satisfying such needs is rewarding for infants and heretofore has seemed a sufficient basis for our looking at the emotional availability system. In technical jargon, this has been referred to as the "drive-reduction," "unidirectional" parent-to-infant point of view. We now appreciate more. Parents do satisfy needs related to hunger, thirst, warmth, and "contact comfort," but they also encourage exploration, and reward the infant in that manner. Parents make opportunities for "interesting spectacles"[28] and for the child to produce effects on the environment in a way we have come to see as intrinsically rewarding for the infant.[33-35] Overall, parents set an expectation that "*good* things will happen," and this rewarding climate leads to a sense of "basic trust" in the infant.[36,37]

Especially during the period of what we have designated as the "awakening of sociability," parents begin to arrange the environment so as to enhance learning. They facilitate contingencies between the infant's actions and useful results. That the infant finds this rewarding has been discussed in a compelling manner by Watson,[38] who demonstrated the relationship of infant smiling to such contingency experiences. In addition, during this time parents reward infants (communicating their love) by talking, smiling, and laughing. They engage in rhythms of eye-to-eye contact, reaching, holding, touching, postural adjustments, facial and hand gestures and they are involved in comings and goings—all of which offer a tuning-in to infant rhythms that must be gratifying.[39]

There are other species-wide adult behaviors that occur in interaction with infants at this age; since they hold infant attention we
might presume they are experienced as rewarding. These include:
"baby talk," particular facial expressions, and looking behavior. Baby
talk involves falsetto speech, extreme variations in pitch with sing-
song intonnations, and long vowel durations; there are many words
like "oh," "ooh," and "ahh."[4,40] Particular facial expressions include
the frequent use of "mock surprise" and a slowing of tempo with
exaggerated eyebrow and mouth movements. Looking is prolonged (as
compared with other social encounters) and long adult-to-baby looks
of 15–30 seconds are not uncommon.

Rewards from Reciprocity

We now know there is a back-and-forth quality in development
between parents and infants. Development does not proceed in a
simple linear fashion, and we increasingly see rewarding behaviors
as a result of sequences of interaction. Reciprocity may be rewarding,
first, from specific interactions and, second, from inherent features in
reciprocal functioning itself.

FROM SPECIFIC INTERACTIONS

One can look at specific interactions from the infant's side and
the parent's side. From the former, we can easily appreciate that the
infant, having been given to in parental interactions, is more apt to
give. Having experienced rewards, an infant is more apt to be rewarding. Further, after experiencing that good things happen pre-
dictably (i.e., having developed a sense of basic trust), an infant is
more predictable, less fussy, and more exploratory.

From the parent's side, there are similar aspects to what is
rewarding. A parent who has been rewarded by her infant is more
likely to feel better about herself as a person and as a fulfilled parent
and is more likely to continue giving in a rewarding manner. But
with parent, there is more complexity. As we know, a parent has also
been parented; there is a longer intergenerational, interactive history.
A parent who can draw upon good parenting experiences from the
past, re-experiences that parenting and is more apt to feel rewarded
and be rewarding to her infant. From a psychodynamic point of view,
we appreciate that through processes of re-experiencing and identification, a mother, for example, in giving to her infant, is also giving to
herself. Optimally, rewards flow back and forth, both because of
identification with the baby who is being pleased, and because of a

reexperiencing with activation of a rewarding store of memories of being parented. We also appreciate that parenthood is a developmental phase in its own right.[41,42] To the extent that this is true, infant interaction is rewarding in still another sense. It is self-fulfilling at an appropriate phase of the life-cycle and it will involve a re-integration of earlier experiences.

INHERENT REWARDS FROM RECIPROCAL FUNCTIONING

As Sameroff[43] has pointed out, there are inherent rewards in exercising reciprocal functioning—intrinsic pleasures in experiencing back-and-forth rhythms and contingencies in social interaction. It is not hard to imagine this in terms of back-and-forth smiling or back-and-forth vocalizing between parent and infant. The point is a more fundamental one, however, rewards may be less obvious to an observer.

To conclude this section on rewards, I offer an example of reciprocity under extraordinary circumstances. This is from a research case report,[44] one in which an infant was born with Down's syndrome and had multiple associated congenital anomalies. The mother was at first shocked and then grief-stricken. She then experienced what was fulfilling to her in a situation of reciprocity which only she and her infant could appreciate.

After the birth of her child, Mrs. D. was told of the diagnosis of Down's syndrome, duodenal atresia, kidney failure, and heart problems. She was told it was likely that her son would not survive. Initially she had thoughts that perhaps, since he was retarded, it would be better if he did not survive. Her view changed dramatically, however, when she first held her son at eight hours. She fell in love with him, knew he needed her and could survive if she could convince him of her loving presence. Leo remained in intensive care for the next seven weeks, had major surgery, and remained critical. He could have nothing by mouth for six weeks. Throughout this time his position was fixed: he was on his back with hands and legs in restraints, so he could not pull the many tubes and wires that were held precariously in place. When our research team visited, we were shocked by the sight. Aside from physical survival, we wondered about psychological survival with this degree of restriction, presumed stress, and pain.

But even more moving than the unsettling sight of Leo was what Mrs. D. did. The nurses had expressed concern that Leo could not get to sleep, that he was awake fretting much of the time. Mrs. D. found that she could insert her arms under Leo's back, avoid disturbing the tubes and wires around his face, and gently pat his buttocks while holding him. She did this for hours and Leo regularly gratified her by going to sleep. Looking back, Mrs. D. later commented that the nursing staff did not have time to do what she did and, after all, they did not love Leo as only she, his mother, could. She felt he was responsive to her; he needed her love and she felt loved.

Leo survived and developed. At a home visit toward the end of the first year, Mrs. D. demonstrated a special way that Leo "knew her." She held him in a somewhat awkward way, with her arms under his back and with his side against her body, she gently patted his buttocks and Leo looked at her and smiled, obviously content. Mrs. D. was clear about the special significance of this posture, seeing an unbroken continuity to the difficult days in the hospital. She said: "I think the patting on the behind is important because I did alot of that in the hospital. Whenever I held him, I rubbed his back and patted his behind. That was about all I could do . . . now he is remembering back to when that was the only place."

EMOTIONAL AVAILABILITY—A BASIC PSYCHOSOCIAL REQUIREMENT FOR DEVELOPMENT

The Adaptive Nature of Emotions

Emotions are adaptive. We assume along with Darwin[45] and many others[46-52] that human emotional states represent complex systems of organized functioning that are useful to the individual and that have been advantageous to the species. An evolutionary history is traceable, especially through primates, wherein emotions seem to have emerged for promoting social interaction in group-living animals. As Hamburg[53] has put it, the formation of social bonds is apt to be experienced as pleasurable and their disruption as unpleasurable. From another perspective, facial expressiveness may have evolved in primates concomitant with the enhancement of daytime vision which allowed for social signaling.[52] The nocturnal prosimian, communicating mostly through sound, smell, and touch, had little in the way of facial expressive musculature. When the ecological niche shifted to daytime life, vision and facial expression of emotion had more prominence. The close ties between emotion and the capacity for social living has been given experimental validation in macaques by Myers,[54] who has shown that emotional and social behaviors are controlled by the same neocortical areas in the forebrain.

The human, as Platt[55] has stated, is the most complex entity evolution has brought forth in the universe. Emotions not only reflect that organized complexity, but are adaptive in an individual sense, telling us about the centered aspect of our being.[56] Not only do they signal others of our interest or disinterest, pain or pleasure, annoyance, fear or surprise, but they tip us off about how we are doing in general. In the words of a current popular book, "feelings" are "our vital signs."[57] Emotional states are ongoing and dynamic rather than intermittent and, as clinicians now appreciate, all meaningful social relationships are affective.[37,58]

Nowhere is the adaptive nature of emotions more apparent than in human infancy. Emotional expressions are the language of the baby, providing messages for survival as well as loving and social bonding. Crying, for example, gives a message of "come change something," a message that is species-wide and peremptory, while smiling gives a species-wide message something like "keep it up, I like it."

Although the baby can't use words to tell us how he feels, we believe that with repeated interactive sequences, mother and infant normally establish modes of reciprocal activity which leave both with a preponderance of pleasurable and positively-toned expectations, rather than negatively-toned ones.

The Concept of Emotional Availability

The view of affects as continuous adaptive features in the lives of infant and parent leads us again to the concept of emotional availability.

From the infant's side, expressing a range of emotions is important for engaging the mother (and father). This includes not only positively-toned emotions of interest, happiness, and surprise, but also negatively-toned ones such as distress, anger, sadness, and disgust. The infant's emotional signaling allows the caregiver to appraise both the current state of contentment and corresponding need for intervention. Less often emphasized, however, is that the infant's emotional expressions in themselves satisfy an important need for the caregiver. For adaptive functioning, it is important that the infant be emotionally available and responsive to the mother, signaling where he is at, how she is doing, and communicating the fact that she is needed and appreciated. Optimally, the infant's expressiveness allows for interchanges that are varied, interesting, dynamic, and, on the whole, rewarding. In a sense, emotional signals confirm that mother is loved and that development is taking place.

From the parent's side, both clinical experience and research have shown us that more than availability is important for fostering development; emotional availability is required. In a recent review of child development research prepared as a background for public policy, Clarke-Stewart[3] emphasized that quality of care was deemed especially important for development. Quality of care was seen to involve playful, responsive, and affectionate parenting with consistent behavior over time. A flexible, rewarding parent is available, responsive to the emotional "language" of the baby, and offers a rich variety of individualized activity in an overall context of parental enjoyment.

A feature of emotional availability that has interested us most recently is the possibility that parenting in early infancy may involve a certain propensity for "reading in" one's own emotions according to situations. Thus, mothers may sometimes attribute infant emotions on the basis of a notion like, "if I were in that situation I would feel angry . . . I would feel afraid . . . I would feel sad. . . ." Different cues may be used for emotion judgments at different ages; situational features may be more important in early infancy and infant response features more important later. In a recent cross-sectional survey of 623 mothers in the Denver area, we asked about infant emotions. Mothers were surveyed with infants at each monthly age from birth through 18 months. We were surprised to find a relatively high amount of emotional attribution in early infancy with more than one-half of mothers in the newborn period seeing interest, joy, surprise, anger, and distress in their infants, and nearly one-half seeing fear.

At first, this result threw us. From our other research, we knew that mothers appeared to have little infant response specificity for such judgments, either in consistent facial expressions or in infant instrumental behaviors. We then realized it would make adaptive sense for mothers to respond emotionally and affectionately to their newborn infants even in the absence of a range of clear cues for a variety of emotions. Acting in this way, perhaps using the mechanism of projective identification, a new parent could begin tuning-in to baby feelings. Presumably, corrections take place with development as infant responses become increasingly specific, related to sequences of interaction, and act as confirmations of maternal interpretations.

The Rewarding Dimension of Emotions

Before considering conditions which interfere with emotional availability, I would like to review some basic research we are now pursuing in our laboratory. This research came about because of the need for understanding the infant's emotional life in terms of messages that are typically available to parents. It is noteworthy that experimental research on emotion has mainly been with adults expressing emotion to other adults and has involved two approaches, those involving the dimensions of emotional expression and those involving discrete emotional expressions. Our research on emotional expressions of infants-to-adults has taken both approaches.

First, for the dimensional approach. Rewards, resting on the balance of pleasure over unpleasure are centrally important in emotions, both as intra-individual states and inter-individual social expressions. In studies of adult-to-adult emotional expression, *hedonic tone* (pleasure–unpleasure) has consistently been found as the central aspect of emotion.[48,49] From a social point of view, this dimension seems to modulate the ebb and flow of rewarding interactions. From an individual point of view, this dimension appears important in motivating instrumental behaviors used in approaching or avoiding. *Activation* consistently emerges as the second main dimension of adult emotional life. This may have to do with both the salience of an emotional signal and the urgency of a message, either to others or oneself. A third dimension in adult-to-adult emotional expressions studies occupies less variance in experimental studies and often seems difficult to label; it is sometimes called "acceptance-rejection," sometimes "control," and sometimes "expressed feeling versus inner feeling." (These three-dimensional descriptions go back to the thinking of Spencer,[59] Wundt,[60] and Freud[61]; and persist through experimental investigations of Woodworth and Schlosberg,[62] Osgood,[63] Frijda and Philipszoon,[64] Frijda,[65] Gladstone,[66] and Abelson and Sermat.[67]

In our dimensional studies of infant-to-adult emotional expression, we have used a multidimensional scaling approach for infant facial expressions of emotion.[68–70] Women who are experienced with children are asked to sort infant pictures into one or more piles, putting those that seem to belong together in the same pile. This allows us to generate a similarity matrix that quantifies the extent to which pairs of pictures are sorted into the same pile; it also allows us to represent these similarities in a spatial configuration using multidimensional scaling. These analyses, reported in detail elsewhere,[71] gave quite different results before and after three months. At two months, scaling solutions are two-dimensional, with dimensions best characterized as "hedonic tone" and "state." At three months (after the period of "awakening of sociability") three-dimensional scaling solutions predominate and these are characteristic of multiple studies we have done at four and twelve months. In the three-dimensional solution, *hedonic tone* carries the most variance, *activation* appears as the second dimension of prominence, and an *internally-oriented/externally-oriented* dimension is third. We feel that it is a reflection of the adaptive significance of emotional expressions and their biological organization that, beginning at three months and afterwards, these results are not only internally consistent but the pattern of results shows consistency with adult emotional expression studies.

Discrete Emotions

Great excitement was given to the field of emotion research in the early 1970s by the findings of crosscultural "species-wide" agreement about specific facial expressions of emotion.[48,49] Using still photographs of adults who posed peak expressions, agreement was found among adults in nonwestern, as well as western cultures and in nonliterate, as well as literate cultures. This universality of agreement suggested a biological basis for emotional expression and recognition, especially for the emotions of joy, surprise, anger, fear, sadness, disgust, and probably for interest. It also suggested the value of looking for the origins of patterned emotional expressions in infancy.

Our infancy work has also found agreement about specific facial expressions of emotion; but, unlike the adult studies, our studies have not used actor-posed peak expressions. Instead, we used infant facial expressions that have been photographically sampled in the home environment under a variety of circumstances. We then made use of these infant photographs to obtain free response judgments about what emotions are seen. These judgments are later categorized, using a technique modified from Izard.[48] Our judges are women experienced with children who are asked to look at the pictures of facial expressions and tell us "the strongest . . . feeling the baby is expressing," if any. Words are categorized automatically according to an accumulated dictionary of words for nine emotional categories plus a tenth of "no emotion." Up to now, we have done studies for infant pictures sampled at three-and-a-half and twelve months of age, with multiple replication studies done at each age, and with 25 judges used in each study.

At three-and-a-half months, our sampling of infant facial expressions yielded agreement about the following emotions: interest (33% of photos), joy (41% of photos), distress (9 % of photos), sleepy (6% of photos), and anger and fear (1% of photos each). Nine percent of the pictures were blends; most of these were for interest combined with joy. At twelve months of age, results were similar, except that four percent of pictures were judged as surprise, one percent as sleepy and one percent each for anger, fear and disgust; 15 percent were categorized as blends. Details of these studies are presented elsewhere.[37,71]

It should be pointed out that our infant photos involved low intensity, mid intensity, and high intensity emotional expressions and that correlations between replication studies were high (ranging from 0.84 to 0.96) for the four major emotion categories. This indicates to us that women who have experience with children have high agreement about these categories of emotion, as well as agreement about the extent of the clarity of emotional signaling.

We are now engaged in a collaborative study with Izard in which he has selected still pictures representing peak emotional expressions from his infant studies; we have exchanged sets of pictures sampled under his conditions and ours and we are estimating the extent of agreement between free response categorizing experiments done in each setting. Preliminary results indicate that agreement levels are high across studies. With the Izard infant pictures major categories of agreement now include fear, anger, and surprise, in addition to joy, interest, distress, and sleepy.

This raises an issue about sampling. Izard sampled for peak emotional expressions; we sampled for more "naturalistic" expressions in the home, but under somewhat arbitrary conditions. But are still photographs meaningful units? We know that emotional life is necessarily embedded in temporal patterns of activity. To explore this concern we did a study comparing still photographs with movies and we were reassured. More than three quarters of our photographs that had met criteria for stability were judged to be in the same category during movie and slide presentations, and disagreements were readily explained by the addition of new information occurring during the movie segments which had preceded the still photographs.[71]

Another question about sampling concerned the representativeness of our sample of group pictures with respect to the infant's usual "behavioral day." This question was partially resolved by doing a time-lapse video recording for a continuous 12-hour period from 8:00 a.m. to 8:00 p.m. for an infant of three-and-a-half months of age. Following the recording, we arbitrarily sampled still photographs at fixed time intervals. Since we established that the recording day was not only typical for this particular infant, but also typical for normative data previously collected from 25 longitudinally-studied infants, we have reason to believe our results provided us with some approximation as to our sampling bias in the three-and-a-half-month-old infant group of pictures. Comparison with this previously collected group data indicated that we had indeed overrepresented joy and underrepresented sleep, but that these two emotion categories, along with distress and interest, were the most prominent categories in both the 12-hour infant data and our group data; we also found that emotion blends were prominent in both methods of sampling.[72]

Our program has taken us in still further directions. A crossvalidation study between our two methods (free responses for categorizing and similarity sorting for dimensional scaling) found a strong tendency for pictures similarly labeled in the free response paradigm to be close together in our multidimensional space.[71] Studies are also being done comparing the infant's response system in relation to judgments of discrete emotions. In one experimental study of fear, surprise, and happiness, there was an encouraging relationship between the number of predicted facial expression components for a discrete emotion and the global judgment of that emotion from videotapes of 10–12-month-old infants.[73] That study, and another involving anger in seven-month-old infants, also found evidence for specificity in the relationship between situations designed to elicit particular emotions and the facial components predicted for those same emotions.[74] We are now studying the action consequences which follow upon the perception of discrete emotional expressions, both for mothers and for infants, as well as individual differences in parental abilities to "read" infant emotional signals and the effects of experience on such abilities. Our search to describe the emotions of infancy may seem a sweeping one; yet, the territory only begins to be charted.

Assessing Emotional Availability

A number of research programs in recent years have taught us about assessing infant-to-mother "attachment" during later infancy.[75,76] and about assessing processes related to separation–individuation during this time.[77] But in thinking about emotional availability, we refer to more general features, perhaps even principles, of the infant–parent system.

A first principle to begin assessment is to take a *"pleasure inventory."* This would address the question: what are the pleasures which infant and parent are finding in their interactions? Parents and infants need to be happy. Taking a pleasure inventory would not only help us "diagnose" problems, it would also help us with our empathic stance when things are awry. Parents as well as infants can be deprived of rewards and the system is sufficiently intricate and interlocked that both will be involved, no matter how that deprivation got started. Overall, there should be a balance of trust, affection, interest, and pleasure in interactions. If there is not, there is likely to be a "turning off," exploration may be inhibited, and in extreme cases, sadness and depression may ensue.

A second principle of assessing emotional availability is to take into account the *individuality* of participants. It is important to assess the mother's individual reward system, for example, in terms of her personality, her past experiences, her view of herself, her expectations, and what is likely to be experienced as pleasurable by her. Similarly, it is important to assess the infant's individuality as best as one can through repeated observations, testing, parental reports, and perceptions of infant temperament.[78]

Third, the *clarity of emotional signaling* needs to be considered. To what extent is each partner able to express what interests, what pleases, and what is being asked for? Fourth, assessment should include consideration of the *range of emotions* expressed and their appropriateness to particular situations. And fifth, the ability of each partner to sustain an *appropriate emotional tone* should be considered, one that fosters reciprocal investment and exchange.[79]

Beyond this, one could assess the operation of *regulatory control* features in the interaction system. If one partner is less emotional does the other readjust with more initiatives and emotional expressiveness?[2]

CONDITIONS WHICH INTERFERE WITH EMOTIONAL AVAILABILITY AND OPPORTUNITIES FOR INTERVENTION

I would now like to give some examples of the usefulness of this kind of approach for thinking about a variety of problematic conditions in infancy. Some conditions interfere with emotional availability and blunt our rewards—rewards we usually take for granted and may even feel "biologically entitled to." In the first group of examples, problems can be thought of as beginning with infants and, in the second group, with parents; but sooner or later all become problems in the interactional arena. Unfortunately, the likelihood is then for emotional *un*availability on both sides. Interactions are not pleasing and corrections are indicated.

Consider the infant with Down's syndrome. We have found that when the "awakening of sociability" occurs in development, this phase is slightly delayed, but the quality is such that it draws attention to itself and is apt to be experienced by parents as disappointing.[44] The smile is dampened. Smiling seems to promise the excitement of social engagement but instead is fleeting. Typically as one approaches there is a bilateral upturning of the corners of the mouth, but the face doesn't "light up" and there is not the bicycling of arms and legs we are used to in the normal infant. Further, eye-to-eye contact is not continued in the face-to-face encounter and eyes do not brighten. As researchers, we experienced a sense of being let down when we saw this in babies we had known since birth. We were empathic with parental disappointment and understood the air of sadness we found in families at this time. Dampened smiling reminded parents again of the expected normal child who was not born; there was a return of sadness and a need for grieving. There was also a corresponding need to find new aspects of what could be rewarding in their Down's baby. (The interested reader is referred to Emde et al.[80] for a photographic display comparing smiling in normal and Down's syndrome infants.) Evidence also suggests that the emotional expression system of the Down's infant is dampened beyond this. When expressions of "focal attachment" appear, they are more obviously delayed (during the middle or end of the second year) and, as with smiling, they are less intense.[80–82]

Let us consider other circumstances where the usual rewards of early infancy are unavailable: the parent whose newborn infant is less cuddly[12] or whose newborn doesn't satisfy by being soothed. Consider the infant whose early fussiness is extreme and does not decline between two and three months, who may be called "colicky," but who may be an extreme instance of a maturationally-related phenomenon.[6] Consider the small-for-dates infant who may be hard to soothe, who may have considerable fussiness, a scragly appearance, difficulty in maintaining his gaze, and a frowning appearance on his face. Parents with such infants may feel they are being "disapproved of" and may experience a sense of failure as Brazelton[83] has observed. Similar irritable states with poor soothability may characterize infants born with a previously undetected syndrome of hyperviscosity or relative polycythemia.[84] We might also consider infants born with physical handicaps (absence of limbs, facial malformations, bony malformations, etc.) that distort their appearance and make them less appealing at the outset. We ought to think of a pleasure inventory in these instances. From a therapeutic standpoint, I believe it helps to acknowledge a deficit in rewards. We can then understand the parental sadness. Parents can then feel freer to talk about this and there can be the beginnings of progress towards an appreciation of other rewarding aspects of their handicapped infants.

Disappointment from a deficit of reward, its potential dire consequences, as well as a strategy for helping parents in "tuning in" to other rewarding features of their infants is beautifully illustrated in the work of Fraiberg[85] with the congenitally blind. Not only is appearance different in the blind baby, but the basic rewarding and

communicating system of eye-to-eye contact is absent. A large proportion of these infants were known to become socially withdrawn
children with stereotypic behaviors, retarded language development,
and were often regarded as "autistic." Fraiberg noticed an interference
in the mother–blind-infant relationship from the earliest postnatal
months. There was a dampening of affective interchange, often a
seeming avoidance of close interaction, and a deficit of interest,
pleasure, and play by mothers. Fraiberg developed a research intervention program in which she helped parents understand cognitive
development in their infants, their nonvisual communicative patterns,
and how these infants were pleasing in a variety of ways. She could
demonstrate developmental accomplishments and, as a result, affective interchange was restored, mothers enjoyed their babies more, and
the so-called "autism" syndrome was eliminated.

Normal infants will have marked individual differences in the
timing, intensity, and nature of rewards they offer to parents. Under
most circumstances the challenge of finding which rewards are prominent in one's own baby is one of the great joys of life. But consider
the particular challenge of those infants who are temperamentally
irregular in their biological functioning, who are slow to adapt to
change and may have a preponderance of negative emotional responses. Such infants have been characterized under the rubric of "the
difficult child" by Thomas and Chess,[86] who found this group to make
up about ten percent of their New York longitudinal study.

The interference with the emotional availability occasioned by
grief provides a bridge to problems on the parental side. The infant
born with a handicap (e.g., Down's syndrome) presents the parent
with a discrepancy from the expected normal baby who was not born
and for whom the parents need to grieve.[87] Energy is tied up in this
grieving process, and emotional availability for other loved ones, and
for the new handicapped infant, is diminished. Similarly, parental
grieving for the death of a sibling or another family member also
interferes with emotional availability. A particular problem has been
observed with twins; when one twin dies in infancy, there is often
enormous difficulty in parents being able to grieve for the lost twin
sufficiently so that there can be full emotional investment in the
survivor.[84] There are also more subtle aspects of grief. Parents often
need to grieve for a brief period following the birth of a child of an
unexpected sex.

Clinically, we know that the grief process, especially if prolonged,
overlaps with depression. Severe depression can result in parental
unavailability in the most profound emotional sense, and this can
have a serious depriving effect on an infant's development. Indeed, a

young child's helplessness in the face of a parent's depression can lead to the child becoming depressed. We known from recent prospective studies that major parental depression conveys a high risk for problematic development.[88,89] From a preventive standpoint, when there is loss it is hard to imagine anything more important than someone's being available to facilitate parental grief. If grieving does not take place, there will be continued suffering, emotional availability will be compromised, and infant incentives for development will be lessened.

We know that parental attitudes can interfere with emotional availability for infants. The Neonatal Perception Inventories[90–92] identify mothers who have less than optimal perceptions of their infants and have allowed for prediction of problematic outcome, as well as for developing a strategy of prevention. In a similar vein, Gray et al.[93] found that negative comments and behaviors on the part of mothers in the delivery room identified risk for later child abuse. But, as we think about risk, we need to know more. What are the sources of these negative parental attitudes? There must be infant effects on these attitudes; in fact, individual differences among infants may account for the greater prediction of the Neonatal Perception Inventory administered at one month as opposed to its being administered at one-to-two postnatal days. Mothers may be influenced for better or worse as they get to know their babies. Other sources of negative attitudes include "ghosts in the nursery," as Selma Fraiberg and her colleagues have put it.[94] Parents re-experience their own parenting and, in many situations of emotional unavailability, it is as if early problematic experiences of being parented are interfering with parental loving in the present. The most dramatic illustration of this phenomenon is found in the well known clinical fact that many child abusing parents were themselves abused by their own parents. But this is only the tip of the iceberg. Unresolved conflicts from the past, even though such conflicts are with shadowy figures from one's own childhood, haunt the present. Unfortunately, it is all too likely that emotional unavailability is transmitted across generations: what is not given, what is not rewarded, what is not learned as pleasurable but instead as unpleasurable, tends to endure.

Thus, more impinges on emotional availability than is immediately apparent. To illustrate the complexity of influences, as well as the reciprocal nature of emotional availability, let us consider recent research on effects of postpartum separation. The work of Klaus and Kennell and their co-workers[95,96] have shown us that, under certain conditions in the modern hospital, postpartum separation of mother and infant can interfere with the later development of parental affective availability. It is as if separation limits new mothers in opportunities for "tuning-in," being rewarded by, and falling in love with their babies. Not having been rewarded by seeing, touching, smelling, and cuddling their babies early-on, they are not as rewarding to them, and show fewer affectionate behaviors when observed at one month and sometimes later than that. But, there are important infant influences as well as parent influences on any outcome. Klaus and Kennell[96] and others in this field[97] have emphasized the importance of early contact and *en face* looking. Our research[98,99] has highlighted that in the first two postpartum hours, the unmedicated infant is not only "wide awake," but is capable of visual pursuit and there is a typical inviting wide-eyed appearance that is often interpreted by parents as a display of "wonderment." To the extent that infants are medicated, or less than awake, one might not expect the same attractiveness. We also know that newborn infants, as well as mothers, are "tuning in." Sander et al.[100] have shown that switching caretakers at ten days can result in disruption of infant rhythms and in increased fussiness. Thus, enforced separations introduced by the technology of intensive care units or by rigid hospital routines, can interfere with the rewarding back-and-forth experiences on both sides. As Leiderman and Seashore[101] have suggested, we would probably do well to consider such situations as involving risk of "interactional deprivation," not just parental deprivation or infant deprivation. Clearly, emotional availability is a reciprocal process.

But influences are still more complex. In experimental studies, enhancing early hospital contact between mothers and babies seems to have more of a demonstrable effect for mothers who are especially needy or socially disadvantaged. The original Cleveland study was done with poor, young, unmarried, and educationally disadvantaged women from the inner city.[95] A subsequent study[96] was done with an impoverished Guatemalan population, which like the Cleveland population, encountered little that was familiar in the modern hospital. These studies and others with disadvantaged groups have found effects. On the other hand, studies with advantaged populations[101-105] have not necessarily found additional affectionate behaviors following enhanced early contact. It would seem that early postpartum physical togetherness may facilitate emotional availability on the part of parents, especially among those who otherwise lack social and educational support systems; but that such early togetherness is not essential for later emotional availability. Many parents are loving and emotionally available to their infants in spite of no early contact (e.g., in the case of Caesarian section deliveries or, even more dramatically, in the case of adoptions). Campbell and Taylor[106] have an excellent discussion of these issues.

Recent research on perinatal separation also highlights the intimate involvement of the family system in emotional availability. Where young mothers do not have family support systems from available fathers of their infants, or from their own parents, things are likely to be difficult. Further, perinatal separation itself is a major stress on the family system. Concomitant with the separation occasioned by prematurity, the incidence of divorce is increased.[107,108] Not only is there a stress on mother when she goes home without her prematurely-born infant, but there is a stress on father, and a stress on the marital relationship.[109]

CONCLUSION: EMOTIONAL AVAILABILITY FOR RESEARCH AND PREVENTION

At the beginning of this chapter we considered emotional availability as a therapeutic principle. In concluding let us consider its role in research and prevention and draw a lesson from the literature on childhood depression. In his now classic papers of the 1940s on hospitalism and anaclitic depression[110-112] Spitz described his infancy research in institutions and related psychopathology to deficits in early parenting. But this stirred scientific controversy. In an evaluation of this work, published in 1955, Pinneau[113] soundly criticized Spitz for inadequate description of environments, samples, and observation methods, as well as for the inappropriate use of a developmental testing instrument. There was little to substantiate Spitz's conclusions, according to Pinneau. In view of subsequent history, with other studies providing convincing evidence for many of Spitz's conclusions, we might ask: What did Pinneau miss? I believe it had to do with emotional availability. Spitz was empathic. In the midst of complexity, he allowed his feelings to guide his clinical pattern perception. He observed that individual infants, after separation, became weepy, immobile, had sad facial expressions, often with dazed looks, and that sometimes they engaged in repetitive and autoerotic activities. Spitz felt saddened. He was reminded of depression in adults and related their plight to the loss of a loved one. He made himself emotionally available so he could feel something communicated by the infants; he then made use of that feeling for a widened perception. A clinical syndrome emerged.

A similar debate about methodology where criticism did not take account of the developmental-empathic data of the researcher, fol-

lowed the dramatic experiment of Skeels[114] wherein orphanage toddlers were raised by foster parents who were retarded institutionalized
adults. These children were contrasted with others who received
routine institutional care. Skeels's initial reports of recovery from
depression and enhanced development in the children raised by the
retarded met with strong methodological skepticism. But an exhaus-
tive follow-up study, done after more than 20 years, revealed not only
successful adoption but successful adult development in the experimental group. Tragically, the contrast group did not fare well.

It is somewhat ironic and sad that we have not absorbed the
research lessons about empathy from Spitz and Skeels. One recent
review,[115] after considering a number of epidemiological studies,
concluded that early childhood depression does not exist! It is stated
that evidence is . . ."insufficient and insubstantial. Consequently, diagnosis of this presumed condition in children would appear to be
premature and treatment unwarranted." The reader will not be
surprised to learn that this review does not consider empathy, emotional availability, and the complexities of individuals changing over
time.

I believe the foregoing example dramatically points up the hazards involved in our becoming abstract. The clinician-researcher and
the clinician-epidemiologist, although dealing with numbers and with
interactions of systems, cannot lose touch with what is personal,
human, and affective. When speaking on this subject I usually show
a selection from Spitz's 1947 movie "Grief: A Peril in Infancy."[116] Even
now, seeing this movie can be a wrenching and horrific experience. I
never show it without there being ample opportunity for discussion.

Thinking about prevention, I would like to offer a few comments
about emotional availability and risk research. We can identify populations at psychosocial risk, at genetic risk for schizophrenia and
manic depressive illness, and at congenital risk for the hyperactivi-
ty–dysfunctional syndrome of childhood.[117] We also know that children
born with physical and mental handicaps are at psychosocial risk, and
that any conditions that interfere with emotional availability may be
studied with profit, for there is risk of adverse development. But there
is an upbeat side which we have often taken for granted: this concerns
what we can learn about *risk-reducing factors*. What makes things go
right in risk populations? How do individuals and families successfully
cope with blunted rewards, handicaps, and stress? Even in circumstances where there is the highest genetic loading for schizophrenia
(i.e., an identical twin who is schizophrenic) there is slightly less than
50 percent outcome for schizophrenia. What are the individual coping

styles which buffer against stress and act as incentives for development? Opportunities abound for studying the development of emotional availability under these circumstances.

The health care professional's other great principle, ranking alongside emotional availability is *concern for individuality*. Our patients might tell it to us in the following voice: "Be there *for me*— I am different from anyone you've ever known before!" The principle is a humbling one, for there will always be privacy and a region of mystery no matter how well we come to understand another. The human organism is extraordinarily complex; the meaning of experience unique; and adaptive solutions to varied environments, multiple and creative. For this reason, in planning intervention, it is difficult to apply solutions in advance and in the abstract. But there is more about individuality and prediction. Therapeutic and other ameliorative processes mobilize transactions among individuals. When we intervene, we not only anticipate change in others, we ourselves change. We experience changing levels of empathy, changing diagnostic assessments, and changing goals as we work with individuals. It is no wonder that we soberly admit our ignorance: we cannot predict solidly in the individual case. How could we expect to?

Herein lies a paradox. In designing prevention programs we are necessarily concerned with the future; but psychosocial prevention begins by helping in the "now," so that individuals and families increase their current options for adaptive choice—so that they become less predictable. To the extent that we help individuals overcome risk and predictability, we feel pleasure. Knowledge of this sustains us. In the field of prevention, it is our reward for emotional availability.

REFERENCES

1. Etzel BC, Gewirtz JL: Experimental modification of caretaker-maintained high-rate operant crying in a 6- and a 20-week-old infant (Infans tyrannotearus): Extinction of crying with reinforcement of eye contact and smiling. J. Exper Child Psychol 5:303–317, 1967
2. Bell RQ, Harper LV: Child Effects on Adults. Hillsdale, New Jersey, Lawrence Erlbaum and Associates, 1977
3. Clarke-Stewart A: Child Care in the Family. New York, Academic Press, 1977
4. Stern DN: Mother and infant at play: The dyadic interaction involving facial, vocal, and gaze behaviors, in Lewis M, Rosenblum L (Eds): The Effect of the Infant on its Caregiver. New York, Wiley, 1974
5. Brazelton TB: The origins of reciprocity: The early mother–infant interaction, in Lewis M, Rosenblum L (Eds): The Effect of the Infant on its Caregiver. New York, Wiley, 1974

6. Vietze PM, Abernathy SR, Ashe ML, et al.: Contingent interaction between mothers and their developmentally delayed infants, in Sackett GP (Ed): Observing Behavior, vol. 1. Baltimore, University Park Press, 1978

7. Emde RN, Gaensbauer TJ, Harmon, RJ: Emotional Expression in Infancy. A Biobehavioral Study. Psychological Issues, A Monograph Series, vol. 10. New York, International Universities Press, 1976

8. Lorenz KZ: Die angegorenen Formen moglicher Erfahrung. Zeitschrift fur Tierpsychologie 5:235–409, 1943

9. Fullard W, Reiling AM: An investigation of Lorenz's "babyness." Child Dev 47(4):1191–1193, 1976

10. Chandler J: Nurturant responses of adolescent children to the young. University of Denver, Department of Psychology, (Doctoral dissertation), 1977

11. Eibl-Eibelsfeldt I: Ethology. The Biology of Behavior (2nd ed). New York, Chicago, Holt, Rinehart and Winston, Inc, 1975

12. Schaffer HR, Emerson PE: Patterns of responses to physical contact in early human development. J Child Psychol & Psychiatr 5:1–13, 1964

13. Winnicott DW: Mother and Child. New York, Basic Books, 1957

14. Erikson EH: Insight and Responsibility: Lectures on the Ethical Implications of Psychoanalytic Insight. New York, Norton, 1964

15. Solnit AJ, Provence S: Vulnerability and risk in early childhood, in Osofsky JD (Ed): Handbook of Infant Development. New York, Wiley, 1979

16. Robson KS: The role of eye-to-eye contact in maternal–infant attachment. J Child Psychol & Psychiatr 8:13–25, 1967

17. Robson KS: Moss HA: Patterns and determinants of maternal attachment. J Pediatrics 77:976–985, 1970

18. Bergman T, Haith MJ, Mann L: Development of eye contact and facial scanning in infants. (Paper presented at the biennial convention of the Society for Research in Child Development) Minneapolis, April 1971

19. Haith MM, Bergman T, Moore MJ: Eye contact and face scanning in early infancy. Science 198:853–855, 1977

20. Emde RN, Harmon RJ: Endogenous and exogenous smiling systems in early infancy. J Amer Acad Child Psychiatr 11:177–200, 1972

21. Tennes K, Emde RN, Kisley AJ, et al.: The stimulus barrier in early infancy: An exploration of some formulations of John Benjamin, in Holt RR, Peterfreund E (Eds): Psychoanalysis and Contemporary Science. New York, Macmillan and Co, 1972

22. Brazelton TB: Crying in infancy. Pediatrics 29:579–588, 1962

23. Dittrichova J, Lapackova V: Development of the waking state in young infants. Child Dev 35:365–370, 1964

24. Paradise J: Maternal and other factors in the etiology of infantile colic. JAMA 197:191–199, 1966

25. Parmelee AH, Wenner WH, Schulz, HR: Infant sleep patterns from birth to 16 weeks of age. J Pediat 65:576–582, 1964

26. Sameroff A, Cavanaugh PJ: Learning in infancy: A developmental perspective, in Osofksy JD (Ed): Handbook of Infant Development. New York, Wiley, 1979

27. Emde RN, Robinson J: The first two months. Recent research in developmental psychobiology and the changing view of the newborn, in Call J, Noshpitz J, Cohen R, Berlin I (Eds): Basic Handbook of Child Psychiatry, vol. 1. New York, Basic Books, 1979

28. Piaget J: The Origins of Intelligence in Children (2nd ed). New York, International University Press, 1952/1936

29. Gaensbauer T, Emde R, Campos J: "Stranger" distress: Confirmation of a developmental shift in a longitudinal sample. Perceptual and Motor Skills 43:99–106, 1976

30. Fouts G, Atlas P: Stranger distress: Mother and stranger as reinforcers. Infant Behav Dev 2: 309–317, 1979

31. Freud S: Beyond the Pleasure Principle. Standard Edition (vol. 18). London, Hogarth Press, 1955/1920, pp 3–64

32. Spitz R: The First Year of Life. Normal and Deviant Object Relations. New York, International Universities Press, 1965

33. White RW: Ego and Reality in Psychoanalytic Theory. Psychological Issues, Monograph No. 11. New York, International Universities Press, 1963

34. Yarrow LJ, Klein RP, Lomonaco S, et al.: Cognitive and motivational development in early childhood, in Friedlander BZ, Sterritt GM, Kirk G (Eds): Exceptional Infant, vol. 3: Assessment and Intervention. New York, Brunner/Mazel, 1975

35. Yarrow LJ, Rubenstein J, Pedersen, F: Infant and Environment: Early Cognitive and Motivational Development. New York, Halstead Press, Wiley, 1975

36. Erikson EH: Childhood and Society. New York, WW Norton, 1952

37. Emde RN: Towards a psychoanalytic theory of affect: I. The Organizational model and its propositions, in Greenspan S, Pollock G (Eds): Psychoanalysis and Development. Current Perspectives (in press)

38. Watson JS: Smiling, cooing, and "the game." Merrill-Palmer Q 18:323–334, 1972

39. Lewis M, Goldberg S: Perceptual-cognitive development in infancy: A generalized expectancy model as a function of mother–infant interaction. Merrill-Palmer Q 15:81–100, 1969

40. Snow CE, Ferguson CA: Talking to Children. London, Cambridge University Press, 1977

41. Erikson EH: Growth and Crises of the Healthy Personality. Psychological Issues, Identity and the Life Cycle, vol. 1. New York, International Universities Press, 1959

42. Benedek T: Parenthood as a developmental phase. J Amer Psychoanal Assoc 7:389–417, 1959

43. Sameroff A: Motivational origins of early cognitive and social behavior, in Immelmann K, Barlow GW, Main M, Petrinovich LF (Eds): Behavioral Development: An Interdisciplinary Approach (in press)

44. Emde RN, Brown C: Adaption to the birth of a Down's syndrome infant. Grieving and maternal attachment. J Amer Acad Child Psychiatr 17:299–323, 1978

45. Darwin C: Expression of Emotion in Man and Animals. London, John Murray, 1904/1872

46. Tomkins SS: Affect, Imagery, Consciousness. The Positive Affects. New York, Springer, 1962

47. Tomkins SS: Affect, Imagery, Consciousness. The Negative Affects. New York, Springer, 1963

48. Izard C: The Face of Emotion. New York, Appleton-Century-Croft, 1971

49. Ekman P, Friesen WV, Ellsworth P: Emotion in the Human Face. New York, Pergamon Press, 1972

50. Plutchik R: Cognitions in the service of emotions. An evolutionary perspective, in Candland DK, Fell JP, Keen E, Leshner AI, et al. (Eds): Emotion. Monterey, California, Brooks/Cole, 1977

51. Kaufman IC, Rosenblum LA: The reaction to separation in infant monkeys:

Anaclitic depression and conservation withdrawal. Psychosom Med 29:648–675, 1967

52. Chevalier-Skolnikoff S: Facial expression of emotion in nonhuman primates, in Ekman P (Ed): Darwin and Facial Expression. New York, Academic Press, 1973

53. Hamburg DA: Emotions in the perspective of human evolution, in Knapp PH (Ed): Expression of the Emotion in Man. New York, International University Press, 1963

54. Myers RE: Cortical localization of emotion control. Invited lecture of the American Psychological Association, Washington, September, 1976

55. Platt JR: The Step to Man. New York, Wiley, 1966

56. Emde RN, Gaensbauer T: Modeling emotion in human infancy, in Immelmann K, Barlow GW, Main M, Petrinovich LF (Eds): Behavioral Development: An Interdisciplinary Approach (in press)

57. Gaylin W: Feelings: Our Vital Signs. New York, Harper and Row, 1978

58. Rangel L: Psychoanalysis, affects, and the "human core." On the relationship of psychoanalysis to the behavioral sciences. Psychoanal Q 36:172–202, 1967

59. Spencer H: The Principles of Psychology. New York, Appleton, 1890

60. Wundt W: Grundriss der psychologie (CH Judd, Transl), as quoted in Izard C: The Face of Emotion. New York, Appleton-Century-Croft, 1971

61. Freud S: Instincts and their vicissitudes. Standard Edition (vol. 14). London, Hogarth Press, 1957/1915, pp 111–140

62. Woodworth RS, Schlosberg HS: Experimental Psychology. New York, Holt, 1954

63. Osgood C: Dimensionality of the semantic space for communication via facial expression. Scand J Psychol 7:1–30, 1966

64. Frijda N, Philipszoon E: Dimensions of recognition of expression. J Abnormal and Social Psychol 66:45–51, 1963

65. Frijda N: Emotion and recognition of emotion, in Arnold MB (Ed): Feelings and Emotions. New York, Academic Press, 1970

66. Gladstone WH: A multidimensional study of facial expression of emotion. Austral J Psychol 14:19, 1962

67. Abelson RP, Sermat V: Multidimensional scaling of facial expressions. J Exper Psychol 63:546–554, 1962

68. Shepard R: The analysis of proximities: Multidimensional scaling with an unknown distance function. Psychometrika 27:125–140, 1962

69. Shepard R: The analysis of proximities: Multidimensional scaling with an unknown distance function. II. Psychometrika 27:219–246, 1962

70. Shepard R: Representation of structure in similarity data: Problems and prospects. Psychometrika 39(4):373–421, 1974

71. Emde RN, Kligman DH, Reich JH, et al.: Emotional expression in infancy: I. Initial studies of social signaling and an emergent model, in Lewis M, Rosenblum L (Eds): The Development of Affect. New York, Plenum, 1978

72. Emde RN: Levels of meaning for infant emotions; A biosocial view, in Collins WA (Ed): Minnesota Symposia on Child Psychology, vol. 13 (in press)

73. Hiatt S, Campos J, Emde RN: Facial patterning and infant emotional expression: Happiness, surprise and fear. Child Dev, 50:1020–1035, 1979

74. Stenberg CR: The facial expression of anger in infancy. Masters Thesis, Department of Psychology, University of Denver, 1979

75. Ainsworth MD, Blehar MC, Waters E, et al.: Patterns of Attachment. Hillsdale, New Jersey, Lawrence Erlbaum, 1978

76. Sroufe LA, Waters E: Attachment of an organizational construct. Child Dev 48:1184–1199, 1977

77. Mahler MS, Pine F, Bergman A: The Psychological Birth of the Human Infant. New York, Basic Books, 1975

78. Carey WB: Clinical applications of infant temperament. J Pediatr 81:823–828, 1972

79. Gaensbauer TJ, Sands K: Distorted affective communications in abused/neglected infants and their potential impact on caretakers. Amer Acad Child Psychiatr 18:236–250, 1979

80. Emde RN, Katz EL, Thorpe JK: Emotional expression in infancy. II. Early deviations in Down's syndrome, in Lewis M, Rosenblum L (Eds): The Development of Affect. New York, Plenum, 1978

81. Cicchetti D, Sroufe LA: An organizational view of affect: Illustration from the study of Down's syndrome infants, in Lewis M, Rosenblum L (Eds): The Development of Affect. New York, Plenum, 1978

82. Cytryn L: Studies of behavior in children with Down's syndrome, in Anthony EJ (Ed): Explorations of Child Psychiatry. New York, Plenum, 1975, pp 271–285

83. Brazelton TB: (personal communication)

84. Lubchenco, L: (personal communication)

85. Fraiberg S: Parallel and divergent patterns in blind and sighted infants, in Eissler R, Freud A, Hartmann H, Kris M (Eds): The Psychoanalytic Study of the Child, vol. 23. New York, International Universities Press, 1968

86. Thomas A, Chess S: Temperament and Development. New York, Brunner/Mazel, 1977

87. Solnit AJ, Stark MH: Mourning and the birth of a defective child. Psychoanal Study Child 16:523–537, 1961

88. Grunebaum H, Cohler BJ, Kauffman C, et al.: Children of depressed and schizophrenic mothers. Presentation, American Psychiatric Association, Toronto, Canada, May 1977

89. Anthony EJ: Childhood depression, in Anthony EJ, Benedek T (Eds): Depression and Human Existence. Boston, Little, Brown and Co, 1975

90. Broussard ER, Hartner MSS: Maternal perception of the neonate as related to development. Child Psychiatr and Human Dev 1:16–25, 1970

91. Broussard E: Neonatal prediction and outcome. Child Psychiatr and Human Dev 7:85–93, 1976

92. Broussard ER: Assessment of the adaptive potential of the mother–infant system: The neonatal perception inventories. This volume, ch. 12

93. Gray JD, Cutler CA, Dean JG, et al.: Prediction and prevention of child abuse and neglect. Child Abuse and Negl 1:45–58, 1977

94. Fraiberg S, Adelson E, Shapiro V: Ghosts in the nursery. J Amer Acad Child Psychiatr 14:387–421, 1975

95. Klaus M, Jerauld R, Kreger NC, et al.: Maternal attachment. Importance of the first postpartum days. New Engl J Med 286:460–463, 1972

96. Klaus MH, Kennell JH: Maternal–Infant Bonding. St. Louis, CV Mosby, 1976

97. DeChateau P, Wiberg B: Long-term effect on mother–infant behavior of extra contact during the first hour postpartum. I and II. Acta Pediatr Scand 66:137–143; 145–151, 1977

98. Emde RN, Swedberg J, Suzuki B: Human wakefulness and biological rhythms after birth. Arch Gen Psychiatr 32:780–783, 1975

99. Butterfield PM, Emde RN, Platt BB: Effects of silver nitrate on initial visual behavior. Am J Dis Child 132:426, 1978

100. Sander LW, Julia HL, Stechler G, et al.: Continuous 24-hour interactional monitoring in infants reared in two caretaking environments. Psychosomat Med 34:270–282, 1972
101. Leiderman PH, Seashore MJ: Mother–infant separation: Some delayed consequences. CIBA Foundation Symposium #33, Parent–Infant Interaction. Amsterdam, Elsevier, 1975
102. Carlsson SG, Fagerberg H, Horneman G, et al.: Effects of various amounts of contact between mother and child on the mother's nursing behavior: A follow-up study. Infant Behav & Dev 2:209–214, 1979
103. Taylor PM, Taylor FH, Campbell SBG, et al.: Effects of extra contact on early maternal attitudes, perceptions and behaviors. Paper presented at the Society for Research in Child Development. San Francisco, March, 1979
104. Svejda MJ, Campos JJ, Emde RN: Mother–infant "bonding": Failure to generalize. Child Dev (in press)
105. Pannabecker BJ, Emde RN: The effects of extended father–newborn contact, in Batey MV (Ed): Communicating Nursing Research: Optimizing Environments for Health: Nursing's Unified Perspective (vol. 10). Boulder, Colorado, Western Interstate Commission for Higher Education, September 1977
106. Campbell SBG, Taylor PM: Bonding and attachment: Theoretical issues. This volume, chapter 1
107. Caplan G, Mason E, Kaplan DM: Four studies of crisis in parents of prematures. Commun Mental Health 1:149–161, 1965
108. Leifer AD, Leiderman PH, Barnett CR, et al.: Effects of mother–infant separation on maternal attachment behavior. Child Dev 43:1203–1218, 1972
109. Harmon RJ, Emde RN: Clinical and research perspectives on perinatal influences on the family. Paper presented at the annual meeting of the American Academy of Child Psychiatry, San Diego, October 1978
110. Spitz R: Hospitalism: An inquiry into the genesis of psychiatric conditions in early childhood. Psychoanal Study Child 1:53–74, 1945
111. Spitz R: Hospitalism: A follow-up report. Psychoanal Study Child 2:113–117, 1946
112. Spitz R: Anaclitic depression. Psychoanal Study Child 2:313–342, 1946
113. Pinneau SR: The infantile disorders of hospitalism and anaclitic depression. Psychol Bull 52:429–462, 1955
114. Skeels HM: Adult status of children with contrasting early life experiences, in Monographs of the Society for Research in Child Development (ser. no. 105, vol. 31, no. 3). Chicago, University of Chicago Press, 1966
115. Lefkowitz MM, Burton N: Childhood depression: A critique of the concept. Psychol Bul 85:716–726, 1978
116. Spitz R: Grief: A Peril in Infancy (film studies of Psychoanalytic Research Project on Problems in Infancy series). New York University, 1947
117. Waldrop MF, Bell RQ, McLaughlin B, et al.: Newborn minor physical anomalies predict short attention span, peer agression, and impulsivity at age 3. Science 199:563–565, 1978

Ross D. Parke, Thomas G. Power,
Barbara R. Tinsley, and Shelley Hymel

6

The Father's Role in the Family System

Until recently there has been little consideration of the nature of the early father–infant relationship or of the impact of the father on the development of the infant. This neglect of the father's role in early infancy stems, in part, from our assumption concerning the primacy of the mother–infant relationship and, secondly, from the belief that paternal influence assumes importance only in late infancy and early childhood.

The purpose of this chapter is to briefly review recent research concerning the nature of father–infant interaction and the impact of fathers on the infant's social and cognitive development and, finally, to note ways in which the father–infant relationship can be modified.

FATHER–INFANT INTERACTION IN THE NEWBORN PERIOD

A number of recent studies have explored the qualitative nature of father involvement with newborn infants. Greenberg and Morris[1] questioned two groups of fathers: (1) those whose first contact with their newborns occurred at the birth (in the delivery room), and (2) those whose first contact with the newborn occurred after the birth

Supported by NICHD Training Grant HD-00244 and Office of Child Development Grant OHD 90-C-900.

when the newborn was shown to them by nursing personnel. Both groups of fathers showed evidence of strong paternal feelings and of involvement with their newborn, with 97 percent of the fathers rating their paternal feelings as average to very high. The majority were generally "very glad" immediately after the delivery and pleased about the sex of their infant (97%). Although both groups of fathers judged themselves able to distinguish their own newborn from other babies by the way he looked (90%), fathers who had been present at birth thought they could do this all the time while the fathers who were not present thought they could do this only some of the time. Finally, there was some indication that fathers who were present at the delivery felt more comfortable in holding their baby. Combined with clinical interview data, Greenberg and Morris suggested that

...fathers begin developing a bond to their newborn by the first three days after birth and often earlier. Furthermore, there are certain character- istics of this bond which we call 'engrossment,'... a feeling of preoccupation, absorption and interest in their newborn (p. 526).

Although suggestive, these verbal reports need to be supplement- ed by direct behavioral observations to determine whether these self- reports of feelings and interest are reflected in behavior. In fact, there is no reason to expect that attitudes and behavior toward infants will be necessarily directly related in any simple fashion.[2]

A series of observational studies by Parke and associates was conducted in order to describe in behavioral terms the nature of father's interaction with his newborn infant. In the first study Parke et al.[3] observed the behavior of fathers in the family triad of mother, father, and infant. Observation sessions lasted ten minutes and occurred during the first three days following delivery. A time-sam- pling procedure was used in which 40 intervals of 15 seconds duration were scored for the following behavior for each parent: holds, changes position, looks, smiles, vocalizes, touches, kisses, explores, imitates, feeds, hands over to other parent.

The results indicated that fathers were just as involved as mothers and that mothers and fathers did not differ on the majority of the measures. In fact, fathers tended to hold the infant more than mothers and rock the infant in their arms more than mothers. Fathers, in short, in a context where participation was voluntary, were just as involved as the mother in interaction with their infants.

There are a variety of questions that could be raised about this study, however. First, the context was unique, since the mother and father were together, and possibly the high degree of father–infant interaction observed was due to the supporting presence of the mother.

Moreover, the sample of fathers was unique in ways that may have contributed to their high degree of interaction with their infants. Over half of the fathers had attended Lamaze childbirth classes, and with one exception all fathers were present during the delivery of the child. Both of these factors are likely to have increased the fathers' later involvement with their infants. Finally, these fathers were well educated and middle class, and their high degree of involvement may be more common in middle-class groups; parental involvement may be less in lower-class samples owing to a typically more rigid definition of parental roles among lower-class parents.

To overcome the limitations of the original study, a group of lower-class fathers who neither participated in childbirth classes nor were present during delivery were observed in two contexts: (1) alone with their infant, and (2) in the presence of the mother.[4] This study permitted a much more stringent test of father–infant involvement and permitted wider generalization of the previous findings. As in the earlier study, the father was a very interested and active participant. In fact, in the family triad, the father was more likely to hold the infant and visually attend to the infant than the mother. Nor was the mother's presence necessary for the father's active involvement; the father was an equally active interactor in both settings—alone and with his wife. Fathers in our studies[3–5] were just as nurturant as mothers. For example, in the first study, they touched, looked, vocalized, and kissed their newborn offspring just as often as mothers did. In the second study, an even more striking picture emerged, with the father showing more nurturant behavior in the triadic context than the mother and an equal amount when alone with the baby. There was only a single nurturant behavior—smiling—in which the mother surpassed the father in both studies.

In a more recent study, Phillips and Parke[6] examined in more detail the types of speech that mothers and fathers use in talking to newborn infants. Fathers, as well as mothers, changed their styles of speech when addressing their new offspring. In contrast to speech addressed to another adult, parents speak in shorter phrases when addressing a newborn, about half as long as the phrases used when speaking with adults. Second, they repeat their messages more frequently and, finally, they slow their rate of speaking when addressing their infants. These shifts in the style of speech probably serve a social function, namely to increase the extent to which the baby visually attends to the speaking parent. In turn, these speech changes may facilitate the infant's learning to recognize the characteristics of his caregivers.

Although there were few differences in the nurturance and stimulatory activities of the parents, fathers did play a less active role in caretaking activities than mothers. In the Parke and O'Leary study[4] in which all infants were bottle-fed, fathers fed significantly less than mothers when they were alone with the baby. Additional support for this mother–father difference comes from another study[5] of father–newborn interaction in a feeding context. Comparisons of the frequencies and duration of specific caretaking activities of mothers and fathers while alone with their infants in a feeding context indicate that mothers spend more time engaged in feeding the infant and in related caretaking activities, such as wiping the baby's face, than do fathers. This suggests that parental role allocation begins in the earliest days of life.

These findings are consistent with the more general proposition that pregnancy and birth of a first child, in particular, are occasions for a shift toward a more traditional division of roles.[7-9] Cowan and co-workers[8] studied couples before and up to six months after the birth of a first child. They reported that the shift was most marked in the household tasks, next in the family decision-making roles, and least in the baby-care items. Of particular interest is the fact that these patterns held regardless of whether their initial role division was traditional or equalitarian:

Despite the current rhetoric and ideology concerning equality of roles for men and women, it seems that couples tend to adopt traditionally defined roles during times of stressful transition such as around the birth of a first child (p. 20).

The lesser degree of father involvement in feeding does not imply, however, that fathers are less competent than mothers to care for the newborn infant. Competence can be measured in a variety of ways, but one approach is to measure the parent's sensitivity to infant cues in the feeding context. Success in caretaking, to a large degree, is dependent on the parents' ability to correctly "read" or interpret the infant's behavior so that their own behavior can be regulated in order to achieve some interaction goals. To illustrate, in the feeding context, the aim of the parent is to facilitate the food intake of the infant; the infant, in turn, by a variety of behaviors such as sucking or coughing, provides the caretaker with feedback concerning the effectiveness and ineffectiveness of their current behavior in maintaining the food intake process. In this context, one approach to the competence issue involves an examination of the degree to which the caretaker modifies his/her behavior in response to infant cues. Parke and Sawin[5] found that the father's sensitivity to an auditory distress signal in the feeding context—sneeze, spit-up, cough—was just as marked as the mother's. Using a Conditional probability analysis, they showed that fathers, like mothers, adjusted their behavior by momentarily ceasing their feeding activity, looking more closely to check on the infant, and vocalizing to their infant. The only difference concerned the greater cautiousness of the fathers, who were more likely than the mothers to inhibit their touching in the presence of this signal. The implication of this analysis is clear: in spite of the fact that they may spend less time overall, fathers are as sensitive as mothers to infant cues and as responsive to them in the feeding context.

Moreover, the amount of milk consumed by the infants with their mothers and fathers was very similar (1.3 versus 1.2 ounces with mothers and fathers, respectively). In short, fathers and mothers are not only similar in their sensitivity but are equally successful in feeding the infant based on the amount of milk consumed by the infant. Invoking a competence/performance distinction, fathers may not necessarily be frequent contributors to infant feeding, but when called upon they have the competence to execute these tasks effectively.

Moreover, fathers are just as responsive as mothers to other infant cues, such as vocalizations and mouth movements. Both mothers and fathers increased their rate of positive vocalizations following an infant vocal sound; in addition, both parents touched the infant and looked more closely at the infant after the infant vocalizations. Mothers and fathers differ in the behaviors that they show in response to this type of infant elicitor, however; upon vocalization, fathers are more likely than mothers to increase their vocalization rate. Mothers, on the other hand, are more likely to react to infant vocalization with touching than fathers. Possibly fathers are more cautious than mothers in their use of tactile stimulation during feeding owing to their concern about disrupting infant feeding behavior. A further demonstration of the modifying impact of the infant's behavior on his caregivers—fathers as well as mothers—comes from an examination of the impact of infant mouth movements; parents of both sexes increase their vocalizing, touching, and stimulation of feeding activity in response to mouth movements. These data indicate that fathers and mothers both react to the newborn infant's cues in a contingent and functional manner even though they differ in their specific response patterns. The interaction patterns in the newborn period are reciprocal. Although our focus in the Parke and Sawin[5] study was on the role of infant cues as elicitors of parent behavior, in a later study[10] it was shown that parent vocalizations can modify newborn infant behavior, such as infant vocalizations. Interaction between fathers and infants—even in the newborn period—is clearly bidirectional in quality; both parents and infants mutually regulate each other's behavior in the course of interaction.

BEYOND THE NEWBORN PERIOD

Many of the features that are evident in father–infant interactions in the newborn period characterize the interaction patterns in late infancy as well. The early differences between mother and father in terms of caretaking are evident in home observations. Fathers spend less time feeding and caretaking than mothers;[11,12] moreover, when they do interact with their infants, fathers spend a greater percentage of their interaction time in play activities than mothers.[11,13] Lamb[14] observed interactions among mother, father, and infant in their homes at 7–8 months and again at 12–13 months of age and reported marked differences in the reasons that fathers and mothers pick up infants. Fathers were more likely to hold the babies simply to play with them, while the mothers were far more likely to hold them for caretaking purposes.

It is not merely the quantity of time per se that discriminates between mother and father involvement in infancy; it is the quality of activity as well. A variety of studies across a wide developmental span from the newborn period to two years of age have explored the qualitative differences in father–infant and mother–infant interaction. A complex, but consistent, pattern of similarities and differences emerges from these studies, with clear role differentiation between fathers and mothers evident from the early days of life.

Not only do fathers devote more time to play than mothers, the style of play during father–infant and mother–infant interaction differs, as shown in a recent study by Yogman et al.[15] These investigators compared mothers, fathers, and strangers in their interactions with infants in a face-to-face play context. Each of five infants was studied for two minutes of interaction with its mother, father, and a stranger from two weeks to six months in a lab arrangement whereby infant and adult faced each other, with instructions to the adult to play without using toys and without removing the infant from the seat. Using videotaped records, a variety of microbehavioral analyses of the adult–infant interaction patterns were scored. Adults differed in their play with infants as indicated by differences in vocalization and touching patterns. Mothers vocalized with soft, repetitive, imitative burst–pause talking (47%) more often than fathers (20%), who did so significantly more often than strangers (12%). Fathers, however, touched their infants with rhythmic tapping patterns (44%) more often than either mothers (28%) or strangers (29%). This appears to be a very promising approach to discriminating subtle differences in styles of interaction of father versus mother.

Power and Parke,[16] in a laboratory playroom comparison of mother–infant and father–infant play, found that mothers engaged in more toy-mediated play, while fathers engaged in more physical (lifting, tossing) play with their eight-month-old infants. Stylistic differences in mother–father play are not restricted to structured laboratory settings. Recent observation of father–and mother–infant interaction in unstructured home contexts indicates mother–father differences in their style of play. In the Lamb[14] study described above, fathers engaged in more physical (i.e., rough-and-tumble type) and unusual play activities than mothers. Similar findings emerged from home observations of the infants at 15, 18, 21, and 24 months of age.[17] Again, fathers played more physical games, and engaged in more parallel play with their infants. Mothers, in contrast, engaged in more conventional play activities (e.g., peek-a-boo, pat-a-cake), stimulus toy play (where a toy was jiggled or operated to stimulate the child directly), and reading than fathers. Similar differences in the style of play patterns were found by Clarke-Stewart[18] in a study of 15–30-month-old infants and their parents.

Not only do fathers and mothers differ in their play patterns, infants react differently to mother and father play. Lamb[14] in his study of 8–13-month-old infants, found that the infants' responses to play with their fathers was significantly more positive than those to play with their mothers. Consistent with Lamb's observations is Clarke-Stewart's finding[18] that 20-month-old children were significantly more responsive to playful social interaction initiated by the father than to play initiated by the mother. At 2.5 years of age children were more cooperative, close, involved, excited, and interested in play with their fathers. Over two-thirds of the children chose to play with their fathers first in a choice situation and displayed a stronger preference for them as playmates. The early emergence of fathers as play partners, in short, is reciprocated by the infants in the first two years of infancy.

SEX OF INFANT AS A DETERMINANT OF FATHER–INFANT INTERACTION

One of the most consistent determinants of parental expectations, perceptions, and organizers of behavior is the infant's sex. There are marked and relatively consistent differences in paternal and maternal reactions to male and female infants.

Evidence of differential parental reactions to males and females is evident even before the infant is born. Parents prefer male offspring across a wide variety of cultures,[19,20] including India and Asia as well as the United States. In a 1975 survey of 1500 women and approximately one-fourth of their husbands in the United States, Hoffman[21] found that there was a 2:1 preference for boys over girls. Coombs et al.[22] reported a similar result. The respondents were given a series of choices about the sexes they would prefer if they had three children; a consistent pattern of choosing more male infants than female babies emerged. Of particular relevance is Hoffman's finding that the pattern of boy preference was more pronounced for men: "Between three and four times as many men preferred boys than girls (p. 11)"[21] Reproduction patterns are revealing as well. According the Hoffman,[21] "Couples are more likely to continue to have children if they have only girls. They will have more children than they originally planned to try for a boy (p. 11)."

After the birth of the infant, parents have clear stereotypes concerning the particular type of behavior that they expect to be associated with infants of different sexes. Rubin et al.[23] asked mothers and fathers to rate their newborn sons or daughters in the first 24 hours after birth. Although male and female infants did not differ in birth length, weight, or Apgar scores, daughters were significantly more likely than sons to be described as little, beautiful, pretty, cute, and resembling their mothers. Fathers who had seen but not handled their infants were more extreme in their ratings of both sons and daughters than were mothers. Sons were rated as firmer, larger featured, better coordinated, more alert, stronger, and hardier, and daughters as softer, finer featured, more awkward, more inattentive, weaker, and more delicate by their fathers than by their mothers.

Next, we turn to evidence of differential *treatment* of boys and girls by mothers and fathers. Differential treatment of male and female children starts as early as the newborn period. Parke and O'Leary[4] in the hospital-based observational study, found that fathers touched firstborn newborn boys more than either later-born boys or girls of either ordinal position. Fathers vocalized more to firstborn boys than to firstborn girls, while they vocalized equally to later-born infants irrespective of their sex. A similar finding emerged from our sequential analyses of the impact of infant vocalizations on parent behavior.[5] Fathers are particularly likely to react contingently to this infant cue by vocalizing, but especially in the case of the male infant. Clearly there may be some basis to the claim that fathers really do prefer boys, especially firstborn boys.

Nor are the differences in father behavior with male and female infants restricted to the newborn period. Parke and Sawin[10] observed parent–infant interaction in a structured bottle-feeding and a toy-play situation at the newborn period in the hospital and again in the home at three weeks and three months of age. Although there were few consistent differences in father and mother treatment of their sons and daughters in a routine caretaking context, there were marked differences in the play context. First, fathers held their daughters closely and snugly more frequently and for longer periods during play than they did their sons, but mothers held their sons closely more than their daughters. In contrast, for visual attending and stimulation behaviors, fathers consistently favored their sons, and mothers more often favored their daughters. Fathers looked at their sons more than their daughters, and they more frequently checked visually on their sons by looking more closely at their sons than at their daughters. Fathers provided more visual and tactual stimulation for their sons, while mothers played a complementary role by providing more stimulation for their daughters. During the play sessions, fathers visually presented the toy and touched their sons more than their daughters. Mothers, on the other hand, more frequently visually stimulated their daughters than their sons with the toy, and touched and moved their girls more than boys. During feeding, the same cross-sex effect was evident: fathers made more frequent attempts to stimulate their sons' feeding by moving the bottle than they did for their daughters; mothers showed the opposite pattern. These findings indicate that parents stimulate their same-sex infant more than the opposite-sex infant; fathers and mothers play complementary roles with their male and female infants.

A similar pattern of father–son involvement is evident in unstructured home observational studies as well. Rebelsky and Hanks,[24] for example, noted that fathers decreased their vocalizations across the first three months of life to female infants more than to male infants. Similarly, Rendina and Dickerscheid[12] reported that fathers spent more time attending to male infants than female infants, while there was a trend for fathers to play more with boys than with girls. A more provocative finding concerns the differential involvement of fathers with temperamentally difficult male and female infants. Using Carey's Infant Temperament Scale, Rendina and Dickerscheid reported that fathers were involved in social activities with tempermentally difficult boys (14.6%) more than with difficult girls (4%). In short, fathers apparently are willing to persist with difficult male infants more than with troublesome female infants. Consistent with these findings are Kotelchuck's data[11] that fathers report that they play about one-half-hour a day longer with their firstborn sons than with their firstborn daughters. Although Lamb[14] found no mother–father differences in infant relationships in his home observations of infants of 8 and 13 months, he did find differences in father and mother treatments of their sons and daughters in his study of 15–24-month-old infants in their homes. Fathers vocalized more to their sons than mothers did, although both parents vocalized to their daughters equally.

These recent observational studies suggest that fathers play a more intrusive and paramount role in the sex-typing process[25]; fathers discriminate more than mothers in their treatment of male and female infants. In addition, boys are treated more discriminatively by their fathers than girls, which is consistent with other studies indicating that pressures toward sex-role adoption are stronger and occur at an earlier age for sons than for daughters.[26]

FATHER–INFANT INTERACTION AND ITS EFFECTS ON THE INFANT

It has already been established that fathers are involved with their infants; do infants reciprocate their fathers' investment? Both laboratory and home-observational studies indicate that infants react positively to *both* mothers and fathers, but the quality of father–infant interaction is an important determinant of the infant's social responsiveness.

Recent evidence indicates that infants can discriminate among mothers, fathers, and strangers at a relatively early age. In a recent study,[27] five infants ranging in age from 2 weeks to 6 months were observed interacting at weekly intervals with either mother, father, or a stranger. Based on a microanalysis of two minutes of playful communication between the adults and the infant, reliable differences in infant behavior were observed as early as two months of age. Using frowning as a measure, Yogman et al.[27] found that infants displayed less frowning to either mother (5.3%) or father (7.8%) than to a stranger (28.2%). They also found that infants older than two months frowned differentially to the mother (2.2%) and to the father (7.7%) as well as to the stranger (30.4%). Infant smiles, vocalization, and limb movement also discriminated between mothers and fathers versus strangers.

It is interesting not simply to determine that infants can discriminate among different social agents but also to explore their preferences for different social agents. Theoretically, it is of interest to evaluate the assumptions underlying the Bowlby-Ainsworth attachment theory[28,29] that infants will be attached to mothers earlier than to fathers and that they will prefer their mothers to their fathers. Both laboratory[11,14,17,30] and home-based[31,32] studies indicate that infants in the first year of life show no consistent preference for either parent and that "there is no evidence to support the popular presumption that infants of this age [8–13 mo] should prefer—indeed be uniquely attached to—their mothers."[14] The degree of infant social responsiveness, however, does vary with the amount and type of father involvement, whether social behavior is assessed in the laboratory[11] or in the home.[13,31,33] Positive relationships between overall proximity to the father for one-year-old infants in the laboratory and paternal caretaking in the home have been found.[34,35] Similarly, Pedersen and Robson,[13] in their study of 8–9 month-old infants, found that father involvement in routine caretaking, emotional investment in his infant, and the stimulation level of paternal play were positively related to his male infant's attachment to his father as assessed by the age of onset and intensity of greeting behavior directed to the father.

Infant cognitive development is affected by the quality of father–infant interaction. In a study of 5–6-month-old male infants,[33] Bayley mental test scores were positively correlated with the amount of father contact. In a more detailed examination of the components of father–infant interaction, in a sample of 16–22-month-old infants, Clarke-Stewart[18] found that the father's social physical play best predicted boys' cognitive development, while the quality of the fathers' verbal interaction was a better predictor for female infants' cognitive status.

In summary, many of the same trends that have been discovered in studies with older children are evident in these investigations of younger infants. Fathers do play an influential role in their infants' cognitive and social development from a *very* early age. The task remains to detail the mechanisms through which this infleunce is mediated, which cognitive capacities and social abilities are most affected by fathers, and at what ages these effects occur. In order to do this, it is important to consider these influences within a family context, since such influences rarely operate in a social vacuum.

BEYOND THE FATHER–INFANT DYAD: THE FATHER IN A FAMILY CONTEXT

Although most research of the father's influence on infant development has centered primarily on direct influences of the father (i.e., the impact of father–infant interaction or the father–infant relationship on the infant's development), it is clear that many of these influences are mediated through the mother or some other family member.[36] For example, the father's relationship with his spouse may affect the way the mother treats the infant. Although very little is known about the nature of such influence patterns, some preliminary work has been done. In two of our earlier studies, we examined the behavior of mother and father alone with the infant and in the mother–father–infant triad.[3,4] In both studies the father was a highly involved participant in the family context and either equalled or excelled the mother in stimulating and nurturing the infant. Of greatest interest were comparisons of the parents in the dyadic and triadic settings. The presence of the spouse significantly altered the behavior of the other parent; specifically, both father and mother expressed more positive affect (smiling) toward their infant and showed a higher level of exploration when the other parent was also present. The family context, in short, appeared to elicit greater affective and exploratory behavior on the part of both parents. Our hypothesis is that the parents verbally stimulate each other by focusing the partner's attention on aspects of the baby's behavior and by commenting on the infant's appearance, which in turn elicits either positive affect directed to the baby or exploration to check out an aspect of behavior noted by the spouse. These results indicate that parent–infant interaction patterns are modified by the presence of another adult; in turn, the implication is that we have assumed prematurely that parent–infant interaction can be understood by our sole focus on the parent–infant dyad alone.

Moreover, other recent investigations underline the importance of studying the family triad by illustrating the impact of the husband–wife relationship on the parent–infant interaction process and the influence of the birth of a high-risk infant on the cohesiveness of the family. Pedersen[37] assessed the influence of the husband–wife relationship on mother–infant interaction in a feeding context. Ratings were made of the quality of the mother–infant relationship in connection with two time-sampling home observations when the infants were four weeks old. Of particular interest was "feeding competence," which refers to the appropriateness of the mother in managing feeding:

> Mothers rated high are able to pace the feeding well, intersperse feeding and burping without disrupting the baby and seem sensitive to the baby's needs for either stimulation of feeding or brief rest periods during the course of feedings (p. 4).[37]

In addition, the husband–wife relationship was assessed through an interview; finally, neonatal assessments (Brazelton) were available. Pedersen summarized his results as follows:

The husband–wife relationship was linked to the mother–infant unit. When the father was more supportive of the mother, that is, evaluated her maternal skills more positively, she was more effective in feeding the baby. Then again, maybe competent mothers elicit more positive evaluations from their husbands. The reverse holds for marital discord. High tension and conflict in the marriage were associated with more inept feeding on the part of the mother (p. 6).[37]

The picture is even more complex, however, as indicated by the observation that the status and well-being of the infant, as assessed by alertness and motor maturity, are also related to the marital relationship. With an alert baby, the father evaluated the mother more positively; with a motorically mature baby, there appeared to be less tension and conflict in the marriage. In Pedersen's view, "a good baby and a good marriage go together."[37]

Both Parke and Pedersen used "normal" healthy, full-term infants. One would, however, expect that the impact of a high-risk infant would have an even more profound impact on the family interaction patterns. Of relevance to this issue is the earlier work of Leiderman and co-workers.[38,39] These investigators examined the impact of the separation that often occurs between parents and premature infants on subsequent mother–infant interaction and family functioning. Two groups of premature infants and their families, as well as a sample of normal infants, were entered on the study. One group of premature infants had contact with their parents during the separation period, while a second group had little contact over a period of approximately three weeks postpartum. Although the study showed the importance of contact for the development of the mother–infant relationship,[40] the finding of particular interest for this section concerned the impact of a premature infant on family cohesiveness. By the time the infants were 21 months old, eight divorces had occurred in the original sample of 66 families: five divorces occurred in families of the separated group, two in the contact group, and one in the full-term group. Leiderman and Seashore suggested "that separation in the newborn period does have a effect, albeit nonspecific, by acting through the family as a stress that creates disequilibrium in the nuclear family structure (pp. 229–230)."[38]

The importance of these findings is clear: in order to understand the father–infant relationship and its effects on the infant's development, the total set of relationships among the members of the family needs to be assessed. Only in this way will the complex nature of such influences be understood.

CULTURAL SUPPORT SYSTEMS FOR FATHERS

In view of the potential role that fathers can play in early infant development and in light of secular pressures toward greater father involvement, it is important to provide cultural support systems for fathering activities. Popular advice-to-father books are currently available, but there is little indication that parents (mothers or fathers) are likely to use these primers as guides for their child care.[31] Aside from this type of primer, there are very few programs that specifically aim at teaching fathers parenting skills. The vast majority of programs are mother-oriented, while fathers are virtually ignored.

Supportive intervention for fathers might assume a variety of forms. First, there needs to be an increase in opportunities for learning fathering skills. Such opportunities might be provided through pre- and postpartum training programs for fathers to learn basic caregiving skills and to learn about normal infant development. Second, there needs to be increased opportunities for fathers to practice and implement these skills. One possibility is the support of paternity leaves, which would provide fathers with opportunities to share in early caretaking of the infant. Opportunities for contact with the infant in the early postpartum period *may* alter subsequent parent–infant interaction patterns. Preliminary evidence from recent studies suggest that father–infant interaction patterns can be modified by hospital-based interventions. Lind[41] found that Swedish fathers who were provided the opportunity to learn and practice basic caretaking skills during the postpartum hospital period were more involved in the care of the infant and in household tasks at three months in the home.

In the United States, Parke et al.[42] recently presented to fathers a videotape of father–infant interaction during the early postpartum hospital period. The videotape provided information concerning the newborn infant's perceptual and social competence, play techniques, and caretaking skills. Observations during structured 10-minute feeding and 10-minute play sessions indicated that fathers who reviewed the videotape learned techniques for maintaining infant feeding. In contrast to control fathers who saw no film, the experimental fathers engaged in significantly more "stimulate feed" behavior, but not only in the newborn period but also at home at three weeks and three months. During play sessions, film fathers vocalized to their infants more than control fathers, especially with firstborn sons. Fathers' knowledge of infant perceptual capacities (e.g., newborn infants can follow an object) was increased as a result of the videotape intervention. In addition, fathers in the experimental group endorsed more strongly the importance of stimulating infants and expressed less resentment and concern about the disruptive impact of the infant on their lives. A final measure concerned the amount of participation in various caretaking activities in the home at three months. Based on a seven-day diary record, it was found that fathers who saw the film were more likely to diaper and feed their sons (although not their daughters) than control fathers. These results illustrate the feasibility and effectiveness of using the postpartum hospital period as a point of intervention for fathers and suggest that similar programs be developed and utilized in the future.

Considerable care must be taken in the implementation of these support systems; the important issue of parent's rights needs to be considered. The infliction on all families of these supports, with their implicit scenario of the liberated, egalitarian family in contrast to more traditional family organization, is not the aim. The goal should be to provide as much support as the couple's ideology and role definition dictates is necessary for the successful fulfillment of these functions. Too often "more" is equated with "improvement;" however, in many families, increased father participation may cause conflict and disruption as a result of the threat to well-established and satisfying role definitions. Intervention therefore should be sensitively geared to the needs of individual families, where the dynamics and ideology of the couple are given primary recognition.

CONCLUSION

This review indicates that the father plays a unique and important role in infancy beginning in the early postpartum period and that the patterns of early interaction between father and infant have an identifiable impact on the infant's social and cognitive development. The nature of father influence patterns must be considered within the family system, since fathers can influence their infant's development in direct and indirect ways. Given the importance of the father's role, the development of cultural support systems that encourage father involvement with their infants is advocated. Only then will the potential benefits of father involvement be fully realized.

REFERENCES

1. Greenberg M. Morris N: Engrossment: The newborn's impact upon the father. Am J Orthopsychiatr 44:520–531, 1974

2. Parke RD: Parent–infant interaction: Progress, paradigms and problems, in Sackett GP, Haywood HC (Eds): Observing Behavior (vol. 1): Theory and Applications in Mental Retardation, Baltimore, University Park, 1978

3. Parke RD, O'Leary SE, West S: Mother–father–newborn interaction: Effects of maternal medication, labor and sex of infant. Proc Am Psychol Assoc 85–86, 1972

4. Parke RD, O'Leary SE: Father–mother–infant interaction in the newborn period: Some findings, some observations and some unresolved issues, in Riegel K. Meacham J (Eds): The Developing Individual in a Changing World (vol. 2): Social and Environmental Issues. The Hague, Mouton, 1976

5. Parke RD, Sawin DB: Infant characteristics and behavior as elicitors of maternal and paternal responsibility in the newborn period. Presented at the Biennial Meeting, Society for Research in Child Development, Denver, 1975 (unpublished)

6. Phillips DM, Parke RD: Parental speech to prelinguistic infants. University of Illinois, 1980 (unpublished)

7. Arbeit SA: Study of women during their first pregnancy. Ph.D. Thesis, Yale, 1975 (unpublished)

8. Cowan C, Cowan PA, Coie L, et al.: Becoming a family: The impact of a first child's birth on the couple's relationship, in Newman L, Miller W (Eds): The First Child and Family Formation. Chapel Hill, University of North Carolina (Carolina Population Center), 1978

9. Shereshefsky PM, Yarrow LJ: Psychological Aspects of a First Pregnancy and Early Postnatal Adaptation. New York, Raven, 1973

10. Parke RD, Sawin DB: The family in early infancy: Social interactional and attitudinal analyses, in Pedersen F (Ed): Father–Infant Relationship: Observational Studies in a Family Context. New York, Holt, Rinehart & Winston (in press)

11. Kotelchuck M: The infant's relationship to the father: Experimental evidence, in Lamb ME (Ed): The Role of the Father in Child Development, New York, Wiley, 1976

12. Rendina I, Dickerscheid JD: Father involvement with first-born infants. Fam Coordinator 25:373–379, 1976

13. Pedersen FA, Robson KS: Father participation in infancy. Am J Orthopsychiatr 39:466–472, 1969

14. Lamb ME: Father–infant and mother–infant interaction in the first year of life. Child Dev 48:167–181, 1977

15. Yogman MJ, Dixon S, Tronick E, et al.: The goals and structure of face-to-face-interaction between infants and fathers. Presented at the Biennial Meeting, Society for Research in Child Development, New Orleans, 1977 (unpublished)

16. Power TG, Parke RD: Toward a taxonomy of father–infant and mother–infant play patterns. Presented at the Biennial Meeting, Society for Research in Child Development, San Francisco, 1979 (unpublished)

17. Lamb ME: The development of mother–infant and father–infant attachments in the second year of life. Dev Psychol 13:637–649, 1977

18. Clarke-Stewart A: And daddy makes three: The father's impact on mother and young child. Child Dev. 49:466–478, 1978

19. Poffenberger T, Poffenberger SB: The social psychology of fertility in a village in India, in Fawcett JT (Ed): Psychological Perspectives on Population, New York, Basic Books, 1973

20. Arnold R, Bulatao R, Buripakdi C, et al.: The Value of Children: Introduction and Comparative Analysis (vol. 1). Honolulu, East-West Population Institute, 1975
21. Hoffman LW: Changes in family roles, socialization and sex differences. Am Psychol 32:644–658, 1977
22. Coombs CH, Coombs LC, McClelland GH: Preference scales for number and sex of children. Population Studies 29:273–298, 1975
23. Rubin JZ, Provenzano FJ, Luria Z: The eye of the beholder: Parents' view on sex of newborns. Am J Orthopsychiatr 43:720–731, 1974
24. Rebelsky F, Hanks C: Fathers' verbal interaction with infants in the first three months of life. Child Dev 42:63–68, 1971
25. Johnson MM: Sex role learning in the nuclear family. Child Dev 34:315–333, 1963
26. Lansky LM: The family structure also affects the model: Sex role attitudes in parents of preschool children. Merrill-Palmer Q 13:139–150, 1967
27. Yogman M, Dixon S, Tronick E, et al.: Development of infant social interaction with fathers. Presented at a meeting of the Eastern Psychological Association, New York, 1976 (unpublished)
28. Bowlby J: Attachment and Loss (vol. 1): Attachment. New York, Basic Books, 1969
29. Ainsworth MD: The development of infant–mother attachment, in Caldwell BM, Ricciuti HN (Eds): Review of Child Development Research (vol. 3). Chicago, University of Chicago, 1973
30. Feldman SS, Ingham ME: Attachment behavior: A validation study in two age groups. Child Dev 46:319–330, 1975
31. Clarke-Stewart A: Popular primers for parents. Am J Psychol 33:359–369, 1978
32. Lamb ME: Interactions between eight-month-old children and their fathers and mothers, in Lamb ME (Ed): The Role of the Father in Child Development. New York, Wiley, 1976
33. Pedersen FA, Rubinstein J, Yarrow LJ: Infant development in father-absent families. J Gen Psychol 135:51–61, 1979
34. Kotelchuck M: The nature of the child's tie to his father. Ph.D. Thesis, Harvard, 1972 (unpublished)
35. Ross G, Kagan J, Zelazo P, et al.: Separation protest in infants in home and laboratory. Dev Psychol 11:256–257, 1975
36. Parke RD, Power TG, Gottman J: Conceptualizing and quantifying influence patterns in the family triad, in Lamb ME, Suomi SJ, Stephenson GR (Eds): The Study of Social Interaction: Methodological Issues. Madison, University of Wisconsin, 1979
37. Pedersen FA: Mother, father and infant as an interactive system. Presented at the Annual Convention, American Psychological Association, Chicago, 1975 (unpublished)
38. Leiderman PH, Seashore MJ: Mother–infant separation: Some delayed consequences, in Hofer MA (Ed): Parent–Infant Interaction. Amsterdam, Elsevier, 1975
39. Leifer AD, Leiderman PH, Barnett CR, et al.: Effects of mother–infant separation on maternal attachment behavior. Child Dev 43:1203–1218, 1972
40. Klaus MH, Kennell JH: Parent–Infant Bonding. St. Louis, Mosby, 1976
41. Lind R: Observations after delivery of communications between mother–infant–father. Presented at the International Congress of Pediatrics, Buenos Aires, 1974 (unpublished)
42. Parke RD, Hymel S, Power TG, et al.: Fathers and risk: A hospital-based model of intervention, in Sawin D, Hawkins RC (Eds): Psychosocial Risks During Pregnancy and Early Infancy (in press)

PART II

Influences of Professional Practices

Peter de Chateau

7

Effects of Hospital Practices on Synchrony in the Development of the Infant–Parent Relationship

L'amour c'est le contact de deux épidermes.
Rabelais

The main purpose of this chapter is to emphasize the influence of a large variety of factors on the development of the relationship between parents and infants. This development can be seen as a continuity from one generation to the next. Pregnancy, delivery, and the neonatal period are but very small parts of this continuous process and progress in time. Many of our own experiences are based on practical day-to-day routine work on the delivery floor and in maternity and neonatal wards. One is impressed to see how newly delivered mothers, both with healthy and with sick newborn infants, very often express feelings about numerous problems and difficulties connected with childbirth and the newborn baby. Many of these questions are of a nonphysical nature and have often to do with existing routines and practices in child-rearing. It therefore seems appropriate to start examining whether or not changes in customary care procedures could influence the parent–infant relationship and the infant's physical and sociopsychologic development.

During recent decades maternal and infant morbidity and mortality have been reduced to a very low level. Hospital personnel have

Supported by funds from the Swedish Save the Children Federation and from the Swedish Medical Research Council. Grant B79-19X-05443-01.

concentrated upon providing a high quality of physical care to mother and infant, but little active interest has been directed toward the importance of the neonatal period for the development of the unique mother–father–infant relationship. Many routines in our neonatal and maternity wards, such as separation of infants from their mothers,[1,2] were introduced to prevent infections and to improve treatment of the newborn. The adverse influences of separation on the mother–infant relationship were recognized,[3,4] yet many parents today are still not allowed to touch, hold, and care for their newborn premature or sick infants. The period immediately following delivery is a particularly sensitive one;[5–12] many changes in our day-to-day care and hospital practices need to be made in order to ensure that mother and infant remain close together during this period. In this chapter we discuss some of the literature together with our own observations during the early neonatal period and the importance of this period for the developing relationship between the newborn and his parents.

A number of factors influence the growth and development of the newborn infant, as well as maternal behavior, during this period. Pitkin et al.[13] and Smith[14] have described the influence of maternal nutrition on the fetus and infant. The use of drugs during pregnancy and the perinatal period[5,6,15] can be to the detriment of mother and infant. Obstetric complications and prematurity are found more often in the history of children with behavior disorders than in controls.[15] Maternal behavior is influenced by a multitude of factors, as described by Bowlby.[16] Others can be added (see Table 7-1), and there must be other factors of which we are not yet aware that also contribute to the final pattern of maternal behavior. Nilsson[17] in his studies of the paranatal emotional adjustment of healthy women found that psychiatric symptoms during the postpartum period, to a greater extent than such symptoms during pregnancy, are connected with conflicts in the reproductive function, i.e., conflicts between the demands of reproduction and ambivalent attitudes toward childbirth. Uddenberg[18] discussed the importance of a psychologic heredity in the etiology of reproductive maladaptation and pointed out that an individual may internalize inadequate adaptational patterns from his parents, with transmission of these patterns from one generation to the next. Mothers who had experienced a large number of crises during pregnancy and who were unable to solve their problems before delivery experienced great difficulty in adapting to the initial needs, both biologic and psychologic, of their newborn infants.[19–21]

Problems of methodology in the study of the mother–infant relationship are many and are far from solved today. Direct observa-

Table 7-1
Some Factors Affecting Maternal and Infant Behavior

Genetic background
Cultural background
Mother's relation to her parents
Relation to infant's father
Education
Occupation
Health
Obstetric history
Pregnancy
Parity
Delivery
Postnatal adaptation and postnatal care
Infant's sex
Infant's state
Infant's development
Infant's age

From de Chateau P: Neonatal Care Routines. Umea University Medical Dissertations, N.S. 20, 1976.

tion is a highly suitable method of studying mother–infant relations.[22–24] The most obvious advantage of observation is that one can see what is happening without having to rely on poorly established indirect techniques. On the other hand, one has to be selective about what is to be observed and recorded, and there is always the risk that valuable information will be missed. The presence of an observer may be disconcerting,[25] but mothers are used to contact with the hospital staff during their stay in the maternity ward and do not usually show any signs of discomfort during observation. For the newborn infant and his mother the maternity ward is a "natural" environment in our culture,[22] since home deliveries are no longer practiced. Later on, the home may be the most appropriate location for both observational studies and interviews.[7,26] The choice of which behavioral items to study is difficult, but some help may be obtained from the literature.[2,7,16,23–30]

Filming and videotape recording may be experienced as a less natural way of observation. Moreover, the camera lens covers a restricted area,[31] and analysis is excessively time-consuming and expensive. When sequences or interactions of behavior are to be studied, a time-sampling technique of direct observation is certainly inferior to the camera. Indirect procedures for studying the mother–infant relationship, such as interviews and questionnaires, have limitations.[22,32] Mothers may have a limited memory of things that have happened in the past and may also give a distorted report of their relationship with their children, being influenced by what they believe is culturally expected mother–infant behavior. No significant differences were found when different groups of mothers were asked about child-rearing practices.[7] This could be due to the limited number of mother–infant pairs investigated, but could also be an illustration of the limitations of a retrospective interview, which almost certainly minimizes the "true" differences that exist.[32] The value of interviews and questionnaires is, however, greater if they are combined with other methods of study, such as scrutiny of hospital records and records from antenatal clinics and child health center.[7]

ANIMAL STUDIES

Several animal species have been studied during the neonatal period in an attempt to identify species-specific maternal caregiving behavior. Studies of variations in neonatal care and their possible impact upon the development of the offspring and their behavior as adults have given further evidence of the special importance of the early postpartum period. A short separation of goat mothers from their young can lead to deviant maternal behavior,[33] whereas a five-minute contact between the goat mother and her own or alien young immediately after birth results in the normal accepting and caregiving behavior of the mother. Herscher and co-workers[34,35] found in goats and sheep that separation reduced the mother's feeding and caregiving ability in about 50 percent of the animals studied. In rats a short separation of mother and infant in the neonatal period has been shown to alter maternal caregiving upon reunion of mother and litter.[36]

The quality and quantity of sensory stimulation during the neonatal period seems to be of special importance to the infant's normal development and subsequent maternal behavior. Harlow et al.[37] showed that after two weeks, during which rhesus monkey mothers who were allowed to see and hear their infants but not to touch them, the mothers also spent less time viewing these infants. Harlow and co-workers[38,39] also showed that contact clinging is the primary variable that binds mother to infant and infant to mother. Infant monkeys were placed together with mother-substitutes of wire and cloth, both equivalent as providers of milk but not equivalent as providers of tactile or psychologic stimulation. The infant monkeys spent significantly more time with the cloth mother-substitutes and clung to the cloth mother-substitutes more often in a frightening or strange situation. These infant monkeys, deprived from tactile contact with their own mothers, failed, when grown up, to rear their own young normally.

Denenberg,[40] in studies of rats, showed that the way of handling the infant during infancy has wide and profound effects upon its behavior and physiology in adulthood. Likewise Levine[41,42] pointed out that handled rats showed more adaptive responses to stress than nonhandled ones, and that stimulated rats grew more rapidly, given the same amount of food, than controls and, using conditional avoidance as a criterion of learning ability, learned more quickly. The consequences of handling (gentle cutaneous stimulation in early infancy) seem to be of more importance where emotional factors rather than matters of cognitivie function are concerned.[42]

MATERNAL BEHAVIOR

In a number of studies Klaus, Kennell, and co-workers[2,8-10,43-46] have questioned whether or not present hospital practices may affect later maternal behavior, and have given evidence that the immediate postpartum period is especially sensitive for the development of the mother–infant relationship. Twelve mothers with healthy full-term infants were filmed during their first contact, and an orderly progression of tactile contact was observed in all mothers.[44] The mothers started with fingertip touch of the infant's extremities, followed by palm contact on the trunk, encompassing of the infant, and eye-to-eye contact. Mothers of normal premature infants followed a similar sequence of behavior, but at a much slower rate. In another study,[45] 14 mothers (control group) had the usual routine contact with their healthy full-term infants after delivery and 14 mothers (extended contact) were given their naked babies for one hour within the first three hours after birth and also for five hours extra contact each afternoon for the three days after delivery. In follow-up studies one month,[45] one year,[43] and two years[46] after delivery, differences were found in maternal attachment behavior and linguistic behavior between the extended contact and control groups.

In a very large prospective study O'Connor et al.[11] are investigating low-income primiparous mothers randomly assigned to either extra contact or hospital routine care. So far over 300 families have been followed for a period of 1–2 years, and abuse, neglect, abandonment, and failure to thrive have been observed more commonly in routine care infants.[11] In an Italian study[47] one month after delivery, these observations were confirmed in a slightly different way, emphasizing that perinatal medicine should be considered an important part of maternal and child health.

In a series of observations by the author,[7,26,28,48-52] an alteration in maternal behavior was also seen when this extra contact was limited to only 20 minutes during the first postpartum hour (Table 7-2). Twenty-two healthy primiparous mothers (P+), with normal pregnancies and deliveries, were given extra skin-to-skin and suckling contact with their infants after delivery ("extra contact"). A control group of 20 primiparous mothers and infants was given routine care (P), as was a second control group of 20 multiparous mothers and infants (M). The subjects were randomly assigned to either the early contact or control group. At 36 hours maternal and infant behavior was observed during breastfeeding. At this stage primiparae with extra contact showed behavior much more like the behavior of multiparae with routine care. Infants of primiparae with routine care cried most frequently.[28] At three months a follow-up study of the two groups of primiparae and their infants was made by means of observation of mother–infant free play and a personal interview with the mothers. Background data concerning pregnancy, delivery, neonatal period, and the first three months at home were comparable in the two groups. Mothers in the "extra contact" group spent more time kissing and looking face-to-face at their infants, and the infants smiled more often and cried less frequently.[26] One year after delivery

Table 7-2
Postpartum Care of Infant

Group	Time Postpartum		
	0–30 min	Next 15–30 min	45–120 min
P (n = 20) and M (n = 20)	Weighing, bathing, Crede-prophylaxis dressing, etc.	Resting dressed in crib or mother's bed	Resting dressed in crib or mother's bed
P + (n = 22)	15–20 min of skin-to-skin and sucking contact with mother	Weighing, bathing, Crede-prophylaxis dressing, etc.	Resting dressed in crib or mother's crib

P, primiparous mothers with routine care; M, multiparous mothers with routine care; P+, primiparous mothers with "extra contact."

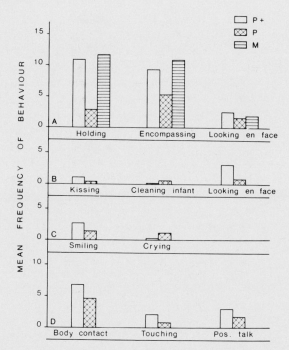

Fig. 7-1. Maternal behavior 36 hours after delivery in maternity ward (A), 3 months later during home visit (B), and 1 year postpartum in the outpatient clinic (D). Infant behavior at 3 months of age (C). P+, primiparous mothers with "extra contact" (n = 22); P, primiparous mothers with routine care (n = 20); M, multiparous mothers with routine care (n = 20).

the primiparous mothers with "extra contact" showed more close body contact with their infants during observation of a routine physical examination. A summary of the most important differences in behavior among these groups is given in Fig. 7-1.

An interesting observation was made when both groups of primiparae were compared according to the sex of the infant. The differences between P+ and P groups were obviously less pronounced in the case of mothers with female infants. Much more marked and statistically significant differences in behavior, however, were seen between P+ and P mothers of boys. This was true on all three occasions. Besides differences in behavior between the two groups, other items included in our studies also showed significant correlation with extra contact. Mean duration of breastfeeding, maternal attitudes to different matters of childrearing, and psychomotor development of the infants up to one year of age are examples of these correlations (see Table 7-3). Breastfeeding was significantly prolonged in early contact mothers, and they also gave night feeding for a considerably longer time and experienced less problems with night feeding as compared to controls. These results could illustrate a more synchronized feeding experience between mother and infant. To our surprise ten control mothers, as opposed to five in the experimental group, had started bladder training of their infants by one year. Bladder training of infants before the age of one year is rather uncommon in our society.

The results of psychomotor development as measured by the Gesell Development Test[53] were surprisingly consistent with the more harmonious results observed in the mother–infant relationship and subsequent child development in the study group. In these studies we also found differences in maternal and infant behavior, duration of breastfeeding, attitudes towards childrearing, and psychomotor development within groups with the same type of postnatal care depending on the infant's sex. This was in itself perhaps not surprising; these differences might be acquired, caused by difference in maternal attitudes associated with different expectations of girls and boys, and

Table 7-3
Some Results of Followup Studies on Early
Postdelivery Contact at One Year Postpartum

	P+	P
Mean duration of breast feeding (days)	180	108
Mean duration of night feeding (days)	42	24
Problems with night feeding		
Yes	1	6
No	20	13
Mothers returned to professional work		
Yes	10	14
No	8	3
Started bladder training		
Yes	5	10
No	13	7
Psychomotor development of infant (Gesell) (wk)	63.8	56.2
Biologic age (wk)	56.4	57.3

P+, primiparous mothers with "extra contact" following delivery; P, primiparous mothers with routine care after delivery.

obviously might also have a more biologic background.[26] On the other hand, the fact that these sex differences were already present at 36 hours after delivery[28] might speak in favor of a genetic cause or at least a prenatal molding. A more interesting and unexpected finding was that a change in care routine influenced boys and their mothers more than girls and their mothers. In our view many of the observed differences in, for example, behavior have an emotional background and a value in the relationship of mother and infant. For instance, behavior that can be expected to have a positive influence and value (smiling) was found to occur more frequently in the extra contact group (P+). At three years still some differences were found during an interview with the parents (Table 7-4). Asked in retrospect parents in the control group (P) found in 60 percent of the cases the time together with the infants immediately after delivery to have been insufficient. In contrast to this, parents in the study group (P+) shared this opinion only in 20 percent of the cases. The general health and development of the children and the number of visits to hospitals and well-baby clinics was comparable in both groups. Mothers in the extra contact group (P+) judged the infants to have a faster language development, however. The number of siblings born during the three-year follow-up period was twice as many in the extra contact group (P+) as compared to the controls (P).

The validity of the results of these and other studies has quite fairly been questioned. Our samples were randomized, a large number of background factors were comparable in both groups, etc., but nevertheless an unknown bias could have slipped into these investigations. Partly because we wanted to meet these criticisms and also to enable us to be more certain and firm about our results, a checkup of the psychologic needs of the mothers was made one year after delivery.[51] For this we used the Cesarec-Marke Personality Scale[54] (CMPS) based on Murray's personality theory,[55] which had been shown to be stable over time when used on the same subjects and with which we were familiar. A summary of the results of this CMPS is given in Figure 7-2). No significant differences between the two groups were found in any of the 12 items (A–L, Figure 7-2), nor did any of the groups differ in any way from the normal range of results. Since the CMPS has been shown to be stable over time,[54] the conclusion from this part of our studies must therefore be that at the time of delivery and randomizing, the two groups were fully comparable as to psychologic needs such as nurturance, achievement, affiliation, autonomy, and succorance.

The importance of direct eye-to-eye contact as a possible releaser of positive maternal feelings has been suggested by Robson.[56] Moss

Table 7-4
Some Results of Personal Interviews with Parents
Three Years after Delivery

	P+	P
Time spent together with infant after delivery insufficient	5/20	12/19
Number of siblings born during follow-up period	9/20	4/19
Language development "two-word sentences" before 18 months	15/20	9/19

P+, primiparous mothers with "extra contact" following delivery; P, primiparous mothers with routine care after delivery. [From de Chateau P: Early post-partum contact and later attitudes, Int J Behav Dev (in press).]

and Robson[57] found a positive correlation between positive maternal attitudes toward infants during pregnancy and frequency of face-to-face contact between mother and infant during a home visit one month after birth. At three months, however, this correlation was statistically significant only for girls and their mothers. Both Rubin[58] and Klaus et al.[44] have pointed out the importance of the development of exploratory touch in the newly delivered mothers. Maternal touch and holding are involved in the progressive handling pattern of the human mother with her newborn baby. Salk,[59-61] Weiland,[62] and de

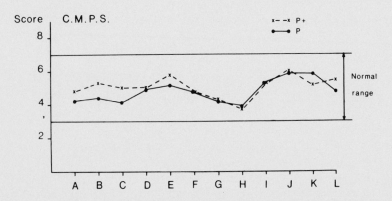

Fig. 7-2. Profile of results of all mothers CMPS one year postpartum. P+, primiparous mothers with "extra contact" ($n = 22$); P, primiparous mothers with routine care ($n = 20$). A–L, 12 factors (affiliation, nurturance, succorance, aggression, etc.) forming CMPS. Stanine score 0–9.

Chateau and co-workers[7,50] found that 80 percent of the mothers studied held their infants to a point to the left of the body midline. Neonatal separation seemed to decrease the incidence of left-sided holding.[7,61] In explaining this left-side preference, Salk[60] discussed the influence of the maternal heartbeat as an imprinting stimulus that has a soothing effect on the infant. Presenting the normal heartbeat constantly during the first days of life to newborn babies, Salk[59] demonstrated a significant increase in weight gain. Palmqvist[63] could not corroborate the effect of the normal human heartbeat sound on the weight development of normal healthy infants. Weiland and Sperber[64] postulated that the preference for left-side holding primarily serves to relieve anxiety in the adult carriers. This can be illustrated by the fact that right-holding mothers, in a follow-up study three years after delivery of their infants, showed more need for contact with the child health center than left-holding mothers.[7] The infants in both groups had been equally healthy. During pregnancy, primiparae who later in the neonatal period held the infant to the right made fewer preparations for delivery and for the baby and also experienced their body as less attractive.[65] Female and male adults differ in holding behavior, and the development of the preference for left-side holding during childhood confirms this observation.[7] Carrying of the infant also seems to follow a given pattern.[50] Mothers carried their infants from one place to another on the left arm, on the right, on "in the hands." Neonatal care influenced maternal carrying in primiparae. Thus 15–20 minutes of immediate postpartum "extra contact" eliminated carrying in the hands and increased the proportion of mothers carrying to the left (Fig. 7-3). Separation, on the other hand, was associated with a slight increase in carrying in the hands and a decrease in carrying to the left.

PARITY

Maternal parity may greatly influence the mother–infant interaction during the first week. Thoman et al.[66] found that multiparous mothers appear to be more sensitive than primiparous mothers to the cues of their infants. Infants of multiparae sucked more during breastfeeding and consumed more during bottle-feeding, even though primiparae spent more time in feeding their infants and stimulated them more to get them to suck. In another study[30] primiparae were found to be more attentive to their infants but had more difficulty in quieting them. Second mothers responded to infant crying more

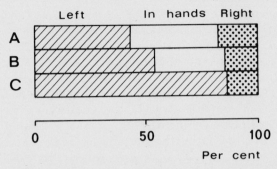

Fig. 7-3. Carrying infant during first week after delivery in three groups of primiparae. A, separated mothers (n = 22); B, nonseparated mothers (n = 125); C, "extra contact" mothers (n = 21), Carrying to left (shaded areas), carrying "in the hands" (blank areas), and carrying to right (dotted areas). [From de Chateau P: Neonatal Care Routines. Umeå University Medical Dissertations, N.S. 20, 1976.]

quickly and more often by feeding than first mothers did.[67] No differences between multiparae and primiparae were found in attempts to achieve visual contact at first contact with their full-term healthy newborn infants.[44] Primiparae and multiparae giving routine care after delivery behaved differently during breastfeeding at 36 hours. An extra naked skin-to-skin and suckling contact with their infants given to primiparae immediately following delivery eliminated this difference.[7,28]

CARETAKER ENVIRONMENT

The facilities for mothers and infants may differ greatly during their hospital stay. Rooming-in long ago proved to be very useful in the prevention of childhood behavior disorders.[68] Rooming-in provides a natural mother–child experience under the supervision of maternity personnel and facilitates the instruction of mothers and fathers in infant care.[69] Primiparae rooming-in with their newborn babies judged themselves, one day prior to discharge, to be more confident and competent in baby care and thought that they would need less help in caring for their infants at home.[70] Rooming-in mothers also claimed to understand the attributes of their baby's cry in a better way than control mothers. During the hospital stay rooming-in mothers showed a higher incidence of breastfeeding,[71] and in the first two months at home, a higher percentage of weaning by control mothers was reported.[29] The importance for the father of a rooming-in hospital practice has been discussed by Lind.[72]

Burns et al.,[73] in a study of infants given up by their mothers for adoptive placement, investigated the effects of multiple and single caregivers on infant distress while feeding during the first ten days. Being cared for by several persons and fixed feeding schedules in the maternity ward resulted in relatively many distress symptoms, such as grimacing, turning away from the nipple, fussing, and crying. Less infant distress in feeding was found when this rigid schedule was changed to a more individualized one. Another group of infants showed an increase in distress when they were switched to the rigid schedule at ten days after first receiving single-caregiver treatment. These studies illustrate that infants react to the kind of care they receive and that the sequence of environments (maternity ward followed by rooming-in and vice versa) influences these reactions. Rooming-in, which is more like the home situation after discharge, and being cared for by only one person (the mother) may therefore be of great importance in the development of mother–infant synchrony.

HOSPITAL STAFF

In studies considering the development of maternal–infant relationships, the hospital staff, like the father,[72,74] is too often a totally forgotten factor of importance. Since home deliveries are not practiced very much in Western societies these days, although there is a tendency in, for instance, California toward an increase in the proportion of home deliveries,[75] most expectant mothers are delivered in the maternity units and delivery wards of our hospitals. In England a number of studies on this subject have been carried out during recent years.[76–78] The sincere wish of many mothers for home confinement is seen merely as a nuisance or a problem by medical officials, and no great effort is made by these officials to meet such demands from families. Hospital deliveries are always said to be safer than deliveries at home for mother and infant. However, it is still very difficult to understand fully how figures on maternal and infant morbidity and mortality can be among the lowest in the world under two obstetric systems so very different as as those of the Scandinavian countries (where most women deliver in hospitals) and the Netherlands (where most women deliver at home).[79,80]

When a woman in labor is admitted to delivery, she is almost always treated as a patient and, like most patients, loses much of her own identity as a human being and an individual. During labor and delivery many women do not have a full understanding of or control over what happens, and decisions are often made by the hospital staff without much discussion. Keefer[81] emphasized three other important factors by which home and hospital deliveries differ: maternal pain medications, uterine stimulants, and lithotomy position. All three are known to have an impact on fetal and infant oxygenation, on maternal and infant behavior, and on lactation.[5,10,82,83]

The canceling of routine weighing of the baby before and after suckling did not seem to influence the mean duration of breastfeeding very much at first.[7,49,84] Early failures during the neonatal week, however, were less common.[49] Mothers accepted the new no-weighing routines very easily, whereas difficulties were encounterd with the staff, who worried a lot about infant weight gain. They seemed to lose some of their professional identity and felt uncertain about their task in the new situation. They observed the infants more closely, however, being afraid the babies would starve. They also became successively more interested and skilled in breastfeeding techniques and in instructing and helping the mothers. Their work demanded more of them than it previously had. After three months the new system without weighing and supplementary feeding had gained their confidence, and the duration of breastfeeding rapidly increased.[7,49]

Many of our more or less unnecessary obstetric and neonatal routines, such as separation of mother and infant after cesarian section, restricted visiting hours, the right of the father to be present in the delivery room, have very little or no support from research. The existence of these routines obviously gives an unwarranted but strong feeling of security and professional status to people working in hospitals. In our own experience the time spent in discussing with the staff the preparation of a change in these routines is very much worthwhile. Such consultation is essential if the full support and enthusiasm of the staff are to be obtained and the new program is to be run successfully. Table 7-5 can serve as an illustration of this statement: During the years 1969–1976, 65 infants were born to 62 diabetic women in the maternity department of our hospital. The mean hospitalization time for infants in our neonatal ward over the past decade was consistently shortened,[85] and during the last few years there have been several instances of children being discharged without ever being transferred from the maternity ward at all. Better resources for obstetric planning and better neonatal care have been important in this development, but the altered views of the hospital

Table 7-5
Length of Postnatal Stay on Neonatal Ward of 65
Infants Born to 62 Diabetic Mothers

Year	Mean Stay (Days) (Range)	No. of Children	No. of Children Never Sent to Neonatal Ward
1969	11.5 (4–22)	7	0
1970	16.3 (5–39)	7	0
1971	18.1 (7–32)	11	0
1972	10.1 (0–33)	13	1
1973	6.1 (2–10)	7	0
1974	6.8 (0–26)	5	1
1975	1.0 (0–2)	3	1
1976	5.6 (0–40)	12	8
Total	10.7 (0–40)	65	11

From Lithner F, de Chateau P, Wickman M, et al:
Opuscula Med 22:119–122, 1977.

staff on the separation of mothers from their newborn infants and a
more individualized assessment of the necessity of hospitalizing these
infants in the neonatal ward have also been important factors.

DISADVANTAGES AT BIRTH

In a study of neonatal separation, Barnett et al.[86] allowed a group
of mothers to enter the premature nursery from the second day after
birth and to touch or handle their premature infants in the incubator.
As compared with mothers without this extra contact, mothers in this
study group showed greater commitment to their infants, more confidence in their ability to mother the infant, and more skill in
caretaking, and they provided the infant with more stimulation.
Leifer et al.[4] found differences in maternal attachment behavior (such
as smiling and close body contact) between mothers of full-term
infants and mothers of preterm infants. In the same study no differences were found in maternal behavior between mothers of premature
infants who had only visual contact and those who had experienced a
nearly full sensory contact during their infant's 3–12 week hospitalization. The incidence of divorce within these families and the proportion of infants given up for adoption sometime after hospital discharge
was much higher in the group that had experienced only visual
contact, however. Lower maternal self-confidence was found in pri-

miparous mothers separated for 3–12 weeks from their premature infants, as compared with primiparous mothers permitted physical interaction and contact during this period.[87] This difference was not found in multiparous mothers.

In a retrospective study Klein and Stern[88,89] found prematurity to correlate strongly with separation and child abuse. In a carefully controlled prospective study of 670 infants, Werner et al.[90] found evidence that if the infant is at some disadvantage at birth—in their study perinatal asphyxia—poor environmental circumstances reinforce the disadvantage already existing, while favorable postnatal social influences can compensate for it. The severity of the infant's illness at birth, the mode of delivery, and the time before the mother is first able to touch her infant seem all to be correlated to the feelings of contact with and importance to the infant during the neonatal period.[7]

A great deal of research has still to be done in this particular field, and with regard to the unique character of the immediate postpartum period,[2,7,12,86] our routines for caring for sick infants and infants at risk deserve increased attention. The benefit of intensive observation in the neonatal ward should be weighed against the possible harmful effects of the associated separation. The balance of benefit between these two factors can be established only after well-designed studies of the whole complex of problems. We are currently carrying out a large multicenter study of elective cesarian section and will try to separate the interrelated factors in such a manner that their possible individual importance can be established.

INFANT FEEDING

Experiences during feeding in the neonatal period may be of special importance; events in the very first feeding of an infant can affect many subsequent feedings.[91] Thoman and co-workers,[30,66,92,93] in a series of observations concerning parity of mother, mode of nutrition, breastfeeding versus bottle-feeding, and sex of infant, found evidence that the relationships observed during the first day of contact between mother and infant may be indicative of subsequent parent–child relationships and significant for the development and personality characteristics of the child. Richards and Bernal[24,94] reported that breastfed and bottlefed infants may differ at birth. Breastfed infants are fed for longer periods and cry more than bottlefed infants right from the start and have a different pattern of interaction with their mothers during the first days of their lives. Differences in infant behavior found on the eighth day can be seen as the result of both or either of these two influences in combination with the nature and quantity of the nutriment received. Infant behavior and development may thus be influenced by early feeding experience. At the time of discharge, the attitude of the nursing staff can influence a mother's decision on whether or not to breastfeed her child,[49,95,96] rooming-in may have a positive influence on the duration of breastfeeding,[29] and hospital practice may subsequently influence infant behavior and later development.

A number of changes in the care of mother and newborn baby have been made in our maternity ward from 1972 to 1975 in order to promote breastfeeding.[7,49,84] The mean duration of breastfeeding during this period has steadily increased (Fig. 7-4). We first canceled routine weighing before and after breastfeeding and supplementary feeding. This was also studied one year later when the staff were fully used to these new routines. Thereafter the impact of additional and prolonged information and support was studied. During this part of our studies, the giving of information to the fathers seemed to influence the duration of breastfeeding. Finally, when mothers and infants were given a naked skin-to-skin and suckling contact during the first hour after delivery, the mean time of breastfeeding increased still further. The trend depicted in Figure 7-4 appears very significant, but in evaluating the results one should remember that during the study period a general trend toward longer breastfeeding was observed in Sweden. According to both our own and official statistics this general trend came later than the trend reported for our maternity population.[84]

One has to be careful in interpreting these results because influences in this field are multifactorial and it is difficult to make experimentation sufficiently simple to justify firm conclusions. An interested and devoted staff may, for example, exert unspecific stimulating influences. The possible effect of canceling weighing before and after breastfeeding came after a rather long period of time. The decrease of the number of early failures, however, came immediately after the change in routines and can hardly be explained by a general swing back to longer breastfeeding.[7,49] During recent years mothers with a high-risk pregnancy have also been able to breastfeed their infants. Our thinking on this matter has changed quite substantially. The diabetic mother may serve as an example. Formerly she was not allowed to nurse her infant; the hospital staff literally forbade her to do so. Medical officials, too, strongly disapproved of lactating diabetics.[97] Recently, however, Miller[98] reported that 17 insulin-depend-

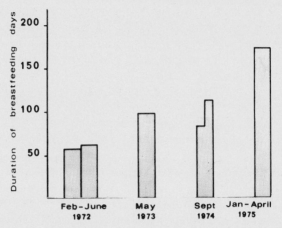

Fig. 7-4.   Mean duration of breastfeeding in groups of mothers with different postpartum care. Periods I to VI from left to right. I, routine care; II, no weighing of infant before and after breastfeeding and no supplementary feeding (n = 203); III, as II, one year later (n = 68); IV, additional and prolonged information (father not present at information) (n = 23); V, additional and prolonged information (father present at information) (n = 20); VI, naked skin-to-skin and suckling contact immediately after delivery (n = 21). [From de Chateau P: Neonatal Care Routines. Umeå University Medical Dissertations, N.S. 20, 1976.]

ent diabetic women could breastfeed without supplementation for periods of 3–24 months. This is fully concordant with our own experience, which includes successful lactation after cesarian section and other complicated deliveries and perinatal events.

SEX OF INFANT

It is still a very common belief that most women wish the expected baby to be a boy. This is obviously very true in many countries and societies, but this is often due to socioeconomic and cultural factors and is not really a free expression of a woman's preference for the sex of her infant. In nulliparous women associations were found during pregnancy between this preference and the sex of the woman's own siblings, her position among them, her education, her intelligence, the degree of her immaturity, and her lack of autonomy. Women wishing prenatally for a son reported that they had experienced a range of mental symptoms even before the current pregnancy, and these women also reported more mental symptoms during the postpartum period. The fulfillment of the wish for a boy seemed, moreover, to be correlated to more symptoms than were found in women wishing for a girl and subsequently having one.[18]

Leiderman et al.[3] found no differences in maternal self-confidence between mothers with male and mothers with female infants. Maternal behavior was different depending on the sex of the infant one week after discharge, mothers with girls showing more ventral contact, although boys and girls were held equally much. At three weeks of age, boys experienced a more extensive and stimulating interaction with their mothers than did girls.[99] Lewis[25] reported differences in maternal holding and vocalizing between mothers with boys and girls at three months, by two years, however, there were no sex differences. This illustrates the change of maternal behavior over time and is a complication in the study of mother–infant behavior.[25] The change in interaction between mother and infant over time has been discussed by Hinde[100]: the mother–infant relationship is dynamic, and each interaction may affect subsequent ones and the course of the relationship. Thoman et al.[66] found that during breastfeeding two days postpartum primiparae talked more to their female than to their male infants and that the duration of breastfeeding and amount of vocalization at two days were positively correlated. In our studies[7,26,28,48,51] boys and their mothers seemed to be more influenced by "extra contact" than girls and their mothers, an exception occurring in the holding and carrying of newborns.[49]

INFANT CAPACITIES

The individual reactive capacity of the newborn and his influence on his environment may be illustrated in a number of ways. If the mother gives birth with a very limited analgesia and without anesthesia, most infants, within minutes after delivery, are in the alert state,[101] able to see and primitively and rather uncoordinatedly to follow slow movements of bright objects and also to turn their heads toward sound, especially the human voice.[102,103] Bowlby[16,104] stated that infant smiling, crying, clinging, suckling, and following are activities that may release and facilitate maternal behavior, which is involved in attachment and maternal care. Although Richards[105] was critical of Bowlby's explanation of all five infant behaviors as being effective in bringing about proximity of mother and child and resulting in their mutual attachment, he agreed that smiling plays a role in the growing mother–infant relationship.

The infant's cry may have different causes and be seen as a way of communicating with the adult. Wasz-Höckert and co-workers[106,107] were able to identify four types of infant cry in a spectrographic study during the neonatal period: the birth cry, the hunger cry, the pain cry, and the pleasure cry. These different types of cry may be specific signals to the mother and may be able to release her response. In lactating primiparous mothers the hunger cry caused an increase in temperature over the breasts.[108] Experience seemed to influence the degree of this reaction; the more mothers had listened to their own infant's cry, the higher the skin temperature.[109] Some mothers were found to react weakly and others strongly to their infant's cry.

Blauvelt and McKenna[110] studied infants' special capacity for response to the environment provided by their mothers. Tactile stimulation of the infant's face from the ears to the lips resulted in the turning of the infant's face toward the mother. This headturning and orienting to the mother's face might be a releaser of maternal response behavior. Turkewitz et al.[111] noted that normal infants were more responsive to stimulation of the right than of the left side of the perioral region. The capacity of a neonate to fix, follow, and alert to a visual stimulus appears to be good evidence of an intact central nervous system.[112–114] Fantz and Miranda[115,116] reported the presence of discrimination ability in neonates and selection of different patterns when vision was tested. Miranda[117] showed that when newborn infants were presented with two identical pictures, the infants more often looked at the one on the right than the one on the left. About 80 percent of mothers have been reported to hold their infant to the left side of the body.[7,50,59–62,118,119] The infant's preference for turning to the right and looking to the right may be a species-specific adaptation to maternal holding to the left—i.e., when looking and turning to the right the baby can see his mother. The infant's preference for right-side looking and turning could also be a signal to the mother to favor holding to the left (Fig. 7-5).

At five days of age, clinically normal babies spent significantly more time turning toward their own mother's breast pad than toward a clean breast pad. This difference was not found at two days. It may be that after birth the infant gradually develops an appreciation for its mother, which becomes more specific the more the infant is exposed to her.[120] The symptoms of distress during feeding by different caregivers observed by Burns et al.[73] may partly be explained by Mac-Farlane's observations.[120] Infants of age 14 months with sleep problems

Fig. 7-5. Signals between infant and mother in lateralization of holding behavior. [From de Chateau P: Paediatricus 8:10, 1978.]

had already been more irritable during the neonatal period and fussy at a neurologic examination and during a sucking test than infants without sleep problems.[67,121] This illustrates the individuality of the newborn infant and shows how careful we must be with the assumption that parents' handling of the infant is always the source of developing problems within a given family.

INFANT SOOTHABILITY

Korner and Thoman[122] found that some newborn infants could be soothed more easily than others. Vestibular-proprioceptive stimulation, as a part of mother–infant body contact, had a highly potent soothing effect. Soothing can be a very important mode of stimulating an infant; when a crying infant during the first weeks of life is picked up and put to the shoulder, it usually stops crying and becomes bright eyed, thus being able to scan its visual surroundings and provide itself with a great deal of visual stimulation.[123,124] Crying infants may therefore need to be picked up more than infants who cry less and thus have more time available to process visual input. Maternal neglect of a crying infant may thus provide the infant with less visual stimulation and influence psychomotor and even affective development.[125] Birns et al.[126] also reported individuality in soothing; a neonate easily soothed by one stimulus (e.g., rocking) tended to be easily soothed by others (e.g., dummy) and vice versa. In another study[127] Birns reported that individual differences in responsiveness to stimulation were found over time and that stability in the individual reactions was evident.

Bell[128] illustrated the social interaction between the neonate and his caregiver. The infant's cry can bring the caregiver into the vicinity and thus start an interaction, although large individual differences have been found, and the tolerance of caregivers to infant crying probably shows a great range. During the first year of life a number of types of behavior by mothers in response to crying, such as picking up, talking, feeding, and touching, were reported by Bell and Ainsworth,[129] illustrating that the individual ways of responding found during the neonatal period also continue later. The early maternal responses to infant signals may therefore influence later social interaction.

EARLY STIMULATION OF INFANT

In recent years increased attention has been paid to the effects of early stimulation on the human infant. Wachs and Cucinotta[130] provided 13 normal newborn infants with 140 minutes of supplementary handling, audiovisual stimulation, and rocking daily for the first three days after birth. At four days of age these stimulated infants showed better-conditioned headturning, and at 30 days their visual attentiveness was greater than that of control infants. By ten months, however, no difference in development was found between the two groups. The authors suggested that permanence of effects may not have been achieved in their study because the optimal amount of critical stimulation may not have been reached. Another explanation might be that the extra stimulation was not given by the infants' own mothers or at the appropriate time. If a special sensitive period for the developing mother–infant relationship exists,[9,45] stimulation by the infant's own mother might be found to produce more lasting advantages. Ourth and Brown[131] found significantly less crying in infants to whom five hours of extra handling by their own mothers was given daily during the first four-and-a-half days of life, as compared with control infants without this extra handling (mild, firm support and rhythmic body stimulation at feeding time).

Distress during feeding in infants with multiple caregivers was pointed out by Burns et al.[73] Enrichment of the infant's hospital environment by means of single-caregiver practices could reduce this distress. In another study[132] infants given extra handling during the first five weeks of life showed significantly more visual interest in their environments than did nonhandled controls. No differences were found in weight gain, development, or general health. In infants of low birthweight, early stimulation might be of extra importance, especially if they are born to mothers of low socioeconomic level or with other disadvantages.

An experimental group of low-birthweight infants were given visual, tactile, and kinesthetic stimulation during six weeks in the neonatal ward.[133] Weekly home visits were also made to improve maternal care during the first year of life. Tests at four weeks and one year indicated greater developmental progress in these infants than in controls without extra stimulation and without weekly home visits.

DISCUSSION

The interpretation of studies on early stimulation is still very hazardous and must be made with great caution. It is notable however, how results of different studies both in humans and in animals tend to fit into a similar pattern.[7,24,26,28,33,39,43,44] A large number of mothers and infants may have individual needs. For example, mothers with an unwanted pregnancy might not be capable of accepting and benefiting from an early "extra contact" with their infants, and in fact we have found that during the period following our first studies[7,26,28] some mothers refused the "extra contact" offered to them. One therefore must be very cautious in offering all mothers this contact immediately after delivery. The offer should be made in an open-minded way, permitting the mother to make her own choice. Since one possible negative side-effect of early contact between mother and infant has been reported,[51] concerning the father's involvement in the day-to-day care of the child at one year, more research must be done and more clear evidence must be gathered on the long-term effects of such early contact on every aspect of the development of intrafamilial relations.

In our view the relatively short period of "extra contact" during the first hour following delivery can hardly in and of itself explain differences in maternal and infant behavior later on. Mothers and infants during this early contact, however, might have an opportunity to exchange signals, that may be of importance for the establishment of mother–infant synchrony. Consequently the development of mother–infant relationship may proceed more smoothly. Other variables such as parity of the mother, family, social background, and parents' age and health may be of equal importance. The same holds true for such factors as the mother's relationship with her husband and her own parents, the planning and course of pregnancy, and the mode of delivery.

From a biologic point of view, taking care of a newborn infant is an extremely delicate task. Critical physical needs, such as environmental temperature and caloric intake, must be met within narrow limits of tolerance to maintain the newborn infant in optimal health. It is reasonable to assume that during the early postdelivery sensitive phase of development the infant is also best served by a pattern of maternal behavior that for the most part is genetically determined and that qualitatively and quantitatively differs markedly from the input he receives from others at this time. It seems just as appropriate to protect the newborn infant against too great departures from his optimal emotional needs as from his optimal physical needs. It is still very common, however, for individuals (nurses, midwives, nurse's aides) other than the infant's own parents to have full access to him after delivery. Certain check-ups must then be carried out that may be important but not absolutely vital from a medical point of view. The extent of the possible permanent psychologic damage to development of the subsequent parent–infant relationship that may be caused by separation after delivery is not known, although the results of recent research strongly support the supposition that there may be some such damage.

The importance of the first hour after delivery cannot be overemphasized. Mothers and infants have a great range of individual patterns of behavior and interaction. The ability to care for the child can be learned, since differences between primiparae and multiparae in this respect are well known. Primiparae with "extra contact" show a behavior during breastfeeding much like the behavior of the more trained and more experienced multiparae with routine care after delivery.[28] This "extra contact" might have put the primiparae in a favorable position that, in a way, could be compared to the position of the multiparae with more training and experience. The "extra contact" might have had other physiologic advantages as well. Through a close skin-to-skin contact the infant is perhaps kept warm so that his unstable temperature regulation immediately after delivery is protected and not disturbed by our routines, like bathing, weighing, and so forth. We usually cover the baby's back with a blanket; a heat panel is not used. No instances of low body temperature were reported in the "extra contact" groups. The regulation of body temperature may have had an economical start through this extra contact.

In the foregoing, many different aspects of the importance of the neonatal period have been discussed. The observations presented have implications for neonatal care as well as for childrearing. Infants differ greatly from each other right from the very start. Their mothers and fathers have different backgrounds and capacities. Flexibility to the individual requirements of each and every family is therefore needed. It is regrettable that the trend in our society is in exactly the opposite direction;[125] certain childcare practices and certain forms of early stimulation and soothing are considered universally beneficial regardless of a given child's particular needs. We should also be very cautious about labeling some interactive patterns as "good" or "bad"[134]; evidence for this is still lacking, and what might be "good" for one infant–parent couple could be "bad" for another.[7] There has also been some discussion about the most appropriate terminology for the processes starting during "early contact," "extra contact," "extended contact," or whatever other terms may be used. So far these discussions have been performed within the scope of our practical hospital work. Efforts have been made to label the early period following delivery as "critical," "sensitive," "imprinting," or "special perceptive" to learning experiences. The mother, in particular, has been put forward as a very powerful carrier of these potentials, whereas the infant has gotten rather little space in the discussion. The family as a whole and their internal interactions should perhaps be looked upon as the real repository of the hidden secrets. A firm theoretical explanation of our empirical observations is also still lacking.

Our future research will have to be built on cooperation between disciplines such as medicine, physiology, psychology, sociology, and anthropology. Within the medical field, combined input from obstetrics, pediatrics, child and adult psychiatry, and social and developmental medicine must be brought together in multicenter investigations. Our ultimate goal has to be a better understanding of and superior service to the families put in our care.

REFERENCES

1. Klaus MH, Kennell JH: Maternal infant bonding. St. Louis, Mosby, 1976
2. Klaus MH, Kennell JH: Mothers separated from their newborn infants. Pediatr Clin North Am 17:1015–1035, 1970
3. Leiderman PH, Leifer A, Seashore M, et al.: Mother–infant interaction: Effects

of early deprivation, prior experience and sex of infant. Early Dev 51:154–175, 1973

4. Leifer A, Leiderman PH, Barnett C, et al.: Effects of mother–infant separation on maternal attachment behavior. Child Dev 43:1203–1218, 1972

5. Brazelton TB, Robey JS: Observations of neonatal behavior: The effect of perinatal variables, in particular that of maternal medication. J Am Acad Child Psychiatr 4:613–618, 1965

6. Brazelton TB: Effect of prenatal drugs on the behavior of the neonate. Am J Psychiatr 126:1261–1266, 1970

7. de Chateau P: Neonatal care routines: Influences on maternal and infant behavior and on breastfeeding. Umea Univ Med Dissert (New Series) 20, 1976

8. Hales DJ, Lozoff B, Sosa R, et al.: Defining the limits of the maternal sensitive period. Dev Med Child Neurol 19:454–461, 1977

9. Kennell JH, Trause MA, Klaus MH: Evidence for a sensitive period in the human mother. Ciba Found Symp 33:87–101, 1975

10. Lozoff B, Brittenham GM, Trause MA, et al.: The mother–newborn relationship: Limits of adaptability. J Pediatr 91:1–12, 1977

11. O'Connor SM, Vietze PH, Hopkins JB, et al.: Postpartum extended maternal–infant contact: Subsequent mothering and child health. Presented at the Forty-Seventh Annual Meeting of the Society for Pediatric Research, San Francisco, 1977 (unpublished)

12. Trause MA: Defining the limits of the sensitive period. Presented at the Biennial Convention of the Society for Research in Child Development, New Orleans, 1977 (unpublished)

13. Pitkin RM, Kaminetzky HA, Newton M, et al.: Maternal nutrition: A selective review of clinical topics. Obstet Gynecol 40:773–785, 1972

14. Smith CA: Effect of maternal undernutrition upon newborn infants in Holland (1944–1945). J Pediatr 30:229–234, 1947

15. Wolff S: The contribution of obstetric complications to the etiology of behavior disorders in childhood. J Child Psychol Psychiatr 8:57–66, 1967

16. Bowlby J: Attachment and Loss, vol. 1. Attachment. London, Hogarth, 1969

17. Nillson A: Paranatal emotional adjustment. Acta Psychiatr Scand [Suppl 220], 1970

18. Uddenberg N: Reproductive adaptation in mother and daughter. Acta Psychiatr Scand [Suppl 254], 1974

19. Lagercrantz E: Kvinnors upplevelse av den första graviditeten, I.A.N. rapport. Stockholm, Pedagogiska Inst, Stockholms Univ, 1973

20. Lagercrantz E: Psykologiska synpunkter på graviditet och för lossning. Lakartidiningen 71:2064–2066, 1974

21. Newton N: Maternal Emotions. New York, Hoeber, 1976

22. Moss HA: Methodological issues in studying mother–infant interaction. Am J Orthopsychiatr 35:482–486, 1965

23. Rheingold HL: The measurement of maternal care. Child Dev 31:565–575, 1960

24. Richards MPM, Bernal JF: An observational study of mother–infant interaction, in Blurton Jones N (Ed): Ethological Studies of Child Behaviour. London, Cambridge University, 1972, pp 175–198

25. Lewis M: State as an infant-environment interaction: An analysis of mother–infant interaction as a function of sex. Merrill-Palmer Q 18:95–121, 1972

26. de Chateau P, Wiberg B: Long-term effect on mother–infant behaviour of extra contact during the first hour postpartum. II. A follow-up at three months. Acta Paediatr Scand 66:145–151, 1977

27. Brazelton TB, Tronick E, Adamson L, et al.: Early mother–infant reciprocity. Ciba Found Symp 33:137–149, 1975
28. de Chateau P, Wiberg B: Long-term effect on mother–infant behaviour of extra contact during the first hour postpartum. I. First observations at 36 hours. Acta Paediatr Scand 66:137–144, 1977
29. Lind J. Jäderling J: The influence of "rooming-in" on breastfeeding. Acta Paediatr Scand [Suppl 159], 1965
30. Thoman EB, Turner AM, Leiderman PH, et al.: Neonate mother interaction: Effects of parity on feeding behavior. Child Dev 41:1103–1111, 1970
31. Cooper ES, Costella AJ, Douglas JWB, et al.: Direct observations. Bull Br Psychol Soc 27:3–7, 1974
32. Yarrow MR: Problems of methods in parent–child research. Child Dev 34:215–226, 1963
33. Klopfer P: Mother love: What turns it on? Am Sci 59:404–407, 1971
34. Herscher L, Moore AU, Richmond JB: Effect of postpartum separation of mother and kid on maternal care in the domestic goat. Science 128:1342–1343, 1958
35. Herscher L, Richmond JB, Moore AU: Maternal behavior in sheep and goats, in Rheingold HL (Ed): Maternal Behavior in Mammals. New York, Wiley, 1963
36. Rosenblatt JS: The basis of synchrony in the behavioural interaction between the mother and her offspring in the laboratory rat, in Foss BM (Ed): Determinants of infant Behaviour, vol. 3. London, Methuen, 1965, pp 17–32
37. Harlow HF, Harlow MK, Hansen EW: The maternal affectional system of rhesus monkeys, in Rheingold HL (Ed): Maternal Behavior in Mammals. New York, Wiley, 1963
38. Harlow HF, Zimmerman RR: Affectional responses in the infant monkey. Science 130:421–432, 1959
39. Harlow HF, Harlow MK: The affectional systems, in Schrier AM, et al. (Eds): Behavior of Non-Human Primates. New York, Academic, 1965
40. Denenberg VH: The effects of early experience, in Hafex ESE (Ed): The behaviour of domestic animals (2nd ed). London, Bailliere, Tindall & Cox, 1969
41. Levine S: A further study of infantile handling and adult avoidance learning. J Pers 27:70–80, 1956
42. Levine S: Stimulation in infancy. Sci Am 202:81–86. 1960
43. Kennell JH, Jerauld R, Wolfe H, et al.: Maternal behavior one year after early and extended postpartum contact. Dev Med Child Neurol 16:172–179, 1974
44. Klaus MH, Kennell, JH, Plumb N, et al.: Human maternal behavior at the first contact with her young. Pediatrics 46:187–192, 1970
45. Klaus MH, Jerauld R, Kreger N, et al.: Maternal attachment—Importance of the first postpartum days. N Engl J Med 286:460–463, 1972
46. Ringler NM, Kennell JH, Jarvelle R, et al.: Mother to child speech at two years— Effect of early postnatal contact. J Pediatr 86:141–144, 1975
47. Kropf V, Negroni G, Nordio S: Influenza della separazione madre-bambino nel periodo neonatale sullo sviluppo di atteggiamenti materni. Riv Ital Pediatr 2:299–305, 1976
48. de Chateau P: The influence of early contact on maternal and infant behavior in primiparae. Birth Family J 3:149–155, 1976
49. de Chateau P, Holmberg H, Jakobson K, et al.: A study of factors promoting and inhibiting lactation. Dev Med Child Neurol 19:575–584, 1977
50. de Chateau P, Holmberg H, Winberg J: Left-side preference in holding and carrying newborn infants. I. Mother's holding during the first week of life. Acta Paediatr Scand 67:169–175, 1978

51. de Chateau P, Cajander K, Engström AC, et al.: Long-term effect of early postpartum contact: One year follow-up, in: Proceedings of the Fifth International Congress on Psychosomatic Obstetrics and Gynecology. New York, Academic Press, 1978

52. de Chateau P, Wiberg B: Long-term effect on mother–infant behavior of extra contact during the first hour post-partum III. One year follow-up. Dev Med Child Neurol. (in press)

53. Gesell A, Armatruda CA: Developmental Diagnosis. New York, Hoeber, 1962

54. Cesarec Z, Marke S: C.M.P.S. Manual. Stockholm, Skandinaviska Testforlaget, 1968

55. Murray HA: Explorations in Personality. New York, Oxford University, 1938

56. Robson KS: The role of eye-to-eye contact in maternal–infant attachment. J Child Psychol Psychiatr 8:13–25, 1967

57. Moss HA, Robson KS: Maternal influences in early social visual behavior. Child Dev 39:401–408, 1968

58. Rubin R: Maternal touch. Nurs Outlook 11:828–831, 1963

59. Salk L: The effects of the normal heartbeat sound on the behavior of the newborn infant: Implications for mental health. World Ment Health 12:168–175, 1960

60. Salk L: Mother's heartbeat as an imprinting stimulus. Trans NY Acad Sci 7:753–763, 1962

61. Salk L: The critical nature of the postpartum period in the human for the establishment of the mother–infant bond: A controlled study. Dis Nerv Syst [Suppl] 11:110–116, 1970

62. Weiland HJ: Heartbeat rhythm and maternal behavior. J Am Acad Psychiatr 3:161–164, 1964

63. Palmqvist H: The effect of heartbeat sound stimulation on the weight development of newborn infants. Child Dev 46:292–295, 1975

64. Weiland JH, Sperber Z: Patterns of mother–infant contact, the significance of lateral preference. J Genet Psychol 117:157–165, 1970

65. de Chateau P, Mäki M, Nyberg B: Left-side preference in holding and carrying newborn infants. III. Mother's perception of pregnancy. Early Human Dev (in press)

66. Thoman EB, Leiderman PH, Olson JP: Neonate–mother interaction during breast feeding. Dev Psychol 6:110–118, 1972

67. Bernal JF: Crying during the first 10 days of life and maternal responses. Dev Med Child Neurol 14:362–372, 1972

68. Klatskin EH, Jackson E: Pediatric and psychiatric aspects of the Yale rooming-in project on parent–child relationship. Am J Orthopsychiatr 25:81–108, 372–397, 1950

69. Committee on Fetus and Newborn: Standards and Recommendations for Hospital Care of Newborn Infants (5th ed). American Academy of Pediatrics, 1971

70. Greenberg M, Rosenburg I, Lind J: First mothers' rooming-in with their newborns: Its impact upon the mother. Am J Orthopsychiatr 43:783–788, 1973

71. Jackson E, Wilkin L, Auerbach H: Statistical report on incidence and duration of breastfeeding in relation to personal-social and hospital maternity factors. Pediatrics 17:700–715, 1956

72. Lind J: Die Geburt der Familie in der Frauenklinik. Med Klin 68:1597–1601, 1973

73. Burns P, Sander LW, Stechler G, et al.: Short-term effects of caretaker environment of the first 10 days. J Am Acad Child Psychiatr 11:427–439, 1972

74. Greenburg M, Morris N: Engrossment: The newborns' impact upon the father. Am J Orthopsychiatr 44:520–531, 1974

75. Mehl LE: Statistical outcome of home-births in the U.S.: Current status, in Stewart L, Stewart D (Ed): Safe Alternatives in Childbirth. Chapel Hill, NAP-SAC, 1976

76. Leading Article, Br Med J 1:55–57, 1976

77. Goldthorpe WO, Richman J: Reorganisation of the maternity services—A comment on domiciliary confinement in view of experience of the hospital strike 1973. Midwife Health Visitor 10:265–270, 1974

78. Kitzinger S: Women's Attitudes to the Place of Birth. London, National Childbirth Trust, 1976

79. Ashford JR, Clayton S, Richman J, et al.: A place to be born. Br Med J 1:279–283, 1976

80. Haire D: Childbirth in the Netherlands: A contrast in care. Chicago, International Childbirth Ed Assoc News, 1970

81. Keefer CH: Pollution of the fetus: The delivery experience. Presented at the Annual Meeting of the American Psychological Association, San Francisco, 1977 (unpublished)

82. Rosen M: Pain and its relief, in Chard T, Richards MPM (Eds): Benefits and Hazards of the New Obstetrics. Clinics in Developmental Medicine No 64. London, Spastics International Medical, 1977, pp 100–115

83. Scanlon JW: Effects of local anesthetics administered to parturient women on the neurological and behavioral performance of newborn children. Bull NY Acad Med 52:231–235, 1976

84. de Chateau P, Holmberg H, Winberg J: Amningsfrekvens, viktutveckling, vägnings-och tillmatningsrutiner på BB. Lakartidningen 72:4388–4390, 1975

85. Lithner F, de Chateau P, Wickman M, et al.: Treatment of pregnant diabetics in a scarcely populated region of northern Sweden. Opuscula Med 22:119–122, 1977

86. Barnett CR, Leiderman PH, Grobstein R, et al.: Neonatal separation, the maternal side of interactional deprivation. Pediatrics 45:197–205, 1970

87. Seashore MJ, Leifer AD, Barnett CR, et al.: The effects of denial of early mother–infant interaction on maternal self-confidence. J Pers Soc Psychol 26:369–378, 1973

88. Klein M, Stern L: Low birthweight and the battered child syndrome. Am J Dis Child 122:15–19, 1971

89. Stern L: Prematurity as a factor in child abuse. Hosp Prac 117–123, May 1973

90. Werner E, Simonian K, Bierman JM, et al.: Cumulative effect of perinatal complications and deprived environment on physical, intellectual and social development of preschool children. Pediatrics 39:490–505, 1967

91. Gunther M: Infant behavior at the breast, in Foss BM (Ed): Determinants of Infant Behavior, New York, Wiley, 1959

92. Thoman EB, Barnett CR, Leiderman PH: Feeding behavior of newborn infants as a function of parity of the mother. Child Dev 42:1471–1483, 1971

93. Thoman EB: Development of synchrony in mother–infant interaction in feeding and other situations, Fed Proc 34:1587–1592, 1975

94. Bernal JF, Richards MPM: The effects of bottle and breastfeeding on infant development. J Psychosom Res 14:247–252, 1970

95. Richards MPM: Feeding and the early growth of the mother–infant relationship, in Kretschmer N, et al. (Eds): Modern Problems in Paediatrics, No. 15. Basel, Karger, 1975, pp 143–154.

96. Sloper K, MacKean L, Baum JD: Factors influencing breastfeeding. Arch Dis Child 50:165–170, 1975

97. White P: What it means to be female and diabetic, part 3. Diab Forecast 14, 1976

98. Miller DL: Birth and long-term unsupplemented breastfeeding in 17 insulin-dependent diabetic mothers. Birth Family J 4:65–70, 1977

99. Moss MA: Sex, age and state as determinants of mother–infant interaction. Merrill-Palmer Q 3:19–36, 1967

100. Hinde RA: Mothers' and infants' roles: Distinguishing the questions to be asked. Ciba Found Symp 33:5–12, 1975

101. Prechtl HFR: The behavioral states of the newborn infant. Brain Res 76:185–189, 1974

102. Brazelton TB: Neonatal behavioural assessment scale, in: Clinics in Developmental Medicine No. 50. London, Spastics International Medical, 1973

103. Condon WS, Sander LW: Neonate movement is synchronized with adult speech: Interactional participation and language acquisition. Science 183:99–101, 1974

104. Bowlby J: The nature of the child's tie to his mother. Int J Psychoanal 39:350–373, 1958

105. Richards MPM: Social interaction in the first weeks of human life. Psychiatr Neurol Neurochir 74:35–42, 1971

106. Valanné E, Vuorenkoski V, Partanen T, et al.: The ability of human mothers to identify the hunger cry signals of their own newborn infants during the lying-in period. Experientia 23:768–769, 1967

107. Wasz-Höckert O, Lind J, Vuorenkoski V, et al.: The infant cry: A spectrographic and auditory analysis, in: Clinics in Developmental Medicine No. 29. London, Spastics International Medical. 1968

108. Lind J, Vuorenkoski V, Wasz-Höckert O: The effect of cry stimulus on the temperature of the lactating breast of the primipara, in: Psychosomatic Medicine in Obstetrics and Gynaecology. Basal, Karger, 1972, pp 293–295

109. Wasz-Höckert O, Seitamo L, Vuorenkoski V, et al.: Emotional attitudes toward the child and childrearing and the effect of cry stimulus on the skin temperature of the lactating breasts in primiparas, in: Psychosomatic Medicine in Obstetrics and Gynaecology, Basel, Karger, 1972, pp 284–286

110. Blauvelt H, McKenna J: Mother–neonate interaction: Capacity of the human newborn for orientation, in Foss BR (Ed): Determinants of Infant Behavior. New York, Wiley, 1962, pp 3–25

111. Turkewitz G, Moreau T, Birch HG: Relation between birth condition and neurobehavioral organization in the neonate. Pediatr Res 2:243–249, 1968

112. Brazelton TB, Scholl ML, Robey JS: Visual responses in the newborn. Pediatrics 37:284–290, 1966

113. Desmond MM, Rudolph AJ, Phitoksphraiwan P: The transitional care nursery: A mechanism for preventive medicine in the newborn. Pediatr Clin North Am 13:651–668, 1966

114. Emde RN, Swedberg J, Suzuki B: Human wakefulness and biological rhythms after birth. Arch Gen Psychiatr 32:780–786, 1975

115. Fantz RL: Pattern vision in newborn infants. Science 140:296–297, 1963

116. Fantz RL, Miranda SB: Newborn infant attention to form and contour. Child Dev 46:224–228, 1975

117. Miranda SB: Visual abilities and pattern preferences of premature infants and full-term neonates. J Exp Child Psychol 10:189–205, 1970

118. de Chateau P: Left-side preference in holding and carrying newborn infants. J Maternal Child Health 2:418–421, 1977

119. de Chateau P, Andersson Y: Left-side preference for holding and carrying
      newborn infants. II. Doll-holding and carrying from 2 to 16 years. Dev Med Child
      Neurol 18:738–744, 1976
120. MacFarlane A: Olfaction in the development of social preferences in the human
      neonate. Ciba Found Symp 33:103–117, 1975
121. Bernal JF: Night waking in the first 14 months. Dev Med Child Neurol
      15:760–769, 1973
122. Korner AF, Thoman EB: The relative efficacy of contact and vestibular-propri-
      oceptive stimulation in soothing neonates. Child Dev 43:443–453, 1972
123. Korner AF, Grobstein R: Visual alertness as related to soothing in neonates:
      Implications for maternal stimulation and early deprivation. Child Dev
      37:867–876, 1966
124. Korner AF, Thoman EB: Visual alertness in neonates as evoked by maternal
      care. J Exp Child Psychol 10·67–78, 1970
125. Korner AF: Individual differences at birth: Implications for early experience and
      later development. Am J Orthopsychiatr 41:608–619, 1971
126. Birns B, Blank M, Bridger WH: The effectiveness of various soothing techniques
      on human neonates. Psychosom Med 28:316–321, 1966
127. Birns B: Individual differences in human neonates' responses to stimulation.
      Child Dev 36:249–256, 1968
128. Bell RQ: Contributions of human infants to caregiving and social interaction, in
      Lewis M, Rosenblum LA (Eds): The Effect of the Infant on its Caregiver. New
      York, Wiley, 1974, pp 1–19
129. Bell SM, Ainsworth MDS: Infant crying and maternal responsiveness. Child Dev
      43:1171–1190, 1972
130. Wachs TD, Cucinotta P: The effect of enriched neonatal experiences upon later
      cognitive functioning, in Williams T (Ed): Infant Care: Abstracts of the Literature.
      Washington, Consortium on Early Childbearing and Childrearing, 1972, pp
      10–22
131. Ourth L, Brown B: Inadequate mothering and disturbance in the neonatal period.
      Child Dev 32:287–295, 1961
132. White BL, Castle PW: Visual exploratory behavior following postnatal handling
      of human infants. Percept Mot Skills 18:497–502, 1964
133. Scarr-Salapatek S, Williams ML: The effects of early stimulation in low-birth-
      weight infants. Child Dev 44:94–101, 1973
134. Hofer MA: Summing up. Ciba Found Symp 33: 309–314, 1975

Roberta A. Ballard, Carol H. Leonard,

Nancy A. Irvin, and Carolyn B. Ferris

8

An Alternative Birth Center: Concepts and Operation

The birth center movement in the United States has grown rapidly during the past ten years, concommitant with a growing public awareness and scrutiny of health care systems and increasing demand for medical services responsive to humanistic concerns as well as physical ones. Family-centered maternity services, such as the perinatal center at Mount Zion Hospital, have sought to respond to these changes by introducing innovative programs to answer the need without compromising high standards of obstetrical and pediatric care. The Alternative Birth Center described here is a program addressed to the needs of healthy women with normal pregnancies.

The measures of a successful pregnancy and delivery for a family are a healthy infant who has made the transition to life outside the uterus in optimal physical condition; a mother physically able to provide a reliable environment for her infant and psychologically ready with some confidence that she can get to know and meet her baby's needs; and a father ready for involvement with his newborn and able to support the mother and, in some instances, siblings in welcoming a new member of the family.

During the past few years, research efforts have led to better understanding of the nature of the infant's characteristics in transaction with his caregivers and of the content of fathers' involvement, and have raised the possibility that mother–infant contact at birth may increase attachment of mother to infant. It follows, then, that obstetric and pediatric practices during pregnancy and the immediate perinatal period should be concerned with creating an environment in which a mother and other caregivers develop sensitivity to and appreciation of the infant. Provision of optimal circumstances for a mother's labor and delivery of her infant is one aspect of this process.

ISSUES OF PERINATAL MANAGEMENT

Historically, most perinatal management policies in the United States have been developed with the chief intention of reducing perinatal mortality and morbidity. A result of these admirable efforts, however, has been a disease-oriented approach to the management of birth with heavy reliance on technologic gains. Consequently, the mother is placed in a passive, "sick" role, rather than a role of an active, protective, decision-making parent. Many of the procedures designed from this high-technology medical base, appropriate in high-risk situations,may have major implications that affect a mother's perception of her childrearing capacities for some time to come when applied to low-risk labor and delivery.[1]

Traditional Interventions

Many medical interventions are based on prevention of complications for mothers and infants at the time of delivery. Often these procedures are based on dogma rather than on scientific evidence and may, under some circumstances, create more complications than they prevent. In re-evaluating obstetric practices, their effects on the physical and psychological environment must be assessed, and their advantages and disadvantages weighed, so that a major goal of the neonatal period—providing a mother with a knowledge of her baby— is optimized. Induction of labor, oxytocic drugs and premature artificial rupture of membranes have inherent medical complications, but, in addition, these artificial interventions may undermine a mother's confidence in her ability to proceed in the natural process. Another much-discussed intervention is the maternal-fetal monitor. A necessary concommitant to its use has been restriction of the mother's free movement, usually requiring that she lie still, often on her back (though improved technology with telemetry may remove this problem). The emotional stress associated with fear for the safety of her monitored infant, plus the mechanical compression of blood vessels by the weight of the gravid uterus, may affect placental circulation adversely. Although in high-risk situations these disadvantages may be outweighed by their necessity, they seem inappropriate for normal labor and delivery. Other obstetrical routines, such as prohibition of any oral intake, mandatory administration of intravenous solutions, shaving, enemas, and transfer from labor to delivery, cause significant discomfort and distraction to the laboring mother and are not based on any demonstrated medical advantage.[2] These and other interventions may undermine the mother's sense of control of labor and delivery, and may increase her need for medication.

Maternal–Infant Relationship

Anesthesia and analgesia may limit a mother's ability to reach out and explore her infant and develop the delicate synchrony so important to her future relationship with her infant. They may also affect the ability of the newborn infant to engage in early behaviors important to maternal–infant attachment, such as eye-to-eye contact.[3] Additionally, contact is impaired by the immediate use of irritating silver nitrate drops which cause swelling of the eyelids and affect this visual attention.[4] The immediate and prolonged separation of mother and infant that has been routine in most hospitals obviously precludes the early contact with the infant which so many mothers desire.

Recently, supported by many health professionals, women have demanded attention to their view of pregnancy as a normal life process, and have sought education through prechildbirth classes to increase their understanding and control of the birth experience. In addition to facilitating their psychological development and preparing them for parenthood, this knowledge may indeed influence the medical course for mother and infant during labor and delivery. For example, mothers who have prepared themselves for childbirth in an organized fashion need less medication during labor.[2] They have also demanded the right to be accompanied in this experience by supportive individuals to help them control their environment and focus on their important tasks during labor and delivery.

Many parents are choosing to deliver at home rather than to fight for control of this experience in the hospital. The Alternative Birth Center (ABC) at Mount Zion Hospital and Medical Center in San Francisco was opened in May 1976 in recognition of the validity of these parents' concerns, and because of our concerns about the risks of home delivery.

THE MOUNT ZION ALTERNATIVE BIRTH CENTER

The primary goal of our ABC is to address the needs of women who seek more sensitive childbirth care in a flexible environment where they can maintain as much control as possible, while safety factors are immediately but unobtrusively available.

Our program encourages the early prenatal care so important for a good medical outcome to pregnancy, but also emphasizes early pregnancy as a time for enhancement and encouragement of a woman's growing appreciation of both herself and her infant. Rather than placing her in a passive role, we encourage her to take active responsibility for planning and making decisions about her pregnancy and childbirth experience.

The birthing rooms are located in close proximity to the high-risk labor and delivery suite and a tertiary intensive care nursery, where both obstetrical and pediatric house staff are available at all times. Attending staff provide 24-hour back-up. The rooms are bed-sitting rooms with a comfortable double bed on which the mother delivers her infant, a sofa bed for the father or support person, pictures, plants, stereo set, and cabinets that house necessary medical and emergency equipment and medications, keeping them out of sight. A Kreiselman resuscitation unit is moved into the room for delivery. An emergency buzzer is connected to the nurses' station in the intensive care nursery and labor and delivery area so help can be summoned if an unexpected emergency arises.

Concerns for safety have been great and have led to the development of strict criteria for registration in the program, transfer in unexpected situation of risk, and early discharge for mother and infant.

Admission Criteria

Low-risk mothers who use the Center must fulfill the following criteria:

1. They must be receiving prenatal care by an obstetrician or by a family practitioner or nurse-midwife with back-up by an obstetrician.
2. They must meet the standard American College of Obstetrics and Gynecology criteria for being medically low risk.
3. They must be taking childbirth preparation classes and attend

Mount Zion's own ABC orientation program given by the birth center nurses.

4. They must understand and *accept* that if their labor status becomes high risk, transfer to the regular labor and delivery area will be necessary.
5. They must sign an informed consent stating that they recognize that the ABC does not have optimal facilities for unforseen complications, and that they accept this risk.
6. Each one must have a support person, either the father or another person who has attended childbirth education and ABC orientation programs with the mother.
7. If children are to be present, a plan for family participation, including an additional support person or persons for the children, must be worked out.
8. The family must choose a pediatrician who is agreeable to the use of the Center and possible early discharge.

Initially an obstetrician was required to attend all births in the Center, but for the past year nurse midwives have been granted privileges to be the professional attending with the back-up of an obstetrician.

Nursing Care

A birth in the ABC is attended by one of a group of obstetrical nurses trained in natural childbirth techniques and intrapartum and postpartum assessment of the mother and her infant. These nurses provide 1:1 care throughout the labor and delivery and stay with the mother and infant for four hours after the birth to assist and support the new family. Following birth, the infant is wrapped in a warm blanket and placed on the mother's chest. The nurse does an initial, brief evaluation of the infant and decides whether the infant meets the following criteria for immediate rooming-in. (1) Five-minute Apgar score greater than seven; (2) weight between 5 and 9.5 pounds; (3) vital signs and color normal and the airway open. If the infant meets these criteria, he/she stays in the room with the parents, and all procedures, including examinations by the pediatrician, are done in the room. Hourly vital signs are obtained by the nurse in attendance. At four hours of age, a hematocrit and Dextrostix are done. If there have been no complications and the mother and infant meet the discharge criteria, they may go home as early as six hours after the birth if the parents so desire.

Early Discharge

Early discharge criteria for the infant require the vital signs, physical examination, and hematocrit and Dextrostix be normal. In addition, there must be no evidence of blood group incompatibility. Feedings must be established, and the mother must be able to handle and care for the infant.

For the mothers, there must be no medical, antepartum, intrapartum or postpartum complications. Specifically, early discharge is not allowed if labor has been prolonged, if there was prolonged rupture of the membranes, if anesthesia other than local was required, if there was blood loss of more than 500 cc, or if postpartum hematocrit is less than 33 percent. The mother must be able to void, have a plan for the administration of RHOgam if appropriate, and have made plans for assistance at home for at least three days.

Nursing staff make a home visit within 24 hours for patients discharged early, and within 72 hours for all patients, to check on the mothers' and infants' conditions and provide emotional support if needed. Blood for the state-required PKU screening is drawn, and if the infant appears jaundiced a bilirubin is done.

Experience in the Center

By August 1979, 800 women had been admitted to the center in labor. Six hundred and seven delivered there, and the remaining 193 were delivered in the regular delivery room. The reasons for the transfer of these 193 women from the ABC are listed in Table 8-1.

Primiparous mothers comprise 79 percent of those transferred out of the center, although they represent only 57 percent of those admitted. The primiparous mothers have a higher incidence of failure of their labor to progress and of cesarean section. Most of the cesarean deliveries were necessary because of cephalopelvic disproportion, so that it is reasonable to expect fewer multiparous women requiring cesarean section for this reason. Women who have previous cesarean sections are not eligible for the ABC, further limiting this group. Among multiparous women, the most frequent reasons for transfer are the need for continuous fetal monitoring and heavy meconium staining.

Some parents experience considerable distress and disappointment and a sense of failure if it is necessary for them to leave the birth center. It is important for the staff to help orient these parents to the different environment in the traditional labor and delivery area

Table 8-1
Reasons for Transfer Out of the ABC

Cesarean section (majority for cephalopelvic disproportion)	68
Maternal or fetal complication during labor	53
Failure to progress	37
Augmentation of labor	20 (51)*
Elective anesthesia	15
	193

*Of 51 women transferred out of the ABC for augmentation of labor in the regular labor and delivery area, 31 returned to the birth center for delivery.

and to help them focus on their primary concern for a healthy infant and safe delivery.

Outcome for both mothers and infants compared favorably with that for similar low-risk mothers and infants cared for in the traditional labor and delivery area. Of the 800 infants, two had Down's syndrome, one had cyanotic congenital heart disease (transportation of the great vessels), and one infant died with a high myelomeningocele that was not treated surgically.

We describe here four of these births, with comments on the issues raised and ways in which they are addressed in the birth center. The first birth is a low-risk one that went smoothly. The second is the experience of a woman requiring cesarean section, the third describes the inclusion of siblings, and the final birth concerns the experience of the family and staff in the case of the infant with the myelomeningocele.

NORMAL BIRTH

This was the third pregnancy for Mrs. N. Her previous deliveries had been in traditional hospital settings. She felt these experiences had been unsatisfactory and would have preferred a home birth this time. Mr. N. wanted to have the safety of a medical setting, so he and his wife chose to deliver at the Birth Center, which offered a compromise acceptable to both.

As the N.'s lived quite far from San Francisco, they decided to come to the Center at midnight when Mrs. N.'s contractions were ten minutes apart. Once in the car her contractions stopped, but the N.'s continued on to the city. Upon arrival at the hospital Mrs. N. was checked, and, as she was not in active labor and not dilated, it was suggested that they return home. The family spent a pleasant day together. That evening Mrs. N.'s contractions began again; this time they were regular. After calling the hospital, they started again for the city at midnight.

When Mrs. N. was admitted she found her doctor already in the Birth Center. He stayed with the family, in the background, for the entire labor.

On admission Mrs. N. found the lights dimmed and the large double bed turned down for her. She tried walking during her labor, but found it uncomfortable and chose instead to lie in bed. She probably would have stayed in the same position during the whole labor, except that the nurse suggested changes in position which proved helpful. Mr. N. sat on one side of his wife; the nurse on the other. Together they supported Mrs. N. during her labor.

The labor and delivery were uncomplicated, and the baby, a girl, was born a little after 5 AM. Mrs. N. remembers that the pediatrician came in and knelt on the floor to examine the baby on the bed. The pediatrician found the baby to be normal except for a heart murmur often heard in the newborn. He explained to the family that this was probably normal, but since they were leaving the hospital only eight hours after birth, he would like them to return the next day so he could recheck the heart. Shortly afterwards, Mr. N. went out for breakfast, giving Mrs. N. time to be alone with the baby. After lunch the family returned home. When they returned the next day, the heart murmur had disappeared.

Comment. A woman preparing for a normal labor and delivery searches for a comfortable physical environment, free from distraction, noises, and unwanted intrusion by ancillary hospital personnel. The ABC has been set up as a quiet room that may not be entered at random by hospital staff. A sign on the door says "Knock and wait," and that is adhered to by all staff, including physicians.

The room itself has been decorated in a casual, comfortable fashion. A stereo set is part of the furnishings, and families frequently bring their own records, as well as some of their own blankets and favorite things to make the room and experience more personal.

The ABC nurse is present in the room during the labor and delivery, but she assumes a background role unless the family desires more active support. The amount of time spent by the obstetrician varies, although from informal observation it appears that physicians tend to spend more time in the room with Birth Center patients than in the traditional labor rooms, sometimes remaining during the entire labor.

During the orientation session, families have indicated on a preference sheet the conditions under which they would like to give birth (low lights, LeBoyer bath, etc.). These plans are reviewed with the family during early labor and are followed as closely as possible. Interestingly, most families requesting a warm bath for the baby do not follow through, not wanting to let go of the newborn infant once it is in their arms.

All examinations of the infant are done in the room. Private pediatricians or pediatric house staff examine the baby with the parents. This has provided these physicians important insights into early attachment behavior and sensitivity to the intimacy of the birth experience.

CESAREAN SECTION

Pam B. chose the Birth Center for the "openness" that it offered; she felt that she could choose the style of birth that she wanted there. Her physician, a family practitioner in a neighboring city, agreed to deliver her at Mount Zion.

Pam described her labor as lengthy. She came into the Birth Center twice, but each time was barely dilated, so she returned home. The third time she came in she was admitted. She brought a neighbor and a friend with her to support her during the birth. She was looking forward to a natural childbirth, with vaginal delivery of her infant.

Pam had a long labor with little progress. She was taken to a labor room for pitocin augmentation of the labor, but this failed. She then had an ultrasound examination that did not reveal anything unusual, followed by an x-ray. She recalled being worried about the effects of an x-ray on her baby and that she felt weak and exhausted. The ABC nurse had been present during the entire labor and was especially supportive to her at this time.

The x-ray revealed an unexpected breech presentation. The doctor discussed the risks of a vaginal delivery with Pam and she elected to have a cesarean delivery. Pam remembers that she did not feel disappointed by this, as her main concern was that her baby be safe.

The ABC nurse stood at the head of the operating table during the section and told Pam about each part of the procedure and how the baby was doing. She remained with Pam and made sure that the baby was able to stay with her in the Recovery Room, where she helped her begin to nurse her baby. Postoperatively Pam returned to the traditional postpartum unit and roomed-in.

Comment. The laboring woman who must have an unanticipated cesarean section has unexpected developmental tasks. The actual time of delivery may be an anxious one with great concern for the safety of the baby. At this time, however, the mother may be so physically depleted that she has little energy left for such important decisions as her choice of anesthesia, who can be with her, and whether or not she may have her baby with her in the Recovery Room.

The ABC nurse plays an important role at this time in acting as an advocate for the family. She is familiar with the hospital rules and not overwhelmed by the sudden transition to an emergency medical setting. The nurse's relationship with the family has become established during labor, and frequently the mother has come to place a great deal of emotional trust in her.

Staffing patterns in the Birth Center, permit the ABC nurse to accompany the family to the operating room for cesarean delivery.

Children are not permitted, but the father is allowed to be present in the O.R. Both father and infant may be present in the recovery room, and the ABC nurse ensures that this occurs if the mothers wishes them to be with her.

SIBLING BIRTH

Sandy and George M. live 30 miles from Mount Zion with their two children, Steve and Heather. Mrs. M. is a LaMaze teacher, and Mr. M. a lawyer. At the time of delivery, Steve was 9-years-old, and Heather 5. The family prepared the children for the birth with books, pictures, and explanations. A close friend of the family, Mary was asked to be the support person for the children.

On the day of delivery, Mrs. M. had mild contractions in the morning. At noon, the family decided to go to the hospital. Steve and Heather brought their pajamas and sleeping bags in case of a long labor.

When the M.'s arrived at the hospital at 3:00 PM, Mrs. M.'s contractions were still mild. Because a sonogram earlier in her pregnancy showed questionable evidence of placenta previa, Mrs. M. went to a labor room for monitoring and observation; Mary and the children waited in an anteroom, since a birth center room was not immediately available. An hour of monitoring revealed no fetal distress and observation disclosed no bleeding, and the obstetrical perinatologist cleared Mrs. M. for delivery in the ABC.

For the next four hours Mr. and Mrs. M. walked up and down the hospital halls. She was checked periodically during this time, during which she had mild contractions and cervical dilatation of 3—4 cm. Mary and the children moved into a birth center room when it became available and waited there.

At 8PM Mrs. M. felt delivery was imminent. She went to the Birth Center room to be checked and was found to have cervical dilatation of 8 cm. As she was preparing to settle in for delivery, her membranes ruptured. Both she and the nurse noted that the amniotic fluid was lightly stained with meconium. The nurse pushed the emergency call button to summon a pediatrician immediately from the Intensive Care Nursery down the hall. The obstetrician, a house officer, was also summoned.

As the meconium was very thin and delivery imminent, Mrs. M. remained in the Birth Center room instead of being moved to the regular labor and delivery area. As the head was delivered, the pediatrician suctioned the baby, and no significant meconium was seen. Immediately after delivery the pediatrician took the baby to the Kreiselman bed nearby and assessed the infant's respiratory status. The baby was fine and was quickly returned to the mother.

During early labor, the children were primarily with the support person. In late labor, Steve and Heather were at the foot of the bed. The children were very excited. Steve rocked back and forth on his heels; Heather stood in front of Terry, more quietly observing the delivery.

When the baby was born, the children followed it to the Kreiselman unit, as did their father. Steve asked many questions about the medical apparatus.

When the baby was handed back to Mrs. M., the children also came back to their mother's side. Mrs. B. was reclining on a large bean-bag pillow used to support her back during the delivery. Steve climbed up on it now and sat on top, peering over his mother's head at his new baby sister. Heather sat at her mother's side, occasionally touching the baby and sometimes looking down at the episiotomy repair. Steve came down from his perch and examined the placenta, which had been delivered while the children were at the Kreiselman.

Shortly following the birth, the family went to sleep, Steve and Heather on the floor in their sleeping bags, baby Emily in her basket.

Comment. Since the inception of the birth center, one of the most controversial aspects has been the presence of children at a sibling's birth. The experience is often presented to children as an unqualifiedly joyous one, and little room is left for expression of any negative or ambivalent feelings the children might have. At home births most children are able to modulate the intensity of the experience by leaving the birth room. In hospital-based birth centers there is generally less freedom, physically or psychologically, to exit. In both home births and hospital-based births, however, very young children frequently require the support of others to translate the birth experience for them. A support person, other than the father, is required for siblings present at birth center deliveries.

Unlike some institutional birth centers, Mount Zion's ABC does not advocate sibling participation during labor and delivery. The frequent request for permission for children to be included in the birth led us, in the spirit of offering choices to the families, to develop a policy that would accommodate their wish safely and still protect the best interests of the laboring mother. We do not encourage sibling presence; it is the initiative of the family and their strong determination that result in children being present. Half of the parents do not follow through with having sibling participation during the labor and delivery, frequently choosing instead to share the new infant with the siblings immediately following the birth.

The reasons given by families for sibling presence are many and varied. A major theme, however, is the wish to reduce sibling rivalry. Popularized notions of "bonding" have been extended to the sibling–sibling relationship. Being there in the beginning, parents hope, will help a deep and positive attachment to form between the siblings, and foster a more conflict-free relationship as the children grow. What is overlooked, of course, is the complexity of such human relationships, and the inevitable stresses and tensions as a family struggles to adjust to the new family configuration.

What may be reflected in these concerns over sibling rivalry is the awkwardness of beginning a sibling relationship out of context—being presented with the product rather than being part of the process. Sibling participation may represent a reaction to the traditional total exclusion of children from the birth process in our culture. Mothers find it uncomfortable to loosen ties to their other children during this critical time of family reformation. Yet during the actual birth process, few mothers are able to undertake the multiple tasks of labor and delivery, greeting of the infant, presentation of the infant to the family and then the larger community, physical recovery, and literal nurturing of the newborn while continuing to be available to her other children. Bringing her other children close to the experience while maintaining enough distance emotionally so she can concentrate on her tasks is perhaps the most difficult challenge for a multiparous woman choosing a birth-center experience. Birth centers need to offer a range of possibilities for sibling participation—the phenomenon of total inclusion of children fits as few families as the traditional one of total exclusion.

The goal of family-centered maternity care is to assist the family in its attempts to master the experience of reforming itself as roles change—as adults become parents, as a family becomes a larger family. The important transaction is, of course, communication to the siblings of the parents' genuine desire for them to share in the birth experience appropriately. Given such communication and sharing, the family should have a good start in its necessary reorganizational process.

Our work with siblings present at a birth has led us to observe that the interpretation of the experience depends a great deal on the developmental level of the child and also on the general family style. We have seen a family in which being present at the birth of her sibling was only one more overstimulating event for a seven-year-old girl whose home life generally tended to be overstimulating. Advice to the parents not to have her present at the birth was, as might have been expected, ignored. We have seen other families where children have been carefully prepared by parents highly sensitive to the issues raised for their children by attendance at a sibling's birth.

For all children who are present at the birth of a sibling, this experience occurs in the context of family life. Some parents shield their children from much; some parents push their children into the thick of things; perhaps the wisest parents follow their children, supporting them where the children feel ready to go.

Careful observation by ABC nurses has indicated that even the most sensitive preparation of children can not always anticipate the occasional difficult moments during labor and delivery. Routine lab work on the mother, for example, is frightening for some children, and labor sounds appear more stressful for some children than sights such as blood or episiotomy. If emergencies arise, it takes great skill on the part of the children's support person to be reassuring.

In summary, while many issues are raised by sibling participation at birth, the overall desire of parents to find a more natural way to integrate the newborn into the existing family structure while continuing to nurture the older siblings must be addressed, and flexible means found to offer appropriate inclusion of previous children in the childbirth setting. Our observations on siblings attending delivery have been published in more detail elsewhere.[6]

CONGENITAL ANOMALY

For Sara K., 19, and her 20-year-old husband, Roger, this had been a planned pregnancy without complications. As with most parents, they had the expectation of a normal birth. They lived close to the hospital and were able to stay at home for the early stages of labor, coming to the birth center when labor was well established.

Sara's membranes ruptured in the birth center, and the nurse noted slight meconium staining. She explained this to the couple who had little anxiety about it. As is the practice, the pediatrician was called to attend the birth.

During delivery a myelomeningocele was noted high on the spine. The nurse who had attended the couple during labor explained in simple terms that the baby had a problem with her back which could sometimes be serious. The anomaly was covered with a sterile blanket and the baby was shown briefly to Sara. The baby was then taken to the intensive care nursery.

The parents were told that a complete examination would be performed, and at that time had no questions. Roger, followed the pediatrician to the ICN while the obstetrician stayed with Sara and the nurse. The pediatrician returned 30 minutes later with the information that the baby was breathing well and was alert, but that consultation with neurological specialists was needed to determine the extent of her problem. When Sara's postdelivery medical procedures were completed, the nurse helped her into a wheelchair and took her and Roger to see the baby. The infant was then one hour old.

The nurse stayed with the family for the afternoon, during which time Sara and Roger cried, requested more information and clarification about the baby's condition and prognosis, and comforted each other. The next morning, after the neurologist and neurosurgeon had evaluated the baby's condition, the pediatrician presented the parents with the difficult medical situation. The infant would probably develop hydrocephalus and other major problems, and paralysis from the waist down was certain. A decision needed to be made about whether to intervene surgically or not. With the support of the ABC and ICN staff, Sara and Roger used their hospital time to contemplate their infant's future. Within a day, they decided against surgical intervention. The next day Sara and Roger left the hospital, prepared for their baby's imminent death. A nurse visited the next day, and other visits were planned for the next two days. Sara and Roger came to see their baby regularly, but decided not to be present when she died.

On the day of the baby's death, the nurse who had cared for Roger and Sara in the birth center was, by her request, the infant's primary nurse in the intensive care nursery. It was she who stood in for the parents and held the baby, calling Sara and Roger immediately after she died.

As is customary in our ICN, the pediatrician, nurse, and social worker met with the family for a conference about six weeks after the death. The purpose of such meetings is to discuss the autopsy findings, to assess parental grieving response and support needs, and to try to bring to a close what has been a sad and traumatic event for the parents. In this instance, the family continued to communicate with several of the staff from the birth center and intensive care nursery, and we were aware of the steps of their grieving process. A year later they decided to have another child, who was born in the ABC. She was a healthy baby girl whom they named for the nurse who had attended their first delivery and cared for the infant they had lost.

Comment. Following a strenuous labor and delivery most mothers are rewarded by the birth of a healthy, vigorous infant. For families of infants born with a congenital anomaly, the physically demanding hours are climaxed with despair. It seems helpful for these families to be able to share their grief with those who have shared their hopeful anticipation during the labor and delivery. The flexible staffing pattern in the birth center permits these nurses to continue to support families whose needs are both greater than customary and also extend beyond the delivery of the infant.

One of the aspects of the family-centered care program in our ICN is provision of support for the parents who experience neonatal loss. For infants who die, the medical staff may be the only ones other than the parents who have seen the child. It is especially important to these families that staff be skilled in facilitating the grieving process. Flexibility in rooming-in arrangements can also allow parents to be close to their dying infant if they so desire and want to hold the baby.

Parents of infants born with major but not fatal anomalies also need to grieve for the perfect child they wished to bear. Families may stay in the birth center until support systems for them have been worked out and they feel ready to leave. The ABC nurse again plays a major role in providing emotional support for the parents. The perinatal staff (obstetrical and pediatric specialists, nurses from the ABC and ICN, social workers), private pediatrician, and any others are ready as needed to work closely with the family. Their efforts are coordinated by the ABC nurse, who is most sensitive to when the family is ready to hear the complex information about their anomalous or terminally ill infant and who can listen to the parents as they begin to make decisions about their infant's care.

ISSUES RELATED TO ALTERNATIVE BIRTH PROGRAMS

In the first three years and 800 births at the Mount Zion Alternative Birth Center, it has become clear that, while reactions and attitudes to the program are overwhelmingly positive, there are difficulties which must be overcome or accepted as inherent in providing this mode of care.

The Problems

ADMINISTRATIVE CONCERNS

Initiation of a birth center requires time and enthusiastic cooperation on the part of the innovators who are undertaking this development, the professional leadership of obstetrical and pediatric medical and nursing staff, hospital administration, representatives of the client population, legal advisors, and state health department personnel. For us, client representatives comprised childbirth educators, midwives, and LaLeche League members.

Policies and procedures must be developed, reviewed and approved, and reassessed once the center is underway. Change is seldom easy, and in this instance even well-intentioned and supportive individuals sometimes find it difficult to change established patterns. Until a program is operating smoothly from all aspects, from the admitting office to the accounting department and record room, a coordinator of knowledge and virtuosity is needed to deal with the myriad details and communications that arise. The coordinator of our ABC responds to all telephone inquiries, provides referral to community resources (such as childbirth educators and classes, obstetrical and pediatric physicians, and parent educators), maintains schedules for classes and orientation provided with the program, orders materials, and collects class fees. She also assures availability of prenatal records and permits from physicians for use of the center, and issues temporary privileges for physicians who care for only an occasional patient and who are not on our staff. Finally, she assists with financial arrangements for families subject to unexpected emergency services and costs.

COST

Although the cost to families of this kind of labor and delivery service is less than that of the traditional hospitalization, initiation of a program involves expense. In our case, the nurses working in the birth center initially remained throughout the labor and delivery and for four hours after the birth. This raised wage issues and the need to have nurses on call at all times. If these nurses are also expected to work elsewhere within the maternity service, the overall staffing plan must be flexible enough to adjust to changing needs in the center.

SPACE

Establishing a birth center within an existing maternity program requires reallocation of space presently used for other activities. Birth center rooms need to be larger than the usual labor room; if rooms are converted to gain space, fewer beds are available for patients in the traditional service areas. We believe strongly in the need for proximity of the birth center to emergency delivery and nursery services; this, too, poses problems in many settings. We had to rapidly expand from our initial birthing room to a second, and are now planning a third. Each time expansion has been necessary, new planning has been needed for space and staffing.

Another aspect of the space problem is that of limited availability. Occasionally our birth center rooms are all occupied when another family arrives. In general, parents have been gracious about moving to a traditional postpartum room after their own delivery, so that the laboring mother can use an ABC room; however, the "mystique" associated with the totality of the ABC experience or the lack of a birth center room has occasionally contributed to disappointment on the part of families. Families not able to use a room in the ABC receive the same 1:1 nursing care in a regular labor room, but the ambience is not the same. Although attitude and preparation are the key elements of a rewarding birth experience, the desire of parents for more birth center rooms is great.

STAFF ATTITUDES

Our ABC nurses have been highly committed individuals. Like many dedicated professionals who cling to traditional roles and modes of care, however, even staff committed to the "Birth Center Way" can become dogmatic and have expectations that are not necessarily attuned to a given mother's own expectations, perceptions, or needs. For example, one of our nurses reported a situation in which she found herself at a loss. She handed a teenage mother her infant, expecting the usual delighted, reaching response, then felt rebuffed and uncomfortable when the new mother did not want to hold her child. Clearly, this very young mother needed some time to sort out her complex feelings and "pull herself together" before she could reach out for her infant. This example, shared by the nurse, underscored the need for staff to follow the lead of the mothers, rather than developing sterotyped assumptions about "ABC mothers."

We found some initial resistance among staff who saw the group of birth center nurses as a separate cadre. Over time, however, the birth center has become more integrated within the overall labor and delivery service, and the ABC staff has gained acceptance and support throughout the perinatal program.

PHYSICIAN INCONVENIENCE

The birth center exists to provide a normal setting for a normal process and therefore is not tailored to provide either physical comfort or emotional aggrandizement for either obstetricians or pediatricians. For example, mothers often choose the position for delivery, the double bed is low, and there are no stirrups. More important, the obstetrician's role is less central in birth center than in traditional delivery; in general, his or her position is that of a support person who provides technical assistance and consultation rather than that of a co-principal with the mother in the cast. Continuing education of medical staff around these issues is of great importance if they are to endorse and participate happily in the birth center.

PATIENT POPULATION

The birth center population tends to be of at least upper-middle class and to be very well educated. These parents are certainly stressed at the time of birth and during the postnatal period, yet they also tend to have many resources, both external and internal, to help them adapt to their new situations. Although the birth center would seem to offer premium care for the new family, it has not proved as yet to be the setting of choice for mothers who might be termed "socially high risk," such as teenage mothers, low-income mothers, or those with limited educational backgrounds who frequently have fewer support systems available to help them with the physical and emotional stresses of parenthood. Thus mothers who might potentially derive the greatest benefit from the ABC and who have the greatest need for the support services provided rarely seek it.

Positive Features of the ABC

SAFETY

Although the establishment of the birth center was an extension of the general philosophy of family-centered care, a major goal from its outset has been to provide those qualities of the birth experience whose absence from traditional settings has led parents to accept the risks of home births. We feel that problems which may result in damage to the infant occur sufficiently often in low-risk deliveries to warrant the ready availability of the staff and facilities of a maternity hospital. We anticipated that the center, located as it is within the perinatal facilities in the hospital, would provide optimal safety for mother and infant. Ongoing monitoring of our experience has confirmed our expectations; details on the 193 women who could not complete delivery have been presented earlier.

PHYSICAL AND EMOTIONAL WELL-BEING

Parents who opt for an ABC delivery tend to have attitudes that permit labor and delivery to be conducted with little or no medication for pain relief. Mother–infant interaction immediately after birth may be richer following a natural delivery than following delivery of a mother who received small quantities of drugs and/or conduction anesthesia for pain relief; this, however, remains to be proved. Natural childbirth may thus add to the positive experience of delivery in a birth room.

Whether or not there are long-term psychological benefits for families using the ABC is unknown. Evaluation of these effects would be extremely difficult, since so many variables influence the evolution of long-term family relationships. Most parents choosing this setting are highly motivated, and we believe that they would be "good parents" regardless of whether or not they chose this delivery service. Few families who might be designated as "socially high risk" and who might thus derive the greatest long-term psychological benefits from the ABC have chosen to deliver there. Motivating such parents to desire ABC delivery is a major challenge for the future.

Fathers who participate in the experience through their preparation in classes, their important support roles during labor, and their assistance in preparing other children to accept the new infant, take pride in their contribution and are eager to assume their changed roles. The families who have chosen an ABC birth are enthusiastic about this choice. In a questionnaire sent to families who have used the center, the most frequent response to the question, "What did you like best about the experience?" was responded to in terms of "family togetherness," "not being separated from one another," "having the baby with us the whole time." Those features of the program designed to foster attachment behaviors have met with enthusiastic endorsement by client families.

The home-like setting and delegation of responsibility to the families have contributed to and supported the view that childbirth is a normal part of family development and removes the "disease-oriented" stigma from hospital births. For many families, a major positive aspect of the ABC experience has been their ability to personalize and control their situation.

Families are enthusiastic about the nursing care. This consistent care and support of one person who also serves as their link with the world outside the birth center has provided great satisfaction.

HUMANISTIC SENSITIVITY

The ripple effect of the program has been seen throughout the maternity and newborn services in the approach and attitudes toward families choosing the traditional service and to high-risk situations. The increased sensitivity of physicians and nurses to patients' needs to be educated and supported, and to participate in the decision-making process, is evident. All the staff have become more sensitive to the value of emotional support and encouragement in reducing the laboring woman's need for analgesia and anesthesia. This has had its positive effect on the condition of mothers and infants in all areas of the program.

The medical and nursing staff have been almost universally supportive of the concepts endorsed by the birth center, and proud to be associated with it. Other departments of the institution are aware of the humanistic philosophy endorsed by the Center, and to take pleasure in its presence in the hospital. This spirit of interest, enthusiastic support, and pride in the center as an innovative, important clinical service has been apparent, too, among the hospital administration and board of directors.

In a larger sense, the program has contributed to the community served and to the public interest by demonstrating responsiveness of the health-care delivery system to public concern and by providing both a model and a stepping stone for health-care planning and public health and legislative agencies.

REFERENCES

1. Cohen RL: Maladaption to pregnancy. This volume, ch. 9
2. Sugarman M: Paranatal influences on maternal–infant attachment. Am J Orthopsychiatr 47:407–421, 1977
3. Robson K: The role of eye-to-eye contact in maternal–infant attachment. J Child Psychol Psychiatr 8:13–25, 1979
4. Butterfield PM, Emde RN, Platt BB: Effects of silver nitrate on initial visual behavior. Am J Dis Child 132:426, 1978
5. Scott J, Rose N: Effect of psychoprophylaxis (Lamaze preparation) on labor and delivery in primiparas. N Engl J Med 294:1205–1207, 1976
6. Leonard CH, Irvin N, Ballard RA, et al,. Preliminary observation on the behavior of children present at the birth of a sibling. Pediatrics 64:949–951, 1979

Richard L. Cohen

9
Parental Experiences in Out-of-Hospital Birth Centers

This chapter reports on the findings of 67 interviews (and other observations) conducted with women and their mates who decided to give birth in out-of-hospital birth centers. Families choosing home delivery were not included in this survey.

The specific purpose of this chapter is to collate information about experiences parents have had in alternative birth centers. Such information may be useful to perinatologists, neonatologists, health planners, obstetric nurses, and others in reviewing current in-hospital practices.

This is a component of a more extensive study. Other reports[1,2] will focus on the decision-making process for parents and on comparisons of women who choose alternative birth centers with those choosing more conventional medical services.

NATURE OF PROGRAM AND POPULATION SERVED

By definition, an "out-of-hospital birth center" is considered one in which one or more professionals trained in childbirth care are in attendance at birth, monitor the progress of labor, and are available to assist and/or intervene as may be required. They may recommend transfer to a backup hospital or request additional consultation as

This work was supported in part by a grant from the Maurice Falk Medical Fund.

circumstances require. Deliveries do not occur within the patient's home or other residence, but in a professional setting designed specifically for child-birthing and with the availability of emergency medication, oxygen, episiotomy trays, and other such basic support supplies and equipment.[3]

Although the author has observed many such programs, only three have been selected for reporting here. Each meets the criteria for an out-of-hospital birth center, yet each has distintive characteristics. Detailed differences are delineated in Table 9-1, as are those basic elements that are considered to be common to most out-of-hospital birth centers. The three birthing programs are characterized below.

Program 1: (27 patients)

This birth center is operated by and physically contained within an obstetric group practice in a large urban area. A portion of the clinic building in which the group practice operates is sequestered as a birthing center and available 24-hours-a-day for use for labor, delivery, and recovery. One of the four obstetricians is always physically available, and much of the direct attendance is provided by nurse midwives. A backup hospital with a modern obstetric service is available less than five minutes away by car and all four obstetricians are on the attending staff of the hospital.

Program 2: (30 patients)

This center is located in a large, converted town house in an urban area and is operated by several nurse midwives with obstetric consultation. Prenatal care is provided onsite with initial medical screening performed by an obstetric consultant. One entire floor of the residence is given over to birthing rooms. A backup hospital is available approximately six minutes by car, though the relationship between this birthing center and the hospital is not a contractual one and is often strained.

Program 3: (10 patients)

This is also free-standing midwife service operating in a small city with obstetric consultation. The center also offers nurse midwives to attend at home deliveries.

Table 9-1
Characteristics of Three Programs for Out-of-Hospital Childbirth Centers

	Program 1	Program 2	Program 3
Large urban area	×	×	
Small city (approximately 100,000 pop.)			×
Physician(s) in charge	×		
Certified Nurse Midwives in charge (M.D. consultants)		×	×
Easily available backup hospital	×		×
Also offers home delivery			×
Discharge within 12 hours	×	×	×
One-to-one nursing care	×	×	×
Constant contact with baby	×	×	×
No separation from mate (or other supports)	×	×	×
Lamaze (or other preparation) required	×	×	×
Labor, delivery, and recovery in same room	×	×	×
Regional anaesthesia on demand	×	×	×

The demographic characteristics of the total sample of 67 patients are summarized in Table 9-2.

It should be emphasized that, in all of the above programs, rather careful prescreening is done by trained obstetricians who make the final decision concerning whether a pregnant woman may be considered "low risk" and therefore eligible for admission to the service. The transfer rate once women have entered into labor is two–three percent.

DATA COLLECTION

Where possible, all women were interviewed during the postpartum period. In some instances, interviews were conducted as much as seven-to-ten days postpartum during home visits. The interviews were semistructured and, when permission was granted, tape recorded for later analysis. The usual demographic data in connection with age, marital status, parity formula, race, educational level, etc. was collected in each instance. In broad outline, the structure of the interview was as follows:

Explain how you learned about the specific professional or service you used.

Indicate all of the other options you considered prior to making this choice.

Describe the specific factors that led you (and your mate) to select this particular option.

Have you had previous experience with other hospitals or birthing centers?

Describe in detail both the positive and negative aspects of that experience.

How did your subsequent experience with the current birthing center develop?

In what way did it prove to be pretty much what you expected?

What was different from what you expected?

Specifically, would you indicate those experiences or components of the service you found most helpful or supportive during your childbirth experience?

Conversely, those which you found least helpful or supportive.

Indicate any recommendations you have for modifying the service.

Would you recommend this service to others? If so, why? If not, why not?

Do you plan to have more children? Would you use this service again? If so, why? If not, why not?

Although the data will not be reported exactly in the form described in this outline, emphasis will be placed on those parental perceptions and experiences found to be either most facilitating to a

Table 9-2
Characteristics of Population of Women
(N=67)

Age	
Under 20	5
20–24	30
25–29	24
30–34	8
Over 35	0
Race	
White	62
Black	4
Other	1
Marital Status	
Married	62
Single	3
Separated	1
Divorced	1
Educational Level	
8–11 Years	6
High School Graduate	28
13–16 years	19
Over 16 years	14
Employment Status	
Full-time homemaker	40
Employed outside home	27
Part-time 7	
Full time 20	
Parity	
Primipara	35
Gravida 2–3	29
More than 2 previous pregnancies	3

good childbirth experience or those which at least partially interfered with it.

FINDINGS

Positive and negative responses are summarized in Tables 9-3 and 9-4 respectively. It is remarkable that the 67 patients reported a total of 462 codable responses and that 94% (433) of these were positive while only 6 percent (29) were negative!

Table 9-3

Positive Responses to Out-of-Hospital Childbirth-Center Care (N=67 Subjects)*

	Rank	Responses
Presence and constant participation of mate (or significant other)	1	52
Uninterrupted contact with neonate	2	49
Positive impact on Lamaze or other preparation	3	48
High level of staff competence	4	45
Continuity of care (both staff and locale)	5	42
Father closer to baby and more help with it	6	41
Ability to participate in decisions concerning care	7	38
Ability to participate in care itself	8	35
Ability to return home within 12 hours	9	25
Open communication with staff	10	22
Home-like (or "non-hospital") quality of environment	11	19
Early contact with older children	12	17

*Total Responses = 433

Table 9-4
Negative Responses to Out-of-Hospital Childbirth Center Care (N=67 Subjects)*

	Rank	Responses
Discontinuity in aftercare if transfer to hospital required	1	9
Tendency to underplay severity of childbirth pain and reinforce overconfidence	2	7
Have to return home before ready	3	5
Make you feel guilty if you don't breastfeed	4a	3
Preparation not specific enough for level of consumer responsibility	4b	3
Expect too much of you (treat you like semiprofessional)	6	2

*Total Responses = 29

195

Positive Responses

RESPONSES RELATED TO AVAILABILITY OF
SUPPORT PERSONS, OTHER OFFSPRING AND
CONTACT WITH NEONATE:

(See items 1,2,6, and 12, respectively, in Table 9-3).

Collectively, this general area received the largest percentage of positive responses (159=36.7 percent). The responses connote the perceived importance of constant involvement of the woman's mate (the usual support person) during the entire labor, delivery, and recovery process. Such perception is not limited to the physical presence of the individual but his active participation in providing emotional support, a communication bridge with professionals, and, often, as a labor coach. For example, the report of this 25-year-old para 2 is typical:

> My husband wasn't at all sure he wanted to be there for the delivery. His stomach was so queasy I couldn't talk at dinner about how the baby (fetus) had been that day. . . . but because everyone here treats birth as such a natural function and expects him to be there he just *was*. . . . When I had my second child here, the midwife held my placenta up and my husband was asking, "What's that part and what's that one?" I couldn't believe this was the same guy that I couldn't discuss normal kinds of medical things with at dinner . . . and the bonding was fabulous . . . my first son opened his eyes and looked at his father first . . . it seemed to make all the difference. He felt more confident about handling the baby than if he hadn't had that early contact and encouragement. It was his experience too, and even though that was three years ago, we still talk about it. By the second one, there was no question . . . actually he was a lousy labor coach, but his being there and part of it made all the difference in the world. For my second one, I needed an epidural and the midwives were trying to coax me to go on without it, but he was able to see that I really did need it and was able to get it across to them. I was just whining at that point and he was able to speak for me.

Receiving almost as many positive responses was the woman's assignment of importance to constant, uninterrupted contact with her new baby. Multiparous women often compared their previous experience with "rooming in" in obstetric hospitals, where the baby might frequently be removed from the room for examination or other procedures, with the experience in the alternative birth center. In the latter, the uninterrupted contact seemed of major importance. Even the physical examination was conducted usually at the bed side or on the mother's bed and within her field of vision. It is difficult to overestimate the importance of this to many families.

A 26-year-old mother had two previous births in conventional obstetric services and, though things had gone well, she and her husband decided to use an out-of-hospital center for their third experience. In describing the impact of uninterrupted contact with her child, she said:

With the first one, got to see her but didn't really keep her until she was six hours old . . . Vicki was definitely ours from the very beginning. We held her for two hours before anyone else . . . She was with us the whole time . . . She never left us . . . Nobody interfered . . . we could really look at her and see her and see all the little parts that you miss when you only see them for 15–20 minutes . . . She just feels, even now, much more like ours than the others did . . . and she's so quiet and calm . . . we didn't have to share it with anybody . . . when she opened her eyes . . . it was our private moment . . . very emotional . . . We (my husband and I) prayed to God for her (cries) . . . she's very special to me. You've been waiting all this time for this little thing and there she was . . . we got to watch as she looked around and moved her little hands . . . She's special in a different way from my other children . . . I would hold her at night after nursing her . . . I had done that with my other children. She'd fall asleep and there'd be a special feeling there that wasn't there with the others. Her behavior maybe wasn't different . . . I just felt different . . . I think it was because she was with me so long when she was first born and she was really mine . . . There was no chance of sneaking anybody else's kid in there . . . My husband feels the same way. He knew every little mark on her. They couldn't have brought us anyone else's baby . . . we would have known.

It was not unusual for mothers to report that husbands who had participated with them in an alternative birth-center experience appeared to be closer to the baby, more physically involved with it and more comfortable caring for it. As if in testimony to this, many fathers indicated that the experience in an alternative birth center answered their needs for greater involvement and participation in the birth and child-care process. Many insisted in taking part in the interviews, although it was often inconvenient for them to do so. The following is quoted from a first-time father.

When I heard about this interview I wanted to be here because I have some things to say too. Right from the beginning, I've been afraid that I would be an outsider . . . you know . . . couldn't be pregnant, couldn't nurse the baby, wouldn't know how to handle it and all that kind of stuff. The wonderful thing about the alternative birth center was that I was completely involved from the start . . . I was really able to take care of my wife during labor and delivery. Cook snacks at the alternative birth centers, etc. . . . that was extremely important to me . . . to feel useful. I cut the cord—it made me feel so involved.

Of lesser importance, but still noteworthy, was the importance that many women attached to being able to have older siblings of the baby present either during the delivery or immediately thereafter. This sense of family participation and intactness, therefore, carried over to the entire family constellation.

RESPONSES RELATED TO INCREASED SENSE OF
RESPONSIBILITY FOR DECISION-MAKING AND SELF-
CARE:

(See items ranked 3,7,8 and 9, respectively, in Table 9-3).

Table 9-3 will again indicate that a large number of responses (146=33.7 percent) were associated with experiences which seem to increase the women's self-confidence and her own sense of participation in decision-making and self-care. Since all three of the birth centers required that the couple attend some form of prepared childbirth classes (usually the Lamaze method), this received a great deal of attention. The classes themselves were perceived as a part of the total experience, and the ability to utilize the alternative birth center was tied intimately in the thinking of parents to the preparation they received in their childbirth classes. With some exception (see below), these were viewed as supportive and positive. Many parents did not believe that their prior life experience would have permited them to use an alternative birth center appropriately and that the prepared childbirth classes not only enabled but enhanced the opportunity.

In this connection, the experience of Magee[4] and a study by Post[5] throw much light on the frequent discrepancies between fantasies, expectations, and actual experience in a childbirth situation.

As can be seen in Table 9-3, many responses were related to the woman's ability to make, or at least participate in, decisions about anesthesia or analgesia; about who would be present at her delivery; about the position she would assume while in labor; about how long she would remain in the alternative birth-center before returning home, and many other decisions that are ordinarily left to professional personnel. As one mother said:

> At our birthing center, they were very personal, very thorough ... they told you everything they were doing ... nothing was a secret, everything was available to you. They made you feel it was the woman doing everything. It was the couple ... almost couple power. They included my husband 100 percent ... even my two-and-a-half-year-old son was welcome.

In some centers, mothers are partially responsible for record-keeping within their charts (which are totally accessible to them), for testing their urine (for which they receive training), and performing other simple record-keeping and diagnostic tasks. In every instance, this was perceived as a positive experience rather than a negative one. The following excerpt from an interview with a 21-year-old first-time mother is illustrative:

My alternative birth center uses a lot of self-help systems. You test your own urine, do your own weight, and you have charge of your chart ... My first reaction was that I didn't think it was all that wonderful, but as I went along in the program, it seemed like a definite plus ... I talked to other women in other programs and many seemed to have no idea what was going on with their pregnancies or their bodies for those nine months.

RESPONSES RELATED TO SPECIFIC ASPECTS OF THE SERVICE

(See items ranked 4,5,10 and 11 respectively in Table 9-3).

A large number of positive responses were related to particular components of the service aspects of the birthing centers (128=29.6 percent). These tended to be rather specific and consistent across the several programs. Many parents emphasized the "surprising" level of competence of the staff, and a few added that they feared that they might be compromising on professional competence by having the baby outside of a hospital setting. They were most gratified by their judgment that this had not been the case.

Continuity of care was emphasized in several respects. The one-on-one nursing care (usually by a nurse midwife) common to birthing centers, without changing shifts or constantly revolving responsibilities for different aspects of care, was viewed most positively. The ability to "nestle down" in one room and one bed for the entire labor, delivery and postpartum period was important to many mothers.

Many parents emphasized a greater openness of communication with the professional staff of the birthing center than they had ever experienced in a hospital. The permissiveness about reading their own records and their sense that questions would be fully answered was a repetitive theme in the interviews. At times, feelings about previous direct or indirect experiences with information-sharing in hospitals ran high. The following two interview responses were not at all unusual:

All the obstetricians I've gone to or heard about kind of listen to you with one ear and then they go ahead and do what *they* want to do, making it look as much as possible that it's what you wanted. In an alternative birth center, I felt that would be less true. Here they really do listen and answer your questions.

The people here are so nice. You can ask any question you want to and they answer it ... I can pick up my chart and read it and nobody gets upset.

They don't keep anything from you. They treat you like a human being . . . Your husband feels a part of everything . . . My mother is a nurse in a university hospital and she told me that they don't like you to know anything there . . . so I know first hand from her that they don't like giving out information . . . many RNs say if the patients know a little bit, then they think they know everything. Then they start self-diagnosing themselves and other stuff . . . also, sometimes they've the same feeling toward families, especially when people are real sick. They think maybe it'll be better if the person doesn't make it and they haven't said anything. It isn't right that they keep things from you, but they do in hospitals.

Although several mothers mentioned the "home-like" atmosphere of some of the birthing centers (as compared to the usual hospital), this really did not seem to be of major importance and was often mentioned in passing.

Negative Responses

Compared to the 443 positive responses received from the the 67 "consumers," there were only 29 responses that could be classified as negative (see Table 9-4). In general, the negative responses may be classified under two broad categories: (1) those relating to the specific nature of the service, and (2) those relating to the content of communication from the staff either during the prenatal period or during labor and delivery.

NEGATIVE RESPONSES RELATED TO NATURE OF
SERVICE

(See items ranked 1,3 and 4b respectively, in Table 9-4).

There was 17 responses which largely pointed to perceived deficiencies in the programs. Nine of these had to do with the fact that some parents saw the birthing center as discontinuous in the sense that it did not provide long-term or ongoing support, counseling or pediatric care following the postpartum period. Important and trusting relationships were developed during the pregnancy and childbirth and there seemed to be no mechanism for ongoing contact once the mother and baby returned home and the immediate postpartum visits by the nursing staff had been accomplished and it was clear that mother and baby were doing well.

In a few instances, parents felt that they had been returned home too soon and were neither physically nor emotionally ready to deal with the neonate. One first time mother had this to say on the subject:

I had no idea that a newborn did anything but sleep and eat and that he

would come out nursing—it wasn't that. I was very tired and he was cranky
and we were both up all the time. We really needed someone who understood
all this and could get us straightened out.

And her husband added emotionally:

> We had to leave in 12 hours. My wife was very tired and we didn't know
> anyone who was really experienced who could help us . . . This was my wife's
> first experience with breastfeeding and even though my mother was with us,
> she hadn't breastfed her kids and didn't know much about it. Eventually one
> of our friends helped. It would have been reassuring if we could have had a
> few days at the alternative birth center to really learn the ropes and help
> find our way . . . or maybe they should have someone move in for a few days
> and get us started . . . our families are too spread out geographically. The
> community has to start supplying some of this guidance.

A few parents were critical of the teaching that had been conducted for postpartum care, believing it to be too "general" and not
covering enough intimate detail for new parents who had little or no
experience caring for small infants.

RESPONSES RELATED TO COMMUNICATIONS FROM STAFF

(See items ranked 2,4a and 6 respectively in Table 9-4)

There were 12 responses which could be viewed as negative
reactions to attitudes or communication from staff members. In a few
instances (7), parents felt that they had been led to believe that the
childbirth would not be very painful if they carefully followed all of
the instructions, exercises, breathing routines, diet, etc. They felt
unprepared for the "violence" and "intensity" of the painful experience, and complained that the painful aspects of labor had been
intentionally underplayed in order to get them to develop positive
attitudes. One father stated rather forcefully:

> I would have preferred if they had not led us to believe, if you'll excuse
> the word, "painless". . . . If it's really that way, then what woman in the world
> would do it this way. Maybe the thing they should stress the most is that this
> is good for the health of the mother and baby and if you want a beautiful,
> natural birth, there are certain things you're going to have to give up—it's
> going to be a lot more painful than if you're knocked out. Nobody was willing
> to say that . . . people who teach childbirth education classes should also be
> trained to teach. I found myself asking more questions than I should have
> had to. A nurse-midwife is not a teacher . . . sometimes it almost became an
> encounter group where too many feelings were allowed to come out and there
> was not enough factual teaching.

Interestingly, a few parents complained that their intelligence and experience had been overestimated by the staff. Most parents who come to birthing centers want as much responsibility and participation as possible, and many have had negative experiences in hospitals where they have felt as though they had been treated "like I was retarded" or "inept." Two parents reported that the staff of a birthing center had expected too much of them and that they had been afraid to ask questions because they did not want to appear "dumb" in front of other more knowledgeable parents. One mother (who had a degree in elementary education) said:

It's okay if you don't mind asking dumb questions, but some people do. They don't work hard enough here to find out what you don't understand. Doctors don't give you enough credit for being bright, and alternative birth centers kind of overestimate you. Either way, it's kind of rough if it's your first baby.

Finally, three mothers reported that they had felt "ashamed" because they had decided not to breastfeed their babies and that this had been reinforced (although subtly) by some members of the nursing staff who had clearly strong biases in favor of breastfeeding. In each of these instances, the mothers believed the nurses were not even aware that they were communicating such disapproving attitudes and that these were transmitted in such an indirect and oblique fashion that the mothers felt "stuck" with their feelings and unable to respond.

DISCUSSION

Since all of the mothers interviewed in this study had already made a clear and informed decision that the use of an alternative or out-of-hospital birth center was the correct place for them to deliver their babies, the heavy weight of responses to the experience would be likely to be in the positive direction. Representative samples of groups of women selecting a wider spectrum of options would undoubtedly display different weightings of positive and negative responses in all categories.

No effort has been made to report here the differences between the three programs with respect to subsequent experience on the part of the parent. Analysis of the responses indicated that there was no significant difference and therefore nothing to gain by separate reporting of the three programs.

The content of the questionnaires and interviews from the three programs was largely indistinguishable from each other. Yet the three programs were different in many respects (Table 9-1). One of the most obvious differences was that one of the three programs was designed and largely operated by four Board-certified obstetricians who are all Fellows of the American College of Obstetricians and Gynecologists. All of them were male, upper middle class, and caucasian. Therefore, although this study does not represent a very large sample, it would *not* appear to bear out the current "myth" that childbirth services are best run by women and that obstetricians cannot be expected to operate family-centered, consumer-oriented, high quality out-of-hospital childbirth services.

It is, of course, possible that all of the above findings have been strongly influenced by the characteristics of the sample of women surveyed. The typical subject in this study was a married, caucasian woman in her twenties. More often than not she was a full-time homemaker with at least a high school education, having her first child. It may be that this does not constitute a representative sample of women who use out-of-hospital birthing centers. The present sample would indeed appear to be a rather "traditional" population of women in the child-bearing age in the United States. Some surveys indicate the women using alternative birth centers are more likely to pursue major careers outside of their home and to be committed to alternative life styles. Nevertheless, despite the possible limitations imposed by this sample, the responses elicited warrant more focused attention in several areas.

Further Observations Concerning Parent–Infant Interaction

In addition to the excerpts from interviews recorded verbatim in an earlier section of this chapter, additional comments and observations are relevant, particularly in view of the major focus of this volume. In some subtle ways we do not yet fully understand, it seems that parental ability to feel close to the child, to be able to read its behavioral cues, and to separate it out as a distinct and unique individual from all other human beings is tied to the parents' own sense of coping, mastering, and confidence as the primary caretakers. They may share this responsibility with professionals, but the whole network of attachment and affiliation to the infant is in jeopardy when the professionals are perceived as being superordinate. When parents perceive that something is being done to or for the baby which they do not understand and over which they have little control, they appear to be saying that this interferes with their capacity to feel close to the baby and to be intimately responsible for it.

A significant percentage (almost 27 percent) of mothers in this study reported that constant contact with the baby immediately following birth did not seem to enhance their ability to feel close to the baby or to care for it. Conversely, a very large percentage did not feel this way. Many mothers described that the period immediately following birth was one of emotional "high" in which they seemed acutely aware of the baby's activity, its physical and behavioral characteristics, and its interaction with the father. These phenomena were noted carefully by them, and the baby was identified as their own. This vigilant state was almost always accompanied by a heightened sense of calmness in the parents (even in the primiparas), a sense of stronger confidence in caring for and understanding the baby and feeling like its mother.

An amazingly high percentage of mothers who gave positive responses (almost 60 percent) emphasized the difference in father–infant interaction in the out-of-hospital birthing centers. The emphasis here seemed not so much on the importance of this for the baby as the importance for the mother. This heightened sense of involvement and participation by the father was taken as concrete evidence that infant caretaking would be a shared experience and that the mother would not be "left" with this new and challenging experience on her own.

Some Lessons for Care of the At-Risk Obstetric Patient in a Hospital Setting

Since most infants are delivered in community or regional hospital obstetric services, it may be worth reviewing many of the above responses briefly for any lessons they may teach us about current hospital attitudes, policies, and practices. Perhaps much of this is self-evident, but a highlighting of the "lessons" may be useful.

AVOIDANCE OF EXCESSIVE FOSTERING OF DEPENDENCY

It is inevitable and perhaps very desirable that people who are ill develop a *healthy* sense of reliance and dependency on the health professionals who are caring for them. This issue involves a delicate balance during pregnancy because the pregnant woman is constantly struggling with what, for her, may be unusual strivings for dependency while at the same time struggling for mastery of a new experience, new skills, new knowledge, and, if she is a first-time mother, a new role in life. Many mothers emphasized that when they had become too reliant on professionals they faced going home with the baby quite apprehensively or feeling bewildered and removed from it. Treating new and prospective parents as responsible adults, involving them every step of the way in the decision-making process, and employing as many self-help procedures as possible, both prenatally and during hospital care, seems of vital importance.

REVISION OF INSTITUTIONAL PRIORITIES THAT ADVERSELY INFLUENCE THE CHILDBIRTH EXPERIENCE

Any professional who has experienced a stay in a hospital as a patient may have occasion to question, on a daily basis, whether his or her own clinical needs are receiving the highest priority. Any attitude or practice within an institution that seems to interfere with childbirth may be particularly destructive. A sense that hospital routines or procedures have higher priority than a maternal patient's questions, discomforts, fears, or concerns may lead her to feel deserted or rejected. This may occur in women who ordinarily would not respond so sensitively and with such intensity were they not delivering a child. Parenthetically, many young women reported that they had used gynecologists for years and had shrugged off what they considered to be unnecessary or irrelevant office practices until they became pregnant. When their gynecologist became their obstetrician, many of these practices became unacceptable sources of irritation and led to feelings of being "not important enough" in the doctor's scheme of things.

AVOIDANCE OF RISKS IN TERTIARY HOSPITAL SETTINGS RELATED TO CLINICAL RESEARCH OR FOCI OF PROFESSIONAL INTEREST

This particular area involves attitudes or practices of individual professionals versus institutional policies and practices mentioned above. One young woman sought an alternative birth center after her obstetrician had toured her through their modern and highly touted obstetric unit in a university hospital. She said "then we went on to the new nursery, which was built largely with research funds. It sounded like any excuse possible was used to get the baby into that intensive care unit so it could be studied (like it was too large, or too small, or too old, or too young, or there was some little scribble in the monitor tracing). It was like a museum or a fishbowl. My husband and I looked at each other and decided right there that this hospital was not for us. We just were not going to subject ourselves and our baby to that kind of experience."

It is obviously important to continue clinical investigation into complications of labor and delivery and into the major neonatal disorders. It seems more likely that parents will participate in such efforts if their interest in it can be enlisted early in pregnancy, if the significance of various studies can be explained to them, and if the studies can be carried out in such a way as to interfere minimally with parent–infant interaction during the first hours and days of the postpartum period.

DEFICIENCIES IN COMMUNICATION

Most professionals believe that they communicate well with their patients, that they give them an opportunity to ask appropriate questions, and that they take special pains to allay fears. Unfortunately, it would appear that in some instances this turns out not to be the case. This may be especially true in high-risk obstetric situations where patients are so apprehensive that they cannot ask appropriate questions or are afraid to and need help to verbalize them. At the same time, the heightened vulnerability of parents to stress during this period makes all professionals, in turn, more vulnerable to their anger, their wishes to find someone to retaliate against, and their need to somehow "balance the books" when they feel they have been short changed in some way.

Most of all, in failing to communicate adequately, professionals may infer a lack of belief in or confidence about the strength of parents. I have come to label this the "flight attendant" syndrome. Many of us have had the experience, when as a passenger on a large airliner, there appears to be something amiss, either with one of the engines or some other piece of apparatus. It is especially degrading to have a smiling, noncommunicating flight attendant offer one a cup of coffee (or a martini) and inform all within hearing that "everything is going according to Hoyle and that all procedures are routine." The passenger is left feeling something akin to a slighly retarded adolescent.

Directions For Further Studies Suggested By These Data

This inquiry would appear to only scratch the surface of a body of knowledge which may be critical to the development of new services for parents and children. There are emerging in this field rather militant schools of thought that high technology approaches are "good" (on one hand) or "bad" (on the other) for infants and parents. Out-of-hospital births are variously described as "disguised forms of child abuse" or "the only way to make a proper start with a new baby."

Popular book stores contain entire shelves of self-help books designed to inform parents about how to choose from the various childbirth options that may be available in their community and often do so with little or no attention to the elements on which parents must make critical decisions.

There appears to be a polarization between the "high technologists" and the "natural childbirth proponents" without regard to whether these approaches are truly antithetical or whether there may be ways of combining them so that the best of both are retained. Systematic and well-controlled long-range studies of the impact of various childbirth approaches on healthy child development are nonexistent.

All of this suggests that, as a minimum, three major areas of investigation should proceed in a parallel interacting fashion:

1. *Parental decision-making and choice of childbirth options.* Comparatively little is known about how parents actually choose the way in which they wish to have their baby (assuming options are available to them and that they know about them). From this study, it would appear that parents are highly influenced by whether or not the particular setting will support their own sense of competence and mastery, whether it meets minimum standards for professional expertise and ability to cope with unforseen emergencies, and whether the staff will communicate and share adequately so that the internalized image of the infant with whom they begin their caretaking efforts is not based on fantasy or supposition, but on the reality-based identity of the child. Much more intensive and systematic work needs to be done both on the timing and the basic ingredients of decision-making for parents. Regardless of the setting, it does seem evident that the way in which parents get started with their new baby is at least one crucial ingredient in subsequent outcome in infant development. There is probably a great variety of desirable settings, but it is crucial to find an appropriate match between parental needs and the specific characteristics of the childbirth program.

2. *The use of high technology approaches to support the adaptive tasks of pregnancy and the neonatal period.* In a world filled with videotape machines, computers, microwave ovens, and electronic

toys, there is no reason why parents cannot be helped to use the latest scientific "hardware" to understand and participate in the appropriate care of themselves and their developing fetus and neonate. Investigation into methods for the training of parents to use technological advances to understand the status of the pregnancy, the needs for various types of intervention, and to monitor their own care seems vital and practicable. The polarization between the tertiary caregivers and "back-to-nature" advocates appears more territorial than necessary and not in the best interests of the families.

3. *Controlled studies for program evaluation.* The strident claims that one approach is highly superior to another require documentation or modulation. The likelihood that one specific procedure (or the absence of it) has a one-to-one relationship to any long-range developmental outcome in a child is extremely remote. Only those approaches and procedures that can be clearly demonstrated to impact either adversely or beneficially on child development should become subjects for modifying childbirth practices. A careful literature search reveals not a single study which indicates that a group of children delivered in a specific birthing environment has a clear advantage in physical, cognitive, and personality development over any other appropriately matched group. Admittedly, studies of this nature are quite difficult to execute, expensive to support, and require extreme patience to administer. There does seem to be enough at stake, however, to give serious consideration to pursuing such studies.

CONCLUSIONS

This chapter summarizes the responses of 67 sets of parents to the experience of giving birth to their babies in out-of-hospital centers. In a series of semistructured interviews aimed at helping them express what they found positive and negative in the experience, a total of 462 codable responses were recorded. Of these, 433 (or 93.7 percent) were positive. This overwhelmingly positive reaction may well be explained by the highly selective nature of the sample. All of these parents had explored other options (approximately one-third had delivered previous births in conventional hospital settings) and had made an active decision that an out-of-hospital birth center offered them opportunities not elsewhere available. They all had invested considerable thought, time, and energy in preparing for the experience, a factor of probable major importance in the positive outcome. Most emphasized the crucial nature of this preparation. All were low risk pregnancies, intact families, and had arrived at rather mature levels of development, permitting rational decision-making and active participation of their own care. The typical woman in this study was caucasian, married, in her twenties, a full-time homemaker, and with at least a high school education.

Although the sample was derived from three different birth centers (one operated by male obstetricians and the others by female, certified nurse-midwives), no significant differences could be found either between the demographic characteristics of the parents using them or in the distribution of positive and negative responses they expressed.

The positive responses tended to cluster in the following areas:

1. Constant availability of marital and kinship supports.
2. Uninterrupted contact with the neonate.
3. Increased sense of responsibility for decision-making and self-care.
4. Program characteristics such as high levels of staff competence, open systems of communication, and the home-like atmosphere of the center.

Negative responses, in the main, focused on:

1. Discontinuities in care resulting from transfer to a hospital for obstetric reasons.
2. Some tendency of the staff to underplay the painful aspects of labor to an unrealistic degree.
3. Overestimating the couple's resources through too little preparation, expecting too much from them during childbirth, or too early discharge home.

REFERENCES

1. Cohen RL: Factors influencing maternal choice of childbirth alternatives. Paper presented at the Annual Meeting of the American Academy of Child Psychiatry, Atlanta, October 1979
2. Cohen RL: A comparative study of women choosing two different childbirth alternatives. (In preparation).
3. Lubic RW, Ernst EKM: The childbearing center: An alternative to conventional care. Nursing Outlook 26:754–760, 1978
4. Magee J: Labor: What the doctor learns as a patient. The Female Patient, December 1976, p 27
5. Post JA: Expectations and reality in the expected day of confinement of a primagravida. Matern Child Nur 1:87–100, 1972

Lesley A. Joy, Sheena Davidson,
Tannis MacBeth Williams, and Susan Lee Painter

10

Parent Education in the Perinatal Period: A Critical Review of the Literature

If you want to grow corn in Kansas, a thousand experts will help you, but if you want to raise a child, you're on your own.[1]

If parenthood is one of the few roles in our society for which little or no preparation is provided, parents nevertheless want and need assistance in learning about parenting—particularly during the perinatal period. This is apparent in three current trends: the increase in popular literature written for parents concerning pregnancy, birth, and infancy; the formation of self-help groups that allow new and expectant parents to discuss the skills and attitudes involved in parental roles; and the development by professionals of a variety of programs and approaches for parent education during the perinatal period.

The purpose of this chapter is to describe the types of parent education programs currently available in North America and to review research on their effectiveness. This review is limited to programs that focus on teaching parents specific skills and those that provide general information about infant behavior. It is also restricted to parent education in the perinatal period, i.e., during pregnancy and the first postpartum month. Since our focus is on evaluating the state of the art of parent education, programs that include formal evaluations will be emphasized.

Unfortunately, relatively few perinatal parent education programs are available, many of those reported have not been evaluated, and the evaluations that have been done have not been free of methodological flaws. This poses problems for people seeking guidance in setting up new programs and for researchers interested in the effects of intervention, but for several reasons the omission of evaluation is understandable. The majority of parent education programs have been offered as a service by persons with little or no training in research methods. The emphasis has been on meeting a need; often, neither funds nor time have been available for evaluation. It is not surprising, therefore, that control groups have seldom been included, random assignment to groups usually was not possible, and self-report measures for assessing program effectiveness may have produced biased results. As funding for social service programs becomes even more limited, however, it will be increasingly necessary that adequate evaluations of parent education programs be carried out as a means of ensuring that public and private money is spent where and when it will do the most good.

The need and desire for parent education have been demonstrated in several studies. J.K. Williams[2] administered a questionnaire early in the postpartum period. The majority of parents (82 percent) said that they felt parent education classes would be helpful, especially in the two-to-four weeks following their infant's birth. Sumner and Fritsch[3] conducted a survey of parents' phone calls to the health care facility where their infants had been born. Fully 88 percent of the primiparous women and 25 percent of the multiparous women called the center during the first six weeks postpartum. The number of calls increased steadily during the first three weeks, coinciding with a time when there is little support available from health care sources. Linde and Engelhardt[4] administered a questionnaire during the hospital stay asking new parents to estimate when 20 developmental milestones typically occur. They were able to give accurate estimations for less than half. They concluded that lack of knowledge of child development could result in less effective parenting, but they did not follow up their sample to see whether this was indeed the case.

In a longitudinal study of 193 families in Seattle, Snyder et al.[5] found that only 13 percent of the expectant mothers believed their babies would be aware of their surroundings from birth, and some mothers did not think it would be especially important to talk to the child before two years of age. More importantly, the mothers' prenatal expectations for their infants were significantly related to the home stimulation they later provided at 4, 8, and 12 months, and to the child's development at one and two years of age in terms of Bayley[6] mental and psychomotor scores. Maternal education was also significantly related to level of home stimulation and to child development, but could not account for the relationship between the latter two variables and prenatal maternal expectations. In other works, even when the analyses controlled for level of maternal education, there was evidence that the quality of the early environment the mother provides and the way in which her child develops are related to her expectations for her child. A clear need for parent education in the perinatal period is demonstrated by the finding that many parents' prenatal expectations for their infants were inappropriate for the infants' capabilities, and that these expectations related to later infant development.

In spite of these findings indicating both the need and desire for parent education, there is as yet no clear consensus concerning what should be taught, by whom, or when. There is, however, enough evidence to suggest the direction for future work. One recurring theme in the available studies is that parents gain confidence through attending either a support group or a more formal parent education program. Our review will emphasize the possibility that one of the critical aspects of parent education is to help parents gain confidence in their ability to care for their infants. This confidence may well be a key factor in the establishment of a healthy parent–infant relationship.

Programs for parents will be discussed in developmental sequence beginning with those intended for the prenatal period. Programs specifically designed for mentally and physically handicapped infants and programs directed toward parents of infants older than one month will not be discussed in this chapter.

PRENATAL PERIOD

An obvious starting point to prepare the couple for parenthood is before the baby's birth. Prenatal classes, however, focus almost exclusively on pregnancy, labor, and delivery. Information we received from hospitals and community programs across North America indicated that prenatal classes entitled "parenting" tend to deal with information about labor and delivery but do not provide information about child development or the problems of parenthood. The trend toward initiation of postpartum parenthood classes covering such topics as caregiving does indicate, however, that organizers of prenatal classes are becoming more aware of the need for parent education programs.

Researchers evaluating the effectiveness of prenatal programs have been concerned primarily with finding differences in the physical outcomes of labor and delivery between women who were prepared by attending a series of classes and women who did not attend classes. Although no consistent differences between groups have been found for such physical variables as length of labor,[7-10] it has been reported that women prepared by prenatal classes go through labor and delivery with less analgesia and anesthesia.[7,10-12] A number of researchers have reported emotional and/or attitudinal benefits for women prepared for the birth experience,[7,10,12-14] but in one study[11] no differences were found between prepared and unprepared women on measures of perception of the baby and concerns about childrearing.

A comprehensive project involving two separate programs was designed to reduce the proportion of low-birthweight infants in Vancouver, Canada.[15] One of the programs focused on prenatal classes. The other was an outreach nutrition and counselling program designed for the hard-to-reach pregnant woman. In the latter case, bilingual paraprofessionals provided counselling during home visits in one of the five languages covered. Both programs achieved low birthweight ratios significantly better than that of the comparison group. The home visit program demonstrated that nonattenders at prenatal classes can be reached with success.

Although it appears logical to provide parent education prenatally, several researchers[2,16,17] have found that expectant parents did not assimilate information about caretaking or material intended to alleviate early parental stress. In Kruse's study,[16] parents attending prepared childbirth classes received information concerning postpartum adjustment that was designed to relieve parental stress. Even though they were "well prepared," they reported on a questionnaire completed during the first few weeks postpartum that they were experiencing stress. For mothers, the main areas of concern were personal appearance, fatigue, and infant crying; for fathers, the main concerns were infant crying and worries about being a "good" father. Kruse concluded that to be effective, teaching should be conducted postnatally, since labor and delivery were the parents' main concerns in the prenatal period. In J. Williams' study[2] 74 percent of parents indicated on a postpartum questionnaire that they wanted information on physical care, even though this is usually discussed during the mother's postnatal hospital stay. Smith and Smith[17] organized prenatal and postpartum classes designed to educate parents about the physical and psychological aspects of pregnancy, childbirth, infant care, and child development. Although the mothers' overall knowledge of child development increased from the prenatal to the postpartum period, parents did not learn the material specifically taught in the classes. There seems to be a need to follow up the programs offered prenatally and in the hospitals after the parents have spent time with their infant and have come to realize what problems might arise.

It is possible that the best time for parent education is when it is most relevant, that is, soon after the baby is born. Some "enlightenment" education in the teenage years also may be useful.[18,19] Only a few programs, however, have attempted to teach parents prenatally about topics other than labor and delivery. Given the demonstration by Snyder et al.[5] that prenatal parental expectations are related to the level of stimulation parents subsequently provide for their infants, and to actual infant development, it is especially important that we answer the question of whether the prenatal or early postpartum period is the optimal time to implement parent education. It may be that special approaches are required for prenatal parent education to be effective. For example, expectant parents may learn about child development and develop appropriate expectations for their infants if they are taught through demonstration but not by books and lectures. At the same time we must be cautious in assuming that teaching parents about child development is an effective mode of parent education. Unless researchers measure changes in parental attitudes and/or behavior, we cannot know whether increased knowledge of child development translates into changes in attitudes and behavior. Infant behaviors should also be assessed. That prenatal parental expectations have been found to be related to subsequent parent and infant behavior suggests that intervention aimed at teaching parents about child development should be effective, but that remains to be demonstrated.

In sum, there is a clear need for parent education in the perinatal period, but the evidence concerning benefits to parents and infants of attending prenatal classes is equivocal. Further research is necessary to clarify the advantages, which seem to depend on the outcomes being studied and the measures used to study them. The increasing number of postpartum parent education classes now being organized suggests that this may be the current trend, although it must be remembered that even with this increase only a very small proportion of parents receive any parent education at all.

NEONATAL PERIOD

Postpartum Stay

Parent education usually begins soon after the baby's birth when the mother is still in the hospital. Nurses help mothers learn basic infant care, such as how to bathe, feed, and burp the baby, but teaching about childrearing and child development is limited. Traditionally the emphasis has been on providing the mother with as much rest as possible. This has meant that hospital personnel have assumed the major caregiving role and mothers have received little caregiving experience. Opportunities for fathers to participate in childcare have been minimal throughout the hospital stay. In contrast, *Family Centered Maternity Care* (FCMC) emphasizes teaching caregiving skills to both mothers and fathers and providing parents with time to practice these skills so that they gain confidence in caring for their new infant. Aspects of FCMC vary at different hospitals, but the mother usually becomes the primary daytime caretaker with support from hospital personnel. Informal evaluations of FCMC programs,[20,21] involving physicians' verbal feedback to the hospitals and parental self-report indicate that the programs are popular with parents. Physicians have also reported their impression that FCMC participants appear calmer and more confident than parents in traditional programs.

Jordan[22] used questionnaires to compare the effects of FCMC with traditional maternity care (TMC) on the reduction of reported parent–child problems during the first two months postpartum. FCMC reported increased confidence in infant care by comparison with parents in the TMC program. Parents in FCMC did not differ from parents in TMC in expressed concern about physical and psychological problems. This finding may have occurred because FCMC hospital nurses encouraged mothers to report their problems, or because FCMC parents had more experience with their infants in the early postpartum period and this resulted in greater awareness of problems. On the other hand, there simply may have been no difference. Unfortunately, there was no assessment of whether parents in FCMC actually learned more about their infants, and no assessment of what they learned. Perhaps the most interesting aspect of these findings is that parents with more experience in caring for their newborn infants had greater confidence about infant care in spite of their reported perception of having the same number of problems.

One difficulty with the few studies designed to evaluate the effectiveness of FCMC is that it differs in several ways from traditional care. For example, FCMC provides more opportunity for teaching caregiving skills, and involves "rooming in," whereas TMC does not. When FCMC is found to be more effective, it will be unclear what components of the program account for the difference unless the research design involves manipulation of the components of FCMC. Several researchers who have compared rooming-in with traditional care[23-25] have found that rooming-in mothers reported feeling more confident with their infants, could better understand the meaning of their infants' cries, and developed maternal feelings sooner. The development of mother-infant interaction also has been found to be facilitated by rooming-in.[26] Greenberg et al.[23] noted that rooming-in seemed to work better in multipatient rooms rather than single rooms, which suggests that mothers may have learned about infants from other mothers as well as from the experience of caring for their own infant in their room. This possibility could be explored by comparing mothers in single and multipatient rooms in traditional versus rooming-in programs using measures of maternal confidence and attachment. Mere exposure to other mothers and infants may produce positive effects. One implication of these studies is that the maternal confidence and competence found in FCMC parents may simply be the result of the rooming-in aspect of the FCMC program. To reiterate, in evaluating any program it is important to assess the contributions of the various components of the program to its overall effectiveness.

The use of television in hospital to teach parents about basic infant care and feeding has been evaluated in two studies.[27,28] Broussard[27] tested the impact of three, half-hour televised anticipatory guidance programs on mothers' perceptions of their newborns using the Neonatal Perception Inventory (NPI).[29] The first videotape showed a group of mothers discussing their feelings about their recent pregnancy, delivery, and the immediate pospartum period. The second tape discussed normal variations in infant behavior and techniques of infant care. The third videotape elaborated on the infant care techniques seen in the second program, with an emphasis on encouraging mothers to have confidence in their ability to meet their infants' needs. The control group consisted of mothers who delivered in the same hospital at a time when the television programs were not available. Counselling by television had significantly enhanced the mothers' positive perceptions of their infants. The Kaiser Foundation Hospital in Haywood, California also used TV as a teaching tool.[28] They showed two videotapes about basic infant care and feeding at the same time every day. Unfortunately, there was no objective evaluation of the effectiveness of these films in terms of maternal behavior, maternal confidence, or the mother–infant relationship.

It is clear from these studies that hospital personnel can play an important role in parent education during the perinatal period. They can teach parents about basic infant care and help parents gain confidence in their ability to care for their infants. In addition, hospitals can be organized so as to maximize parents' learning opportunities, for example, by offering FCMC, "rooming-in," and televised guidance programs.

Several authors[30–34] have stressed the importance of helping parents of infants who are in an intensive care nursery learn how to interact with their newborns. In some reports no specific teaching approach has been outlined[30] and in others there has been no formal evaluation of the approach used.[31-33] In contrast, researchers at the Hospital for Sick Children in Toronto[34] have recently completed an evaluation of a program in which mothers whose infants were in the intensive care nursery attended self-help groups. The groups were designed to assist parents in coping with the stresses associated with having a small premature infant and in learning about community resources. The 32 mothers who participated were randomly assigned to the self-help program (experimental group) or to a control group that received routine hospital care. Mothers who attended the self-help groups visited their infants in the nursery significantly more often than mothers in the control group. They also were more knowledgeable about their infant's condition, interacted more with other parents of infants in the intensive care unit, were more comfortable with their own ability to care for the baby at home, and had better knowledge of community resources. That this model program has now been taken over by the parents themselves indicates its popularity. In addition, the parents and researchers have produced a booklet for parents of premature infants that has been published and is being distributed by the Ontario government to all parents of prematures in the province. Evaluations of approaches used by other intensive care units, such as formal teaching sessions and/or providing written information, still need to be carried out.

Well-Baby Programs

Following discharge from the hospital, sources of professional advice for new parents are mainly the family doctor, the office nurse, and community-health nurses. The ways in which these health care professionals provide support and information to parents have been evaluated in a number of studies.

One early investigation[35] involving direct observation of private pediatricians revealed that 72 to 82 percent of the average well-baby visit was spent on medical-physical concerns, whereas less than 25 percent of the visit consisted of personal, social, and emotional concerns. However, a more recent study of pediatric practice,[37] indicated that pediatric nurses and physicians spent 50 to 60 percent of the visit on behavioral-developmental problems, substantially more than was found in the earlier study. Unfortunately the pediatricians and nurses in this latter study were aware of the authors' interest in the content of the visits, and may have altered their normal patterns.[37] Nevertheless, these results indicate a shift in the approach of pediatricians to child-health supervision in keeping with what Brazelton first advocated more than a decade ago: as part of well-child care, parents need supportive information, choices concerning how to nurture and provide optimal environments for their infants, and help in decreasing their anxiety. Unfortunately, changes in current practices in child-health supervision seem to be based largely on consensus about what ought to be done rather than on research designed to determine the effectiveness of current practices.[37] Our review of the current pediatric literature revealed relatively few studies in which the pediatrician's role in parent education was assessed. Some programs were based on informal discussion group formats.[38-40] Other programs[41-45] were more research oriented, investigating the effect of pediatric well-child care on mother–infant relations and the infant's cognitive development.

Cronin,[38] Hancock,[39] and Stein[40] conducted informal group discussions on well-baby care with parents of infants varying in age from two weeks to one year. The topics covered included breastfeeding, infant sleep patterns, stranger anxiety, infant reflexes, crying and physical care, father's role in infant care, infant stimulation, and so on. Physical examinations of the infants were also routinely carried out. Although there were no formal evaluations of the effectiveness of these group discussions, parents verbally reported feeling better and more confident, and in one study the pediatrican noted that the parents' overall trust increased.[40] In another study,[39] fewer infants were found to have problems at the six-week well-baby clinic, there were fewer "unnecessary" visits to the hospital, and parents reported feeling more confident after attending group meetings. In a third study,[38] the advantages of using group discussions were shown to include an increased number of well-baby care visits and coverage of more topics than was possible in the traditional individual visits. Mothers also reported receiving more support from one another. Disadvantages were reported to be minimal, e.g., having to organize group meetings limited the flexibility of appointment times (a particular disadvantage for working parents), and loss of the one-to-one relationship between the parents and pediatric nurse.

For all of these studies it is important to note that since the pediatrician, pediatric nurse, and parents would have a vested interest in observing or feeling positive effects from attending group discussions, informal reports that the groups were successful are likely to be biased. In addition, the research reports give no indication of what aspects of the group discussions may have contributed to the reported positive effects. Increased pediatrician attention, e.g., two hours each month for one year compared to the norm of perhaps ten minutes every few months,[40] might on its own be expected to contribute to increased parental awareness and self-confidence. Furthermore, there was no evaluation of how much parents learned, or of the effects of the group meetings on parent–infant relationships. It would be worthwhile to separate the evaluation of the material presented in the groups from the evaluation of the effects of physician contact and group support.

These three studies suggest that increased contact with pediatric staff may have positive effects on parental feelings of confidence in infant care; however, before conclusions can be drawn and recommendations offered, programs such as these need to be more thoroughly evaluated. We need to know which aspects of the program are most effective in changing parents' attitudes, knowledge of child development, and behaviors.

Chamberlin and Szumowski[42] evaluated the effectiveness of various pediatricians' programs designed to increase mothers' knowledge of child development. Pediatricians were interviewed to assess the extent of their teaching programs, and, depending on the number and variety of techniques used to teach child development (planned discussions, handouts, books, group sessions, etc.), were divided into three groups: high, medium, and low input. A questionnaire given immediately after the birth and one year later assessed the mother's knowledge of child development, her techniques of modifying behavior, her childrearing style, and her perception of her child's behavioral characteristics. When the infants were 18-months-old their mothers completed the Minnesota Child Development Inventory designed to assess infant developmental status. The level of physician's input was related to the mother's gain in knowledge of child development, but not to the number of concerns she had about her child nor to the child's level of development. Only the mother's self-report of her own childrearing behavior (as assessed by the questionnaire) was found to be related to the child's level of development. Given that the mother's contact with the pediatrician in this study was limited (approximately one 10–15 minute visit every two months), it is possible that the use of trained lay home visitors to augment the pediatrician's input, as the authors suggested, also would have an effect on the mother's behavior.

Gutelius et al.[43,44] conducted a longitudinal study to evaluate the effects of three years of well-baby care and a cognitive stimulation program on young, unmarried women and their first-born infants. Mothers were randomly assigned to an experimental or control group.

The intervention began in the third trimester of pregnancy. For the infant's first three years the same pediatrician and nurse provided complete well-baby care (nine visits in the first year, seven in the second year, and five in the third year). In addition, the same nurse conducted the same number of home visits for the cognitive stimulation program, in which she demonstrated infant visual, auditory, tactile, and motor stimulation. The control subjects were referred to prenatal clinics and received one pediatrician home-visit a year to collect information concerning child care practices and to examine the infant. The control group mothers reported receiving some well-baby care at various clinics, but the number of visits was approximately half the number of well-baby care visits received by the experimental group. There were no significant differences between the two groups in infant development at six months. At one and two years, however, the experimental infants scored significantly higher on the Bayley[6] mental and motor scales, and they also scored significantly higher at three years on the Stanford-Binet intelligence test. The home-visit data revealed that the experimental group families had more appropriate diets and eating habits and fewer developmental problems (e.g., regarding toilet training), the parents played more with their infants, took them out of the house more often, read more to their infants, and the mothers were seen as demonstrating increased self-confidence and assurance. The authors concluded that the results of their program indicated a causal relationship between intervention and these few favorable findings, and contended that if a larger study had been conducted (actual N = 95), favorable trends would have reached significance. By most research standards, however, this is not a small sample.

This study was one of the earliest to evaluate the effectiveness of intervention with parents in the context of child-health supervision, and it has some methodological problems. For example, the input received by the control group was not controlled and the pediatrician and nurse who collected some data were not blind to group status. Ironically, from the point of view of evaluation it is unfortunate that this project was so comprehensive. The results give no indication of optimal timing for intervention or what the most effective intervention might be. As funding for programs of all kinds becomes less available, it might not be feasible or practical to provide extensive care and teaching over a long period of time, especially if the same results could be achieved with less extensive intervention timed more optimally. Gordon et al.[46] conducted a cognitive stimulation program with older children that involved eight different groups varying in time of initiation of intervention so that the effect of length and timing of parent education could be systematically evaluated. A similar design could be adopted by pediatricians in child-health supervision. In evaluating the Gutelius et al.[43,44] project it is difficult to conclude that the gains achieved justify the effort and expense.

The effectiveness of the Yale Child Welfare Research Program[45] is also difficult to assess because of its comprehensiveness. This program aimed at inner city children was initiated at birth and continued for 30 months, with unstructured home visits every two weeks for the first year and monthly thereafter, pediatric well-baby care visits once a month for the first year and every three months thereafter, day care and toddler school, and regular developmental testing throughout the 30 months by a pediatrician and psychologist not involved with the families (using the Yale Developmental Schedules). A matched comparison group was added after the intervention ended at 30 months, hence assignment to groups was not random. Experimental group infants had significantly higher language scores than comparison group infants, but there was no differences in basic cognitive-perceptual capacities. A continued effect of the intervention program on children's scores on the Peabody Picture Vocabulary Test and in school achievement was demonstrated in a five-year follow-up.[47] Families also showed gains in several indices of upward mobility relative to their position at the beginning of the project (e.g., mother's education and source of support). While this would appear to be an indication of project success, it is possible that changes would have occurred anyway. Since the control group was added after the project ended, it is impossible to know. There were some definite methodological problems with this study, but the goals of the program are admirable and there is an indication of some long-term success in preventing or alleviating the intellectual impairment often associated with poverty and/or inadequate care.

In a study conducted by Casey and Whitt[41] mother-infant pairs were randomly assigned following hospital discharge to an experimental or control group. Parents in both groups visited the same pediatrician six times over a seven-month period. The control group received a standard visit during which the pediatrician examined the infant and discussed physical and preventive care. The experimental group received the standard visit and, in addition, the pediatrician discussed methods to enhance mother–infant interaction and child development (e.g., maintaining eye contact, vocalizing in response to infant vocalization, methods for quieting a crying infant, infant's developmental sequence). The pediatrician spent approximately 30 minutes on each visit for both groups. An assistant who was blind to group status assessed the mother–infant relationship by observing the pair in the pediatrician's office through a one-way mirror just prior to the last visit (27 weeks postpartum). Experimental group mothers scored significantly higher than control group mothers on four of the eight Ainsworth scales used to assess maternal sensitivity (appropriateness of interaction, cooperation, appropriateness of play, and maternal sensitivity). Thus there was some evidence that a brief pediatric intervention affected maternal behavior.

In 1972 the American Academy of Pediatrics defined the goals of child-health supervision as (1) lowered child mortality; (2) reduced disability and morbidity; (3) promotion of optimum growth and development; and (4) help for children to achieve longer, fuller, and more productive lives.[37] The Academy indicated that these goals were to be achieved by early disease detection, preventive health measures, health education, counselling, anticipatory guidance, and continuity of care. If pediatricians are to follow these guidelines, further research needs to be conducted to learn more about a number of important issues; what pediatricians should teach in well-baby visits; whether it is sufficient for parents to receive support and teaching from a paraprofessional or lay person; when child-health supervision by pediatricians should begin; how long this supervision should continue; and what the short- and long-term goals of intervention should be. We need to know the specific implications of health-care intervention for parent–child relationships and for child development. However, as Casey et al.[37] state: "Unfortunately, relatively few data are available upon which to base conclusions concerning the effectiveness of many aspects of current practice or to make recommendations for change" (p. 6). Further research is clearly indicated.

Cognitive Stimulation Programs

With the exception of programs designed to teach parents how to stimulate their low birth-weight newborns, programs to stimulate infant cognitive development generally have not been initiated with infants younger than one month. Scarr-Salapatek and M.L. Williams[48] randomly assigned low birth-weight infants of young mothers with little formal education and low socioeconomic status to an experimental or control group. Nursery staff were instructed to give experimental group infants special visual, tactile, and kinesthetic stimulation while in hospital during eight half-hour stimulation sessions per day. Control group infants received standard pediatric care. Upon discharge from the hospital, approximately six weeks after birth, a social worker visited experimental group mothers weekly at home to demonstrate stimulation techniques. Control group infants scored slightly higher on the Brazelton Neonatal Assessment Scale[49] at one week, but at four weeks the experimental group infants scored higher. They also scored significantly higher on the Cattell IQ test at one year. Although this study demonstrates the effectiveness of early intervention in enhancing infant cognitive development, it also raises several interesting issues. First, what were the relative contributions to the infant I.Q. gain of the hospital and home-based programs? Second, as T.M. Williams[50] has suggested, it would have been helpful to have had home observations at one year to assess whether maternal education in stimulation techniques resulted in lasting effects in spheres other than cognitive development.

In sum, there is some evidence that programs to stimulate the cognitive development of infants less than one month old can be successful.[48] The majority of programs have been initiated with older infants, however,[46,51] Further research is needed to ascertain when interventions should begin and whether the effects of early intervention have lasting results.

Programs Designed to Teach Parents about Infant Behavior

Based on Brazelton's work, several researchers have argued that teaching parents about the behavior patterns of their newborns will facilitate the development of maternal attachment and maternal behavior.[52-55]

Studies by Edelstein[53] and Ryan[55] shared some common features. In both cases mother-infant pairs were randomly assigned to an experimental or control group. Within the first few days postpartum, all infants were assessed on the Brazelton Neonatal Behavioral Assessment Scale. (BNBAS) The intervention consisted of demonstrating the BNBAS to the mother in the Edelstein study, and a teaching session based on the BNBAS in the Ryan study. In both cases there were no significant differences between the experimental and control groups at one-month postpartum on the outcome measures used, i.e., the Broussard-Hartner NPI[29] in both studies, and, in addition, the Schaefer-Manheimer Postnatal Research Inventory[56] in the Edelstein research, and the BNBAS in the Ryan research. Both authors concluded that there was no evidence that intervention based on the BNBAS affects maternal perception at one-month postpartum. There were methodological problems with both of these studies, however. In particular, the intervention may have occurred too soon after delivery for the mothers to be able to benefit from the teaching, e.g., they may have been suffering from the after effects of anaesthesia. Broussard's finding[27] of differences in maternal perceptions at one month related to televised anticipatory guidance programs seen in the first few days postpartum suggests that the form and content of intervention may be an important factor to consider along with timing. Finally, the very small sample studied by Ryan may also account for the negative results.

A study conducted by Kang[54] improved upon these two studies in several ways. The intervention was given to both mothers and fathers and allowed for slower assimilation of the material presented. In addition, several different outcome measures were used. On the first or second day postpartum (time 1), randomly assigned pairs of parents completed the NPI and received a written form of a revised version of the BNBAS. A nurse observed mother-infant pairs during feeding and then assessed the infants on the BNBAS without either parent being present. Two weeks later the nurse visited experimental group parents in their homes to conduct a teaching session based on the revised BNBAS. (This teaching procedure was also used by Ryan.) At one-month postpartum (time 2) parents in both groups again completed the NPI, mother-infant pairs were observed, and the nurse again assessed the infants on the BNBAS. There were no significant differences between the groups in perception of the infant (NPI) at time 1, but at time 2 more experimental group parents than control group parents rated their infants as better than average. There were no significant differences between the groups at time 1 or time 2 in BNBAS scores or in mother–infant interaction during feeding. Differences in procedure may explain why Kang's teaching session produced changes in parental perceptions but Ryan's did not. Kang introduced her teaching session at two-weeks postpartum after mothers had some time to recover from the birth experience. Furthermore, Kang gave all parents a written form of the revised BNBAS, which alone was not sufficient to alter parents' perceptions of their infants (that is, no differences on the NPI were found at time 1), but when given in conjunction with the teaching session resulted in parents rating their infants more positively. Unfortunately, again because of the small sample size, conclusions from this study can be only tentative. The findings are suggestive enough to warrant replication with a larger sample, especially in light of the conflicting results obtained by Ryan[55] and Edelstein.[53]

A more complex intervention study with a much larger sample (86 families) was conducted by Davidson.[52] Four groups of parents (two experimental, two control) differed with respect to the number and content of home visits during the first month postpartum; group assignment was random. All mothers completed a series of prenatal questionnaires in their last trimester of pregnancy and were interviewed in their homes about their prenatal experience. Information concerning labor and delivery was obtained from hospital charts. The two control groups differed in terms of whether they received a home visit at twelve-days postpartum. The pure control group did not, and the placebo group received a visit from the project nurse, scheduled when both mother and father could be present. During this visit the hospital and birth experiences were discussed. The placebo group was included as a check on whether the content or merely the contact provided in the experimental group visits was responsible for the results. The home visits for the two experimental groups, experimental and follow-through, both included a teaching session based on the BNBAS that had three components: (1) information about the general behavioral patterns of newborns, (2) discussion and demonstration of the individual infant's response patterns, and (3) discussion of how the parents could best respond to these individual patterns. The follow-through group received an additional two visits, one week apart. The project nurse did not do additional teaching during the follow-up visits, but reinforced earlier teaching by discussing infant behaviors and the parent–infant relationship. At one-month postpartum, observers who were blind to the mothers' group status observed mothers from all four groups in interaction with their infants for one hour at home. The observers also completed the Maternal Care Rating Scales designed by Ainsworth[57] to assess aspects of maternal behavior, sensitivity, and interaction with the infant. At this time mothers also completed postpartum questionnaires: the Schaefer-Manheimer PRI,[56] the Broussard-Hartner NPI,[29] and a self-report measure designed by the researchers. Only the results pertinent to the intervention will be discussed here (for a full report of our longitudinal study see Williams et al.[58]). Prenatally, there were no differences among the groups except that the experimental group mothers predicted they would take *longer* than control group mothers to feel close to their infants. At one-month postpartum a set of 22 variables significantly differentiated the two experimental from the two control groups. These variables included observations of mother–infant interaction (e.g., mothers who had received teaching engaged more often in auditory stimulation and social engagement with their infants); observer ratings of maternal sensitivity based on the Ainsworth scales[57] (e.g., experimental mothers were rated as providing more encouragment to their infants for sensorimotor achievement and as providing a more stimulating environment); maternal report of confidence in caregiving (experimental mothers reported themselves as more confident in caring for their infants, that feeding was progressing more smoothly, and that they found it easier to quiet their fussy/crying infant); maternal report of attachment (contrary to the prenatal prediction experimental mothers reported feeling closer to their infants at one month); self-report of adjustment to the maternal role (experimental mothers obtained better scores on several of the PRI scales); and maternal report of perception of the infant (experimental mothers perceived their infant as having changed more in the first month and as more different from the average baby on the NPI). This study was designed to separate the effects of the nurse's visit per se from the specific teaching effects of the intervention and, since no systematic differences were found between the two experimental groups (the follow-through group had three visits while the experimental group had one) or between the two control groups (the placebo group had one nonteaching visit, the pure controls had no visit from the nurse), we may conclude that it was the teaching session that contributed to the differences found between the two treatment and two control groups. It is still not clear, however, which aspects of the teaching session were responsible for producing these differences. The results of this study nevertheless reinforce Kang's findings,[54] showing that both timing and structure of intervention are important. If teaching parents about their infant's responses to the environment is indeed beneficial to their postpartum adjustment, public health nurses could incorporate an intervention of the type used by Kang and Davidson in their home visits during the postpartum period. (In Canada, where Davidson's study was conducted, mothers delivering in the hospital receive a home visit from the community health nurse at one–two-weeks postpartum. This service and hospital care expenses are provided by the government, so an intervention could be incorporated into an already existing health care program).

Schaefer[59] is currently conducting a study to assess the effects of both extended early mother–neonate contact in the hospital and home visits from a paraprofessional infant-care worker upon maternal attachment and child development. Mothers from low-income families are randomly assigned to one of four groups: (1) hospital and home intervention (one hour of mother–infant contact during the first three hours after delivery, at least five additional hours of contact each remaining day in hospital, and home visits from the infant-care worker for the first three months); (2) hospital intervention but no home intervention; (3) home intervention but no hospital intervention; and (4) no intervention. During home visits the infant-care worker discusses with the mother ways of coping with stress, and works with the mother to promote involvement with her infant. Preliminary results indicate that extended contact may be effective in eliminating extreme cases of noninvolvement and hostile detachment, but there is no evidence as yet that the home visiting program affects maternal attachment at four-months postpartum. Because the program is still continuing, and only preliminary data have been obtained, more definite conclusions await the completion of this study.

The studies reviewed in this section illustrate the importance of specifying precisely the content of any educational procedure, the timing of intervention, the goals of the program, and the measures used to evaluate the outcome. There is some indication in the results of several studies that teaching parents about their infant's behavior can affect parental perceptions of the infant and the parent–infant relationship.

Informal and Self-Help Programs

The need for parent education and support can be seen in the number of informal groups and community health programs established in recent years. Some are highly structured, offering classes in child development and new-baby care, but more often the course content and focus are determined by the group as the program progresses. These programs for parents with young infants usually have a varied format, including group discussions, lectures given by invited professionals, peer modeling (employing the presence of experienced parents), and role-playing techniques.[60–66] On the whole, formal evaluations of program effectiveness have not been done, and they are needed to document the fact that the majority of organizers and parents report these programs to be successful. Anecdotally, parents report feeling more confident and are observed to be more calm and competent after attending group sessions, and the enrollment in the classes is usually good and maintained. Parents who participate may be reluctant to report no benefits from attending the groups however, and the organizers clearly wish to believe that their programs are helpful. In addition, the question of self-selection needs to be addressed in evaluating informal parent programs. It may be that parents who attend are highly motivated to change, or perhaps especially competent and likely to do well in any event. On the other hand, these programs may attract those most in need of help and likely to benefit from any form of intervention. In evaluating these and other parent education programs, the target group must be taken into consideration.

A program for parents of infants one-to-four-weeks-old is currently being offered by Stranik and Hogberg.[65] Weekly classes run by an obstetrical nurse and a pediatric nurse cover the mother's labor and delivery experience, the immediate concerns of parents about their infant's behavior, and long-range needs of the infant (for example, toilet training). Only four classes are offered at present, but plans are in progress for instituting a follow-up program.

Even more informal groups exist, usually run by interested parents. The major function of these groups is to provide support for parents through sharing experiences and knowledge in discussion groups.[67-69] Contacts made by parents in prenatal classes are often maintained and the groups reestablished in the postpartum period. Again, there are no formal evaluations of these lay groups, but they do seem to provide an important service, as indicated by their popularity. In our own longitudinal research from the prenatal to early postpartum period we found that even mothers who perceive themselves prenatally to be well prepared for childbirth and childrearing experience considerable loneliness and self-doubt in the first postpartum month.[70]

Another type of informal support program is nurse-initiated telephone follow-up of postpartum women.[71-73] In these programs, the maternity nurse-caring for mother and infant in the hospital provides notes to the follow-up nurse concerning the mother's and infant's progress in hospital, teaching received, and potential problems. During the follow-up call, made within the first week after discharge, the nurse can assess the mother's progress, reinforce previous health education, and provide additional teaching if necessary. If more contact is needed, the mother can be referred to a community agency. These programs, which aim to promote parental confidence and competence, are simple to initiate and can easily reach a large number of people,[72] but unfortunately have not been formally evaluated.

Informal programs, because they already exist, and because they do not require much in the way of funding, may be a very important form of parent education in the perinatal period. Objective evaluations of the effectiveness of these programs need to be conducted, and should include random assignment to groups, observers blind to group status, objective measures of parental behavior, self-report of parental feelings and attitudes, and the use of control groups. The characteristics of parents attending informal groups also need to be analyzed to determine whether certain groups of parents who might benefit from the support and parent education provided are not aware of or able to take advantage of the opportunity (e.g., immigrant families). The results of such evaluations will be helpful in establishing the most appropriate format for parent education programs, either self-help or structured, and who should organize them. The anecdotal finding that parents report gaining confidence should be followed up to see if there are any changes in parental behavior that may contribute to or result from this increased confidence.

INFANCY

As the focus of this chapter is on parent education in the perinatal period, only brief mention will be made of programs designed for parents of children one-to-eighteen months. The majority of such programs focus on teaching parents, usually during home visits, how to stimulate their infants to enhance cognitive development and ameliorate class differences. The content and effectiveness of these infant programs have been reviewed extensively elsewhere.[50,74-81] Some of the more salient issues regarding the effectiveness of programs designed for parents of older infants are relevant for parent education in the perinatal period. The question of timing of intervention was mentioned earlier in this chapter. The design of a study conducted by Gordon et al.,[46] with parents of children as young as three months of age, may be helpful to persons wishing to address the question of when in the perinatal period parent education should begin, and how long it should be maintained.

A study from the infancy period with particular relevance for the perinatal period was conducted by Dickie and Carnahan.[82] They assessed the effect on mothers, fathers, and their 4-to-12-month infants of training to improve competence in dyadic interactions. Competence was defined as occurring when both parent and infant provided contingency experiences for one another, for example, the parent vocalized in response to the baby's gurgle. The competent parent was seen as one who could assess and predict infant behavior. The competent infant was seen as one who provided readable, predictable cues to parents and responded to parents and the environment. Training was given over eight weeks to parents randomly assigned to an experimental group, and consisted of teaching parents about their infant's temperament and cues given, variations in infant behavior, and what effect the infant has on the parent. Parents with training increased their interaction with their infants and were able to read infant cues and respond contingently. Infants also differed; they sought interaction least with untrained fathers and most with trained fathers. Although there was a significant increase in objective parents' behavioral competence assessed via home observations and videotapes, the parents' own feelings of competence (questionnaire data) did not increase. Training did result in a change in judgments of the *spouses'* competence, however. Trained parents thought their spouses were more competent than did untrained parents. The question arises whether it is more important to increase parents' own feelings of competence which may then lead to improved feelings of self-esteem, or whether it is sufficient to increase behavioral competence. Obviously, it would be maximally beneficial to increase both. This discrepancy between the results of observed competence and self-report of competence is especially interesting in light of the anecdotal reports from parents, organizers of informal discussion groups, community health programs, and other parent education programs that, after participation in the programs, feelings of confidence, competence, and self-esteem increased. A possible explanation for this descrepancy is that the definition of what is meant by competence may vary. Alternatively, given that the children in this study were 4-to-12-months-old when training began, it is possible that the parents had already established whether they thought of themselves as competent in the parent–infant dyad, and although training altered their behavior, it did not change their own perceptions.

CONCLUSION

What have we learned from our review of the literature, and what remains to be done in the field of parent education in the perinatal period? There is considerable evidence that education for childbirth and parenting can positively affect parental behavior, attitudes, and parent–infant relationships.

One recurring theme is that parents participating in educational programs and informal support groups report feeling increasingly confident and competent in infant caretaking. Our own previous research has indicated that confidence in caregiving is related to the development of maternal attachment and adjustment of the maternal role.[83] The mediating factor in parent education programs, regardless of content, quite possibly may be parental self-confidence. This needs to be tested, but the question is not completely clear-cut. We do not know whether specific feelings of confidence in the parental role, general self-esteem, or some combination of the two is most critical for parental competence and thus for parent education programs. Painter[84] is currently asking this question in relation to parents of toddlers; further research is warranted.

The role of self-confidence in adaptation to parenthood raises a second important question, namely the relationship between self-report and behavior. In our own research we found that observations of mother–infant behavior are not necessarily related to maternal attitudes and perceptions of the infant.[85] Dickie and Carnahan[82] found that competence as assessed by an observer may not necessarily coincide with self-report of feelings of competence. The issue of the nature of parental self-perception is important because self-report measures are frequently used in evaluations. In order to develop successful educational programs we probably need to use both attitudinal and behavioral assessments.

We also need to know how parental knowledge of child development relates to parental behavior. Teaching parents about child development is a major component of many parent education programs, presumably based on the assumption that such knowledge will be translated into appropriate parental behavior. The finding by Snyder et al.[5] that prenatal maternal expectations regarding child development were related to the environment provided postnatally for the baby, as well as to infant development, supports the assumption that knowledge of child development is important. Chamberlin and Szumowksi,[42] however, concluded on the basis of their research that what a mother reports she does with her baby is more important for the baby's development than what she reports to know concerning infant development; so teaching parents about child development is by no means the sole answer to parent education. It is important to remember that the evidence of Synder et al.[5] concerning the role of parental expectations was based on correlational description rather than on intervention. *How* parents learn about child development undoubtedly is very important and may provide a clue to the apparently equivocal findings. When the results from several studies are combined, one gets the impression that teaching parents in the abstract about child development is much less effective than demonstrating infant capabilities. In sum, we need to understand the relationships among parental knowledge of child development, parental behavior, and parental self-report of variables such as emotions and feelings of competence.

If parent education is to be optimally effective, we also need to know when to initiate it and how long to maintain it. There is evidence that using books and lectures to teach parents prenatally about child development is not particularly effective.[2,16] In this case we do not know whether the time or the method of intervention is inappropriate. Again, the evidence that prenatal parental expectations are important for subsequent infant development and that prenatal predictions of competence in caregiving are important for postpartum maternal attachment and adjustment to the maternal role indicate that much more effort needs to be made in developing and evaluating prenatal parent education programs. The most appropriate timing and methods for parent education after childbirth also need to be worked out through further evaluation research.

Who should be assessed in the evaluation of parent education? The answer to this question requires knowledge of the program goals. If the goal is to improve the parent–infant relationship, then evaluation should entail an assessment of the program's impact on both parents and children. The possibility that a program may have a negative influence also should be borne in mind. For example, a parent may only partially learn some infant-rearing principles and then misapply them. Perhaps a more serious possibility is that a program may serve to make parents feel inadequate or guilty about what they have failed to provide for their infants. If, as we argue, parental self-confidence is so important, we must be careful to build up rather than undermine parents' feelings about the quality of parenting they are providing for their children.

Finally, program evaluators must be cautioned not to repeat the mistakes of others. For example, standardized tests are sometimes used because they are readily available, even though they are not appropriate indicators of treatment. Evaluators should be prepared to design their own outcome measures, tailored to the goals of their own program, As Lewis[86] observed, IQ tests are not used to evaluate the progress of school children in geography courses, Similarly, tests of infant behavior are not appropriate to evaluate the quality of parent–infant relationships.

In sum, objective evaluations of program effectiveness are needed. The fact that most programs have been offered as a service, rather than with the intention of conducting research on parent education, may explain our current lack of knowledge of program effectiveness, but will not serve as an excuse for the future. As funds become increasingly tight, program evaluation will become a necessity rather than an academic frill.

Our review of programs and research dealing with parent education in the perinatal period convinces us that this is a burgeoning enterprise. Because the questions still outnumber the answers, future efforts need to be designed systematically to address some of these unanswered questions. It is our hope that by integrating the work that has been done and pointing out some of the gaps in our knowledge, this chapter will provide an impetus toward further program development and evaluation. There is no doubt that parent education can be effective and that parents need and want education for childbirth and parenting. The only question is how best to provide it.

REFERENCES

1. Horowitz FD: Directions for parenting. Paper presented at the Banff International Conference on Behavior Modification. Banff, Canada, Spring, 1976
2. Williams JK: Learning needs of new parents. Am J Nurs 77: 1173, 1977
3. Sumner G, Fritsch J: Postnatal parental concerns: The first six weeks of life. JOGN Nurs 6: 27–32, 1977
4. Linde DB, Engelhardt, KF: What do parents know about infant development? Ped Nurs 5: 32–36, 1979
5. Snyder C, Eyres SJ, Barnard K: New findings about mothers' antenatal expectations and their relationship to infant development. Mat Child Nurs 4: 354–357, 1979
6. Bayley N: Bayley scales of infant development: Birth to two years. New York, Psychological Corp, 1969
7. Enkin MW, Smith SL, Dermer SW, et al.: An adequately controlled study of the effectiveness of PPM training, (abstract) in Morris N (Ed): Psychosomatic Medicine in Obstetrics and Gynaecology. Basel, S. Karger, 1972, pp 62–67
8. Halstead J, Fredrickson T: Evaluation of a prepared childbirth program. JOGN Nurs 7: 39–42, 1978
9. Shapiro HI, Schmitt LG: Evaluation of the psychoprophylactic method of childbirth in the primigravida. Connecticut Med 37: 341–343, 1973
10. Scott JR, Rose N: Effect of psychoprophylaxis on labor and delivery in primiparas. N Engl J Med 22: 1205–1207, 1976
11. Stark AJ: Styles of health care offered to pregnant women and mother-child health outcomes. PhD thesis, University of North Carolina, Chapel Hill, 1976
12. Huttel FA, Mitchell I, Fischer WM, et al.: A quantitative evaluation of psychoprophylaxis in childbirth. J Psychosoma Res 16: 81–92, 1972
13. Doering S, Entwisle D: Preparation during pregnancy and ability to cope with labor and delivery. Am J Orthopsychiat 45: 825–837, 1975
14. Thorardson L, Costanzo GA: An evaluation of the effectiveness of an educational program for expectant parents. Cana J Pub Health 67: 117–121, 1976
15. Warnyca J, Ross S, Bradley C: Healthiest babies possible: The Vancouver Perinatal Health Project. Can Nurs 75: 18–21, 1979
16. Kruse DC: Anticipatory guidance in fourth trimester adjustment. Master's thesis, School of Nursing, Arizona State University, 1976
17. Smith D, Smith HL: Toward improvements in parenting. A description of prenatal and postpartum classes with teaching guide. JOGN Nurs 7: 22–27, 1978
18. Epstein AS: Pregnant teenagers' knowledge of infant development. Paper presented at the meeting of the Society for Research in Child Development, San Francisco, March 1979
19. MacLachlan EA, Cole EP: Learning about children and family life: The Salvation Army Education for Parenthood Program. Children Today 7: 7–11, 1978
20. Candy MM: Birth of a comprehensive family centered maternity program. JOGN Nurs 8: 80–84, 1979

21. Ratsoy B: Personal communication, 1979

22. Jordan DA: Evaluation of a family centered maternity care hospital program. JOGN Nurs 2(1): 13–35; 2(2): 15–27; 2(3) 15–23, 1973

23. Greenberg M, Rosenberg I, Lind J: First mothers rooming-in with their newborns: Its impact on the mother. Am J Orthopsychiat 43: 783–788, 1973

24. Schroeder MA: Is the immediate postpartum period crucial to the mother–child relationship? A pilot study comparing primiparas with rooming-in and those in a maternity ward. JOGN Nurs 6: 37–40, 1977

25. Vietze PM, O'Connor S, Falsey S, et al.: Effects of rooming-in on maternal behavior directed towards infants. Paper presented at the meeting of the American Psychological Association, Toronto, August 1978

26. O'Connor S, Altemeier W, Sherrod K, et al.: How does rooming-in enhance the mother–infant bond? Paper presented at the meeting of the Society for Research in Child Development, San Francisco, March 1979

27. Broussard ER: Evaluation of televised anticipatory guidance to primiparae. Commun Ment Health J 12: 203–210, 1976

28. Idea Forum: Untitled article. Hospitals (J Am Hosp Assoc) 52: 16–17, 1978

29. Broussard ER, Hartner MSS: Further consideration regarding maternal perceptions of the first born, in Hellmuth J (Ed): Exceptional Infant: vol. 2, Studies in Abnormalities. New York, Brunner/Mazel, pp 432–444

30. Miller C: Working with parents of high risk infants. Am J Nurs 78: 1228–1230, 1978

31. Meier PP: A crisis group for parents of high-risk infants. Mat Child Nurs 7: 1978

32. Slade CI, Reide CJ, Mangurter HH: Working with parents of high risk newborns. JOGN Nurs 6: 21–26, 1977

33. Whaley P, Gosling C, Schrener R: Relieving parental anxiety: A booklet for parents of an infant in NICU. JOGN Nurs 8: 49–55, 1979

34. Minde K, Shosenberg N, Marton P, et al.: Self-help groups in a premature nursery. Paper presented at the meeting of the American Orthopsychiatric Association, San Francisco, 1978

35. Bergman A, Probstfield JL, Wedgewood RJ: Performance analysis in pediatric practice. J Med Educ 42: 249, 1967

36. Foye H, Chamberlin R, Charney E: Content and emphasis of well child visits. Am J Dis Child 131: 794, 1977

37. Casey P, Sharp M, Loda F: Child health supervision for children under 2 years of age: A review of its content and effectiveness. J. Pediatr 95: 1–9, 1979

38. Cronin CM: Cluster well-baby clinic. Pediatr Nurs 5: 56–57, 1979

39. Hancock K. A new direction for postnatal infant care. Pediatr Nur 5: 49–51, 1979

40. Stein MT: The providing of well-baby care within parent–infant groups. Clin Pediatr 16: 825–828, 1977

41. Casey P, Whitt JK: Effect of pediatric well-child care on the mother–infant relationship and infant cognitive development. Paper presented at the meeting of the Society for Research in Child Development, San Francisco, March 1979

42. Chamberlin RW, Szumowski EK: Effects of educating mothers about child development in physicians' offices on mother and child functioning over time. Paper presented at the meeting of the Society for Research in Child Development, San Francisco, March 1979

43. Gutelius MF, Kirsch AD, MacDonald S, et al.: Promising results from a cognitive stimulation program in infancy. A preliminary report. Clin Pediatr 11: 585–593, 1972

44. Gutelius MF, Kirsch AD, MacDonald S, et al.: Controlled study of child health supervision: Behavioral results. Pediatrics 60: 294–304, 1977

45. Provence S, Naylor A, Patterson J: The Challenge of Day Care. New Haven, Yale University Press, 1977
46. Gordon I, Guinagh B, Jester RE: The Florida Parent Education Infant and Toddler Programs, in Day MC, Parker RK (Eds): The Preschool in Action (2nd ed). Boston, Allyn & Bacon, 1977
47. Trickett PK: The Yale Child Welfare Research Program. An independent follow-up five years later. Paper presented at the meeting of The Society for Research in Child Development, San Francisco, March 1979
48. Scarr-Salapatek S, Williams ML: The effects of early stimulation on low birth weight infants. Child Dev 44: 94–101, 1973
49. Brazelton TB: Neonatal Behavioral Assessment Scale. London, William Heinemann Medical Books, 1973
50. Williams TM: Infant Care: Abstracts of the Literature (2nd ed). Washington, Child Welfare League of America, 1974
51. Schaefer ES, Aaronson M: Infant education research project: Implementation and implications of a home tutoring program, in Day MC, Parker RK (Eds): The Preschool in Action (2nd ed). Boston, Allyn & Bacon, 1977
52. Davidson S: An experiment in teaching parenting skills, in Williams TM (Ch): The development of maternal attachment: A longitudinal study. Symposium presented at the meeting of the Society for Research in Child Development, San Francisco, March 1979
53. Edelstein JM: The effect of nursing intervention with the Brazelton Neonatal Behavioral Assessment Scale on postpartum adjustment and maternal perception of the infant. Masters thesis, School of Nursing, Yale University, 1975
54. Kang RR: The relationship between informing both parents of their infant's behavioral response patterns and the mother's perception of the infant. Master's thesis, School of Nursing, University of Washington, 1974
55. Ryan LJ: Maternal perception of neonatal behavior. Master's thesis, School of Nursing, University of Washington, 1973
56. Schaefer ES, Manheimer H: Dimensions of perinatal adjustment. Paper presented at the meeting of the Eastern Psychological Association, New York, 1960
57. Ainsworth MDS: Systems for rating maternal care behaviors. In Boyer EG, Simon A, Karafin G, Karafin R (Eds): Measures of Maturation: An Anthology of Early Childhood Observation Instruments (vol. 1). Philadelphia, Research for Better Schools, Inc. 1973, pp 73–172
58. Williams TM, Painter SL, Davidson S, et al.: The development of maternal attachment: A longitudinal study. Symposium presented at the meeting of the Society for Research in Child Development, San Francisco, March 1979
59. Schaefer ES: Infancy intervention, attachment, and school adaptation. Research grant application funded by U.S. Dept. HEW, being conducted in School of Public Health, University of North Carolina, 1979
60. Charnley L, Myre G: Parent–infant education. Children Today 6: 18–21, 1977
61. DeSocio CA, Hollen P: What is a peds program? Pediatr Nurs 4: 16–19, 1978
62. Johnston M, Kayne M, Mittleider K: Putting more PEP in parenting. Am J Nurs 77: 994–995, 1977
63. Levenson P, Hale J, Hollier M, et al.: Serving teenage mothers and their high risk infants. Children Today 7: 11–15, 1978
64. McAbee R: Rural parenting classes: Beginning to meet the need. Mat Child Nurs 2: 315–319, 1977
65. Stranik MK, Hogberg BL: Transition into parenthood. Am J Nurs 79: 90–93, 1979
66. Zinner E, Hertzman R: PACE, a model for parent–infant support groups during the first months of life. Clin Pediatr 17: 396–400, 1978

67. Cronenwett IR: Transition to parenthood, in McCall LK, Galeener JT (Eds): Current Practice in Obstetric and Gynecological Nursing. St. Louis, C.V. Mosby Co., 1976

68. Garrand S, Sherman N, Rentchler D, et al.: A parent-to-parent program. Fam Commun Health 1: 103–113, 1978

69. Miller DL, Baird SF: Helping parents to be parents—a special center. Mat Child Nurs 3: 117–120, 1978

70. Williams TM, Painter SL, Davidson S, et al.: Feasibility study for a prospective investigation of parent–infant bonding. Vancouver, Final report to Health & Welfare, Canada, 1979

71. Donaldson NE: Fourth trimester follow-up. Am J Nurs 77: 1176–1178, 1977

72. Haight J: Steadying parents as they go—by phone. Mat Child Nurs 2: 311–312, 1977

73. Rhode MA, Groenges J: Nurse initiated telephone follow-up of postpartum women. Unpublished paper, University of Utah, School of Nursing, 1976

74. Bronfenbrenner U: A Report on Longitudinal Evaluations of Preschool Programs (vol. 2). Is early intervention effective? Washington, DHEW Publication No. (OHD) 74-25, 1974

75. Chilman CS: Programs for disadvantaged parents: Some major trends and related research, in Caldwell BM, Ricciuti HN (Eds): Review of Child Development Research, (vol. 3), Chicago, University of Chicago Press, 1973

76. Day MC, Parker (Eds): The Preschool in Action (2nd ed). Boston, Allyn & Bacon, 1977

77. Horowtiz FD, Paden LY: The effectiveness of environmental intervention programs, in Caldwell BM, Ricciuti HN (Eds). Review of Child Development Research (vol. 3). Chicago, University of Chicago Press, 1973

78. Ryan S: A Report on Longitudinal Evaluations of Preschool Programs (vol. 1). Longitudinal evaluations. Washington, DHEW Publication No. (OHD) 74-24, 1974

79. Williams TM: Infant Care: Abstracts of the Literature (1st ed). Washington, Child Welfare League of America, 1972

80. Williams TM: Infant development and supplemental care: A comparative review of basic and applied research. Hum Dev 20: 1–30, 1977

81. Zigler E, Trickett PK: IQ, social competence and evaluation of early childhood intervention programs. Am Psychol 33: 789–798, 1978

82. Dickie JR, Carnahan S: Training in social competence: The effect on mothers, fathers and infants. Paper presented at the meeting of the Society for Research in Child Development, San Francisco, March 1979

83. Williams TM: Continuities and discontinuities related to the development of maternal attachment, in Williams TM (ch): The development of maternal attachment: A longitudinal study. Symposium presented at the meeting of the Society for Research in Child Development, San Francisco, March 1979

84. Painter SL: Adaptation to parenthood during the toddler period. Doctoral dissertation in progress, Department of Psychology, University of British Columbia, Vancouver, Canada

85. Painter SL: The measurement of maternal attachment: Attachment versus attachment behavior, in Williams TM (Ch). The development of maternal attachment: A longitudinal study. Symposium presented at the meeting of the Society for Research in Child Development, San Francisco, March 1979

86. Lewis M: Infant intelligence tests: Their use and misuse. Hum Dev 16: 108–118, 1973

Jerome H. Wolfson and Lee W. Bass

11

How the Pediatrician Can Foster Optimal Parent-Infant Relationships

Other chapters in this volume have dealt with the issues of maladaptive responses to pregnancy, acceptance of pregnancy, affiliation with the fetus, and eventual bonding to the baby. It is our intent in this chapter to outline how we, as practicing pediatricians, deal with these issues and work to foster optimal parent–infant relationships.[1]

Parent–infant relationships represent the focal point of childrearing practice, and the pediatrician is in an exquisitely sensitive position to use his medical expertise to have a major effect in preventive pediatrics. The pediatrician's role in monitoring physical health care is clearly defined. He provides immunizations, follows growth and development, advises about various milestones, and provides care for sick children. This is a clear delineation of his duties and of the work he must do to maintain his patients in good health. Today, however, the breadth and scope of pediatric care is much greater. Physical care is only one part of his work. In order to be truly effective as a pediatrician and as an expert in child health needs, he must involve himself in behavioral pediatrics as well. He must be part of the psychosocial growth and development of his patients from the very beginning. The measure of a successful childhood is growing up physically and emotionally, becoming ready to go into the world, and achieving independence and self-fulfillment whether it be at college, in a job, or in marriage. The degree to which children will achieve their potential and realize their uniqueness will be related to the childrearing methods practiced by their parents. These in turn can be

239

influenced, to a great extent, by the pediatrician, who is one of the earliest and most attended advisors.

Pediatric training over the years, unfortunately, has not prepared the young pediatrician to deal adequately with the psychosocial aspects of practice. He has no idea in his hospital world of the magnitude of the problem. On the basis of a survey of seven pediatric practices in Pittsburgh (by L. W. B.), as many as 40 percent of the patients will come with problems of this nature in the routine, everyday practice of pediatrics.

To prevent or solve such problems, the pediatrician must obtain necessary information about the infant and his family. He must be aware of the potential problems therein, and he must formulate a role for himself in fostering optimal parent–infant relationships.[2]

The pediatrician must perceive himself as an important figure in the childrearing constellation, and as such he must know a great deal about the family and all about the child. In order to learn about the family he is working with, he must take the time to ask: What has happened to them? How do they react to what has happened? What would they like to accomplish with their family? He thus creates an atmosphere in which he says to the parents that he is interested in them and their child. He wants to know how they respond to each other and how they handle events. By knowing what goes into each person's individuality and uniqueness he can use his experience and knowledge to help resolve situations more appropriately for this family. This approach to pediatrics not only serves to inform the pediatrician but also benefits the parents because it establishes a partnership between the two. Both parents and pediatrician are working in a strengthened way for the child's enhancement.

The single most important tool in achieving this partnership is an adequate history focused on the child and recognizing the contributions each family member makes. It is most important to start the doctor–patient relationship on the right foot. The pediatrician spells out, in his original contract with the family, his intention to spend enough time to establish an exchange of information and a rapport that will be the basis for their ongoing relationship. Because it is important to start as early as possible in the beginning of family life, we prefer to have a prenatal visit[3] with both parents, if possible. The next contact with the family is the daily visit to the hospital after the baby is born. Barring complications, the final contact in this initial information-gathering process comes when the infant is one month of age. Both parents are urged to bring the baby into the office for the first post-hospital visit, which is scheduled for one hour.

THE PRENATAL VISIT

We feel that the prenatal visit is the most helpful for several reasons. The relationship between the pregnant woman and her obstetrician is usually an extremely good one; at the end of gestation, this relationship is suddenly dropped and she is left at the start of a very complex and long-term task with a new physician whom she has not met. A prenatal visit helps bridge this gap in care. The visit should come sometime during the last trimester, and preferably should be with both mother and father. At the time of this visit, "front-sheet" information is obtained that includes the mother's and father's age, length of marriage, religion, place of birth, duration of time lived in Pittsburgh, location of home, number of bedrooms, where the baby is to sleep, employment of both parents, and, if the mother is employed, whether or not she will return to work after the baby is born. A history of previous pregnancies is also obtained.

The history of the present pregnancy follows. Was it planned and, if so, why at this time? If unplanned, how has it been accepted and how have the parents felt about it? Has there been vomiting, spotting, bleeding? When was the time of first movement and quickening? How much weight was gained? In general, how has the pregnancy gone during the last trimester? We ask the mother about concerns she may have about herself, her baby, or what is going to happen. Does she picture herself with the baby? Is she concerned with clothes and furniture? Has she thought about the baby's sex and has she picked a name? Does she call the baby anything now? Has there been any adverse experience in previous pregnancies or in previous childrearing practices? Is the mother concerned about things she has heard about other mothers with adverse experiences? How helpful is the father? If she is living in the town of her parents and her in-laws, are they helpful? Has she had any previous experience in caring for children? Does she have health problems that may be aggravated by the pregnancy? Will she breast- or bottle-feed? We then give the mother an instruction sheet containing information about her newborn. If the father is present, he is asked how the pregnancy has been for him. How much is he involved in preparing for the baby? We urge the father to participate as fully as possible in all aspects of the pregnancy, including labor and delivery. We recommend rooming-in for our first-time parents so that both parents can be more comfortable handling the baby by the time they are ready to go home.

At the conclusion of the prenatal visit the mother and father are both given an opportunity to ask questions. It is important to pay close attention to what we call OTD (out the door) comments; this is often the time that highly charged emotional concerns will be revealed that may not come out in the ordinary history-taking process. The parents are told that at the time of the first visit, when the baby is about one month old, further history taking will be done and one hour will be spent at that time. Fees are also discussed.

HOSPITAL VISITS

The next interaction occurs at the mother's bedside following delivery. We see the mother within the first 24 hours after delivery and then daily. At the time of the first visit, we examine the baby at the mother's bedside, if appropriate, sharing findings step by step. The history of labor and delivery is elicited, and the concerns about early infant care are discussed. We explore, with the mother, the concepts of bonding. When we give discharge instructions, we *sit down* and allow enough time to talk with her about what to expect from her new baby. It is also important for her to know that we care about what will happen when they get home. We emphasize our availability for consultation and stress appropriate utilization of the telephone. The mother is given instructions and again told about the first office visit, at which time we will take a complete history of the baby and discuss the parents' own backgrounds and their new childrearing role. We discuss the importance of this first visit in allowing us to understand the baby and the parents. We allot one hour for this procedure and charge appropriately.

FIRST OFFICE VISIT

The first office visit, when the child is about one month old, should include the father as well as the mother. We like to include the father at these first visits because we feel that he is an important person in his family's life and his input is valued. It is also more helpful to get his family history directly from him. At the beginning of the hour we repeat the explanation of the purpose of the history-taking.

The interview is well disciplined and flows in a specific fasion. Although disciplined, it must be conducted with empathy and understanding. Questions must be open-ended, and the pediatrician must not inject his own attitude or bias into the history, no matter what he hears. If he does, the parents may begin to tell him what they think he wants to hear, may edit their comments, and may interrupt the free flow of information. The focus of discussion is always on the baby; then any questions such as sexual relationships, religious matters, and in-law relationships are more easily answered by the parents.

If this is the very first contact, with no previous prenatal visit or hospital care, we start with the front-sheet information. If there has been a prior prenatal visit, we continue with the history of the hospital stay and of the present period. We ask about the end of the pregnancy? How was labor? How did they know when to go to the hospital? What was it like? We try to keep questions simple and open-ended because we never know what kind of answers we will get. If our questions allow it, whatever comes to mind will pop out, sometimes surprising even the parents. What did you think when you saw the baby? Did you want a boy or girl? What was the hospital like for you and your baby? How was your care in the hospital? How was the obstetric care and then the pediatric care? This may bring out areas of concern regarding this important subject. By this time the parents usually understand the intent of the interview, focused on the child, and the questions and answers are not uncomfortable for us or for the parents, even though their answers have at times been critical. Invariably the parents are glad to have their say. If there were problems in the delivery room or the baby had to stay in the premie nursery, feelings about this are discussed in detail. Whenever questions about feelings come up, the parents are asked individually and encouraged to speak for themselves. It may be very revealing when one or the other dominates the hour and seems to speak for both.

Then we talk about going home. What was it like? How long did it take for things to settle down? Did they have any help? Which grandparents were involved, and were they helpful? How did they get along with each other? It is amazing how many new parents have difficulty relating to their own parents and how many grandparents love their grandchildren but have difficulty thinking their own children are adequate to the job of parenting. This may cause conflict within families and result in maladaptive parenting. At this point, before discussing the baby's present day routine, we obtain the history of each parent.

First we talk with the mother and ask her to comment briefly on what growing up was like and to discuss the ages, health, and occupation of all family members. How did she feel about the way her parents raised their children? Did they share responsibility for the children? Did they have a good marriage? To whom was she closer as she grew up? Did her mother prepare her for adolescence and puberty?

What was her schooling background? What did she do after high school, and was it her choice? Did she go away to school, and how was her adjustment to leaving home? (This is a good measure of whether or not her parents made her independent by age 18.) We ask her about memorable events of her childhood and particularly about any family experience with death and how she handled it. This may reveal grief that has not yet been worked through, even though years may have passed since the death of a sibling or a parent. It is important to be aware of this because these kinds of hidden feelings may influence parent's attitudes toward their children. We talk about her relationships with men leading up to her courtship and marriage. A similar discussion is held with the father if he is present; if not, we obtain as much information as we can from the mother.

We then talk about their adjustment to marriage and how their marriage is now. How much is the father involved in the active care of the child? How content are they with their living situation, their job situation, housing, and relationships with grandparents and extended family? We are also concerned with things they are interested in, outside activities or hobbies.

We then ask about the child. We ask them to describe a typical 24-hour period. This includes information about eating, sleeping, bowel movements, and adaptation to receiving the bath and the vitamins. We are also interested in the parents feelings about the baby. We defer answering their questions until after the baby is examined. (Information about the baby's typical day is discussed at each subsequent visit, and with this discussion we get an understanding of the uniqueness of the baby.)

At this time in the initial history-taking and at subsequent follow-up visits, we introduce the important concept of primary reactive patterns as described by Thomas et al.[4] and recently elaborated by Carey.[5] Descriptions of the actions of the baby, rather than the parent's interpretations are sought. This helps the parents understand the personality characteristics of their child and why he behaves as he does. At the same time we try to recognize why parents behave as they do, and we discuss the melding of the two. Difficult behaviors therefore must be accepted and dealt with for what they are. The parents are relieved to know that they are not the cause of some difficult behavior. Once this guilt is relieved, they may find themselves much better able to cope with their children, able to tolerate and even influence the very same difficult behaviors.

Finally, we sum up with goal-oriented questions. How many children do you plan to have? What stands out most in your mind over the past year? (Most will look at their child and smile, but some will give very unexpected answers, such as "my new job" or "I hated my body.") The last questions are: What are your goals for your baby? Do you think your parents did a good job in raising you? Will you improve on what your parents did? These last questions often bring up a wealth of new feelings and information. The main value for the parents, however, is to bring out into the open feelings that they have but not previously thought about in just this way. This is a very important part of the interview.

At this point we talk with the parents about *our goals* for the child's growing up, which are health maintenance, fostering independence in the child, and teaching the child how to get along with other people. In the neonatal period sleep is an activity that is easily tied into these goals and is one of the first developmental stages discussed. We recommend that the child sleep in his own room from the very first night home if possible. Being in his own room is an early step in independence, recognizing both his and his parent's need for privacy. Also, being away from traffic areas helps him sleep through the night, which is in a sense an expression of his ability to fit into family routine and get along with others.

The child is examined and his individuality, even at this early age, is discussed, and the importance of recognizing this is stressed. The baby is seen frequently during the first year; during these visits the questions about eating, sleeping, and bowel movements are discussed, but there are always questions as to what is going on in the household, how the child is acting, and how the parents are reacting.

CONCLUSION

We believe the history-taking process as described carries great benefit for all involved in the childrearing constellation—the pediatrician, the parents, and the child. When we have this information, we become much more aware of what is going on within the family unit. In a brief period we get a glimpse into the family dynamics and are in a good position to anticipate problems and understand to a fair extent how the family's coping mechanism operates. The parents, on the other hand, have been taken through a review of familiar material that has been reorganized in a way that they may not have thought of before. Now, in the context of their own child, they too have become to some degree more aware of the significance of their own experience, background, and feelings. Finally, the child is better understood by both the pediatrician and the parents.

Our approach to practice encourages our parents to become more knowledgeable about the psychosocial implications of their own actions and reactions. The advantages of this process are intangible and difficult to measure, but they are there nevertheless. As a result of the process, parents tend to interact differently with their children. They recognize the individuality and worth of each family member, including themselves. They tend to be better parents, more self-assured, and less demanding. Working with families in this way seems to generate more satisfying relationships for parents, children, and physician. For these reasons, we feel that the ultimate outcome of childrearing is more likely to be successful.

REFERENCES

1. Bass LW, Wolfson JH: The Style and Management of a Pediatric Practice, Pittsburgh, University of Pittsburgh, 1977
2. Rose JA: On the initial contact interview in pediatric practice. Prepared for the Joint Seminar on Postgraduate Education in Pediatrics, University of Pittsburgh and University of Pennsylvania, November 1962
3. Wessel MA: The prenatal pediatric visit. Pediatrics 32:926–930, 1963
4. Thomas A, Birch HG, Chess S, et al.: Behavioral Individuality in Early Childhood. New York, New York University, 1963
5. Carey WB: A simplified method for measuring infant temperament. J Pediatr 77:184–194, 1970

PART III

Relationships at Risk: Approaches to Intervention

Elsie R. Broussard

12

Assessment of the Adaptive Potential of the Mother–Infant System: The Neonatal Perception Inventories

The longitudinal studies of Pittsburgh firstborns begun in 1963 are epidemiologic studies that focus on the silent majority of newborns—those healthy, full-term infants born without physical defect who traditionally have not been considered at high risk for psychosocial disorder. This chapter summarizes selected aspects of these studies and the implications of the findings for clinical practice.

BACKGROUND

Within my private practice of pediatrics and later as an Assistant County Health Officer, I was often puzzled when observing the functioning of mothers in regard to their newborns. My clinical work suggested that the mother's perception of her newborn often was determined by factors coming from within herself rather than the

Supported by the Benedum Foundation, Buhl Foundation, Amelia Miles Foundation, Pittsburgh Foundation, Staunton Farm Foundation, through private donations, and by NIH General Research Support Grant FR 5451.

actual physical condition of the infant. Her perception did *not* seem related to race or economic status, although these variables may impact on the child's later development.

Some mothers made a smooth transition from pregnancy to motherhood and had pride and pleasure in raising their infants, and the infants thrived. Others lacked pride in their infants and had little pleasure in motherhood, although we the physicians had judged the infants' biologic endowments to be normal and saw them as appealing. Physician and mother looked at the same infant and saw different things, as though the beauty lay in the eye of the beholder.

With the cooperation and assistance of many, the Pittsburgh firstborn studies evolved as I attempted to answer my "puzzlement" about maternal perception: How do mothers perceive their babies? What influences their perception? Is their perception related to the infant's subsequent development? If so, can it be modified?

Instrument of Measure

As a first step, in 1963, I developed the Neonatal Perception Inventories (NPI) to measure maternal perception of the neonate as compared to her concept of the average infant and provide a measure of the adaptive potential of the mother–infant unit during the first month of life.

There are two distinct inventories, (1) the Neonatal Perception Inventory I, administered during the immediate postpartum hospital stay (days 1–4), and (2) the Neonatal Perception Inventory II, administered approximately 1 month postpartum (4–6 wk). Each inventory consists of two forms designed to be used together: the "Average Baby" and "Your Baby" forms. Each of the forms consists of six single-item scales. The behavioral items included in these Inventories are crying, spitting, feeding, elimination, sleeping, and predictability.[1] These items were selected on the basis of clinical experience with the concerns young mothers expressed about their babies. These are crucial areas in the neonatal period that reflect the state of functioning of the mother–infant unit.

The NPI may be viewed as a projective measure. The mother is presented with a set of ambiguous stimuli—the Average Baby and Your Baby—upon which she projects her concept of what most little babies are like and her expectation of what her newborn will be like. Understandably these vary from mother to mother and are influenced by her past, as well as her current life experiences.

The NPI score is obtained by determining the discrepancy between the mother's ratings of her own infant and the average baby. If a mother rates her baby as better than average, her perception is considered to be positive. If she does not rate her baby as better than average, her perception is considered to be negative. Thus at either time I or time II the infants can be categorized as having mothers with positive or negative perceptions of them.

The next step in developing the NPI was to determine if it would discriminate among mothers in regard to the perception of their neonates. Inventories were administered to 318 mothers delivering healthy, full-term, firstborn infants in five local hospitals during a specified two-and-a-half month period. All socioeconomic and racial groups were included. Selecting physically healthy neonates weighing 2500 g (5.5 lb) or more was an attempt to insure that infants were within the range of normal endowment, biologically equipped to elicit response from the mother, and not handicapped in their ability to respond to her care.

These inventories were completed by the primiparae on the first or second postpartum day (time I), while they were still in the hospital. Of these mothers, 46.5 percent rated their infants as better than average. At the end of the neonatal period, home visits were made by trained interviewers. The average age of the infants at the time of this interview (time II) was 32.3 days (median 29.9, SD 2.59). The mothers completed the Degree of Bother Inventory and the Neonatal Perception Inventory II. At this time 61.2 percent of the women rated their infants as better than average. Thus we were able to compare NPI data collected at two different times.

One hypothesis was that mothers who originally rated their babies as not being better than average at time I would experience a dissonance between their expectations of the average baby and perception of their babies immediately after delivery. One could further expect that these mothers would attempt to reduce the dissonance.[2] Those who were successful in doing so were expected to have low problem scores at time II. On the other hand, if mothers were unable to reduce the dissonance or if they experienced an increase in dissonance, the problem score would be expected to be high.

Since the threshold of parental annoyance varies widely in accordance with a parent's emotional orientation to the child, the ultimate decision as to what constitutes a problem for a specific mother varies among mothers. In order to measure problems in infant behavior, a Degree of Bother Inventory (DBI) was designed to assess the degree to which mothers were bothered by their infants' behavior in regard to the same six behavioral items; it was administered when the infants were one month old.

Relation of Maternal Perception of the Neonate to Problems in Infant Behavior at One Month of Age

The maternal perception of her infant at time I was not correlated with problems in infant behavior at one month of age, but the perception of her infant at time II was correlated with the problems in infant behavior at one month of age. Those mothers who rated their infants as better than average were less bothered by their infants' behavior than those mothers who did not view their infants as better than average (χ^2 significant at $p < 0.001$).

Stimulus for Further Research

The findings (1) that changes occur in the maternal perception of the firstborn during the first month of life, (2) that 40 percent of the mothers did not view their one-month-old infants positively, and (3) that the DBI was correlated with maternal perception at time II but not at time I, suggested that the maternal perception of her infant at time II could serve as a predictive instrument to identify a group of primiparae whose infants would be at high risk for subsequent emotional disorder.

Infants were categorized as high risk if their mothers did not perceive their behavior as better than average at time II. Infants whose mothers had rated their behavior as better than average at time II were identified as low risk.

Relationship of Maternal Perception of the Neonate to Later Development

Follow-up studies were designed to test the hypothesis that maternal perception of the neonate would be related to the child's subsequent psychosocial development. These findings have been reported elsewhere and are summarized briefly.[3-5]

Except for racial distribution due to the loss of the 20 black subjects in the original population, the demographic data for the original population were comparable with the data for the subpopulation evaluated at 4.5 and 10–11 years. The proportion of children rated as high risk was almost identical in the original and follow-up groups (39 percent versus 40 percent). There was no statistically significant difference between the groups with regard to other descriptive data (e.g., health of mother, type of delivery). With respect to these data, the children evaluated at 4.5 and 10–11 years were judged representative of the original 318 subjects.

Findings at 4.5 Years

At age 4.5 years 120 children from the original 1963 population were evaluated by two child psychiatrists who had no knowledge of the NPI ratings. More infants classified as high risk at one month of age were diagnosed as having emotional disorder than those who were at low risk ($\chi^2 = 16.43, p \leq 0.001$).

Outcome at 10–11 Years

In order to determine to what extent the mother's perception of her infant continued to be predictive of the child's emotional development up to the preadolescent phase, 104 of the firstborns were evaluated when they ranged in age from 10 years 3 months to 11 years 9 months.

The children were evaluated by one of three psychiatrists who had no knowledge of the NPI risk rating or of the previous evaluation conducted at age 4.5 years. After completing the clinical evaluation, the psychiatrists rated each child according to a four-point Probability of Mental Disorder Scale adapted from the Stirling County Study.[6] The categories were (A) high confidence mental disorder, (B) probable but less certain, (C) doubtful but suspicious, and (D) high confidence no disorder. There was a statistically significant association ($\chi^2 = 4.09, p < 0.05$) between the predictive risk rating at one month of age and the child's emotional development at age 10–11 years, indicating that the mother's perception of her one-month old firstborn continued to be associated with psychosocial disorder.

There was no statistically significant association between the NPI rating on the first or second day of life (time I) and the psychiatric assessment of the child at either 4.5 or 10–11 years.

It is also possible to combine time I and time II ratings to form four groups; positive-positive, negative-positive, positive-negative, and negative-negative. It is to be noted that some mothers maintain a consistent view of their infants at each time; for others the maternal perception is in a fluid state from time I to time II, with shifts occurring in either direction. When the combined ratings of the mother's perception at both time points were used, a more discriminating predictor of the child's subsequent development resulted.

Figure 12-1 shows the joint distribution at age 10–11 years of the psychiatric ratings and the combined maternal perception for males and females spearately and for the total population of 104 children. For the total population there was a stepwise decrease in the percentage of children having no disorder as the negative valence of the maternal perception increased. Among those infants viewed positively by their mothers at both time I and time II, 46.2 percent were considered emotionally healthy at 10–11 years, while only 7.7 percent were considered emotionally healthy among those infants viewed negatively at both times. For statistical analysis, the A, B, and C categories, pooled into one group representing gradations of mental disorder, were compared with the D category, representing no disorder. The combined maternal perception was associated with the psychiatric rating of the child ($\chi^2 = 11.08, p < 0.02$; 3 df).

Comparison Between Sexes at Ages 10–11 Years

Among those children viewed positively at both time I and time II, 40 percent of males and 54.5 percent of females were free of disorder. Among those viewed negatively at both times, the percentage without disorder was identical for males and females, 7.7 percent. Where there was a shift in perception from time I to time II, 38.1 percent females and 9.7 percent males were free of disorder ($\chi^2 = 4.48$, $p < 0.05$). Among males there was a sharp drop in the percentage of those free of disorder with the appearance of a single negative perception at either time, whereas there was a gradual stepwise decrease for females.

Some Implications of the 1963 Study

In this study the critical variable associated with the child's psychosocial development is judged to be the mother's early perception of him. No association was found between the following variables and either the psychiatric rating or the NPI: type of delivery, religious preference, maternal age at delivery, educational level of parents, father's occupation, prenatal or postpartum complications, moves or deaths of significant others during the year prior to pregnancy or after delivery, frequency of hospitalization of the child, illness within the nuclear family, changes in income since delivery.

The data indicate that the association between the maternal perception of the neonate and the subsequent emotional development

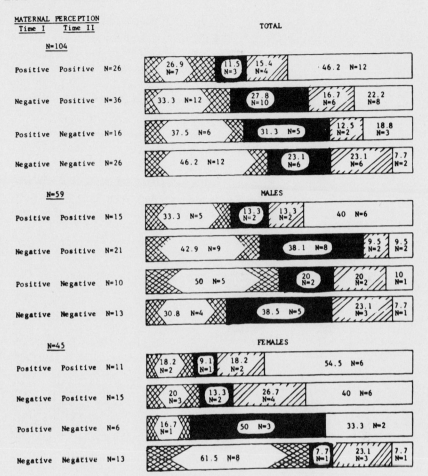

Fig. 12-1. Psychiatric ratings and combined maternal perception at age 10–11 years. ▨, High confidence mental disorder; ■, probable but less certain; ◩, doubtful but suspicious; ☐, high confidence no mental disorder. (Reprinted with permission from Child Psychiatry and Human Development.[7]

of the child persists over time and is predictive of the probability of mental disorder at ages 10–11 years among these firstborns.

The research with the 1963 population did not establish the basis for the mother's perception of her firstborn. Many factors contribute to the functioning of the mother–infant system.

It can be postulated, on the one hand, that certain innate genetic characteristics are detected very early by the mother, and that her rating represents a "true" picture of the child. On the other hand, it can be postulated that her expectations become a self-fulfilling proph-ecy—that is, these influence her handling of her infant, which in turn influences his behavior. The fact that these infants were considered to be "normal" by the physicians providing health care tends to support the latter theory, that maternal perception has an influence on development. In either event, the fact that we can predict a high-risk population as early as one month of age offers a basis for planning programs aimed at primary prevention.

The presence of a positive maternal perception during the first month of life does not guarantee that there will be no difficulties in the child's subsequent development, but the absence of a positive maternal perception of the neonate is associated with a very high rate of subsequent psychosocial disorder.

The NPI does not predict the precise nature of the psychosocial disorder. The complexity of human development makes such predic-tive specificity impossible. The NPI can serve to screen for potential failures in psychosocial adaptation stemming from disorders in the earliest mother–infant relationship, disorders that may exist unde-tected at an early stage. It is essential to view the NPI as a screening measure to predict the adaptive potential of a given mother–infant pair. A screening procedure is the first step. The next step is to conduct a careful clinical assessment of the adaptive potential of a specific mother–infant pair and establish the level of need for inter-vention. The clinician can then decide how to proceed.

The findings of the 1963 study led me to explore the possibility of early intervention as an attempt to minimize the development of psychosocial disorder.

PREVENTIVE INTERVENTION PROGRAM FOR NEONATES AT HIGH RISK

It is important to emphasize that our preventive intervention program was not designed for infants already designated as patients in need of help by the parents or referred by an agency. This unique feature of providing intervention to infants not designated as patients has influenced much of our method of procedure.

First, we recognized that the NPI was a screening instrument and as such was but the first step—a way to select a population of infants for more careful assessment—to see if indeed further intervention was warranted.

It is not feasible to tell parents of a healthy, full-term firstborn that their infant is considered a high risk for subsequent emotional difficulty. This might have the potential for establishing a self-fulfilling prophecy—that is, the mother's already negative perception of her newborn would be compounded by such a prediction. In addition, this would fail to take into account that there are a multiplicity of life variables with impact on development that may modify the effect of the negative maternal perception, such as the presence of other family members, various support systems, or some unique capacity within the infant.

Method of Procedure

In 1973, using the NPI as a screening measure to identify infants at high risk, we began a preventive-intervention program. The 1973 population consisted of 281 healthy, normal, full-term firstborns delivered during a specified two-and-a-half-month period. All were single births.

Based on the NPI at one month of age, 205 infants (73 percent) were categorized into a low-risk group and 76 (27 percent) into a high-risk group. The 76 infants in the high-risk group were randomly divided into an experimental group of 39 to whom intervention was offered and a comparison group of 37 to whom no intervention was offered.

Each mother had been visited at home when the infants were one month old. Following this visit, I telephoned each mother whom we had randomly selected and asked if she wished to participate in the firstborn program being offered for first-time parents. The program was described as an opportunity for parents to talk with other parents and staff about their concerns regarding childrearing.

Of the 39 mothers in the experimental group, 17 elected to participate in the intervention program. Intervention contacts consisted of an initial individual interview with one or both parents, participation in mother–infant group meetings, and home-based intervention. Dr. Cleon Cornes and I served as co-leaders for two groups, each composed of seven or eight mothers and their infants. Groups met every other week for 1–1.5 hours. They began when the infants were 2–4 months of age and continued until they were 3.5 years old. Home visits were made by child development specialists. The details of the intervention program have been reported elsewhere and are beyond the scope of this chapter.[7] During the process of intervention, we actively observed the functioning of the mother–infant pair and intervened with each individual dyad according to our understanding of their developmental needs. This understanding influenced our timing as well as the nature of the interventions. We used basic principles of child development and knowledge of the parenting process to guide our responsiveness to changing parent and infant needs.

Throughout the project, we continually monitored the developmental progress of the infants. In order to measure the impact of the intervention, formal evaluations were conducted when the infants were 1 and 2.5 years old.

Evaluation Findings at Age One Year

At age one year, 67 subjects (26 low risk, 41 high risk) were evaluated during office visits. The high-risk children were distributed in groups as follows: intervention ($n = 11$), intervention refused ($n = 12$), and comparison ($n = 18$).

The sequence of the evaluation procedure was structured as follows: (1) a period of free play for mother and infant, (2) administration of the Bayley test with mother present, (3) observing child's reaction to mother leaving the room with the examiner present, (4) observing mother–child reunion.

The entire evaluation interview was observed via a one-way-vision mirror by a single observer-rater (rater I) who recorded sequential detailed notes during the entire semistructured evaluation. These observations served as the basis for her subsequent rating of each child on single-item graphic scales.

In addition, 14 infants were rated by a second observer-rater. Budgetary restriction and difficulties in scheduling part-time available personnel resulted in the second observations being made by one of three observers. This resulted in five subjects being observed by raters 1 and 2, another five by raters 1 and 3, and another four by raters 1 and 4. None of the observer-raters had any knowledge of the original risk-rating or group membership of the children.

Instrument of Measure

Sixteen single-item graphic scales were designed, each in the form of a perpendicular continuous line, each on a separate page. The top of the scale represented the optimal rating for the specific item. Raters marked each scale with a horizontal line.

Each scale was superimposed over a transilluminated millimeter scale and each item was measured at the point of rater-mark inter-section to the nearest 0.5-mm score. The raters used a wide range (0–130) on the scales. Higher numbers were considered less optimal.

On the basis of my clinical judgment, the 16 items were grouped into clinical clusters for analysis of data. These clinical clusters were (I) appropriate and specific attachment to mother, (II) separation indicators, (III) aggression, (IV) implementation of contacts with the nonhuman environment, and (V) investment in mastery of motor functions. Cluster I contained six items, cluster II, three items; cluster III, two items; cluster IV, three items; and cluster V, two items. Subsequent statistical analysis supported these as valid groupings. The intercorrelations between items within each cluster was high. In addition, factor analysis was performed for each of the clusters having more than two items (clusters I, II, and IV). In each case a single significant factor was identified.

Rater Agreement

To test for mean rater consistency on the five clinical clusters, 15 multifactor ANOVAs with repeated measures were performed (α = 0.05). This resulted from pairing rater 1 with the other three raters for each of the five clusters. With respect to clusters I and II there were no significant rater differences for the three rater pairs. In the other three clusters two of the three pairs were not significantly different on the ratings.

Analysis of Data

A cluster score was calculated for each subject by obtaining the mean of the natural logarithms for the items in each cluster. The natural logarithmic transformation was used because of the observed proportionality between the item means and standard deviations.[8] Using the cluster scores, the data were analyzed using a two-way (group and sex) multivariate analysis of variance. None of the multi-variate tests were significant. The test for group differences yielded an F ratio of 1.24 ($p < 0.25$). The F ratio for sex was 0.22 ($p < 0.95$), and for interaction was 0.87 ($p < 0.60$).

Although the four groups were not significantly different, the low-risk group always had the more optimal scores, whereas the comparison group generally had the least optimal. In order to test for the difference between the low-risk and the high-risk infants, the intervention, intervention refused, and comparison groups were pooled into one combined high-risk group. The cluster index scores for the low-risk and combined high-risk groups were then examined. This yielded a multivariate F of 1.98 significant at $p < 0.09$. The univariate F ratios are given in Table 12-1. Thus we see that for four of the five clusters there was a statistically significant difference, with cluster V approaching significance. The low-risk group cluster scores were more optimal than those of the combined high-risk group.

Even though there was no significant sex difference, the females did have more optimal scores than the males for each of the five clusters.

The Bayley Scale of Mental Development was also administered. A two-factor (group and sex) univariate ANOVA was performed. None of the F ratios were significant. The overall mean scores were as follows: intervention, 110.70; intervention refused, 103.08; comparison, 105.35; low risk, 103.81. The intervention group had the highest Bayley scores, and the intervention refused group the lowest. Females had higher scores than males (107.70 versus 102.04).

Evaluation Findings at Age Two-and-a-half Years

At age two-and-a-half years 68 subjects [25 low risk and 43 high risk (13 intervention, 12 intervention refused, and 18 comparison)] were evaluated. The entire evaluation interview was observed via a one-way-vision mirror and notes recorded by an observer-rater. The interview again consisted of (1) a period of free play for mother-infant, (2) administration of the Bayley tests, (3) observing child's reaction to mother leaving room with examiner present, (4) observing mother–child reunion.

The observer-rater, who had no knowledge of the one-month NPI

Table 12-1
Univariate F Tests for Group Differences on the Five Clinical Clusters at One Year in Preventive-Intervention Program

Variable (Cluster)	Univariate F	p
I	6.1151	<0.0161
II	7.4739	<0.0081
III	5.8999	<0.0180
IV	9.5074	<0.0031
V	3.1992	<0.0784

Table 12-2
Univariate F Tests for Group Differences on the Eight
Clinical Clusters of Evaluation at Age Two-and-a-half
Years

Variable (Cluster)	Univariate F	p
Separation/individuation	5.0569	<0.0035
Confidence	5.0353	<0.0036
Implementation/environment	6.4875	<0.0008
Aggression	6.6374	<0.0007
Affective balance	7.7534	<0.0002
Language/communication	5.8003	<0.0016
Coping	9.0424	<0.0001
Play	8.4291	<0.0001

risk rating or the group membership of the children, rated the children
on 15 single-item graphic scales that were then grouped into eight
clinical clusters: (I) separation-individuation process (Mahler), (II)
confidence, (III) implementation of contacts with the nonhuman environment, (IV) aggression, (V) affective balance, (VI) investment in
use of language for communication, (VII) coping, and (VIII) play.

A two-way multivariate analysis of variance for the four groups
and sex was performed. The logarithmic transformation was not used
for these data because the problem of proportionality between means
and standard deviations was not present. The test for the equality of
group mean vectors yielded an F ratio of 2.84 (p < 0.0001). The
univariate F ratios are given in Table 12-2. As Table 12-2 indicates,
all of the univariate F tests were significant. The individual group
means for each of the clusters are given in Table 12-3. In all cases the
low-risk and intervention groups had the lowest scores (low scores
reflect more optimal functioning). The comparison and the intervention-refused groups had similar scores, with both groups having scores
considerably higher than those of the first two groups.

The test for interaction between group and sex was not significant
(multivariate F ratio = 1.57, p > 0.05). The multivariate F ratio for
sex was 2.47 (p < 0.0235). Although the multivariate test for sex was
significant, none of the univariate F tests were significant. The means
for males and females are shown in Table 12-4. In general, the females
scored better than the males. Only on the play variable did the males
score more optimally than the females.

The Bayley Scale was also administered when the infants were
two-and-a-half years. The two-way ANOVA gave results similar to
those observed at age one year. None of the F ratios were significant.

Table 12-3
Means for Eight Clusters for Each of the Four Groups at Age Two-and-a-half Years

Variable (Cluster)	Low Risk	High Risk		
		Intervention	Intervention Refused	Comparison
Separation/individuation	40.32	50.98	84.60	79.82
Confidence	41.38	50.69	85.96	86.06
Implementation/environment	35.32	43.23	84.79	82.19
Aggression	36.52	44.96	85.79	83.61
Affective balance	35.40	45.50	89.83	90.61
Language/communication	28.52	26.00	64.50	63.39
Coping	36.80	39.31	85.50	90.11
Play	45.40	19.38	84.83	80.33

Table 12-4
Means for Eight Clusters for Males and Females at
Age Two-and-a-half Years

Variable (Cluster)	Males (n = 25)	Females (n = 43)
Separation/individuation	64.63	58.15
Confidence	68.58	59.31
Implementation/environment	60.88	56.17
Aggression	65.50	55.45
Affective balance	62.04	61.25
Language/communication	50.19	39.55
Coping	63.96	57.52
Play	52.50	59.19

Although the groups were not significantly different, the intervention group still had the highest Bayley scores and the intervention-refused group the lowest scores. The difference between these groups increased from 7.62 at age one year to 11.8 at age two-and-a-half. The individual group means were as follows: intervention, 111.63; intervention refused, 99.83; comparison, 104.88; low risk, 106.74. The females still had better scores than the males (107.78 versus 102.30).

Although this preventive work was a pilot project, the findings suggest that early intervention can be of value.

Our work with this Pittsburgh First Born Project has showed that there are clinical signs of the adaptiveness of mother–infant dyads visible in the earliest weeks of life. We learned that the earlier we examine systemic functioning, the earlier we can evaluate the needs of given mother-child pairs and thus begin appropriate early interventions.

The following section discusses some of the clinical signs indicative of the functioning of mother-infant pairs.

Clinical Signs

Clues to the differences between NPI high-risk and low-risk mother-infant pairs are evident during the neonatal period. During interviews one month postpartum mothers of infants at high risk were noted to (1) have poor self-esteem, lack confidence in themselves as mothers, and be dependent on the external world, yet often not able to use help when offered; (2) view their environmental support systems as less helpful than the mothers of low-risk infants (they make many references to the health professionals as being of no help or not to be trusted, and husbands and mothers are often considered to be "not much help"); (3) report having more trouble in caring for their infants in regard to sleeping, feeding, colic, crying, and elimination; and (4) often seem depressed and anxious.

We observed spatially what seemed to be going on psychologically. In mothers of infants at high risk, we saw difficulty in tolerating the closeness required during mothering—i.e., a fear of proximity, holding, spitting, feeding, cleansing, etc.—repeatedly acted out in interaction with their infants.

The clinical pictures presented by mothers of infants at high and low risk are dramatically divergent. Research has shown that while some signs of impairment in the mother–infant relationship are visible during the neonatal period, others may not be evident until later. Differences in functioning shown by mothers of infants at high and low risk may appear in the mother's ability to (1) anticipate or fulfill the child's needs, (2) anticipate threat or danger to the child, (3) establish appropriate limits, (4) engage in mutually satisfying games, and (5) provide a positive verbal mirror.

ANTICIPATE OR FULFILL THE CHILD'S NEEDS

In mothers of high-risk infants this is evidenced by inattentiveness or failure to recognize clear cues from the child, excessive delay or failure to respond, an intolerance of age-appropriate limitations in the child's ability, and difficulties in recognition of the child's needs— e.g., fatigue, hunger, discomfort, or amount of stimulation.

When feeding their neonates, mothers of low-risk infants are often observed to modify their actions according to changes in their babies' states—e.g., during a pause in sucking or the infant's exploration of the surroundings. Conversely, mothers of high-risk infants do not seem to base their actions upon their babies' cues. A mother of a high-risk infant was observed to continue to spoon feed her five-week old infant as she drifted off into sleep. The mother would use the spoon to pry open the sleepy baby's mouth, and when the baby did not swallow, mother would say, "You're getting lazy."

ANTICIPATE THREAT OR DANGER

Mothers of infants at high risk often "lose" their babies from their perceptual field, unaware of impending danger. This is evidenced in mothers of high-risk infants by failure to prevent accidents through sufficient precautions. At a routine checkup a pediatrician asked a mother of a high-risk infant what had caused the large raised bruise on the forehead of her one-year-old son. The mother reported that she had heard the baby fall down the stairs but had not gone to him because he had not cried. Mothers of low-risk infants are generally available to their babies, allowing the infants to explore the environment while vigilantly watching for potential hazards.

ESTABLISH APPROPRIATE LIMITS

Some mothers of high-risk infants fail to recognize the child's potential for inflicting injury to others and have difficulty modulating the child's aggression. One mother of a high-risk infant sat idly by as her eight-month-old repeatedly hit and pinched another infant. The mother of the latter infant, also at high risk, did not intercede or comfort her crying child.

MUTUALLY SATISFYING GAMES

The mother of a high-risk infant may repeatedly interfere with the child's task completion when he is involved in self-initiated activity. She may push the child to perform when he is not interested, fail to maintain contact that she has initiated, or not respond when the child initiates contact. Some of these mothers show an impaired ability to permit the child the normal exploration of the mother's body. One mother repeatedly tickled her little boy's stomach until he began to cry; another began a "game" with her 15-month-old son in which she pulled on a rubber bat that he held clenched between his teeth, suddenly letting go so that the little boy fell backwards, hitting his head on the wall.

POSITIVE VERBAL MIRROR

Mothers of high-risk infants make statements such as "You're so bad," "You're a stinker," "She's a wild woman," "I feel like giving him away," "Can't you leave me alone?" Contrast these with the statements of mothers of low-risk infants: "Who's that pretty girl in the mirror?" (to a four-month-old playing happily on the floor with a mirror rattle) or "You're not ready for me to go? I'll sit here where you can see me."

Infants at high risk present a considerably different clinical picture than those at low risk. Areas of dissimilar functioning include (1) affective expression, (2) ability to engage in explorative play, (3) ability to cope with stress, and (4) body management.

AFFECTIVE EXPRESSION

Some high-risk infants display few signs of pleasure; others may have frozen, fixed smiles, apparently not demonstrating true enjoyment. Infants at low risk exhibit a range of affective responses.

EXPLORATIVE PLAY

Some high-risk infants are immobilized and unable to explore the environment; others do not engage in sustained play with objects but flit from one item to another. Infants at low risk progressively show an interest in the environment and can ultimately engage in prolonged play with objects.

ABILITY TO COPE WITH STRESS

Infants at high risk have a restricted range of coping mechanisms and poor frustration tolerance, and they are often unable to accept comfort when it is offered. Conversely, when under stress low-risk infants cope in a variety of ways—e.g., going to their mothers for comfort, using self-comforting activities such as thumbsucking, or temporarily withdrawing from a stressful situation.

BODY MANAGEMENT

High-risk infants may be stiff and awkward in their movements. They are often unable to manage their bodies and get themselves into precarious positions. They sometimes seem unaware of their body boundaries and walk into objects. These infants show aggression toward themselves. When frustrated by his mother's withdrawal of a toy, a one-year-old boy repeatedly pinched his abdomen.

Infants at low-risk often appear to be more fluid and graceful. They are able to engage in physical activity, yet tend to keep themselves safe from harm, as though they had learned to care for themselves as their mothers had protectively cared for them.

DISCUSSION

The mother–child relationship develops as a cyclic system—each participant having the potential for influence upon the other. At birth the infant evidences the capacity to initiate and regulate his interaction with the environment. The mother provides the immediate environment critical to the child's survival. Her sensitivity to the infant's needs influences her ability to provide an optimal environment in which the infant develops. When a woman becomes a mother she has certain expectations as to what kind of mother she will be and what kind of child she will have. The way the mother relates to the child will be modified by her perception of his appearance and behavior. His behavior will affect and, in turn, be affected by her handling of him.

During the first few weeks of life, the mother and infant are intimately involved in a "getting to know you" interchange. Initially, mothers are concerned with the problems of the infant's basic activities of sleeping, feeding, spitting up, elimination, crying, predictability. During this time there is a reciprocal interchange, characterized by a periodicity or rhythmicity.

The extent to which the infant is helped in beginning to determine aspects of his own regulation is important in laying the foundations for a sense of his own potency. As the infant experiences repeated gratification of his needs he learns to confidently expect that his cues will be understood. The extent to which a mother acquires a sense of confidence in her ability to "know" and meet her baby's needs is important in facilitating an optimal mutuality between mother and child.[9,10]

The mothers who did not have a positive perception of their infants (as measured by the NPI) had difficulties in being able to respond to the infants' needs. Many seemed in a state of "postpartum paralysis," bewildered and depleted. Given such a state, it is unlikely that the mother can provide the reliable, steady environment appropriate to the infant's needs that is essential for the establishment of an optimal psychophysiologic equilibrium in the infant. Such a failure can lead to difficulty in the establishment of synchronization between the infant and mother.

The mother's early perception of her newborn seems to reflect her own sense of well-being. Mothers of infants at high risk have negative self-images that appear to be projected onto their infants. Their inability to believe that what they have created is of value is impressive. The negative self-images of mothers of infants at high risk are not identical. In each there is a different source, resulting in different ranges of adult behavior.

The Neonatal Perception Inventories provide an easily administered screening measure that can identify a population of infants at high risk for subsequent psychosocial difficulty and predict the adaptive potential of a given infant-mother pair.

Many factors may interfere with the smooth functioning of the infant–mother system. Each is unique and there can be no simplistic intervention. When the system is judged in distress, a careful clinical appraisal is needed to determine the specific nature and etiology of the dysfunction. Only then can appropriate intervention be planned and implemented.

REFERENCES

1. Broussard ER: A study to determine the effectiveness of television as a medium for counseling groups of primiparous women during the immediate postpartum period. Doctoral dissertation, University of Pittsburgh, 1964 (unpublished)
2. Festinger L: A Theory of Cognitive Dissonance. Evanston, Ill., Peterson, 1957
3. Broussard ER, Hartner MSS: Maternal perception of the neonate as related to development. Child Psychiatr Hum Dev 2:16–25, 1970
4. Broussard ER, Hartner MSS: Further considerations regarding maternal perception of the first-born, in Hellmuth J (Ed): Exceptional Infant. Studies in Abnormalities (vol 2). New York, Brunner/Mazel, 1971
5. Broussard ER: Neonatal prediction and outcome at 10/11 years. Child Psychiatr Hum Dev 7:85–93, 1976
6. Leighton DC, Harding JS, Macklin DB, et al.: Psychiatric findings of the Stirling County Study. Am J Psychiatr 119:1021–1026, 1963
7. Broussard ER: Primary prevention program for new born infants at high risk for emotional disorder, in Klein D, Goldston S (Eds): Primary Prevention: An Idea Whose Time has Come. Washington, USGPO, 1977, pp 63–68
8. Brownlee KA: Statistical Theory and Methodology in Science and Engineering. New York, Wiley, 1961
9. Sander LW: Infant and caretaking environment, in Anthony EJ (Ed): Explorations in Child Psychiatry. New York, Plenum, 1975
10. Basch MF: Toward a theory that encompasses depression, in Anthony EJ, Benedek T (Eds): Depression and Human Existence. Boston, Little, Brown, 1975

Peter A. Gorski,

Martha F. Davison,

and T. Berry Brazelton

13

Stages of Behavioral Organization in the High-Risk Neonate: Theoretical and Clinical Considerations

Recent advances in the care of neonates have led to rapid increases in survival rates and decreases in neurologic sequelae of immature and sick infants. Sophisticated treatment of neonates is based on the monitoring of physiologic and biochemical parameters. Since constant monitoring is necessary, the environments that we are presently providing for these immature, fragile infants are likely to be relentlessly instrusive. Since we have become impressed with the powerful organizational capacities of the full-term neonate as he organizes to react with positive social stimuli, we have been wondering if an environment sensitive to these capacities might not benefit the immature and sick neonate.

As one observes a neonate as he interacts with an attractive visual or auditory stimulus, the improvement in his autonomic and neurologic behavior as he attends provides observers opportunities for learning about his neurologic organization. Providing care geared to the state of neurobehavioral organization of these fragile, disorganized infants may be therapeutic. We have seen such infants begin to improve after prolonged periods of no weight gain, static oxygen requirements, and other indications of fixed respiratory disease after

Supported in part by grants from the Johnson Foundation, The Carnegie Foundation, and the National Institute of Mental Health.

providing them programs of sensitively positive experience, such as gavage feeding on "demand" (i.e., when the premie becomes active), gentle handling and sensory experiences shaped to the baby at each feeding time, and visual and auditory feedback geared to the infant's own initiation. These preliminary observations point to the potential for increasing the behavioral and neurologic organization of such premature babies. Such behavioral improvement might lead to better outcomes for high-risk neonates by improving their neurologic and autonomic organization on which to build toward improved interaction with their environment and providing improved behavioral feedback at discharge for their already stressed parents to offer them a better focus for their parenting.

Serious disturbances in parent–child interaction, such as child abuse and neglect, are more common with low-birthweight than with healthy full-term infants.[1] Prematures and minimally brain-damaged infants seem less able than well-equipped neonates to compensate in disorganized, depriving environments,[2] but even in families where no gross pathology exists, these infants present a challenge to caregivers. Kaplan and Mason[3] described the birth of a premature infant as an emotional crisis for a mother. One of the important tasks in dealing with that crisis is coming to understand how the premature infant differs from the normal expected infant in terms of its special needs.

Several studies have compared the performance of preterm infants at 40 weeks conceptual age with full-term infants at birth. The electroencephalogram of a preterm infant at 40 weeks conceptual age includes more immature patterns than that of the term newborn.[4,5] Components of the sleep cycle are less well organized in the preterm infant.[6] Preterm infants have less visual attentiveness at 40 weeks conceptual age than full-term infants at birth.[7] Visually evoked electroencephalographic response has a longer latency in preterm infants at 40 weeks conceptual age than in full-term neonates.[8] These neurologic delays cause disordered or violated feedback when preterm infants interact with anxious parents. Perhaps we could improve the behavioral feedback at discharge by programs in the nursery that lead to more responsive babies.

The professional often struggles with the complex challenges of improving development of newborns at risk armed only with a stimulation program for specific neuromotor handicaps. In hopes of providing the clinician with a richer conceptual base for understanding the recovery from illness and the potential for development in such infants, we will elaborate upon a three-stage model of neurobehavioral development for high-risk neonates. The three stages of (1) physiologic organization, (2) the beginnings of organized behavioral responsiveness, and (3) active reciprocity with the infant's social environment form the structural framework for this chapter. Our intention is to appreciate the process that these infants face at each stage of development and how and when the caregiver environment might best foster his maximal potential for development.

We must emphasize the crucial importance of recognizing the individual variations in challenges to normal infant development and parent–infant bonding. Observing the unique capacities and deficits in each parent–infant relationship will allow a therapeutic approach appropriate to cementing the particular strengths in the system that can mobilized toward successful recovery from or coping with the weaknesses identified.

ASSESSMENT OF INTEGRITY

Recent refinements of the standard neurologic exam are now contributing to an appreciation of subtle differences in the neurologic organization of the preterm infant at 40 weeks conceptual age compared to the healthy full-term at birth. Prechtl and Beintema[9] examined neurologic responses in the context of the infant's ongoing state of consciousness. These states range from deep sleep to active arousal. They noted that the quality of responses on standard reflex items and the infant's muscle tone vary with his state of consciousness, and observed that infants with CNS damage have difficulty controlling their states and that the quality of their reflexes is often quite different from the graded responses seen in an intact baby.

Parmelee[10] designed an examination to evaluate neurologic func tioning with respect to muscle tone, reflex patterns of behavior, and states of arousal. The items are prescribed in a standardized order, and states are recorded at specified times. All administered items are scored as (1) normal, (2) exaggerated, (3) weak, or (4) absent.

When the performance of 97 preterm infants tested at 40 weeks conceptual age was compared with the performance of 97 full-term infants at 40 weeks gestational age, preterm infants had weaker responses despite higher activity levels and were more difficult to soothe.[10] The differences in the preterm as compared to full-term infants were subtle, but it was suggested that the differences indicate uneven neurologic maturation or delayed development of integrating systems in the preterm infants.[11]

The Brazelton Neonatal Behavioral Assessment Scale[12] was designed to evaluate the integrative processes evidenced in neonatal behavior and is based on the concept that the full-term healthy infant shows a range of complex behaviors that allows him to elicit the kind of feedback from his environment that is needed for his social and cognitive development. We feel that these behaviors reflect the integrity of his central nervous system.

These behavioral responses include (1) the capacity to respond reliably and selectively in a social interaction with a nurturing adult or with attractive auditory or visual stimuli, (2) the capacity to regulate his state of consciousness in order to be available for positive stimulation and to defend himself from negative stimulation, (3) the capacity to maintain adequate tone, to control motor behavior, and to perform integrated motor activities such as hand-to-mouth maneuvers, and (4) the capacity to maintain physiologic homeostasis.[13]

The infant's performance on the examination articulates his individual temperament and organizational style and may have direct implications for understanding the infant's effect on his environment.

Als et al.[14] proposed that there is a hierarchy of levels of organization in the developing infant. The full-term infant's ability to elicit social responses from his environment depends on his having achieved control over his autonomic, motoric, and state regulation. The preterm infant has not yet achieved integrated functioning in all these areas; he is dealing with different developmental tasks.

In an effort to learn more about the emergence of behavioral organization, the Neonatal Behavioral Assessment Scale is being modified for use with premature infants and infants at risk.[15] The examination taps into the emerging organization by delineating in detail not only the quality of the infant's response but also the duration of the response, the difficulty with which it is elicited, and the effort and cost involved in achieving and maintaining responsivity. Since the examination is conducted within an interactive framework, the nature of the organization that the examiner has to provide in order to bring out the infant's best performance becomes an indication of the integrative functions that the infant still lacks. Repeated assessment over time provides a window into newly emerging capacities that appear as development proceeds. Our own experience in examining a group of ten premature infants at regular intervals from shortly after birth until 42–44 weeks conceptual age convinced us of the usefulness of looking at individual patterns of development as an indicator of prognosis for CNS intactness and as a guide to delineating the kind of support that the infant needs from the environment.

With these assumptions in mind, we would like to organize our observations into a model that includes the parent's participation as critical to the infant's outcome.

"IN-TURNING"—THE PHYSIOLOGIC STAGE

The normal term infant is born with individual as well as species-specific mechanisms for eliciting care from its protectors. Osofsky and Danzger[16] found that term infants judged in the first days of life on the Brazelton Neonatal Behavioral Assessment Scale to be more responsive to visual, auditory, and tactile stimuli had more attentive and stimulating mothers. The developmental consequences of the quality of such reciprocal parent–infant relationships are clearly documented although still poorly understood. Beckwith and Cohen[17] found the recovery process in a population of infants at risk to be strongly influenced by the caregiver–infant relationship. They found that cognitive development in prematurely born infants tested at two years with the Gesell Infant Development Sclaes, Bayley Mental Scales, and Piagetian tests did not correlate with the usual measures of infant neurologic integrity: an Obstetric Complications Scale as adapted from Prechtl, a Postnatal Complications Scale assessing difficulties within the first month of life, a newborn neurologic scale, neurophysiologic sleep measured at full-term conceptual age including activity, eye movements, state of consciousness, and EEG pattern, and a measure of the duration of visual attention in newborns. Instead, prediction of cognitive development correlated better with measures of social interaction with the parent, as in holding, touching, talking, and eye contact, rather than with the neurophysiologic measures.

Our research into the development of premature infants has shown (and warned) that the stressed premature infant may be unable to participate reciprocally with caregivers in establishing a bond of mutually satisfying interaction early on. The high-risk infant must first develop sufficient physical integrity and internal stability before he is able to use caregiver support and input needed to make continuing developmental gains. Let us examine and identify, then, the challenges of and efforts toward physiologic organization, the first stage of development for the high-risk infant.

The use of repeated tests to evaluate the premature infant's capacities for recovery and for eliciting interaction can be demonstrated in an "optimal" baby.

At 33 weeks, the infant lay motionless as he slept, propped on his side in the isolette with arms and legs flexed. As a light was shined in his eyes, he blinked his eyes tightly but did not move. Noise from a rattle produced immediate extension and relaxation of the fingers of one hand, followed after a couple of second by a generalized startle reaction involving both upper and lower extremities. After that, he responded only intermittently to repeated auditory stimuli with small, isolated movements of a hand or foot. As the infant was placed in the supine position for administration of the last of the response decrement items, his face and upper torso reddened slightly, and the rate and depth of his respirations increased, but within a few seconds these changes subsided. The first pinprick applied gently to the sole of one foot produced almost no response. With the second pinprick, there was rapid withdrawal first of tbe stimulated leg, then of the other leg as well. With each succeeding pinprick, more of the infant's body was involved in the response. The fifth stimulus produced an evanescent grimace and brief shimmer as well as generalized motor activity. As soon as the response subsided, the infant fell into a flaccid frogleg posture, his face immobile with the eyes shut and the mouth open. His color had changed to a generalized acrocyanosis. Although he seemed depleted, he recovered rather quickly and testing could be resumed.

The next portion of the examination involved testing of his reflexes and he was disturbed as little as possible. Suck was weak, with poor coordination of suction and stripping action. As the infant was lifted gently to a standing and walking position, his head rolled forward and his arms and legs hung limp. He made no crawling efforts in the prone position. Certain of the reflexes elicited irritable responses with furrowing of the brows and tightening of the lips accompanied by a weak cry, but the grimace faded almost instantaneously.

After a period, the infant was wrapped in a blanket, taken out of the isolette, and gently rocked up and down in an effort to bring him to an alert state. Although his color remained good and there was no change in his respiratory or heart rate, his arms hung limp outside the blanket and his eyes remained shut, his cheeks sagged, and his jaw dropped. The infant's name was called in a soft voice; his mouth rounded slightly and he slowly brought both hands close to his face with his fingers smoothly fanning open and shut, but he never opened his eyes and he made no attempt to turn to the sound. Even with increased vestibular and tactile stimulation, as with elicitation of Moro and tonic neck reflexes, he did not become aroused. He lay flaccid when his face was covered with a cloth. Even after a long latency, there was no active protest to this intrusive stimulus; in the absence of any motor response, we noted only that the infant began to breathe rapidly and appeared more exhausted. The examination was terminated, and our impression was that of a fragile infant unable to organize himself for any social response.

At 35 weeks, the infant was examined at home. His physical appearance had become more robust. His color was pink. His face had filled out considerably and, as he slept, he would wrinkle his forehead or smack his lips together in REM sleep.

The first light stimulus produced an isolated movement of one hand. Following this, blinks and respiratory changes were noted until the eighth stimulus, when his face contorted in a strong grimace and there was a generalized startle reaction involving the whole body. On the next two stimuli, the infant reverted to the barely perceptible, isolated movements of the hand.

A similar pattern was seen in response to presentation of the rattle as a stimulus. The first three stimuli produced minimal responses, but on the fourth, after a brief delay, there was a generalized startle reaction with motion starting in the right arm and spreading to the trunk and other extremities. As the startle subsided, he grimaced, let out a weak, staccato cry, and then began to yawn and stretch. After about 50 seconds, the motion ceased and his face relaxed, the jaw dropping slightly. He had no further responses to the rattle for the next five presentations.

On the first presentation of the bell, he again began to writhe and whimper, and he became increasingly irritable and active. As he worked himself into a strong crying state, he became red in the face. The cry subsided and his color quickly returned to normal. He grimaced and whimpered occasionally as tone and reflexes were examined, but his reflex responses were all easily elicited and appeared to be average in quality.

He was able to hold his head up for 10 seconds when pulled to a sitting position. He did not become tremulous with handling. On the contrary, as he was picked up and put through the various maneuvers of standing and walking, he became quiet and alert, with his eyes wide open. When placed in ventral suspension, his movements became jerky and he began to fuss, but he calmed down quickly when he was cuddled.

His responses to social stimulation were variable. When the examiner brought him into a face-to-face position, he initially averted his gaze. He then turned back to the examiner, he eyes lidded slightly and his mouth opened, and followed the examiner's face horizontally for 60°. Having accomplished that, he yawned. As the examiner began to talk softly to him, his eyes widened and brightened, he pursed his lips, and his hands, which had been hanging at his sides, began to make smooth sweeping movements. He slowly followed the examiner's face and voice and, as he did, the corners of his mouth lifted slightly in what appeared to be a faint trace of a smile. This bright alerting quality lasted only 15 seconds. After that the limbs began to droop again.

The infant followed a bright ball horizontally, but the eye movements were jerkier and he tended to lose the stimulus. Several attempts were required to get him to focus on it. His responses to sound were also difficult to elicit and variable when he did respond. On some trials, his body would be still but he would keep his head and eyes straight ahead. On other trials, he would turn his head and eyes to search but would go past the source of the sound as he pursued it.

In contrast to his performance two weeks earlier, aversive stimuli such as the elicitation of tonic neck and Moro reflexes brought him to a state of strong, sustained crying and vigorous activity. Even in that agitated state, however, he was easily calmed. He did not appear fatigued at the end of the exam. He remained alert and active when he was put back in the crib. We felt his progress had been dramatic.

When the infant was examined at 42 weeks, he appeared plump and hearty. As he slept, he responded to the first bright light stimulus with a discrete generalized startle. His motor responses diminished gradually for the next two stimuli and disappeared completely by the fourth stimulus. In response to the rattle, he began to slowly stretch his body, opening and shutting his eyes, rubbing his head with his hands. As his movements subsided, he lifted his head up, opened his eyes wide, and flashed a broad grin. He remained bright-eyed and alert throughout the testing of muscle tone and reflexes, and his movements remained smooth and unrestricted as he was handled. When cuddled, he snuggled up close with one arm reaching toward the examiner's face and the other arm wrapped around the examiner's arm. He gazed directly into the examiner's eyes, blinking his eyelids vigorously and smiling broadly. He turned consistently to follow the examiner's face with smooth movements of the eyes, both horizontal and vertical. He seemed to show a clear preference for the face over inanimate objects. In order to get him to follow the ball, it was necessary to hold him so that the examiner's face was not visible. In response to the rattle, his body stilled, his eyes widened, and a broad smile gradually came over his face as he turned to search for the source of the soft noise.

The infant appropriately protested aversive maneuvers. When his eyes were covered with a cloth, he immediately arched his back, squirmed, and swiped at the cloth with both hands, crying lustily all the while. As soon as the cloth was removed, however, he turned his head to the side and locked onto the examiner's face with his eyes, while he slowly brought his hand up to his mouth, inserted his thumb, and began to suck on it to quiet quickly. He appeared as robust at the end of the exam as he had in the beginning, with good color, easy respirations, smooth movements, and a bright-eyed facial expression.

Although there were aspects of his initial examination that were worrisome, such as poor tone, weak and absent reflexes, his depressed states, and his failure to achieve alertness, his rapid and consistent progress, shown on repeated examinations over time, did much to dispel worries about the integrity of his nervous system. His ability to elicit responses from his environment and to respond consistently to his environment by the second examination led us to predict that he would not be at risk for interactional problems, a prediction borne out over the year he was followed.

A more typical pattern of development was shown by a second infant in the study. At 33 weeks of age, he appeared quite fragile. He was tremulous and startled easily in all states of consciousness. Even such distal stimuli as a bright light in his eyes during sleep produced color changes that resolved only slowly. He was flaccid when he was not handled and he lay in a frogleg posture much of the time. The arms were more hypotonic than the legs and trunk. His suck was weak, and he showed minimal reflex responses to placing, standing, and walking. In a sleep state, the infant's initial response to light consisted of strong blinks with delayed jerky movements of a hand. On the third stimulus, movement of the hand spread to the arms and torso. As that sequence of movement was subsiding, jerky movements began again in the hand and spread again to the arms and trunk, then to the legs. After three cycles of movement, the infant quieted. Thereafter, only isolated movements of the extremities occurred and, after the seventh stimulus, movement responses shut down. Shutdown of movement occurred even sooner in response to rattle and bell, but marked respiratory changes were worrisome as testing proceeded; by the end of that portion of the examination the infant appeared very fatigued.

Despite frequent rest periods and gentle handling the infant maintained low levels of arousal throughout the examination and was only barely responsive. After a rest, he was wrapped and taken out of the isolette for a short time. As he was gently rocked up and down, he opened his eyes for a few seconds at a time. During one of these brief episodes he did track the examiner's face over a narrow (15°–20°) arc. The infant's eyes remained dull, hence it was difficult to determine whether or not the eye movement was purposeful pursuit. He began to hiccough and his face paled, so he was placed back in the isolette. As he went back into the isolette, his eyes opened a little wider and his color came back to normal. He tracked a red ball horizontally for almost 30° with jerky movements to one side and then made no further attempts.

The infant's responses to sound were not consistent. To the soft shake of the rattle, his first response was to turn his head immediately to the side away from the sound. In contrast, when his name was called softly in a high-pitched voice, his eyes widened slightly and after a delay of several seconds his head turned slowly to the source of the sound. On subsequent trials, however, he closed his eyes and yawned. Even with aversive stimulation he never reached a vigorous crying state. He did exhibit some arching and took a few swipes at the cloth that was put over his face, but then became completely flaccid when the cloth was removed. He appeared exhausted at the end of the examination.

At 35 weeks, the infant was examined in an open crib. His face was starting to fill out a little. His color was pink, and color changes brought about by handling or fussing resolved quickly. He still exhibited frequent tremors and startles, and the tremulousness was present in the most alert states.

The infant again was able to habituate to distracting stimuli during sleep. There was little change in his muscle tone and he still had diminished standing, walking, and crawling reflexes, although by this time his suck was strong and well-coordinated. His movements were still very jerky most of the time, especially with wrapping or handling. Turning him from prone to supine in the crib and holding him suspended horizontally in the air triggered an increased activity, with a very jerky quality to the movements.

The infant's activity in relation to handling became very much an issue when trying to interact with him socially. He would maintain his color and regular respirations when unwrapped but was not able to inhibit his disorganized motor activity in order to attend to stimuli. As his arms and legs flailed about he would shut his eyes. When he was swaddled or held close to the body to restrain some of his movement, he would open his eyes and focus briefly on the face or a red ball. At one point he was able to follow a face for 60° horizontally.

He was quite sensitive to the amount of stimulation he could tolerate. Although he would follow a face or turn to a voice, when those two stimuli were presented together he would close his eyes and yawn or turn his head in the opposite direction. Even when presented with only one stimulus at a time, he had difficulty maintaining alertness. After a brief period of responsiveness, the muscle tone would decrease throughout his body, his jaw would drop, his cheeks would sag, and he appeared fatigued.

By 37 weeks, the infant was still tremulous and continued to startle easily, but he no longer appeared to fatigue with handling. His muscle tone was improved, and he showed little fluctuation throughout the examination. His movements were smoother in most states, although he still became quite jerky with changes in position.

Although he never actually reached a state of intense crying, even with aversive maneuvers, he was irritable throughout much of the examination, in marked contrast to his low level of arousal earlier. He was more easily brought to an alert state, but he needed to be consoled frequently with cuddling to maintain alertness. When presented with the examiner's face alone, his eyes became bright and focused and he would follow it with smooth movements of the eyes. He consistently turned his head to the voice as well. When the examiner's face and voice were presented together, he maintained an alert expression, but he turned his head away, as if he were overloaded.

By 42 weeks of age, the infant appeared sturdy. He was gaining weight rapidly, his color was good, and he was no longer tremulous. His movements were smooth, with unrestricted arcs of movement most of the time, although he still became disorganized with sudden changes in position. He was able to habituate promptly to the bright light and to the rattle or bell in a sleep state and to register vigorous protest to such aversive stimuli when he was awake.

He was better able to maintain an alert state. It was no longer necessary for the examiner to work to bring him up from a drowsy state (as in the earliest examinations) or to use frequent consoling maneuvers to calm him down from an irritable state (as in the 37-weeks examination). There were still a few types of handling, such as sudden changes in position, that would set him off, but his responses were quite consistent and predictable.

It was notable, however, that the quality of his responsiveness in an alert state was still variable. The variability in quality of facial expressions was more subtle than previously. He would be wide-eyed and focused one moment, attending to a stimulus, and then gradually there would be slight narrowing of the eyes, a loss of luster, a few rapid eye blinks, and slight tightening of the lips with the corners starting to turn down a little. Despite the lack of any dramatic change in the infant's facial expression, there was a significant change in the way the infant seemed to the examiner. When he was dull-looking, he seemed to be much less involved in the interaction. Sometimes he would spontaneously revert back to a brighter quality of alerting. At other times he would go on to give more obvious signals such as yawning or turning his head away to indicate that he wanted to terminate the interaction.

Over the course of time, this infant showed a more gradual emergence of the capacity to control his physiologic and motoric processes than the infant previously described. At 42 weeks, he still had more difficulty with state control than one would expect in a full-term infant of comparable age. However, if attention was paid to his cues and the right stimulus was presented, he could interact positively and consistently. Knowing something about this infant's organizational style was helpful in working with his parents. They were able to see what his developmental tasks were and to take the cues from him as to what they should be providing.

A more worrisome pattern was shown by a third infant in the study. On the initial examination at 32 weeks, she appeared very fragile. In quiet sleep, stimulation with light, rattle, and bell produced either no movement or barely perceptible responses in the form of facial grimaces or isolated jerks of the extremities. At the same time, the infant's color was very labile and she showed marked changes in rate and depth of respirations and heart rate. She had a withdrawal response in both legs to pinprick. Each stimulus produced a fleeting grimace, but there was no cry. There was no decrement in startles over five trials.

The infant was hypotonic. She had no walking reflex and incurvation was weak, but otherwise reflexes were within normal limits. She did have a strong, well-coordinated suck.

Although she lay still when left alone, any sort of tactile stimulation set off jerky, flailing movements of the extremities that would subside as suddenly as they had begun.

The infant remained in a drowsy state throughout most of the examination, but when wrapped and brought out of the isolette she did come to an alert state for a brief time. Her eyes would come open briefly and she would fix on a stimulus, but then her lids would droop, her jaw would drop, and after a few seconds she would close her eyes. When gently rocked up and down, she made repeated efforts to alert and at one point followed a face for 60°, although there was very little investment of energy in the response. By this time, the muscles in her face were so lax that as she exhaled her cheeks ballooned out. Her eyes kept popping open, but since she was hiccoughing and beginning to turn pale around the mouth, she was returned to the isolette.

When examined again at 34 weeks, the infant was still in the isolette, but she was dressed and maintaining her body temperature without heat from the isolette. During the initial observation she lay quietly in a prone position for a time, then she lifted her buttocks off the mattress and, as she did, her right arm extended and her upper torso rotated slightly, after which she extended both legs slowly to become quiet again.

On the first light stimulus, her eyes blinked tightly and the fingers of her right hand fanned out and then relaxed. There was no further movement response until the fifth stimulus, when she stretched her neck. Only slight respiratory changes were noted after that. The first two stimuli with the rattle produced only slight extension of the fingers of one hand, but on the third stimulus, her upper torso and then her hips raised slightly off the mattress, followed by extension of both legs and stretching of the neck. As that cycle of movement subsided, her hips raised up, there was a slow rotation of the torso, and the legs swung out again, the movements becoming jerkier. As the movements became jerkier and more intense, the infant grimaced and there was some reddening of her whole torso. A third cycle of movement began that was more global, with first an arm flinging out and in, then a leg. Eventually, the movement subsided. On the fourth stimulus, the infant raised her hips slightly, but this time there was no generalized response. By the fifth stimulus, only slight movements of the toes and fingers were observed, and by the sixth, the only response was a delayed motion on the left foot. No further movement responses were noted after that. A similar pattern, with several cycles of increasingly disorganized movement in response to a single stimulus, was seen with the bell.

The infant's tone had improved since her initial examination, but it still fluctuated a good deal during the examination. At times when awake, she lay quite flaccid. With certain kinds of tactile stimulation, her whole body would stiffen and her face would contort in a grimace. This stiffening was particularly evident when she was held horizontal in a supine position to test her response to auditory stimulation. As her name was called softly, however, her body gradually relaxed, her movements became smooth, and at that point she was able to turn her head and eyes to search for the source of the sound.

The infant made repeated attempts to come to an alert state, but these periods of alertness were difficult for her to maintain. She would track both animate and inaminate objects with her eyes, but her responses were delayed and she appeared stressed with an open-mouthed, dull-eyed look. At one point, as she was gazing at the examiner, she suddenly became limp, so interaction was terminated. As soon as she was put back in the isolette, she opened her eyes again and began to look around.

A week later, when examined at home, her behavior was even more disorganized. Her color was stable, but she startled and became tremulous in all states. As soon as she was touched, her movements became disorganized, with cogwheel-like jerkiness and overshooting of her arms and legs. Talking to her in a soothing voice did not produce any improvement in the quality of her movement. She grimaced and cried loudly when attempts were made to engage her in social interaction and was consoled only briefly with holding and rocking by the examiner. On one occasion, she was able to follow the examiner's face and voice both horizontally and vertically, but in order to do this she had to be swaddled and given a pacifier to suck upon.

When examined again at 40 weeks, she appeared fragile. She

showed some improvement in her use of states. In sleep, she was able to suppress her motor responses to each noxious stimulus within a few trials, and as she was turned to a supine position she gradually awoke with smooth stretching movements rather than the previously observed flailing movements of her extremities. As she was undressed her movements again became jerkier, and she became irritable during the testing of her reflex behavior. When she was picked up and held, she calmed and for a few seconds her eyes brightened. Her face softened and body movements smoothed out as she attended to the examiner's face and voice. Then suddenly she began to thrash and grimace, and it was only with swaddling and a pacifier that she was able to be calmed to a quiet, alert state. Her eyes brightened again as she followed the examiner's face with her eyes, sucking all the while on her pacifier. Soon, however, her eyelids began to droop and her eyes took on an appearance of staring right through the examiner. The pacifier was removed in an attempt to focus her attention on the face of the examiner, but immediately she screamed. She calmed with difficulty when the pacifier was put back in her mouth.

This infant showed a marked unevenness in the emergence of her behavioral organization. This continual unevenness raises the question of possible subtle neurologic impairment and alerts us to the need for careful followup. Her parents are certainly alert to this difficult baby's problems in organization and find her unrewarding and unpredictable to play with. As a result, they have left her alone as much as possible. They say that she is difficult to feed but that she eats well finally. They rarely play with her except at feeding times, and they are frightened by her crying periods, which they try in vain to handle. She is already fixed in their minds as a "problem." Although they blame themselves for their inability to handle her, their concerns about her neurologic status are near the surface and keep cropping up in such questions as "Is she really all right?"

"COMING OUT"—THE FIRST ACTIVE RESPONSE TO THE ENVIRONMENT

Once having mastered a minimum capacity to control and maintain his or her physiologic systems, the infant must then begin to build upon these basic organizational patterns. This second developmental stage implies a more active response to outside stimuli, both nutritional and social. This is the period when changes in the caregiver environment critically affect the physical well-being and growth of the high-risk infant.

Most high-risk infants experience this second level of developmental progress and of potential vulnerability in the special care nursery. The time frame spans the period from the time when the baby is no longer acutely ill and is able to breathe effectively and to absorb enough calories from the gastrointestinal tract to gain weight to the time when he can be discharged home. The parents are urged to assume responsibility for the care of the infant during this period. This is the time when behavioral observations can point to caregiver interventions that can foster the infant's physical as well as social-interactive development. Several examples illustrate our experience to date.

An infant born at 34 weeks gestation had required a short course of mechanical ventilation for hyaline membrane disease. At the time of our behavioral observations he was two weeks old, breathing spontaneously and gaining weight slowly. The infant was still considered fragile because of frequent apneic spells. Fully half of the apneic episodes required intervention ranging from gentle stimulation to positive pressure oxygen delivered by mask. He was afebrile and evidenced no physical, radiologic, bacteriologic, or metabolic signs of acute illness. Neurobehavioral assessment showed an infant who at rest appeared pink and well nourished with smooth, organized movement of all extremities. He was able to spontaneously come from quiet sleep to quiet alert states and when irritable could use postural change and visual locking into his immediate environment to successfully calm himself. The examiner made some striking observations, however. The infant could maintain a quiet alert state for moderate periods of time and visually track animate and inanimate stimuli in a coordinated manner *only* if the infant–examiner interaction began with the baby already in the alert state, apparently ready and organized for processing and using outside cues. When on other occasions the examiner attempted to manipulate, call to, or present visual or auditory stimuli to the infant while the child was in light sleep or a fussy awake state, the infant responded by sudden reddening or paling, uncoordinated jerky movements, tachypnea, and a facial hypotonia expressive of total exhaustion. Skin color, respirations, and movements recovered more rapidly when the infant was left alone in his isolette than when active consoling was attempted by the examiner. In addition, the medical staff remarked that most of the serious apneic spells in this infant seemed to occur during times of morning work rounds and evening sign-outs at the bedside.

On the strength of these observations, we recommended that rounds be diverted from this baby's vicinity and that his sleep–awake cycles be respected so as to interlock with caretaking procedures at times when he appeared behaviorally stable enough to process them positively. Within days the child's apneic spells became rare and self-limitingly brief. These episodes had previously proved refractory to respiratory, pharmacologic, and extranutritional measures. We feel our success lay in attending to the level of external sensory input stressing this infant's autonomic controls while he was still in a vulnerable organizing stage of neurologic development.

"High-risk" infants display varying levels and forms of developmental susceptibilities (e.g., their state control, motor organization, caloric absorption from the gut or respiratory control centers). Therefore we can effect positive changes in infant care by first learning the unique capacities and needs of individual babies. Routine intervention in nurseries, no matter how well intentioned, may adversely affect some infants while helping others. Some infants require regular patterns of feeding schedules, sleep, and handling, while others fail to thrive unless care is organized around the infant's idiosyncratic demands for feeding and activity. Some infants can tolerate only one or two sensory inputs from the environment and respond by physiologic decompensation to overloading stimuli that other infants might turn to with alerting in request for still more stimulation.

Stressed premature infants in special care nurseries do indeed respond positively or negatively to caretaking interventions. We must recognize that especially early in their course these responses often get expressed on a physiologic rather than an interactive level. We have made some surprising observations during a study in which state, motor tone and activity, motor maturity, skin color, and respirations were recorded continuously over 24 hours every five days during hospitalization of a recovering premature infant. If a nurse or physician took care to contain the infant's limbs while slowly turning the baby supine in preparation for an intravenous injection, the infant's heart rate, respirations, and skin color remained stable during the actual procedure, as contrasted with the marked signs of autonomic lability noted when the infant was abruptly turned with limbs uncontained. This occurred despite similarly adequate thermal regulation. Current work utilizes a computer-programmed observational scale of continuous recording of behavioral and physiological data about infants in an intensive care nursery. Preliminary results support our earlier correlation of physiological stability and caregiving environments. We hope to use our measures to demonstrate that such untoward responses to caregiving interventions as apnea, vomiting, irritability, and dangerously low pO_2 can be reproducible and predictable. Furthermore, we are documenting the ability to protect infants from such negative effects through caregiving behavioral plans instituted as a result of behavioral data analysis.[18]

The infant who develops chronic lung disease, such as bronchopulmonary dysplasia, in the newborn period serves as an example of the successful integration of behavioral observations with overall medical care. These infants pass through several stages of physical and developmental risk as they grapple with emerging behavioral capacities and begin to process environmental input that may severely stress their respiratory system. Many of these infants are unable to physically tolerate eye-to-eye contact or close cuddling in the early weeks. Diverting nonessential noise from their isolettes and limiting contact to a few primary caregivers can limit the life-threatening respiratory distress triggered by irritable crying and disorganized movement.

Failure to feed successfully and gain weight often plagues infants with chronic lung disease. Again we have found that focusing on the infant's behavioral responses to and interactions with caregivers often influences nutritional recovery when calorie counting fails. Spacing and timing of feedings around spontaneous alert periods are often important to successful absorption of calories. With other babies, the distance from caregiver during feeding and the absence of much extra noise in the area influence the success of feeding. By five or six months, such stressed infants whose care has been provided contingent to their physiologic and developmental needs will respond to programs designed to challenge hand-to-eye coordination and reaching and exploring behavior without exceeding their physical limits.

When assessing the developmental progress of high-risk infants, it is important to recall McGraw's observation that the neuromaturation of normal infants proceeds in spurts followed by plateaus and even essential regressions before succeeding times of progress.[19] As the infant advances in a particular area of development, he may also temporarily show evidence of increased vulnerability, so that we must expect moments (or days) of renewed difficulty during the recovery of stressed infants. Therefore, serial neurobehavioral assessments during the neonatal period guide our plans and indicate prognosis much more reliably than the results of a single exam. The examples above clearly illustrate the value of repeated assessments of the neurobehavioral recovery of high-risk infants.

"RECIPROCITY"—THE ULTIMATE STATE OF ENVIRONMENTAL OPPORTUNITY

We now have an infant strong enough to breathe, feed, and respond to caregiver behaviors in specific and predictable ways, yet who is still faced with overcoming the remaining handicaps of a difficult start in life. The developing relationship between parents and infant plays a key role in this final phase of early development of high-risk infants.

The importance of understanding the early developmental processes of high-risk infants and the impact of environmental conditions upon these processes stems from a conviction that eventual cognitive and affective outcome is at least as determined by the postnatal social environments of the infants as by the obstetric and perinatal physiologic stresses upon them. Current studies support the principle that the impact of perinatal risk factors can be reduced by a nurturant caretaking environment. On the other hand, noncontingent caretaking can amplify the effects of intrinsic pathology. Studies by Drillien[20] and Werner et al.,[21] and the Johns Hopkins Study of Premature Infants (Harper et al.[22] and Wiener and co-workers[23-25]) all make a direct association between social status and ultimate developmental quotient, cognitive, and perceptual-motor development and IQ in populations of premature and term infants with perinatal complications. Each study showed that low social status of the family was associated with greater developmental delay than that seen in infants from families of high social status. Low social status exaggerated the effects of prematurity or of perinatal complications, while privileged environment tended to erase earlier developmental deficits by the third or fourth birthday.

A deprivation model that arose from investigations of orphans was applied initially to answer the question as to *how* social status affects development. The deficits of lower social status children were felt to be based on lack of appropriate stimulation. Then an increasing number of studies using naturalistic observations[26,27] indicated that poverty was not analogous to stimulus deprivation. Infants in lower social status families do not differ from those of higher social situations in the amount of physical contact received through holding, soothing, or affection,[28,29] nor do infants in upper social status families necessarily receive more verbal input. Infants in upper social status families, however, seem to be exposed to more reciprocal vocal exchanges and face-to-face vocalization.[30] Indeed, we suspect that excessive nonreciprocal stimulation rather than deprivation contributes to the strong effect of social status on developmental outcome of normal as well as high-risk infants. Our findings concerning the negative responses of premature infants to the often "overstimulating" environment of the special care nursery may apply here. Perhaps in an overstimulating home environment not sensitive to their needs these vulnerable babies are too easily overloaded and must withdraw. The behavioral disorganization of such an infant can set off parental responses that attempt to reorganize him too quickly. The overwhelming parental responses stem from caring too much, not too little. With proper direction, they can easily be turned into responses appropriate to the vulnerable infant's particular needs.

Even the full-term, but underweight, neonate may offer an example of initial behavioral distortions that can challenge and frustrate parents in the earliest weeks after delivery. Als et al.[15] found that a significant percent of these infants failed to muster an alert awake state for social interaction when tested over the first weeks of life. Such infants are difficult to rouse, and even when roused present an unrewarding set of responses to their caregivers. Hence, a caring parent may leave them alone or overstimulate them in an attempt to reach them. A few weeks or months later, these same infants show ceaseless, irritable, and no less disorganized activity spontaneously or when engaged socially. The parent who complains that her newborn, in the beginning, sleeps constantly and does not respond to caregiving situations often later faces a paradoxic dilemma with a seemingly hyperactive child who refuses to rest quietly. Therapeutic intervention, which we have found to be of help in this problem, offers an excellent example of how strongly the infant's behavioral recovery can be shaped by the caregiver response to the baby's behavior. Neurobehavioral examination as well as parental observations show the baby's poorly controlled neurologic development. One observes the infant's attempts to stay in lower sleep states, his respiratory and skin color instability in the face of environmental stimuli such as noise or handling, and his increasingly disorganized irritable behavior when the examiner or caregiver attempts to console him.

Reassuring the parent that this disorganization is in the baby and is not the parent's fault relieves the parents of the guilt and frustration they are bound to feel. One can then offer them several successful recommendations—e.g., swaddle the infant whose uncontrolled activity or startles interfere with his holding a quiet alert state, use spontaneous alert periods to advantage for interactive play and attempt to stretch these organized periods, and allow the unconsolable baby to exercise self-quieting mechanisms. We believe that the disorganized behaviors of such stressed infants represent an overload of sensory input to their central nervous system. Indeed, we guess that the sleepy, unresponsive behavior of many of these infants is an effort to protect the CNS from the demands of responding to such overload.

Parents blame themselves when their baby's message appears to be "leave me alone." Therefore in performing and integrating a behavioral assessment of such a newborn one should be prepared to identify and demonstrate the infant's *strengths* and capacities as well as discuss his disturbing behaviors. This makes the situation more tolerable and fosters the positive attachment feelings the parents might otherwise be unable to find.

Parents of high-risk babies are undergoing a profound adaptive process at the same time that they are learning the difficult behavioral messages by which their newborn responds to and elicits their nurturing. By making the effort to understand and appreciate parents' difficult emotions, especially during earliest hospitalization of their infant, we give them the message that their feelings are worth expressing and, more importantly, that these feelings are worthy of our attention. This message is itself important in supporting the awesome challenges for the initial period of parent–infant attachment, since we must help parents feel better about themselves for them in turn to develop more confidence to parent their special infant. Parents of infants at risk must be psychologically free enough to attend to the often confusing and unusual needs of their babies. We strongly believe that stressed infants are more dependent than normal infants upon the positive effects of newborn care offered *contingently* with their developmental needs and likewise more vulnerable to the disorganizing consequences of routinized, inflexible care.

REFERENCES

1. Klein M, Stern L: Low birthweight and the battered child syndrome. Am J Dis Child 122:15–18, 1971
2. Greenberg NH: A comparison of infant–mother interactional behavior in infants with atypical behavior and normal infants, in Hellmuth J (Ed): Exceptional Infant (vol. 2). New York, Bruner/Mazel, 1971, p 390
3. Kaplan D, Mason E: Maternal reactions to a premature birth viewed as an acute emotional disorder. Am J Orthopsychiatry 30:539–542, 1960
4. Dreyfuss-Brisac C: The bioelectrical development of the central nervous system during early life, in Falkner F (Ed): Human Development. Philadelphia, Saunders, 1966, p. 286
5. Parmelee AH, Schulte FJ, Akiyama Y, et al.: Maturation of EEG activity during sleep in premature infants. Electroenceph Clin Neurophysiol 24:319–329, 1968
6. Dreyfuss-Brisac C: Ontogenesis of sleep in human prematures after 32 weeks of conceptual age. Dev Psychobiol 3:91–121, 1970
7. Kopp CB, Sigman M, Parmelee AH, et al.: Neurological organization and visual fixation in infants at 40 weeks conceptual age. Dev Psychobiol 8:165–170, 1975
8. Engel R: Maturational changes and abnormalities in the newborn electroencephalogram. Dev Med Child Neurol 7:498–506, 1965
9. Prechtl HFR, Beintema O: The Neurological Examination of the Full-Term Infant. London, Heinemann, 1964
10. Parmelee AH: Newborn Neurological Examination. UCLA, 1974 (unpublished)

11. Howard J, Parmelee AH, Kopp CB, et al.: A neurologic comparison of pre-term and full-term infants at term conceptual age. J Pediatr 88:995–1002, 1976

12. Brazelton TB: The Neonatal Behavioral Assessment Scale. London, Spastics International, Medical Publications monograph 50, 1973

13. Als H, Tronick E, Lester B, et al.: The Brazelton Neonatal Behavioral Assessment Scale (BNBAS). J Abnorm Child Psychol 5:215–231, 1977

14. Als H, Lester B, Brazelton TB: Dynamics of the behavioral organization of the premature infant. A theoretical perspective, in Field TM, Sostek AM, Goldberg S, Shuman HH (Eds): Infants Born at Risk, New York, Spectrum, 1979

15. Als H, Tronick E, Adamson L, et al.: The behavior of the full-term yet underweight newborn infant. Dev Med Child Neurol 18:590–602, 1976

16. Osofsky JD, Danzger B: Relationships between neonatal characteristics and mother–infant interaction. Dev Psychol 10:124–130, 1974

17. Beckwith L, Cohen SE: Pre-term birth: Hazardous obstetrical and postnatal events as related to caregiver-infant behavior. Inf Behav Dev 1:4, 1978

18. Gorski P, Leonard C, Hole W: Premature infant behavioral and physiological responses to caregiving interventions in the intensive care nursery. Presented at the First World Congress on Infant Psychiatry, Portugal, April, 1980

19. McGraw M: The Neuromuscular Maturation of the Human Infant. New York, Columbia University, 1943

20. Drillien CM: The Growth and Development of the Prematurely Born Infant. Baltimore, Williams & Wilkins, 1964

21. Werner EE, Bierman JM, French FE: The Children of Kauai: A Longitudinal Study From the Prenatal Period to Age Ten. Honolulu, University of Hawaii, 1971

22. Harper PA, Fischer LK, Rider RV: Neurological and intellectual status of prematures at three to five years of age. J Pediatr 55:679–690, 1959

23. Wiener G, Rider RV, Oppel W, et al.: Correlates of low birthweight: Psychological status at 6–7 years of age. Pediatrics 35:434–444, 1965

24. Wiener G, Rider RV, Oppel W, et al.: Corelates of low birthweight: Psychological status of 8–10 years of age. Pediatr Res 2:110–118, 1968

25. Wiener G: The relationship of birthweight and length of gestation to intellectual development at ages 8–10 years. J Pediatr 76:694–699, 1970

26. Tulkin SR: An analysis of the concept of cultural deprivation. Dev Psychol 6:326–339, 1972

27. Wachs TD, Uzgiris IC, Hunt JM: Cognitive development in infants of different age levels and from different environmental backgrounds: An explanatory investigation. Merrill Palmer Q 17:283–317, 1971

28. Lewis M, Wilson CD: Infant development in lower class American families. Hum Dev 15:112–127, 1972

29. Tulkin SR, Kagan J: Mother–child interaction in the first year of life. Child Dev 43:31–41, 1972

30. Cohen SE, Beckwith L: Maternal language in infancy. Dev Psychol 12:371–372, 1976

Klaus K. Minde

14

Bonding of Parents to Premature Infants: Theory and Practice

Studies examining the interaction of parents with their prematurely born infants have appeared only recently in the literature.[1] This is due to a number of developments: There has been a remarkable increase in the survival rate of these infants during the past decade and a parallel improvement in the outlook of those who do survive.[2,3] Thus substantial numbers of infants born prematurely have become available for study. Furthermore there has been a clinical awareness of the differences in these small infants later on, highlighted by reported increased incidence of behavioral abnormalities[4] and an allegedly abnormal high rate of abuse and neglect to which these infants are subjected.[5,6] In addition, however, the increasing interest of both developmental psychologists and physicians in these infants may also stem from changes in our understanding of the processes guiding the development of children. Since these changes seem especially pertinent for the understanding of behavioral studies dealing with premature infants and their primary caretakers, a brief review of some recent concepts of child development is indicated.

Traditionally, development was seen as an interaction between a particular environment and an essentially passive organism endowed with specific genetically determined characteristics. More recently, however, a growing literature has documented the importance of

This research was supported by Medical Research Council of Canada Grant number MA 6003 and the Laidlaw Foundation.

considering the effect the child's behavior has on his primary caretaker. For example, investigators who had initially studied parent–infant interaction and its effect on the child's later cognitive and social behavior[7,8] became more interested in the nature of the interaction itself and the feedback systems of the interacting partners.[9,10] Finally, Sameroff and Chandler[11] argued that development is a series of interactive states between the partners or dyads. They suggested that each interaction results in a change of state in the dyad that in turn influences the next state. To differentiate their model of development from others, they have called it transactional. One important aspect of this model of development is the concept that the human organism is endowed with an inherited "self-righting concept." This capacity can best be compared with the principle of homeostasis found in many of the human body's feedback systems. However, Sameroff and Chandler have expanded this concept to include all interactions between an organism and his environment. Consequently, a sense of homeostasis or "making up" is sought not only within different physiological systems within a child, to use one concrete example, but also between the behaviors of this child and his caretaker and/or other people with whom he comes in contact.

While Sameroff and Chandler's transactional model in development is only the latest of many attempts to provide a unifying concept to the laws governing child development, scientists have always sought empirical data to validate their particular developmental model. It is here that the study of premature infants has an added benefit of providing the researcher with a population which has many characteristics of a natural experiment. For example, these infants' early birth allows a more detailed examination of issues related to questions of nature and nurture. Thus medical complications, so frequent in these children, and the response of primary caretakers to them can be studied using different developmental models. Finally, possible precursors of later behavioral abnormalities can be identified and validated against a variety of theoretical assumptions.

This chapter will review some studies that have investigated the initial relationship between parents and their premature infants and relate the results to the transactional model. We will first examine studies that have suggested that the relationship between premature infants and their caretakers is indeed different from full-term dyads and then examine in more detail those studies that identify factors thought to be responsible for these differences. Finally, the implications of these factors for everyday clinical practice and for possible intervention strategies will be discussed.

Initial Relationship Between Parents and Their
Premature Infants: Why Should It Be Different?

With the advent of neonatal intensive care in the 1950s, a number of clinical studies have focused on the early relationship of parent to premature infants. This process was investigated because premature infants were initially separated from their parents for a substantial length of time and the consequences of this separation were unknown. The data from these studies were interpreted to suggest that preterm infants were over-represented in populations of abused children and those failing to thrive. An additional assumption was made that these conditions resulted from inadequate "bonding" of the mother to the infant. The term bonding was used to denote a rapid process which creates a unique affectional relationship between a primary caretaker and his/her infant shortly after birth.[12] The term thus referred to a phenomenon which primarily affected the caretaker and not the child.

Two studies in particular[5,6] have been cited as documenting the causal relationship between prematurity and later physical abuse. A more critical review of these studies, however, reveals a number of methodological difficulties. Elmer and Gregg[5] in the first study to link prematurity with later child abuse examined the records of 50 children who had been seen at the Children's Hospital in Pittsburgh from 1949 to 1962 with unexplained bone injuries and a history of gross neglect. Many of the children had *not* been identified as abused or battered at the time of diagnosis but in the review were classified as abused retrospectively (i.e., had suffered skeletal damage or severe bruising).

When we look at the data more closely, however, we find that of the 50 children identified as battered by Elmer and Gregg from the medical records, 19 could not be re-examined since the families either refused to participate in the study, the children had died, or had been admitted to institutions for the mentally retarded. Thirty-one of the remaining children were then examined at the hospital and 11 were now thought to have had "genuine accidents." This reduced the sample of "abused children" to only 20. Of these children, only six were premature, having birthweights ranging from 1644 to 2381 grams, with "the majority" weighing more than 2041 grams. Thus they were fairly large premature infants. Two of the prematurely born children, however, were different in other ways: i.e., mentally retarded, prior to their injuries. This leaves 4 out of 20 children with a clear association of prematurity and a history of possible abuse. While this figure is obviously above the rate of prematurity in this community, the vague definition of abuse, the substantial sample loss, and the low number of remaining subjects make any conclusions about the causative association between prematurity and abuse highly questionable.

In the second study associating prematurity and abuse, Klein and Stern[6] studied the charts of all children who had been diagnosed as "battered children" at the Montreal Children's hospital between 1960 and 1969. Battering was defined as unexplained skeletal trauma, severe bruising, or both. Of the 51 cases so identified, 12 cases (23.5 percent) were born prematurely. Ages of the children at the time of the abuse varied from 2 to 48 months. Three of the 12 prematurely born infants died of their injuries. Nevertheless it is interesting to note that factors other than prematurity characterized the abused infants. For example, of the 12 prematurely born infants, three had birthweights above 2000 grams and remained in hospital for only seven days, hence were not separated from their parents for an unusually long time. Another infant weighed more than 2300 grams at birth and was discharged after only two weeks. Six other infants were known to have been mentally retarded prior to their injury. Thus some 75 percent of the battered premature infants either had a very brief hospital stay, and consequently no significant separation, or suffered from associated chronic medical conditions which also could explain abuse. The three remaining infants in Klein and Stern's study who were not retarded and had an initial hospitalization of two or more weeks represent seven percent of the total abused group and therefore correspond to the expected incidence of prematurity in the population served by the hospital under study.

The three most frequently cited studies of the syndrome "Failure to Thrive" associated with prematurity[13-15] are plagued with even more methodological uncertainties than are those that examined abused children. For example, both Ambuel and Harris[13] and Shaheen et al.,[14] who cite figures of 27 percent and 36 percent of premature infants among their samples of 144 (Ambuel and Harris) and 44 (Shaheen et al.) failure to thrive children, did not use the generally accepted definition of the syndrome. This definition encompasses the failure to *gain* weight and grow adequately in conjunction with signs of physical as well as emotional deprivation such as apathy, poor hygiene, and withdrawing behavior.[16] In other words, the accepted definition clearly states that an infant must have shown a significant change in his growth pattern to be labelled failure to thrive. In addition, for the present purpose, this change in growth pattern must not be accompanied by any medical condition that could by itself cause such a change in growth and weight gain. In the studies cited, however, the diagnosis of failure to thrive was made if the child presented with a height *or* weight below the third percentile. This is clearly inadequate. The authors of both the studies also failed to differentiate infants who were born as small for gestational age (SGA) from true premature infants. Such infants are by definition born with weight and heights below the third percentile. They also diagnosed premature infants from age three months onward on their weight alone as failure to thrive, and included them in their sample although it is well known that such infants take up to two years to catch up in height and weight with their full-term peers, and thus cannot be compared on the same growth charts.[17] Furthermore, Ambuel and Harris[13] also stated that 68 percent of their total sample had an associated medical diagnosis, such as fibrocystic or congenital heart disease (33 cases) or mental retardation (22 cases), each of which can by itself cause an arrest in the gain of height and weight. In a footnote they remark that premature infants had more of these complications, but give no exact figures. Shaheen and her colleagues also mention that 50 percent of all their pregnancy histories were abnormal and four infants were the smaller of twins. Because of the imprecise diagnosis of failure to thrive and the confounding of other diseases as complications, the link between prematurity and failure to thrive is not clear.

In a third study Evans et al.[15] mention prematurity to be present in 9 out of their 40 subjects diagnosed as failure to thrive. The authors, however, do not define their criteria of a premature birth and do not discuss this unusually high percentage of premature infants in their sample. Hence one again cannot exclude the possibility that the "premature" infant were SGA infants born at or near term who had always scored below the third percentile on standard weight and height charts.

These articles are widely quoted as giving the best documented evidence of the association between prematurity and parenting disorders. Yet other investigators have not confirmed this association. For example, Steele and Pollock,[18] members of the group of Kempe and Helfer in Denver, mention prematurity only as an example of a condition which may require extra care from parents and hence tax their caretaking skill more severely. Douglas and Gaer,[19] in their 15-year follow-up study of all 88 surviving premature infants born in the first week of March 1946 in England matched on six variables with full-term peers, also found no difference in the rate of abuse or failure to thrive in their sample. Likewise, Bidder et al.[20] compared mothers' attitudes to their preterm and full-term infants using the semantic differential. The average age of their preterms was 2.8, their full-terms 3.5 years. The only statistical significance was in the concept "strong–weak," indicating that these mothers saw their preterm child as being weaker than their term child.

Despite the methodological inadequacies of some of the above cited studies, however, they have sparked a number of investigations examining the development of the initial parent–infant bond. The possible contribution of various factors to this bond is the topic of the next section.

Separation and The "Critical Period" of Parent–Infant Bonding

Faced with growing concern that the premature infant is at risk for parenting disorders, a number of investigators began to examine the current medical management of such infants and their families. Klaus and Kennell[12] followed Bowlby's example[21] in conceptualizing attachment as an ethological process. They too used the construct "bonding," and in addition hypothesized that there exists a sensitive period immediately following birth, during which the mother–infant bond is formed. They concluded that the early separation of an infant from his mother during the sensitive period could lead to serious difficulties in a mother's later caretaking abilities.

Part of Klaus and Kennell's concern[12] was based on medical practice in the 1950s and 60s which, among other things, strongly emphasized the control on infection in premature infants. Consequently parental visits to neonatal units were generally not permitted. However, Barnett et al.[22] at Stanford University Medical Center wondered whether mothers visiting their premature infants would indeed increase the number of bacteriologically positive cultures in these babies, as it seemed unlikely to these authors that mothers would neglect to wash their hands and refuse to participate in any other procedures preventing cross-infection prior to visiting their babies. Consequently, they initiated an investigation during which some mothers could visit and touch their premature infants as early as the second day after birth, and recorded the percentage of positive cultures and potential pathogens isolated from the infants and the equipment used in the nursery. Results showed a decrease rather than an increase of culture pathogens in the nursery following the intro-duction of liberal visiting practices.

The awareness of the apparent safety to let parents into the nursery made it possible to examine the difference in commitment, feelings of competence, and actual behavior in mothers who had different amounts of early exposure to their premature infants. Leiderman and associates[23] compared three groups of mothers: 24 normal full-term dyads, 20 preterm dyads where mother could not enter the nursery for one month (separation group), and 22 preterm dyads whose mothers were allowed to handle their infants from the second day after birth in the nursery (contact group). All families were seen in their homes one week postdischarge, in the pediatric clinic one month later, and at home 3, 6, 8, 11, and 15 months after their expected date of birth. The results of the study suggested that providing mothers with the opportunity to make early contact with their infants did not influence the mother's general later caretaking behavior, although during the period of separation the separated mothers felt much less confident in their ability to care for their infants.[24] However, this difference disappeared after the infants had been home for one month. The only other difference in the behavior between early and late contact mothers was seen nine months after discharge when the contact mothers touched their first-born premature infants more than did the separated mothers. This disappeared at 11 months. In fact, a number of other variables such as sex and whether the infant was the first or later born child had a far more pronounced impact on maternal behavior after discharge home than did the early contact in the nursery. Furthermore, Leiderman and Seashore[25] also showed there were fewer differences in parental and infant behavior between the contact and noncontact premature dyads than between the full-term group and any of the preterm dyads. These authors conclude that the concept of bonding as derived from ethological theories cannot account for their data because of the variation in maternal behavior related to sex and birth order. Especially the consistent finding that mothers of second or later born infants had significantly more confidence in their initial contact with their infants made the authors believe that the variations in the mothers' behavior can best be understood by a learning theory model which is modulated by the culturally conditioned expectations of mother–infant roles.

The second major project investigating the effect of early maternal contact on premature infants was carried out at Case Western Reserve Medical Center under the direction of Klaus and Kennell.[12] Klaus had participated in the original work at Stanford and was deeply concerned about some of the possible consequences of neonatal intensive care on the parents of premature infants. The studies of Klaus and his group investigated two separate phenomena: (1) the degree to which visiting frequency predicts later parenting skills and (2) the consequences of early (prior to 20 days postpartum) and late (after 20 days postpartum) maternal contact on maternal behavior and the child's development.

One-hundred-and-forty-six high-risk infants were involved in the visiting study,[26] 41 of their mothers visited their infants less than three times every two weeks (low visitors), 105 visited more frequently (high visitors). No figures of the actual number of visits for each group were given, however, at follow-up, which ranged from 6-to-23 months and was done by an unspecified number of private physicians, as well as in the premature follow-up clinic, 9 of the 41 families in the low-visiting group versus only 2 of the 105 frequent visitors showed disorders of mothering. Five of the nine infants in the low-visiting group were described as failure-to-thrive children, two as battered, and one each as fostered and abandoned. Unfortunately, the results of this study can only be accepted with great caution, as much necessary information is not supplied. For example, the authors give no definition of failure to thrive and do not document the reliability of their follow-up sources. Nevertheless their work suggests that a mother's attitude toward her baby and her visiting frequency may be taken as an early index of maternal involvement. This finding is contradicted somewhat, however, by the results of their second project, which examined the consequences of early maternal visiting to the premature nursery. In this study, Klaus and his colleagues[12,27] studied 53 mothers, dividing them into an early contact (N = 27), allowed to visit from birth onwards, and a late contact group (N = 26) in which the first mother–infant contact occurred after more than 21 days. All mothers were observed during a feed just before discharge and one mother later. Bayley developmental examinations were performed after 9, 15, and 21 months, and the Stanford Binet test administered at 42 months. Results showed that early contact mothers spent more time looking at their infants during the first feeding and that this was positively correlated with a higher IQ at 42 months. Yet early and late contact mothers did not vary in the number of visits to the nursery, and Kennell reports no difference in their later mothering behavior. In addition both groups of infants behaved similarly during the second feeding and received similar scores on the Bayley at 9, 15, and 21 months. As 18 of the 53 families were lost at the time of the 42-month follow-up, the later intellectual differences among the groups can only be accepted with great caution.

Further interesting work dealing with the possible effect of early mother–infant separation on later caretaking comes from Field in Miami[28]. This investigator hypothesized that infants were most responsive in those feeding situations which showed mothers contingently responding to their full-term infants by imitating or amplifying their behavior. In practice this meant that mothers normally followed their infant's leads and did not interrupt or intrude into the "mutual behavioral conversation."[28] To test this hypothesis Field observed 12 full-term, 12 postmature, and 12 high-risk premature infants at three-and-a-half months postgestational age in an interaction situation in which mothers were requested to play with their infant as she would do at home, keep their infant's attention as if they tried to make a movie, and imitate all their infant's behaviors.[29] Her results indicated that the attention-getting and imitation manipulations modified considerably the face-to-face interaction of all the dyads. For example, mother's differing amount of activity directly modified the amount of her infant's gaze; i.e., when mother imitated the baby his attention to her virtually doubled; when she tried to get his attention it decreased. However, both post- and premature infants showed significantly more gaze aversion than the full-terms in all three situations. Since both post- and prematures had received very low scores on subtests of the Brazelton Behavioral Assessment Scale which tap an infant's interactive abilities, the author concluded that the interactional difficulties shown by both high-risk groups were not due to initial mother–infant separation (the postmature group had been in hospital for only three days), but to their basically poor CNS organization. In the later study the author[28] confirmed her earlier results and showed that premature high-risk infants had a higher heart rate in all interaction situations and their mothers showed a greater amount of general activity than did the full-term mothers. During video-taped mother–child interactions of the same infants at four months, mothers of the premature infants were still significantly more active and less imitative, and at two years they used more imperatives and fewer statements when talking to them than the full-term controls. The children, in turn, averted their gaze more often than their full-term peers, and at two years corrected age had shorter "mean length of utterance" and a smaller working vocabulary.

It is clear from the studies presented above that the interval between birth and the initial contact between a mother and her premature infant is of little consequence for her later caretaking skills and the development of the neonate. A "sensitive" period of bonding between mothers and those very small infants likewise thus receives little support, confirming the conclusions of Campbell and Taylor[30] following their review of work dealing with bonding in full-term infants.

The Premature Infant as a Shaper of His World

There has been much interest recently in infancy research in describing the behavior of the infant and its contribution to the caretaking it receives. This interest derived from a number of sources.

Clinicians such as Thomas et al.[31] had reported on the effect of a child's temperament can have on his interactions with his family, an effect which was later confirmed by Carey[32] on an infant population. Brazelton and his colleagues[33] published their Neonatal Behavioral Assessment Scale, which documented the great variety of behaviors available to the newborn and the possible effects this has on his environment. Others have stressed the effect of parity and differences in initial state organization have on later parent–child interaction.[34-36] Only very recently, however, have there been any attempts to assess specific behavioral patterns in premature infants and compare them with those shown by full-term neonates. For example, Frodi et al.[37] showed videotapes of crying and calm full-term and preterm infants to fathers and mothers. Physiological recordings taken during the showings of the video-tapes indicated that the cry of a preterm baby was more arousing to these parents than the cry of a full-term infant. Since the preterm infants cried less often, the authors speculated that the special quality of that cry may compensate for this lack of frequency or the adversive nature of the cry may trigger parental abuse.

While Frodi and her colleagues[37] examined a very specific behavior of these infants, Als and her colleagues[38] attempted to modify Brazelton's Neonatal Assessment Scale for the use of premature infants; following one premature and one full-term infant in great detail for nine months and documenting with a number of interaction paradigms that the premature infant is far less responsive than the full-term. Als also showed how this lack of responsiveness correlated with the increased attempts of the preterm infant's parents to engage this infant in various interactive processes although they rarely succeeded in holding the baby's attention for any length of time. In contrast, the full-term infant was able to organize her interactive processes soon after birth and consequently was able to socially engage with relative ease.

In another investigation Brown and Bakeman[39,40] studied 26 preterm and 23 full-term dyads. Their sample came from a low-income black population and was followed for 12 months. They reported that in hospital and one month after discharge their preterm infants were more difficult to care for and less responsive than the full-term infants. For example, they showed fewer gross motor movements and looked less often at their mothers and their surroundings. As a possible consequence, mothers of preterms were more active than the mothers of full-terms during all observations, while the preterm infants were somewhat less active than the full-terms. When these authors examined the interactions of their mother–infant dyads with the help of a sequence analysis, they confirmed that mothers of preterms were more often acting alone, trying to initiate interactive behavior in their children. Furthermore, although these infants increased their rates of activity over time, approaching the rate of the full-terms, the pattern of interaction between the mother–infant dyads did not change. These data in many ways confirm the results by Field and Als.

Our own group[41-44] has attempted to examine the impact these very small infants have on their caretakers in two different ways. We initially developed a computer-compatible event recorder and a coding system that allowed us to make continuous observations of a large number of behaviors of both infants and their caretakers.[41] Our aim was to record all those behaviors of both the infant and his caretaker that may be socially meaningful to each other. Twelve infant and ten maternal behaviors were finally selected. In order to describe the changes in the behavior of preterm infants as they mature, we observed 21 infants during their first few weeks in a premature nursery for 40 minutes two times per week at specified times.[42] Seven infants were born after 26–27 weeks gestation, seven after 28–30 weeks, and seven after 31–32 weeks. All infants were free of any but the mildest medical complications. We hoped that this study would tell us (1) how the behavior of relatively well premature infants changes during the first weeks after birth; (2) whether this rate of development is dependent on the length of gestation. For example, it seemed possible to postulate that an infant born after 27 weeks gestation would be neurologically more mature at 33 weeks than an infant born after 32 weeks gestation. Results, however, showed no difference in the behaviors among the three gestational groups during their first three weeks after birth. Furthermore, the infants did not show any developmental behavioral changes up to 34 weeks postconception. Finally, we found that at least up to their fifth visit in the nursery mothers and fathers could not initiate or change any behavior in their infants although they often seemed to try. Rather, in these very small premature infants it was the parents who primarily responded to their infant's signals, and in this way were steered by their infant's behavior.[42,43]

The importance and influence of the behavior of a premature infant on his caretaker could be seen even more clearly in an almost natural experiment on our unit.[44] In this investigation we compared the behavior of ten very small infants who were critically ill during their initial stay in the nursery with the behavior of ten relatively well controls matched for gestational age at birth and age after birth. Not unexpectedly, the "sick" infants were significantly less active

during our observations; i.e., showed fewer arm, leg, and head movements, and also opened their eyes less often than did their relatively
healthy controls. The parents of the sick infants likewise did much
less with these babies during their hospital visits; i.e., they talked to
and touched them only very sporadically. However, while the behavior
patterns of the original "sick" groups of infants changed following the
improvement of their medical condition and closely approximated the
behavior of the healthy group, the parents of the formerly ill infants
interacted much more than the control parents with these infants
during their later visits to the nursery. Although we do not yet know
to what extent such an initial "set" of parental interactive response
patterns is retained by various groups of caretakers, these data at
least suggest the possibility that the cues parents receive from their
infants may determine to an important degree their later attitudes
and behavior toward them.

In this context, the work of Parmelee and associates[45-49] at
U.C.L.A. becomes important. In 1971 Parmelee had begun, together
with a group of co-workers, to evaluate the relative impact of biological
and social events on the cognitive development of 126 preterm infants.
Although his definition of prematurity was rather broad, including
all infants born less than 37 weeks post-conceptual age and weighing
less than 2500 grams, his precise and innovative methodology of
measuring specific cognitive functions in these infants until two years
of age makes this study one of the most productive investigations on
the field. While not all data of the U.C.L.A. study have yet been
analyzed, presently available results clearly reflect on the issues
examined in the present chapter. For example, Littman[45] showed that
there was no relationship between developmental outcome at 18 or 24
months and well-defined obstetrical and neonatal complications. However, infants with higher rates of medical complications during later
infancy (at four and nine months) performed less well on measures of
development at 18 and 25 months. At the same time Beckwith and
Cohen[46] observed these infants at home for an average of 74 minutes
at one month as calculated from their expected date of birth. Maternal
behaviors recorded were grouped into clusters such as social interactions (e.g., contingent vocalizations), responsive holding (e.g., attentiveness), verbal stimulation, mutual gazing, and stressful holding
(e.g., interfering touches). Beckwith and Cohen found that caregiver
behaviors were significantly related to prior obstetrical and neonatal
hazards. Thus infants who had more neonatal complications received
more verbal stimulation from their primary caretaker at one month
of age. Here again the infant proved to be an important mediator,
however, since babies who were awake a great deal of time received

relatively less positive social interaction than those who had shorter waking periods. It seemed as if mothers had to transmit a defined number of interactive stimuli and, when dealing with an infant who slept less, would spread the stimuli out over a longer period.

Further work by the same authors showed that the way mothers interacted with their premature infants at two years of age was highly correlated to their behavior toward these infants at one month after discharge from hospital.[47] For example, mutual gazing at one month was highly related to vocalization and intellectual functioning of the infant at age two. This again suggests that mothers who show a great deal of interest in their infants early on in infancy continue to stimulate and encourage their infants and in this way assist them in their cognitive and psychological development. The most interesting suggestion coming from the work of Beckwith and Cohen, however, a suggestion that has recently been confirmed by Sigman and Parmelee[48,49] in a different context, is that a special event in an infant's life, such as a severe medical complication after birth, often triggers an apparently compensatory mechanism within its primary caretakers. This may take the form of special stimulation, with subsequent superior intellectual functioning of the medically more compromised infant.

In summary, there is good evidence which suggests that premature infants, like their full-term peers, significantly contribute to the caretaking they receive, and that transactional phenomena as suggested by Sameroff and Chandler[11] can function as important modifiers of a potentially abnormal developmental process.

THE PARENTS OF PREMATURE INFANTS

Are They Different?

Traditionally, parents of premature infants have been described as poor and disadvantaged.[17] Their poverty is related to the comparatively inadequate prenatal care poor women receive during their pregnancy, which in turn leads to a higher incidence of prematurity.

In conjunction with the generally lower socioeconomic background of parents of premature infants, however, it has also been suggested that the caretakers of these small infants lack certain other characteristics important for adequate parenting. For example, they have been described as having fewer social support systems within the community[50] or to have undergone more personal deprivation.[51]

Much work has been done to isolate characteristics of those parents who find themselves in difficulties with their small infants. Most studies examining these issues have focused on socio-demographic variables traditionally associated with high psychiatric morbidity, and have found parents of preterms to score higher on variables such as marital maladjustment, past history of abuse or separation, or alcoholism.[50-53] Others have looked at the emotional response of mothers following the birth of such a small infant[54] and at the cultural background (e.g., Spanish versus English speaking) of various U.S. samples.[48] Not surprisingly, the studies have generally found that the majority of mothers who have problems in parenting their infants showed many socio-demographic adversities. Studies, however, have not dealt with the many women who, despite the lack of adequate past and present support systems, prove to be adequate in the rearing of their children, nor do they specify exactly what these "poor" mothers do with their children that is wrong.

Our own group has attempted to approach the issue of how such past parental experiences influence their present caretaking style somewhat differently. We initially decided to study only infants whose birthweight was less than 1501 grams and who were not small for gestational age. This allowed us to increase the homogeneity of our sample, since virtually all our infants were at risk for medical complications. The exclusion of bigger premature infants also eliminated those low-weight births that are traditionally associated with possible sociological factors. Finally, this method also allowed us to observe our infants for several weeks in the nursery.

Results indicated that the mothers of these very low birthweight infants became involved with their babies through a gradual process; i.e., they increased the length of their visiting time to the nursery from 19 to 28 minutes over the first five visits, and during their visits spent an increasing percentage of time touching, looking en face, and vocalizing to their infants.[55] More importantly, however, about 20 percent of our mothers interacted (i.e., smiled, touched, look en face, vocalized) a great deal with their infants from their first visit on. Another 25 percent of our mothers were equally consistent in showing little interaction vis-à-vis their infants, and 55 percent took a middle position. Most important to us, however, was the finding that both high, low, and medium interactive mothers remained in their respective positions at least during the first three months following their infant's discharge home. In examining the background factors associated with these three activity groups, we found that the level of an individual mother's interaction is not related to the perinatal complications of her infant. However, low interacting mothers during a psychiatric interview consistently reported poor relationships with their own mother and with the father of the infant, while high interactive mothers reported much more satisfying previous interpersonal relationships. In order to specify the infant's possible contribution to his mother's interactive pattern we performed a sequential analysis of the nursery visits of the high, medium, and low activity groups of mothers.[43] This analysis showed that high activity mothers exhibited a greater number of behaviors that co-occurred with the infant behaviors which can be considered social signals (e.g., eye open, smile). This seems to indicate a greater sensitivity of behavior for this group. Further analyses of this data allowed us to determine the direction of influence of behavior between the infant and his mother. Again, the data suggested that high activity mothers primarily responded to their infant's social and gross motor behaviors, while lower activity mothers interacted more randomly.

In summary, the above-mentioned data suggests that a mother's activity towards her preterm infant in the nursery may be a good indicator of her initial adjustment to this infant. Furthermore, they demonstrate a high correlation between important past and present interpersonal relationships of the mother and her caretaking involvement.

The Father of The Premature Infant

The bulk of the studies that have examined caretaking behavior of parents with their full-term infants have focused only on the mother. In fact, while a number of studies have found that the paternal esteem for the mother's competence as caretaker was related to her actual caretaking competence,[56,57] fathers still tended to have only little direct contact with their infants. For example, Ban and Lewis[58] claim fathers only spent 15 to 20 minutes a day with their one-year-old infants. The reason for this differential involvement of fathers and mothers is obviously multidetermined, although society's expectations undoubtedly play an important part.[59] Yet premature infants are a population in which the parental roles and experiences during the early postpartum period differ considerably from the full-term infants. For example, preterm infants are often separated from their mothers after birth and are severely ill. During this time the father has an opportunity to visit the infant and is recognized by the medical and nursing staff in the nursery as a legitimate intermediary between the nursery and the mother. This in turn may shape his later involvement with the child.

In an ongoing study on our own ward, we have compared 10 full-term and 10 preterm father–infant dyads. Preliminary results indicate that the fathers of preterm infants in a nursery interacted with these infants as much as their mothers. Three months after discharge home, these fathers also changed about 25 percent of all the diapers, gave one in three feeds, and played about half as much with the baby than did the mother.[60]

Although, these findings are very preliminary, they nevertheless indicate that fathers of premature infants as a group may be more involved with their infants than are fathers of full-terms. Their support of the mothers of these babies furthermore may be of major importance for these woman and, in this way, significantly contribute to the infant's later physical and mental health.

PRACTICAL IMPLICATIONS

This chapter has provided good evidence that prematurely born infants, at least during their early life, are more difficult to look after than are full-term infants. It is not yet clear, however, to what extent this is due to the possible differences in the neuro-integrative capacities of these infants or to the changes in parental expectations due to the very special early environment. The work by Field[28] and Als[38] demonstrate clear differences in the ease with which these infants can be engaged in interaction during the first year of life. This lack of responsiveness is attributed primarily to differences in the biological make-up between preterm and full-term infants. Our own work[61] examined those factors which influence the caretaking style of parents. We have emphasized the interrelationship between the infants' medical status, their actual behavior, and parental response pattern.

Remediation programs based on the hypothesis that the atypical development of the premature infant is due to an inadequate postnatal environment[62] have attempted to provide supplementary therapeutic experiences. Both the type or frequency of the additional stimulation best suited for these infants, however, has been a cause of much debate. Some of the researchers felt that any additional stimulation should primarily "compensate" for these infants' lack of the intra-uterine environment, while others reasoned that these infants have to adjust to an extrauterine existence, and hence should be helped to do so by providing them with the qualitatively important increased visual and social stimulation.[63] On the basis of these theoretical positions a number of different stimulation programs have been evaluated. These have recently been reviewed by Masi.[64] The investigators in these studies have employed a great variety of stimuli such as rocking,[65,66] stroking,[67] or the playing of a recorded female voice.[68,69] They differed in the amount and duration of stimulation they provided their infant populations and also used samples of various sizes and postconceptional age. As outcome criteria in these studies have also varied from growth measurements or length of sleep to scores on specific developmental assessment scales, the individual investigations are difficult to compare. In general, however, the authors of these studies report some benefit to the stimulated infants. These benefits range from an improvement of motor development measured by neonatal assessments[70] and weight gain[71] to the increase in specific cognitive functions.[72]

A significant failing of these studies is that they have not tried to objectively assess the capacity of these very immature organisms to utilize extra stimulation. This seems important since the very meticulous ethological observations of Prechtl and his group,[73] as well as our own work,[42] has documented that it is most unlikely that premature infants show any consistent response to any type of cognitive input at least up to the 34th week postconception. This is in part due to the grossly immature internal state organization of these infants up to this age.[74,75] Since cognitive stimulation is most effective, however, if it is applied to an alert organism, any type of extra stimulation before the 34th postconceptual week seems to be of doubtful value for that reason alone. In addition, the work by Lawson et al.[76] found that preterm infants receive a great deal of stimulation provided by the continuous illumination of the nurseries, the high amount of auditory stimulation, and fairly consistent handling by the staff. Furthermore, Marton et al.[77] have also shown that these very small infants do receive a fair amount of stimulation from the day-to-day caretaking routines of the nursing staff in the neonatal intensive care unit.

A second strategy of remediation has been to provide the parents of these very small infants with experiences that can facilitate their development of a responsive caretaking pattern. The potential usefulness of this approach has been documented by the stimulation studies which showed the most sustained improvement in those infants whose mothers involved them in longer term at-home stimulation.[78,79] The work by Field[28] and Als[38] also clearly suggests that under normal circumstances a good number of parents seem to try to make up for their infant's initial smallness by overstimulating them, and in that sense depriving them from developing a sense of their own behavioral autonomy. Instructions to parents of how to help these infants to cope with their immature behavioral repertoire by, e.g., gaining their attention through imitating their spontaneous behavior rather than forcing them to attend to novel stimuli, has also had documented beneficial effects on both the infants' and mothers' behavior.

The final hypothesis discussed dealt with the possibility that parents of premature infants are psychologically different from parents of full-term infants. It is here that Klaus and Kennell[12] and their associates and Leiderman and Seashore[25] and associates have proposed changes in hospital routines to promote parent–infant bonding. This is clearly best achieved if both parents are allowed to actively contribute to the care of their infants from birth onward. The provision for the active participation of both mothers and fathers in the care of their small infants, however, can take place most easily when these infants are delivered in a perinatal unit that has facilities for the after-care of these high-risk infants. In such units the infant can remain within the same hospital for its neonatal care, and consequently the initial contact between the infant and his parents is much more easily arranged than in those instances where the infant has to be moved to another hospital after delivery.

While the opportunity of parents to partake in the initial care of their infant is obviously a cornerstone of modern day neonatal intensive care, the work of Klaus and Kennell,[12] as well as our own studies,[61,80] have demonstrated that this opportunity alone will often not be sufficient to allay the anxieties and fears of such parents. What seems to be required initially is to allow the parents of these very small infants to develop a feeling that their infants have a life ahead of them which contains some sense of the future. The feeling of "not knowing what is in store" and the frequent perception that these infants are "completely different from normal babies" does not allow parents to conceptualize their proper role in the caretaking process, and hence makes them unsure of how to interact and deal with their small infants. A very effective way to bring about a feeling of competence within such parents is through group meetings with other parents of premature infants, led by a mother or father who have had such a small infant within the last 12 months. Such "veteran" parents invariably establish a rapid and intense relationship with the new parents by sharing their own experiences following the birth of their infant. This sharing in turn enables the new parents to work through some of their own grief and gradually sense and incorporate the possibility of a real life for their infant. Once this has been achieved the new parents can focus on the present, and consequently retain information which can significantly assist them in their later caretaking tasks.[80] For example, in our study parents who had participated in such groups visited their infants significantly more frequently for longer periods during their stay in the nursery than did the control parents. They also reported themselves to be more satisfied with the care their infants received during their nursery visits, and touched, smiled, and talked to their infants more. Likewise, they showed a more contingent behavior towards their infants during the first three months of their baby's stay at home and could use available community facilities more freely.[80] In fact, a very recent one-year follow-up investigation of parents who participated in such a self-help group showed them still to be more sensitive and appropriately stimulating to their infant at that time.[81]

We hope that this chapter has demonstrated the behavioral plasticity of premature infants. In practice this means that infants who show little spontaneous activity when ill during their early infancy, or exhibit difficulties in their spontaneous interpersonal interaction during the first year of life, nevertheless may become responsive if appropriately handled at home. It also means that the role of the caretaker for these children's later development cannot be overemphasized. As many parents who feel diffident or incompetent toward their premature infants can be recognized during the first month of the child's life with fairly good reliability,[50] the medical staff of any modern intensive care unit must see the facilitation of parental involvement with their infant as one of their primary treatment goals. It is only when the care for the emotional and cognitive needs for these infants equals the concern that is presently shown toward their physical ills that we will provide the optimal care for these infants and their families.

REFERENCES

1. Goldberg S: Prematurity: Effects on parent–infant interaction. Pediat Psychol 3:137–144, 1978
2. Fitzhardinge P: Follow-up studies on the low birthweight infant. Clin in Perinat 3:503–516, 1976
3. Pape KE, Buncie RJ, Ashby S, Fitzhardinge PM: The status at two years of low birthweight infants born in 1974 with birthweights of less than 1001 gm. J Pediatr 2:253–260, 1978
4. Drillien CM: The growth and development of the prematurely born infant. Baltimore, Williams and Wilkins, 1964
5. Elmer E, Gregg GS: Developmental characteristics of abused children. Pediatrics 40:596–602, 1967
6. Klein M, Stern L: Low birthweight and the battered child syndrome. Am J Dis Child 122:15–18, 1971
7. Lewis M, Goldberg S: Perceptual-cognitive development in infancy: A generalized

expectancy model as a function of the mother–infant interaction. Merrill-Palmer Q 15:81–100, 1969

8. Bell SM, Ainsworth MDS: Infant crying and maternal responsiveness. Child Dev 43:1171–1190, 1972

9. Lewis M, Rosenblum LA: The Effect of the Infant on Its Caregiver. New York, Wiley, 1974

10. Goldberg S: Social competence in infancy: A model of parent–infant interaction. Merrill-Palmer Q 23:163–177, 1977

11. Sameroff AJ, Chandler MJ: Reproductive risk and the continuum of caretaking casualty, in Horowitz FD, Hetherington M, Scarr-Salapatek S, Siegel G (Eds): Review of Child Development Research vol. 4. Chicago, University of Chicago Press, 1975

12. Klaus MH, Kennell JH: Maternal–infant Bonding. Saint Louis, C. V. Mosby Co., 1976

13. Ambuel JP, Harris B: Failure to thrive. A study of failure to grow in height or weight. Ohio State Med J 59:997–1001, 1963

14. Shaheen E, Alexander D, Truskowsky M, Barbero GJ: Failure to thrive: A retrospective profile. Clin Pediatr 7:255–261, 1968

15. Evans S, Reinhart J, Succop P: A study of 45 children and their families. J Am Acad Child Psychol 11:440–454, 1972

16. Barbero GJ, McKay RJ: Failure to Thrive, in Vaughan VC, McKay RJ, Behrman RE (Eds): Nelson Textbook of Pediatrics. Philadelphia, W. B. Saunders Co., 1979, pp 311–312

17. Behrman RE: Prematurity and low birthweight, in Vaughan VC, McKay RJ, Behrman RE (Eds): Nelson Textbook of Pediatrics. Philadelphia, W. B. Saunders Co., 1979, pp 404–413

18. Steele BF, Pollock CB: A psychiatric study of parents who abuse infants and small children, in Kempe CH, Helfer DE (Eds): The Battered Child (2nd ed). Chicago, University of Chicago Press, 1974

19. Douglas J, Gaer R: Children of low birthweight in the 1946 cohort. Arch Dis Child 51:820–827, 1976

20. Bidder RT, Crowe EA, Gray OP: Mothers' attitudes to preterm infants. Arch Dis Child 49:766, 1974

21. Bowlby J: Attachment and Loss (vol. I). Attachment. New York, Basic Books, 1969

22. Barnett C, Leiderman P, Grobstein R, Klaus M: Neonatal separation: The maternal side of interactional deprivation. Pediatrics 45:197–205, 1970

23. Leifer AD, Leiderman PH, Barnett CR, Williams JA: Effects of mother–infant separation on maternal attachment behavior. Child Dev 43:1203–1218, 1972

24. Seashore MJ, Leifer AD, Barnett CR, Leiderman PH: The effects of denial of early expectancy model as a function of the mother–infant interaction. Merrill-Palmer Q 15:81–100, 1969

25. Leiderman PH, Seashore MJ: Mother–infant separation: Some delayed consequences, in Parent-infant interaction. Ciba Found Symp No 33. New York, Elsevier, 1975, pp 213–239

26. Fanaroff AA, Kennell JH, Klaus MH: Follow-up of low birthweight infants: The predictive value of maternal visiting patterns. Pediatrics 49:287–290, 1972

27. Kennell J, Trause M, Klaus M: Evidence for a sensitive period in the human mother, in Parent–infant interaction. Ciba Found Symp No 33. New York, Elsevier, 1975, pp 87–101

28. Field TM: Interaction patterns of preterm and term infants, in Field TM (Ed): Infants Born at Risk. Jamaica, NY, Spectrum Publications Inc., 1979, pp 333–356

29. Field TM: Effects of early separation, interactive deficits, and experimental manipulations on infant–mother face-to-face interaction. Child Dev 48:763–771, 1977

30. Campbell SBG, Taylor PM: Bonding and attachment: Theoretical issues, in Taylor PM (ed): Parent–Infant Relationships. New York, Grune & Stratton, 1980, p 3

31. Thomas A, Birch HG, Chess S, Hertzig ME, Korn S: Behavioral Individuality in Early Childhood. London, University of London Press, 1963

32. Carey WB: A simplified method for measuring infant temperament. J Pediatr 77:188–194, 1970

33. Brazelton TB: Neonatal Behavioral Assessment Scale. London, Heineman, 1973

34. Thoman E, Turner A, Leiderman P, Barnett E: Neonate–mother interaction. Effects of parity on feeding behavior. Child Dev 41:1103–1111, 1970

35. Korner AF: Individual differences at birth: Implications for early experience and later development. Am J Orthopsychiatr 41:608–619, 1971

36. Osofsky JD, Danzger B: Relationships between neonatal characteristics and mother–infant interaction. Develop Psychol 10:124–130, 1974

37. Frodi A, Lamb M, Leavitt L, Donovan W, Neff C, Sherry D: Fathers' and mothers' responses to the faces and cries of normal and premature infants. Develop Psychol 14:490–498, 1978

38. Als H: Assessment of behavioral organization in preterm and full-term infants. Presented at meeting of the American Academy of Child Psychiatry, Atlanta, 1979

39. Bakeman R, Brown J: Behavioral dialogues: An approach to the assessment of mother–infant interaction. Child Dev 48:195–201, 1977

40. Brown J, Bakeman R: Relationships of human mothers with their infants during the first year of life: Effects of prematurity, in Bell R, Smotherman W (Eds): Maternal Influences and Early Behavior. Holliswood, N.Y., Spectrum, 1980

41. Celhoffer L, Boukydis C, Muir E, Minde K: A portable computer-compatible event recorder for observing behavior. Behav Res Meth Inst 9:442–446, 1977

42. Hines B, Minde K, Marton P, Trehub S: Behavioral development of premature infants. An ethological approach. Dev Med Child Neurol (in press)

43. Marton P, Minde K, Ogilvie J: Mother–infant interactions in the premature nursery—a sequential analysis, in Friedman SL, Sigman M (Eds): Preterm Birth and Psychological Development. New York, Academic Press, 1980

44. Whitelaw A, Minde K, Brown J: The effect of severe physical illness on the behavior of very small premature infants. Dev Med Child Psychol (in press)

45. Littman B: The relationship of medical events to infant development, in Field TM (Ed): Infants Born at Risk. Jamaica, N.Y., Spectrum Publications Inc., 1979, pp 53–65

46. Beckwith L, Cohen SE: Preterm birth: Hazardous obstetrical and postnatal events as related to caregiver—infant behavior. Inf Behav Dev 1:403–411, 1978

47. Cohen SE, Beckwith L: Preterm infant interaction with the caregiver in the first year of life and competence at age two. Child Dev 50:767–776, 1979

48. Sigman M, Parmelee AHJ: Longitudinal evaluation of the preterm infant, in Field TM (Ed): Infants Born at Risk. Jamaica, N.Y., Spectrum Publications Inc. 1979, pp 193–217

49. Sigman M, Parmelee AH: Evidence for the transactional model in a longitudinal study of preterm infants, in Friedman SL, Sigman M (Eds): Preterm Birth and Psychological Development. New York, Academic Press, 1980

50. Hunter RS, Kilstrom N, Kraybill EN, Loda F: Antecedents of child abuse and neglect in premature infants: A prospective study in a newborn intensive care unit. Pediatrics 61:629–635, 1978

51. Lynch M, Roberts J: Predicting child abuse: Signs of bonding failure in the maternity hospital. Brit Med J, 1:624–626, 1977

52. Baldwin JA: Child abuse: Epidemiology and prevention, in Graham PJ, (Ed): Epidemiological Approaches in Child Psychiatry. London, Academic Press, 1977, pp 55–106

53. Schmitt D, Kempe HC: Neglect and abuse of children, in Vaughan V, McKay R (Eds): Nelson Textbook of Pediatrics. Philadelphia, W. B. Saunders Co., 1975, pp 107–111

54. Kaplan DM, Mason EA: Maternal reaction to premature birth viewed as an acute emotional disorder. Am J Orthopsychiatr 30:539–547, 1960

55. Minde K, Trehub S, Corter C, Boukydis C, Celhoffer L, Marton P: Mother–child relationships on the premature nursery: An observational study. Pediatrics 61:373–379, 1978

56. Lynn O: The Father: His Role in Child Development. Monterey, California, Brooks/Cole Publishing Co., 1974

57. Pedersen F: Mother, father and infant as an interactive system. Paper presented at the meeting of the American Psychological Association, Chicago, 1975

58. Ban P, Lewis M: Mothers and father, girls and boys. Attachment behavior in the one-year-old. Merrill-Palmer Q, 20:195–204, 1974

59. Parke R: Perspectives on father–infant interaction in Osofsky J (Ed): Handbook of Infant Development. New York, Wiley, 1979, pp 549–590

60. Marton P, Minde K, Perotta M: Paternal behavior with premature and full-term infants. (in preparation)

61. Minde K, Marton P, Manning D, Hines B: Some determinants of mother–infant interaction in the premature nursery. J Am Acad Child Psychiatr 19:1–21, 1980

62. Rothchild BT: Incubator isolation as a possible contributing factor to the high incidence of emotional disturbance among prematurely born persons. Genetic Psychol 110:287–304, 1967

63. Cornell EH, Gottfried AW: Intervention with premature human infants. Child Dev 47:32–39, 1976

64. Masi W: Supplement stimulation of the premature infant, in Field TM (Ed): Infants Born at Risk: Behavior and Development. Jamaica, N.Y., Spectrum Publications Inc., 1979, pp 367–388

65. Korner AF, Kraemer HC, Faffner ME, Cosper IM: Effects of waterbed flotation on premature infants. A pilot study. Pediatrics 56:361–367, 1975

66. Freedman D, Boverman H, Freedman N: Effects of kinesthetic stimulation on weight gain and on smiling in premature infants. Paper presented at the American Orthopsychiatric Association, San Francisco, 1966

67. Solkoff N, Yaffe S, Weintraub D, Blase B: Effects of handling on the subsequent development of premature infants. Develop Psychol 1:765–768, 1969

68. Katz V: Auditory stimulation and developmental behavior of the premature infant. Nurs Res 20:196–201, 1971

69. Segall M: Cardiac responsivity to auditory stimulation in premature infants. Nurs Res 21:15–19, 1972

70. Powell LF: The effect of extra stimulation and maternal involvement on the development of low birthweight infants and on maternal behavior. Child Dev 45:106–113, 1974

71. Barnard KE: The effect of stimulation on the duration and amount of sleep and wakefulness in the premature infant. Unpublished doctoral dissertation. University of Washington, 1972

72. Siqueland ER: Biological and experiential determinants of exploration in infancy,

in Stone L, Smith H, Murphy C (Eds): The Competent Infant. New York, Basic Books, Inc., 1973, pp 822–823

73. Prechtl HFR, Fargel JW, Weinmann HM, Bakker HW: Postures, motility and respiration in low-risk preterm infants. Develop Med Child Neurol 21:3–27, 1979

74. Saint-Anne Dargassies S: Neurological Development in the Full-term and Premature Neonate. Amsterdam, Excerpta Medica, Elsevier/North Holland, 1977

75. Parmelee AH: Neurophysiological and behavioral organization of premature infants in the first months of life. Biol Psychiatr 10:501–512, 1975

76. Lawson K, Daum C, Turkewitz G: Environmental characteristics of a neonatal intensive care unit. Child Dev 48:1633–1639, 1977

77. Marton P, Dawson H, Minde K: The interaction of ward personnel with infants in the premature nursery. J Infant Behav Dev (in press)

78. Scarr-Salapatek S, Williams ML: The effects of early stimulation on low birthweight infants. Child Dev 44:94–101, 1973

79. Rice R: Neurophysiological development in premature infants following stimulation. Dev Psychol 13:69–76, 1977

80. Minde K, Shosenberg N, Marton P, et al.: Self-help groups in a premature nursery—a controlled evaluation. J Pediat (in press)

81. Minde K, Shosenberg N, Thompson P. Self-help groups in a premature nursery—infant behavior and parental competence one year later. Paper presented at the First World Congress on Infant Psychiatry, Lisbon, April 1980

Paul M. Taylor

and Barbara Lee Hall

15

Parent–Infant Bonding: Problems and Opportunities in a Perinatal Center

Survival of high-risk infants delivered in community hospitals is increased when neonatal referral centers are utilized fully; survival is greater still if such infants are delivered at hospitals containing neonatal intensive care units.[1] Transfer of critically ill or very small newborn infants from community hospitals to neonatal referral centers is an integral component of regionalized neonatal care systems. Maximal neonatal care is thus afforded many infants, indeed, most infants in sparsely populated areas, at the expense of separation from their parents. Parents' emotional reactions to the birth of a premature or otherwise high-risk infant, profound under the best of circumstances, are intensified if the infant must be transferred to a neonatal referral center.

In this chapter we will present certain approaches we have found of value when working with parents of infants admitted to the Infant Referral Center at the Magee-Womens Hospital. We will emphasize principles and techniques of communicating with these uniquely stressed parents. Our communications with parents will be most appropriate and supportive if we have a grasp not only of the usual emotional reactions of parents to the birth of a premature infant but also of the meaning of this event to each particular parent. Therefore, we will focus on means by which we may understand parents' idiosyncractic reactions to this crisis and the sources of their individual concerns. We will conclude by suggesting that the parents of premature and other high-risk infants may cope best with the crisis of the infant's birth if the mother is referred to a perinatal center for delivery; and, when antenatal referral is not possible, that the mother, too, be transferred with the infant to the referral center.

First, we must review the conceptual framework within which we attempt to understand the reactions of parents of premature infants. For this, we draw heavily on the work of Klaus and Kennell, who effectively led the movement to humanize the hospital care of infants sick and well. Their book, *Parent-Infant Bonding*,[2] contains chapters entitled "Caring for parents of a premature or sick infant" and "Caring for parents of an infant who dies," which are prerequisites for the following discussion and indeed for anyone who wishes to provide total care to premature and sick infants. Many of the concepts and techniques presented below are amplified by Klaus and Kennell.

CONCEPTUAL FRAMEWORK

Normal Pregnancy

It is useful to initially consider the mother's psychologic adaptation to a normal full-term pregnancy. We can then better understand the impact on the mother of the premature interruption of this very dynamic process, which, thinking teleologically, we assume prepares her to optimally nurture her full-term newborn infant.

Bibring[3] considered pregnancy to be a normal developmental crisis, in Erikson's sense of that phrase. In her words,

Pregnancy is a crisis that affects all expectant mothers, no matter what their state of psychic health. Crises, as we see it, are turning points in the life of the individual, leading to acute disequilibria which under favorable conditions result in specific maturational steps toward new functions. We find them as developmental phenomena at points of no return between one phase and the next when decisive changes deprive former central needs and modes of living of their significance, forcing the acceptance of highly charged new goals and functions. Pregnancy as a major turning point in the life of the woman represents one of these normal crises, especially for the primigravida who faces the impact of this event for the first time. We believe that all women show what look like remarkable, far-reaching psychological changes while they are pregnant. The outcome of this crisis, then, has profound effects on the early mother–child relationship.

Bibring also pointed out that pregnancy shares with the maturational crises of adolescence and menopause, which begin and end the childbearing years, "the quality of inevitability." She and her co-workers[4] noted, "Once an adolescent, you cannot become a child again; once menopausal you cannot bear children again; and once a mother you cannot be a single unit again." Pregnancy differs importantly, however, from adolescence and menopause in that it takes place over a relatively short, fixed span of time, is impossible to deny, and has a usual outcome, a normal baby, which is tangible but not inevitable.

Many women feel negative or ambivalent about their pregnancy until quickening, and then rapidly come to accept it with happy anticipation. Between the time pregnancy is suspected or confirmed and quickening, the woman makes a major narcissistic investment in which she regards the fetus as an integral part of herself and not as a separate individual. Self-interest and self-absorption continue throughout the pregnancy and seem to complement rather than compete with the affiliation with and investment in the fetus as a separate and unique being that begins at about the time of quickening and increases for the duration of the pregnancy. Investment in the fetus is reflected by active, practical preparation for the new baby, or "nesting behavior." Throughout the gestation, but most notably during the second half, and with a crescendo during the final weeks, women actively fantasize about the fetus and develop expectations for the infant and child-to-be. Most of the conscious fantasies deal with the expected, hoped-for infant. Coexisting fantasies about the "feared" infant who may be sick or malformed and who may die are usually also at the conscious level, but may be restricted to dreams in which these threatening ideas are presented symbolically.[5] Concerns about the effect of pregnancy on her own health, and about being mutilated or dying during childbirth, are almost universal, yet frequently are expressed only symbolically in dreams. It is not surprising, then, that psychoanalytic evaluations of normal women detected a buildup of anxiety late in pregnancy.[4,6,7] Unresolved conflicts are stirred up during developmental crises: the developmental crisis of pregnancy features reawakening and hopefully constructive reworking of unresolved neurotic conflicts the woman may have with her mother.[4,6,7] These reactivated conflicts may also contribute to the anxiety of late pregnancy. Brazelton[7] suggested that this anxiety is adaptive in that it generates energy that helps the parents cope with complications of labor or delivery or with a sick or malformed infant, and that if this energy is not expended on such contingencies, it is then available to invest in the first contact with the newborn baby.

When pregnancy has progressed to within a month of term, women begin to actively wish that the baby would come. The dynamics of this feeling are probably incompletely understood. Mothers usually explain it on the basis of physical discomfort (and that may be sufficient), yet it is intriguing that the onset of the desire to have the pregnancy end usually coincides with the attaining of that gestational age at which chances for neonatal survival become maximal. Prior to that time, when delivery would have been associated with greater risk of neonatal death, women wish to retain the pregnancy. We speculate that the intensity of the mother's desire to retain the pregnancy or "let it go" might affect her attitude toward her delivery and new infant. Thus she might well construe delivery after onset of the desire to let the pregnancy go as active fulfillment of her wish and as an indication that she controlled the timing of the birth. On the other hand, delivery when she actively wanted to continue the pregnancy could be considered by the pregnant mother as loss of control over a production in which she is the main attraction.

Figure 15-1 is a schematic representation inter-relating the time-courses of the main psychologic processes that occur during pregnancy. Usual affective and mood changes such as increases in dependency, passivity, introspectiveness, and anxiety have been omitted for simplicity.

Premature Birth

Parents lose much when their infant is born prematurely. The psychologic work that goes on during the last trimester must serve an important purpose; hence, we infer, the earlier the delivery the greater the frustration of that purpose. Consider, for example, the maternal emotional preparation that must be completed following delivery at 28 weeks that would have been completed antenatally if the infant had been delivered at full term. Affiliation with the fetus is waxing and narcissism is waning at 28 weeks, while the urge to let the pregnancy go is still weeks away. Failure to produce the expected full-term baby might exacerbate neurotic conflicts with her own mother that the pregnant woman may be reworking, and contribute to the grief and depression usually experienced after the birth of a premature infant.

When an infant is delivered prematurely, unexpected realities replace expectations—and each of these replacements represents a futher loss (Table 15-1):

A scrawny, underweight, "high-risk" infant, who is either seriously ill or likely to become so, replaces the expected healthy full-term infant.

An unreactive or under-reactive infant replaces the responsive

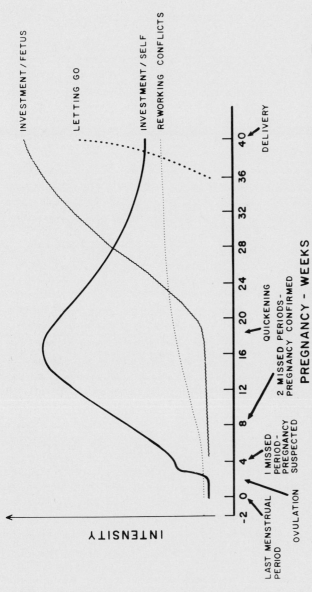

Fig. 15-1. Relationship between basic psychologic processes and milestones of pregnancy. There is general agreement as to the sequence and time courses of the processes of investment in self, investment in fetus, and letting go as represented here. The process of reworking unresolved conflicts with her own mother is represented only tentatively: we know of no systematic investigations of changes in the intensity of this process during pregnancy. Likewise, we are unaware of studies that permit quantitative comparison of the other processes as pregnancy progresses. For this reason, "intensity" is included in this schematic representation only to depict usual changes in strength of a process as pregnancy advances, not to imply comparisons of the intensities of different processes.

319

Table 15-1
Parents' Usual Emotional Reactions and Adjustment to Full-Term and Prematur
Births—Some Contributory Factors

	Full-Term Delivery	Premature Delivery
Perceptions of event	Gain, success	Loss, failure
Reactions to birth	Joy, relief	Grief, concern
Emotional preparation	Complete	Incomplete
Expectation confirmed	"Wished-for" baby	"Feared" baby
Self-esteem	Increased	Decreased
Baby's primary caregivers	Mother, father	Nurses, doctors
Parents and infants	Together	Separated
Baby's social responsiveness	Well-developed	Decreased or absent
Parents go home with	Baby	Empty arms
Major psychological tasks remaining	Reconciling real baby and fantasized baby	Grieving for expected baby; anticipatory grieving for baby; individualizing and accepting baby

and reactive infant with whom the parents had expected to
actively interact.

Separation of the premature infant from his parents replaces the
anticipated frequent close contact between them.

An incubator in a sophisticated neonatal intensive care unit
replaces the expected bassinette beside the mother's bed in a
rooming-in unit.

Nurses and doctors, strangers but awesomely knowledgeable and
competent, replace the parents as primary caregivers.

The mother, especially, has failed to produce the expected baby;
hence in the parents' perception, failure and its accompanying
loss of self-esteem replaces the expected success and increase of
self-esteem.

From observations of parents of premature infants and discussions
with them about their feelings and concerns, we know that in addition
to fearing that the infant will die or survive severely handicapped,
parents are also guilty, angry, depressed, and preoccupied with the
infant. Kaplan and Mason[8] were perhaps the first to note that these
usual feelings of parents after the birth of a premature infant were
symptomatic of grief—under these circumstances grief both for the
loss of the expected infant and in realistic anticipation of the loss of
the newborn infant. Benfield et al.[9] recently documented the perva-
siveness of anticipatory grieving by mothers and fathers of infants

transferred to a regional neonatal referral center. The Kaplan and Mason study was published in 1960, before parents were allowed to visit and participate in the care of infants in premature nurseries. Parents were separated from their infants by glass walls in that study and by miles (although visiting was encouraged) in Benfield's population. Since the work of Kennell and Klaus[10] suggests that frequent visiting accelerates parents' working through their anticipatory grief and accepting and relating to their premature infants, separation of parents from infants may have contributed to the parents' grief reactions in those two studies.

Anticipatory grief is caused by more than early separation, however, since it occurs regularly even when separation is minimized by the mother's delivering in a perinatal center and with the parents' having unrestricted access to the premature infant. We feel, in agreement with Klaus and Kennell, that early bonding of parents to premature infants is enhanced under these circumstances, yet the long-term improvement in the quality of the parent–infant relationship that might be expected to result from the earlier development of a secure parent–infant bond remains to be convincingly demonstrated.

WORKING WITH PARENTS OF PREMATURE INFANTS

Goals

The ultimate goal of our work with parents of a premature infant is to facilitate their developing a secure bond to their infant. That goal cannot be achieved until the parents have largely resolved their grieving over the loss of the expected baby and their anticipatory grieving for the real baby. Our immediate goal, then, is to facilitate their working through their grief. To accomplish this, we encourage parents to express and discuss their feelings of fear, anger, guilt, and sadness between themselves and with us, and let them know that their feelings are shared by most parents of premature and sick infants.

Caregiver–Parent Relationship

It is important that parents have identified members of the nursery team with whom they regularly discuss the infant's clinical condition. The infant's physician, plus the social worker and nurse, must also be committed to helping them adjust to and accept the infant so that they may become meaningfully involved in his care and stimulation. The team members have the important responsibility of making the parent feel welcome in the nursery, not only as concerned observers but also, if even in the smallest way, as active participants in their baby's care. We must be supportive, show empathy based on understanding of specific concerns, and be comfortable in permitting parents to temporarily develop some degree of dependecy on us.

The crises that the births of premature infants cause in parents' lives have basic features in common, yet the manifestations of such crises in individual parents and the aspects of such crises that trouble and perplex them most will vary greatly. Before we can constructively assist an individual mother or father in working through such a crisis, we must know certain basic information about the parents' health, family history, education, occupation, previous experience with sick infants and hospitals, and support available from family and others. From the nature of our contact with parents in nurseries it is almost inevitable that important background material will emerge piecemeal at a pace determined by how rapidly the parents accept us as trustworthy, concerned, and nonjudgmental, and by their specific needs related to the infant's changing clinical condition.

Each relationship between parents and care-givers will differ, but each should reward and enrich both parties. Beyond that, only one statement about our work with parents can be made with certainty: it takes time. There is no way to avoid making a considerable investment of time and effort if we personalize the support and guidance parents of premature infants so urgently need. Confusion in the parents' minds and misunderstandings between parents and staff resulting from garbled communications have results ranging from unproductive to destructive. The results of communication failures may take an inordinate amount of time to correct and may not be totally correctible no matter how great the effort. The extra time that must be spent with parents early in the infant's course if we are to understand them as particular parents of a particular baby is later returned to us many times over during the infant's stay. Much that follows will illustrate our conviction that unless we understand individual parents' feelings and concerns, our attempts to help them may indeed be misdirected and thus ineffectual or counterproductive.

Communicating With Parents

PRINCIPLES

Years ago we cared for Mary S., a premature infant transferred from a community hospital for management of severe hyaline membrane disease.

Her parents were young and healthy; this was Mrs. S.'s first pregnancy. Mary had improved so by her sixth day that frequent samplings of arterial blood and continuous measurement of blood pressure via umbilical artery catheter were no longer necessary. Her umbilical artery catheter was removed and a scalp i.v. started.

Mr. and Mrs. S. had been kept fully informed about Mary's condition during frequent visits and seemed to have an adequate grasp of her lung problem and to be pleased with her progress. Mr. S. had touched and stroked her on his first visit and called her by name; he seemed progressively less anxious and more enthusiastic about her with each visit. Mrs. S. touched Mary only after much encouragement, and then very tentatively. She relaxed very little on subsequent visits and seemed guarded and concerned. She commented on two occasions that Mary's head "seems so large," but she was told reassuringly that all premature babies' heads are relatively large. We were delighted to tell them about the removal of the umbilical artery catheter and expected that this good news of a milestone passed would hearten them. Mr. S. reacted as we had anticipated, but Mrs. S. did not. She seemed dazed and concerned when shown that a safe scalp i.v. had been substituted for a potentially dangerous deep catheter. She seemed not to hear us repeat the message that this was very good news and did not touch Mary that visit. She called that evening to ask only "if that needle is still in her head."

Mrs. S. did not accompany her husband when he visited Mary the next day. Mr. S. told us that Mrs. S. had cried most of the night because of the news we had given her. We were perplexed and put out by Mrs. S.'s inability to understand good news presented simply, directly, and with enthusiasm. We urged Mr. S. to bring his wife that evening. She came reluctantly, but refused to enter the nursery and met with us in the parents' lounge. She opened the conversation by tearfully asking, "If she lives, will she have convulsions and be retarded?" This concern seemed irrational. After all, we had been relentlessly optimistic about Mary and had gone to some trouble to point out to Mr. and Mrs. S. that Mary's grasping their finger, normal spontaneous activity, responses to being touched and stroked, and beginning to open her eyes and look around, all indicated that her brain was functioning perfectly normally. We briefly reviewed the excellent progress and added, "Of course she will live, and there is absolutely no reason to worry about seizures and mental retardation." Mrs. S., unconvinced, persisted, "But what about that needle in her head?" Our answer, irritation hopefully disguised: "We told you that we give her the extra sugar and salt solution through that needle." Then, finally, the cause of Mrs. S.'s "irrational" concern came out: "But my cousin's premature baby was sent to an intensive care nursery too and had to have a needle in his head. The doctors found he had water on the brain. They operated on him a couple of times. He's four now and he can't walk or talk and he takes convulsions a lot."

With this information available, we were able to address ourselves to Mrs. S.'s particular concern. We immediately removed the i.v. needle from Mary's scalp and started it in her hand. We encouraged Mrs. S. to go into details about her cousin's child and pointed out obvious differences between his condition and Mary's. We showed Mrs. S. several other infants receiving scalp vein infusions and we looked together at the "large" heads of other premature infants in the nursery. Mrs. S. seemed somewhat relieved, but would not touch Mary for another three days. She continued to voice concerns about Mary's head and neurologic outcome. When Mary was a month old, Mrs. S. had finally relaxed enough to enjoy her thriving, attractive, and responsive baby, and had finally accepted her as healthy. The nursery social worker, nurses, and Mary's physician devoted many hours to Mrs. S. during that month.

On review of our management of Mr. and Mrs. S., it was obvious that we had not met a cardinal requirement of effective communication: we had not bothered to learn Mr. and Mrs. S.'s perceptions of their daughter's condition and prognosis. We talked *to*, not *with* them. We assumed that simply telling them our perceptions of Mary's excellent progress and prognosis would be sufficient to reassure them. We "gave them talks," simple little lectures pitched at their level of sophistication, did this sincerely, and did not begrudge them the hours we spent with them, but we had lectured them without knowing their specific worries. We proceeded with a progressively more ineffectual and confusing "communication" by not checking frequently to learn from Mr. and Mrs. S. what they were hearing from us and others about their baby. We realized that we should have immediately sought the explanation for the jarring dissonance between Mrs. S.'s reaction to the "good news" on day six and the reaction we had expected. We then appreciated that we would have uncovered Mrs. S.'s preoccupation, which was probably too threatening to her to articulate spontaneously, even earlier if we had gone beyond the manifested content of her repeated expressions of concern about Mary's "large head."

Finally, we agreed that we could have easily obtained this important information that so strongly influenced Mrs. S.'s set toward her sick baby if we had asked her a few basic screening questions before she entered the nursery to see Mary for the first time. We would then have heard Mrs. S.'s questions in the context of this deep concern and would have directed our supportive effort accordingly. In other words, we could have prevented much of the anxiety that kept Mrs. S. from developing a secure bond of attachment to Mary during her first week of life.

From this and similar experiences and from the teaching of others we have come to the conviction that we communicate best with parents when we observe the following principles:

1. Determine and address the *parents'* perceptions.
2. Begin each discussion by listening to the *parents'* perceptions of the infant's condition and of what you and others have told them about him.

3. Check frequently during discussions to determine the parents' interpretations of what they are hearing and modify input as indicated.
4. Don't lecture.
5. Avoid information overload, statistics, vivid modifiers.
6. Regularly communicate both medical information and the approach to working with these particular parents to the nursery team and to referring physicians.

TECHNIQUES

The management of the parents of an infant referred to the Infant Referral Center several months ago illustrates the techniques by which we apply those principles. Our approach to parents of infants being transported is similar to that of Kennell and Klaus[10] and will be mentioned only in passing.

Alan C. was an 1800-g male delivered to a 21-year-old married secundagravida at 32 weeks gestation by cesarean section because of premature separation of the placenta. The first pregnancy, three years previously, produced a 3000-g stillborn female at term; the stillbirth was unexplained. The father was 23 years old and employed. The infant was asphyxiated at birth, required resuscitation, and developed severe respiratory distress while in the delivery room. The transport team consisting of doctor, nurse, and respiratory therapist arrived when the infant was three hours old and found it necessary to transfuse him and to intubate and ventilate him by intermittent positive pressure. The referring physician assisted with the stabilization. Alan was taken briefly to his mother's room, where his condition was described in simple terms to the parents. They were briefly told about the Infant Referral Center and given pamphlets describing it in detail. The father was urged to visit the infant within the next few hours.

Mr. C. arrived on schedule. The physician responsible for Alan's care and one of the unit's social workers greeted Mr. C. and then talked with him for a few minutes in the parents' lounge. He looked pale and anxious.

Neonatologist: Alan is doing pretty well now. His condition seems stable. We've given him some more blood and more oxygen and he responded well to that. How is Mrs. C.?

Mr. C. Okay, the doctor says. But she's very sore and worried about the baby.

Social Worker: I'm sure she is. All moms and dads worry when a baby is sick and has to be sent to another hospital. Have you or your wife had any experience with sick babies or premature babies?

Mr. C.: No, unless you count our little girl who was stillborn. This is the first living grandchild in my family and my wife's family, too.

Social Worker: Have you ever visited anyone in an Intensive Care Unit before this?

Mr. C.: (after nodding gravely in assent several times and swallowing

hard): I visited my Dad every day for the three weeks he was in the
Intensive Care Unit back home. He was on a respirator too. He had
emphysema. He was getting worse and worse. I think he was really glad
to go when he finally died.

Neonatologist: What was your father's name, Mr. C.?

Mr. C.: Alan.

The neonatologist assured Mr. C. that most infants of 32 week gestation
with hyaline membrane disease severe enough to require a respirator survive
intact.

They then went to Alan's isolette in the Intensive Care Unit. Nothing
was said for two minutes while Mr. C.'s eyes were riveted on his son. Then:

Neonatologist: How does Alan look to you?

Mr. C.: He certainly is nice and pink. Toward the end my father was
blue all the time, even with the oxygen turned all the way up.

Neonatologist: We're pleased that he's so pink. He's only getting 45
percent oxygen now. We turned it down from 50 percent a half-hour ago
and his color stayed fine.

In this case a few open-ended, nondirective screening questions
brought out the recent tragic losses that the father could relate
directly to his sick infant. Knowing this, the nursery team had a fair
grasp of this particular father's specific concerns and associations and
were thus better prepared to be of help to him.

A polaroid color print of Alan was taken for Mr. C. to take to his wife.
The monitoring equipment was not explained, since we knew of his recent
ICU experience. Mr. C. was encouraged to call the unit whenever he wished
and to return the next day. He touched Alan's legs tenderly before leaving.

Alan's neonatologist phoned the referring pediatrician about two hours
later. Alan's oxygen requirement had increased slightly, but he was otherwise
unchanged.

Neonatologist (after giving medical details): We take a pretty optimistic
approach here with parents. I pointed out the hopeful signs to Mr. C.—
good color, good birthweight for his 32 weeks, good response to transfu-
sions and the respirator. I didn't have to tell him we were worried about
the baby. There was plenty of evidence of that in the past eight hours.

Referring Pediatrician: That doctor who picked the baby up talked the
same way. I'm really not too sure that's the right approach to these
parents. But I'll go along with it. We really should be saying the same
things to them. I'll stop by the hospital and see Mrs. C. on my way home.
How about calling me about him tomorrow, sooner if anything happens?

The neonatologist then called Mrs. C.'s obstetrician and told him of Alan's
condition.

Neonatologist (after providing medical information): And how's Mrs. C.
doing?

Obstetrician: Okay as of two hours ago, but too groggy from the Demerol to pay much attention to what I said. I'm going to check on her soon. I'll prepare her for the worst, don't worry about that! You just can't be sure how those babies will do this early, and I wouldn't want his death to come as too much of a shock to her.

Neonatologist: Whoa—!

He then gave the argument for a cautiously optimistic approach to obviously seriously ill infants,[11] which the obstetrician did not buy but did agree to go along with for the sake of consistency.

Communication between the parents and Alan's and Mrs. C.'s physicians was fortunately coordinated in time to spare Mr. and Mrs. C. the enormous confusion of having one physician prepare them for Alan's death while another prepared them for intact survival.

The infant required a transfusion for mild hypotension and an increase in respirator pressure because of an increased arterial PCO_2 during the night, but he was stable by morning.

The social worker and neonatologist spoke together with Mrs. C. by phone:

Social worker: How are you feeling, Mrs. C?

Mrs. C.: I'm achy and sore. Mainly, I'm worried about the baby.

Social Worker: What did your husband tell you about Alan?

Mrs. C.: He said his color was good and that he was a pretty baby. It's hard to tell from that picture. My OB doctor and the baby's pediatrician from up here were both in and they seemed to think he was doing fairly well.

Neonatologist: He did okay overnight. He needed a little more blood, but that's not unusual with these babies. He's nice and pink this morning, too.

Mrs. C.: When will he be over the critical period?

Neonatologist: Well, we really don't think in terms of a critical period. Right now he's stable and we're pleased about that. Babies with this lung disease usually start to get better gradually during the first week. We think he's doing well at this stage of the game.

There were no apparent communication misunderstandings to correct as yet. The neonatologist ducked the mother's question of a critical period and would have similarly evaded any attempt to have him provide statistics on prognosis. He also scrupulously avoided use of vivid modifiers such as "critically," "seriously" (ill), and "extremely" (well); in fact, he did not use a single modifier. He realized that he was talking to a parent under the stress of an intense crisis and hence in a period of high arousal, during which perceptions (be they accurate or distorted) of an infant likely to die may be retained intact as the infant survives and thrives. This sequence of events may lead to the parents continuing to be convinced of the child's vulnerability and cause serious distortions in the parent–infant relationship and the child's emotional and social development. This has been termed the "vulnerable child syndrome."[12]

Alan's case was presented by a pediatric resident on work rounds that morning. Aspects of the psychosocial issues discussed here were explained by resident and social worker, and the special needs of Alan's parents were made clear to all who might be in contact with them. The infant's admission record contained a form on which nurses, social workers, and physicians would regularly record the frequency of parents visiting and calling and observations on the parents' interaction with Alan and their progress in providing care for him and their special needs and concerns. This permanent record form has helped us keep a running tab on psychosocial aspects of case management.

That morning the nurse caring for Alan phoned the nurse in charge of the postpartum nursing unit at the referring hospital. She was anxious that Mrs. C.'s nurse reinforce the information that the C.'s were getting from the Infant Referral Center and to get her assessment of Mrs. C.'s feelings about Alan. She learned that Mrs. C. seemed somewhat depressed and had cried a few times about Alan but that she was talking more about the stillbirth three years ago than about him; this important information was recorded and shared with others. Infant Referral Center and the referring hospital nurses maintained daily phone contact until Mrs. C. was discharged.

Mr. C. visited again that afternoon at the end of Alan's first day in the Intensive Care Unit.

Neonatologist: What did you tell Mrs. C. about Alan after you saw him yesterday?

Mr. C.: I told her he had a lung disease lots of premature babies get and that it's serious enough for him to be on a respirator and he needs a lot of special attention. I also told her he was pink and pretty and that he probably wouldn't start to get better for a few days yet. You won't believe what she said then. She said, "Does he look like the little girl?" and she started to cry. (Pause, and then reflectively) You know, I've been thinking a lot about her too these past couple days. I saw her but my wife didn't.

"What did you tell (whomever) about the baby?" is a standard opener to check on what parents heard us and others tell them previously about their infant. Mr. C. had heard what we said and had not denied or distorted the information. He, too, then volunteered that both he and his wife were painfully reliving the stillbirth of their first infant.

Alan began to improve on the third day and was weaned completely from the respirator by the seventh day. When Mrs. C. first visited him two days later he was breathing easily in room air and was pink, active, and gaining weight regularly on nasogastric feeding.

Mrs. C. had accurate perceptions of Alan's course and excellent prognosis. She had never been in an ICU before. We anticipated that her flat affect would lift when she saw her handsome, active boy and that she would begin to refer to him by name. We were wrong. She stood dejectedly by Alan's isolette, shook her head repeatedly, cried quietly, and did not want to touch or hold him. She finally turned to her husband and asked, "Did she look at all like him?" Her second visit two days later was a repeat of the first; she again referred to the stillborn baby girl. The neonatologist and social worker suggested to Mr. and Mrs. C. that they might like to sit down and talk about the first baby. They readily agreed, and a full hour was then spent discussing that pregnancy and delivery and their feelings about the stillbirth. They had not systematically reviewed or organized that material previously, nor had they shared their feelings of deep grief over her loss and their concern that Alan, too, would be stillborn. Both returned to Alan's isolette, and Mrs. C. asked a few questions about him and smiled before she left. Within the next three visits she called him by name and rocked, fed, and obviously enjoyed him. Mr. C. became enthusiastic about Alan only when he was removed from the respirator. They were competent, caring parents by the time of discharge.

We have worked with several other families who needed attention given to a previous stillbirth or neonatal death (or recent loss of other family members) before they could focus fully on the new infant, no matter how healthy. We have also had the somewhat analogous experience of needing to spend considerable time discussing a previous neonatal death or stillbirth to facilitate grieving for a current loss.

IMPACT OF SEPARATION ON THE MOTHER

About 1600 premature and 400 sick full-term infants have been referred to the Infant Referral Center during its decade of operation. Most were transported during their first day of life from hospitals from 5–100 miles away. Most fathers visited the infant during his first or second day here. Mothers first visited, on average, when the infant was 5–6 days old. About 500 of the 2000 infants died, and about 200 of the deaths occurred before the infant was 72 hours old. None of the mothers but many of the fathers of these 200 infants who died early saw their infants in the Infant Referral Center.

We have listened carefully to many of the mothers of infants referred here describe the period between their infant's birth and the mother's first visit to the Infant Referral Center. Many of the fathers were not present during the delivery. Most mothers saw the infant only fleetingly at birth. Many were aware that there was concern about the infant's condition while still in the Delivery Room. A few touched their infant before he left the Delivery Room. Most of the infants were ill at birth or within the first few hours. The mother usually next saw him when the transport team visited her room in route to the transport van or helicopter. She and the father usually briefly touched the infant in the transport incubator, afraid of dislodging monitor probes and leads, catheters, peripheral i.v. infusions, and endotracheal tubes. She felt "dazed," "overwhelmed," "as if it were unreal," and then "empty" when the baby was taken away.

From then on the stories varied little. Her huband usually stayed with her a few hours and then went to visit the infant as the transport team had suggested. He was gone about six hours, but it seemed an eternity. She felt "too numb and confused to cry" and "scared the baby was going to die; I just kept waiting for the phone to ring." She had mixed feelings about her husband and the concerned and efficient nurses and doctors he told her about. She was glad her husband cared so much about the baby but envious that he, not she, was involved with the baby. She felt "helpless" and "useless" enough as it was, and this caregiving role-reversal made her feel all the more "a failure." She felt guilty enough as it was, and the growing anger and ambivalence toward her husband ("and even [the husband's] *mother* saw the baby twice before I ever got out of the hospital!") made her feel more guilty still. She couldn't get the baby off her mind: "I kept thinking about all those wires and gadgets and how hard he was breathing; I knew he might die," and "I couldn't stop thinking about what I did, or didn't do, maybe, to cause him to be so early and sick."

She "cried a lot and had a lump in my throat and a heavy chest, especially when I heard babies cry and when my roommate got her baby to nurse. I really envied her. That made me feel like I was a terrible person, but I just couldn't help it." "I couldn't wait until you people called from Pittsburgh every morning. And I just couldn't keep from calling you a couple of times a day. But I was always terrified when I called that he might be worse."

Most mothers were discharged home with instructions to "relax, take it easy, and get rested up for a week before going to Pittsburgh." None could or would follow this advice. Most first visited their baby within a few days of being discharged; some came here directly from the hospital.

Almost all mothers showed and expressed relief when they first saw their baby in the Infant Referral Center, no matter how sick he might be. "I was afraid before that he was in a lot of pain with those tubes in his chest." "He looks so much better than I though he would." "It was hard to believe there was someone with him almost all of the time," We concluded that no descriptions or series of photos could give mothers an adequate mental picture of the Infant Referral Center and that their fantasies about the infant's appearance, suffering, and general condition were almost always far worse than reality; subsequent interviews verified that conclusion.

Many of the infants had recovered partially or completely from their acute illness when their mother first visited. A mother who already feels herself "useless" and "a failure" may feel her maternal role and value further diminished by her frail infant's having been pulled through a life-threatening illness without her by his side. It is not hard to understand the ambivalence mothers feel toward their infant's doctors and (especially) nurses: they are appreciated for having saved the infant, resented for being the surrogate for the "useless" mother in the most basic of maternal caretaking tasks.

The early reactions to separation described by mothers whose infants live are similar to but less intense than those described by mothers of infants who died; perhaps their feelings during separation are magnified when recalled after the infant's death. Mothers whose babies died in the Infant Referral Center before they could visit have the usual reactions to the death of an infant. In addition, they often spontaneously comment on their intense frustration and sense of having failed the infant because he died alone (without family), in a distant hospital, attended by strangers. At the close of the conferences, held about one month after neonatal deaths,[13] we offer to accompany parents who were unable to visit the infant to the Infant Referral Center so that they may see the exact isolette their baby occupied and the sort of intentsive care he recieved. No parent has refused this offer. Most have indicated that the brief visit to the unit was helpful. We feel that these visits remove much of the parents' uncertainty about the type and quality of care the infant received and the place in which it was given, and provide them a picture about which they can organize some of their grieving. This may be a step, albeit belated, toward confirming the death of an infant whose corpse the parents may not have seen.

IN PRAISE OF ANTENATAL REFERRALS

We have no reason to suspect that separating a high-risk infant from his mother helps her in any way to cope with the crisis of his birth and illness. On the contrary, we consider that the increment of emotional turmoil caused by separation impedes her coping with and beginning to adapt to this crisis. Cramer's findings[13] that mothers progressively withdrew their investment in premature infants from whom they were separated has particularly troubling implications for the quality of the subsequent parent–child relationship. The argument against separation would be strengthened if there were incontrovertible evidence that it is associated with poor developmental outcome in the child. Suggestions that such an association may exist are presented with more[10] or less[14] conviction elsewhere.

We do not need sure proof of adverse long-term effects of mother–infant separation to urge that it be avoided whenever possible. Unnecessary separation is adequately indicted on the charge of inhumanity alone. That sentiment would be quixotic, given the improved survival of premature and other high-risk infants referred from community hospitals to neonatal centers,[1] if acceptable alternatives to neonatal transport were not available. Two acceptable alternatives exist: antenatal ("in utero") referral, and referral of the mother to the perinatal center with her newborn infant. We had had experience with increasing numbers of antenatal referrals during the past four years and limited recent experience with postnatal mother/baby referrals.

High-risk status of the fetus and newborn can be first anticipated or detected in one-third of pregnancies before onset of labor, in another one-third during labor, and in the final third at birth. By rough estimate, half of the women who develop obstetric complications that might compromise the fetus or whose fetuses show evidence of compromise during labor could be transported to perinatal centers for delivery. There is no compelling practical reason why all pregnant women with high-risk status confirmed before onset of labor could not be referred for management of the later part of pregnancy, labor, and delivery. All told, then, approximately half of the infants transported *to* a center because of prematurity or critical neonatal illness could be delivered readily *at* that center.

The obvious and overarching psychologic advantage of delivery of a high-risk infant in a perinatal center is the close proximity of the mother to her infant during his first days of life. The mother's (and father's) involvement with the sick or small infant is facilitated in this setting by postpartum nursing unit and nursery staffs deeply committed to encouraging the bonding of parents to infant. Moreover, important communications between caregivers and parents, and between perinatologists and neonatologists, are more likely to be fruitful when they are frequent and face-to-face, as they usually are in a perinatal center.

We feel that the psychologic benefits to a high-risk mother of delivery in a perinatal center are potentially greatest when referrals can be made before birth. We draw here on experience with a large population of women with diabetes mellitus hospitalized routinely at

34–35 weeks gestation for observation and studies to determine the optimal timing and route of delivery. Our approach to these women illustrates the supportive care of any woman admitted before onset of labor because of a high-risk pregnancy.

At the time of a woman's admission on a combined Medical/Perinatal Service, Neonatology and Social Service are routinely consulted. The neonatologist and social worker discuss case management with internist and perinatologist. Beyond this, we attempt to facilitate the woman's adjustment to the hospital and to determine her particular needs and concerns. We visit frequently to discuss her progress and learn how well she is tolerating tedious and uncomfortable procedures such as sonar evaluation of fetal head circumference, anniocentesis, and fetal stress tests. We take the attitude that these studies are done to assure fetal well-being (which they usually do) rather than to find fetal compromise—a distinction most women are pleased to accept. A copy of the neonatologists' consultation report is filed in the Infant Referral Center for future medical use and to alert the unit's Nurse Parent Instructor, who provides liaison between nursery and obstetric floors, to visit the patient. During that leisurely visit and subsequent visits the nurse discusses hospital and nursery routines (or, thankfully, relative lack of routines), previous pregnancies, babies in general, babies of diabetic mothers in particular and how they are usually managed here, the mother's previous experience with infants, expectations for and concerns and questions about the coming baby, and whatever else is on the mother's mind. The nurse then takes the pregnant woman into the Infant Referral Center, where they look at babies and equipment together and discuss any further questions the mother may have. This visit to the unit where her baby may spend some time intrigues mothers and decreases anxiety in most. Many choose to return on their own while awaiting delivery. The Nurse Parent Instructor will also follow this mother daily after the baby is born, as she follows all mothers of infants in the Infant Referral Center while they are hospitalized here following delivery.

Perinatal centers offer medical benefits to high-risk infants and emotional benefits to their parents. Delivery at a perinatal center, in contrast to referral of the infant to a center, provides the important psychologic advantage of enhanced mother (and father)–infant contact plus the bonus of more frequent and direct communication between parents and the infants' caregivers. Taken together, the tangible benefit of increased infant survival and the intangible emotional benefit of earlier and closer parent–infant contact, which should promote parent-to-infant bonding, far outweight the inconvenience of delivery in a strange hospital away from home.

Within the past year a mother insisted on being transferred to our hospital with her critically ill infant just six hours after delivery by cesarean section. The parents felt they benefited greatly by being close to their infant during her acute illness and early convalescence. On the basis of this positive initial experience with baby *plus* mother transfer, we have subsequently offered this opportunity to other parents. The several who accepted transfer likewise felt the relief that accompanied enhanced contact with their sick infant more than outweighed the discomfort and complicated logistics of the maternal transport. In those cases in which antenatal transfer is not possible, our preliminary experience suggests that postnatal maternal transfer is usually feasible and safe, and emotionally better for the mother than remaining in the referring hospital after her infant has been sent to the referral center.

REFERENCES

1. Usher R: Changing mortality rates with perinatal intensive care and regionalization. Semin Perinatol 1:309–319, 1977
2. Klaus MH, Kennell JH: Parent–Infant Bonding. St. Louis, Mosby, 1976
3. Bibring GL: Some considerations of the psychological processes in pregnancy. Psychoanal Study Child 14:113–121, 1959
4. Bibring GL, Dwyer TF, Huntington DS, et al: A study of the psychological processes in pregnancy and of the earliest mother–child relationship. I. Some propositions and comments. Psychoanal Study Child 16:9–24, 1961
5. Deutsch H: The Psychology of Women (vol 2). Motherhood. New York, Grune & Stratton, 1945
6. Benedek T: The psychobiology of pregnancy, in Anthony EJ, Benedek T (Eds): Parenthood. Boston, Little, Brown, 1970
7. Brazelton TB: The parent–infant attachment. Clin Obstet Gynecol 19:373–389, 1976
8. Kaplan DM, Mason EA: Maternal reactions to premature birth viewed as an emotional disorder. Am J Orthopsychiatry 30:539–552, 1960
9. Benfield DG, Leib SA, Rentor J: Grief response of parents following referral of the critically ill newborn. N Engl J Med 294:975–978, 1976
10. Kennell JH, Klaus MH: Caring for parents of a premature or sick infant, in Klaus MH, Kennell JH: Parent–Infant Bonding. St. Louis, Mosby, 1976
11. Green M, Solnit AJ: Reactions to the threatened loss of a child: A vulnerable child syndrome. Pediatrics 34:58–66, 1964
12. Kennell JH, Klaus MH: Caring for parents of an infant who dies, in Klaus MH, Kennell JH: Parent–Infant Bonding. St. Louis, Mosby, 1976
13. Cramer B: A mother's reactions to the birth of a premature infant, in Klaus MH, Kennell JH: Parent–Infant Bonding. St. Louis, Mosby, 1976
14. Campbell SBG, Taylor PM: Bonding and attachment: Theoretical issues, in Taylor PM (ed): Parent–Infant Relationships. New York, Grune & Stratton, 1980, p3.

Jane D. Gray, Christy A. Cutler,
Janet G. Dean, and C. Henry Kempe

16

Prediction and Prevention of Child Abuse

Child abuse is a major problem affecting many thousands of children from all social strata. Increasing knowledge of the general factors that operate in causing children to be abused has resulted in earlier and more accurate diagnosis. Effective therapy is now being instituted at the first indication of injuries in an attempt to break the cycle of parent-induced child abuse and neglect. Although the overall dynamics operating to produce child abuse and neglect are becoming better understood, the specific factors that allow us to predict abnormal childrearing patterns in certain families have not been generally established. The ability to make accurate predictions of abnormal parenting practices will greatly facilitate the initiation of effective intervention before significant damage has been allowed to occur.

This study examines the feasibility of predicting the potential for some abnormal childrearing practices, of which child abuse and neglect is one extreme. It concentrates on the perinatal and early neonatal periods, since these offer an excellent opportunity to make assessments of a newborn infant's behavior, to observe the mother's and father's responses to their child, and to study the interaction between them. The perinatal period also provides easy accessibility to individuals as they become a family, permits observations of the

This is a very slightly modified version of the original paper of the same title by the same authors that appeared in the journal Child Abuse and Neglect: The International Journal [1:45–58, 1977]. The findings of this study, although not as yet replicated, are so provocative that it seemed warranted to present them again in this forum. – Ed.

mother and child during a critically sensitive time,[1] and allows pediatric intervention to begin early whenever there is indication that potentially harmful childrearing patterns may occur. Intervention at this time can be aimed at increasing strengths within the family so that a child may have the opportunity to reach his physical, emotional, and intellectual potential.

MATERIALS AND METHODS

From November 1971 to March 1973 a population sample was drawn from 350 mothers who were having either their first or second child at Colorado General Hospital. Infants with neonatal conditions severe enough to require transfer to the neonatal intensive care unit were excluded from the study.

Some or all of the following screening procedures were carried out to determine which of them were most likely to be predictive of "abnormal parenting practices."

1. *Collection of prenatal information.* Data were gathered regarding the parents' upbringing, feelings about this pregnancy, expectations for the unborn child, attitudes toward discipline, availability of support systems, and the present living situations. Important warning signs are presented in Table 16-1. It is obvious that many of these facts can be obtained and observations made throughout the perinatal period.

2. *Administration of a questionnaire.*[2] A 74-item questionnaire was administered to the mother during the prenatal or early postnatal period. The questions covered information similar to that obtained in the prenatal interview (see above).

3. *Assessment of labor and delivery room information.* These data were collected by one or more of the following methods:

    a. Mother–infant forms were completed by the labor and delivery room nurses. The nurses recorded the parents' verbal and nonverbal interactions with their child during their first encounter with him/her (Table 16-2). The nurse also added any additional pertinent observations about the parents' behavior.

    b. In a number of instances, with the parents' permission, videotapes were made of mothers' and infants' interaction so as to be able to carry out a more thorough assessment of the quality of this interaction and to check the accuracy of observations made by labor and delivery room nurses and physicians.

Table 16-1
Warning Signs During the Prenatal Period

Mother seems overly concerned with the baby's sex or performance
Mother exhibits denial of the pregnancy (not willing to gain weight, no
    plans for the baby, refusal to talk about the situation)
This child could be "one too many"
Mother is extremely depressed over the pregnancy
Mother is very frightened and alone, especially in anticipation of delivery.
    Careful explanations do not seem to dissipate the fears
There is lack of support from husband and/or family
Mother and/or father formerly wanted an abortion or seriously considered
    relinquishment and have changed their minds
Parents come from an abusive/neglectful background
Parents' living situation is overcrowded, isolated, unstable, or intolerable to
    them
They do not have a telephone
There are no supportive relatives and/or friends

c. The delivery room staff was encouraged to provide anecdotal
information regarding their observations of the parents and children. This information was also utilized to assess parenting
potential (Table 16-2).
4. *Observations and/or interview during the postpartum period.* During the postpartum period the parents were again interviewed to

Table 16-2
Warning Signs During Delivery

Written form with baby's chart of parent's reaction at birth:
    How does the mother LOOK?
    What does the mother SAY?
    What does the mother DO?
    When the father attends delivery, record his reactions as well
Passive reaction, either verbal or nonverbal: Mother
    doesn't touch, hold, or examine baby, nor talk in affectionate
    terms or tones about the baby
Hostile reaction, either verbal or nonverbal: Mother
    makes inappropriate verbalization, glances, or disparaging
    remarks about the physical characteristics of the child
Disappointment over sex of the baby
No eye contact
Nonsupportive interaction between the parents
If interaction seems dubious, talk to the nurse and doctor
    involved with delivery for further information

obtain or expand on information gained during the prenatal interview (see above and Table 16-3). Information obtained from direct observation of the mother–infant interaction during the postpartum stay in the hospital was also recorded. The warning signs listed in Tables 16-1–16-3 are indications of possible problems. A high-risk situation is created by varying combinations of these signs, the family's degree of emphasis upon them, and the family's willingness to change. The interviewer took into consideration the mother's age, culture, and education as well as her affect and the importance she seemed to attach to her problems.

From the data gathered in two or more of these areas, parents

Table 16-3
Warning Signs During the Postpartum Period

Mother doesn't have fun with the baby

Mother avoids eye contact with the baby and avoids the direct "en face" position

Verbalizations to the infant are negative, demanding, harsh, etc.

Most of the mother's verbalizations to others about the child are negative

Parents remain disappointed over the sex of the child

Negative identification of the child: significance of name, who he/she looks like and/or acts like

Parents have expectations developmentally far beyond the child's capabilities

Mother is very bothered by crying; it makes her feel hopeless, helpless, or like crying herself

Feedings: the mother sees the baby as too demanding; she is repulsed by his messiness, or ignores his demands

Changing diapers is seen as a very negative, repulsive task

Mother does not comfort the baby when he cries

Husband's and/or family's reactions to the baby have been negative or nonsupportive

Mother is receiving little or no meaningful support from anyone

There are sibling rivalry problems or a complete lack of understanding of this possibility

Husband is very jealous of the baby's drain on mother's time, energy, and affection

Mother lacks control over the situation. She is not involved, nor does she respond to the baby's needs, but relinquishes control to the doctors or nurses

When attention is focused on the child in her presence, the mother does not see this as something positive for herself

Mother makes complaints about the baby that cannot be verified

---

were assessed as to their parenting potential. One hundred mothers identified as having psychologic, interactional, and lifestyle dynamics[3-5] that might result in "abnormal parenting practices" were randomly assigned to a "high-risk intervene" (HRI) group (n = 50) or a "high-risk nonintervene" (HRN) group (n = 50). Fifty mothers who also delivered their first or second child at the hospital in the same time period and who were assessed as low risk (LR) in terms of abnormal parenting potential were selected as controls. Positive family circumstances that predominated in the low-risk families are listed in Table 16-4.

"Intervention" in this study meant the provision of pediatric care by one pediatrician at the Medical Center where the child was born. This pediatrician examined the infant during his stay in the newborn nursery, talked with the parents on the postpartum ward, and scheduled the first pediatric clinic visit to take place before the infant was two weeks old. Thereafter the pediatrician saw the child at scheduled bimonthly visits. Additional pediatric visits took place whenever the doctor or the mother felt that the child should be seen. In addition to seeing the child during visits to the clinic, the pediatrician also contacted the family by telephone two or three days after discharge from the hospital as well as during the subsequent weeks when a clinic visit was not scheduled. Additional telephone calls were initiated by the pediatrician to ascertain the status of any problems that may have become apparent in previous clinic visits and/or telephone conversations. The physician also contacted the family to provide support to them whenever a medical or other crisis was known to be present. It was not pointed out to the study families that this service was exceptional; it was simply provided as part of the child's well-baby care. The special care given high-risk families is summarized in Table 16-5.

In addition to the contact between the pediatrician and the family, "intervention" also included weekly visits to the home by the public health nurses. The public health nurses had been notified of the pertinent findings obtained by the interview, assessment of the delivery room interaction, and the questionnaires. Whenever necessary, referrals were made to other medical facilities or mental health clinics. Lay health visitors[6] (lay persons who visited in the homes to assess the general health status of the child, to offer emotional support to the entire family, and to provide liaison with the professional health system) were utilized whenever indicated.

"Nonintervention" meant that the investigators did nothing directly for the family after discharge. All of the available information, however, was routinely shared with attending hospital staff, commu-

Table 16-4
Positive Family Circumstances

Parents see likable attributes in baby, see baby as separate individual
Baby is healthy and not too disruptive to parents' lifestyle
Either parent can rescue the child or relieve the other in a crisis
Marriage is stable
Parents have a good friend or relative to turn to, a sound "need-meeting"
    system
Parents exhibit coping abilities; i.e., capacity to plan and understand need
    for adjustments because of new baby
Mother's intelligence and health are good
Parents had helpful role models when growing up
Parents can have fun together and enjoy personal interests or hobbies
This baby was planned or wanted
Future birth control is planned
Father has stable job
Parents have their own home and stable living conditions
Father is supportive to mother and involved in care of baby

---

nity agencies such as visiting nurse services, and the family physician
or clinic.

When a child was between the ages of 17 and 35 months (mean
age 26.8 months) a home visit was made to 25 randomly selected
families in each of the three categories: HRI, HRN, and LR. During
this home visit, the mother was interviewed and medical and social
information involving the entire family was collected. Also, observations of mother–child interaction were made and the Denver Developmental Screening Test (DDST) was administered to the child.

The incidence of various findings was determined for each child
during the first 17 months of life (at the time of detailed evaluation,
the youngest child was 17 months old). In order to determine whether
or not a group at risk for deficient parenting had actually been

Table 16-5
Special Well-Child Care for High-Risk Families

Promote maternal attachment to the newborn
Contact the mother by telephone on the second day after discharge
Provide more frequent office visits
Give more attention to the mother
Emphasize accident prevention
Use compliments rather than criticism
Accept phone calls at home
Provide regular home visits by public health nurse or lay health visitor

---

predicted, children were assessed for the presence of incidents of "abnormal parenting practices," which included all verified reports of abuse and neglect to the Center Child Abuse Registry, injury secondary to lack of adequate care and supervision, injuries suspicious for inflicted trauma, failure to thrive that was thought to be secondary to deprivation,[7] relinquishments, foster care placements, and parental kidnappings. Children were also assessed as to the number of incidents of trauma thought to be true accidents, reasons why children were no longer in their biologic homes, their immunization status, and their performance on the DDST.

Central Child Abuse Registry reports and indications of "abnormal parenting practices" involving medical concern were categorized for all three study groups as a comparison of the effect of intervention.

Data were also compiled to help indicate which of the four screening procedures (prenatal interview, questionnaires, baby and delivery room observations, or postpartum interviews and observations) resulted in the greatest percentage of correct predictions of "parenting potential."

The three groups were compared by ordinary χ^2 tests appropriate for 3 × 2 contingency tables (Table 16-6). These "total" χ^2 were partitioned into single-degree-of-freedom χ^2 appropriate for comparing the two high-risk groups with tbe low-risk group (HR versus LR) and HRI versus HRN, as discussed by Kastenbaum.[8]

RESULTS

Ability to Predict

INDICATIONS OF ABNORMAL PARENTING

By the time of detailed evaluation there were 22 indications of "abnormal parenting practices" in the high-risk groups (25 HRI and 25 HRN) and 2 indications in the control group of 25. The high-risk groups differed significantly from the low-risk group ($p < 0.01$). In the total population sample (150 children) 8 high-risk and no low-risk children were reported to the Central Child Abuse Registry ($p < 0.04$).

There were three cases of failure to thrive (weight below the third percentile, height and head circumference above the third percentile) thought to be secondary to deprivation[7] in the HRI group. Although children in the HRN group were not followed as closely, information was obtained by chart review and contact with the child's physician

Table 16-6

Summary of Statistical Analyses

Item	HRI	HRN	LR	Partitioned χ² Results (p Values)		
				HR-LR	HRI-HRN	Total
Total study population (150):						
Central Registry reports	6	2	0	< 0.04	< 0.08	< 0.03
Detailed evaluation of population (25 in each category)						
Central Registry reports:						
At time of home evaluation						
(mean 26.8 mo)	2	1	0	< 0.22	< 0.48	< 0.36
By 17 mo of age	1	1	0	< 0.60	< 0.99	< 0.30
Indications of abnormal parenting practices:						
By time of home evaluation	11	11	2	< 0.01	< 0.99	< 0.01
By 17 months of age	10	10	0	< 0.01	< 0.99	< 0.01
Failure to thrive	3	2	0	< 0.20	< 0.60	< 0.30
DDST not normal:						
By test manual (see Ref. 9)	3	3	0	< 0.08	< 0.99	< 0.20
By failed items	7	3	0	< 0.02	< 0.10	< 0.02
Accidents:						
By time of home evaluation	16	15	11	< 0.14	< 0.78	< 0.33
By 17 months of age	12	10	4	< 0.02	< 0.56	< 0.05
Not in biologic home	5	3	0	< 0.04	< 0.36	< 0.07
Appropriate immunization status at 1 year	25	22	24	< 0.72	< 0.16	< 0.16
Inpatient treatment for injury	0	5	0	< 0.11	< 0.01	< 0.01

that two of these children had failure to thrive thought to be secondary to deprivation. There were no such cases in the low-risk group.

ACCIDENTS

There were 31 children in the high-risk groups and 11 children in the low-risk group who had sustained at least one accident that required medical attention during the time period of the study. During the first 17 months of life 22 children in the high-risk groups and 4 in the low-risk group had at least one accident requiring medical attention ($p < 0.02$).

IMMUNIZATION STATUS

At one year of age 47 of the 50 high-risk children (25 HRI and 22 HRN) were up-to-date with their immunizations. In the low-risk group 24 of 25 had similar immunization status. The difference between the groups was not statistically significant.

DENVER DEVELOPMENTAL SCREENING TEST

DDST assessment of high-risk children showed 3 whose results were recorded as questionable, 3 who were untestable, and 44 who were normal.[9] In the low-risk group, all 25 were normal. There was no statistically significant difference between these results. If the results of the DDST are examined by counting the number of clear failures (test items to the left of the child's chronologic age), 10 high-risk children versus no low-risk children had clear failures ($p < 0.02$).

REASONS FOR NO EVALUATION

There was a significantly increased incidence ($p < 0.04$) of infants assessed as being at risk for "abnormal parenting practices" not being in their biologic home at the time of the follow-up evaluation. All low-risk children were in their biologic home, but eight high-risk children were either in foster care, permanently living with relatives, or had been legally relinquished.

Results of Intervention on the Incidence and Outcome of Abnormal Parenting Practices

INCIDENCE

Between the HRI and HRN groups there were no significant statistical differences on the basis of Central Child Abuse Registry reports, indications of "abnormal parenting practices," accidents, immunizations, or DDST scores.

OUTCOME

Another way to measure the effect of intervention within the high-risk groups is to describe the quality of differences in the types of "abnormal parenting practices" that occurred. No child in the low-risk group and no child in the HRI group suffered an injury thought to be secondary to "abnormal parenting practices" that was serious enough to require hospitalization for treatment. Five children in the HRN group, however, required inpatient treatment for serious injuries ($p < 0.01$). These injuries included a fractured femur, a fractured skull, barbiturate ingestion, a subdural hematoma, and third-degree burns. Although these five injuries were treated in local hospitals, only two of them had been reported to the Central Child Abuse Registry.

Screening Procedures

Information from observations of labor and delivery room interactions was analyzed individually and resulted in 76.5 percent correct predictions of parenting potential; the questionnaire alone resulted in 57.5 percent correct predictions; the prenatal interview alone resulted in 54.4 percent correct predictions; and the postpartum interview/ observations resulted in 54 percent correct predictions. If all four parameters are included together, they resulted in 79 percent correct predictions.

During the initial interviews and observations, four factors were considered as possible indicators of high risk; the mother's race, the family's socioeconomic status (as determined by the hospital's financial ratings), the mother's marital status, and the mother's age. In the study population, the mother's race did not prove to be a significant variable. There was a trend toward "financial difficulty" in mothers in the high-risk groups. The mother's marital status and age differed significantly between the high-risk groups and the low-risk group; single and young mothers were considered to be at higher risk for abnormal parenting practices.

DISCUSSION

Child abuse is now being reported approximately 300,000 times each year in our country. The figure rises to one million if neglect is included. About 60,000 children have significant injuries; about 2000 die and 6000 suffer permanent brain damage.[6] Multidisciplinary research (sociologic, pediatric, nursing, psychiatric, and legal) has made possible earlier diagnosis and more successful treatment programs; however, as in many other aspects of medicine, prevention is the ultimate goal.

Medical and nursing staff who work in the prenatal area, labor and delivery area, and the neonatal nursery are ideally situated to make sensitive observations of a family's interactional behavior. The assessment of attitudes and feelings has been a part of pediatrics for many years. It is now time to formally utilize these assessments in the implementation of supportive intervention for families in need. Systematic use of prenatal interview, questionnaire, labor and delivery observations, and postpartum interviews/observations can identify a population of risk for "abnormal parenting practices." These data show that accurate prediction of families in need of extra services is possible, as evidenced by the statistical differences between the high-risk groups and the low-risk group in the areas of "abnormal parenting practices," Central Child Abuse Registry reports, number of accidents (by 17 months of age), children no longer in their biologic homes, and children with clear failures on the DDST.

It is a belabored point that battering parents tend to lack motivation toward initiating helping services. When the health care providers (pediatricians, public health nurses, and lay health visitors) initiate an outreach approach with high-risk families, however, a comprehensive medical program can be successful.

Recently there has been an increased awareness of the abnormal behavior characteristics and the developmental lags seen in abused children.[10,11] This has been observed in the children after documentation of abuse, but with the assumption that the children have been living in an "abusive environment" prior to the physical abuse. In this study, 20 percent of children thought prospectively to be at risk for abnormal parenting had at least one clear failure on the DDST. These are children thought to be living in an environment deficient in parenting.

Now that it is largely possible to identify a population at risk for "abnormal parenting practices," the next step is to determine the success and practicality of initiating early intervention with these families. Although there was no statistically significant difference in the incidence of "abnormal parenting practices" between the HRI and the HRN groups, there was a qualitative difference in the injuries in the study groups. In the HRI and the low-risk groups, no child required hospitalization for treatment of a serious injury thought to be secondary to "abnormal parenting practices." In the HRN group, however, five children required treatment for trauma or poisoning. One of the five serious injuries (the burns) was preceded by relatively minor inflicted trauma, including cigarette burns, scratch marks, and strap marks. These all received medical attention but were never reported, nor was an attempt made to involve other helping agencies in an effort to prevent further injuries. There is a possibility that the third-degree burns and the resulting contractures could have been prevented if intervention had been initiated promptly. In another case, a subdural hematoma and its resulting intellectual deficit and neurologic handicap might have been prevented if intervention had been instituted during a "social admission" to a hospital just prior to the injury. If appropriate interventions to alleviate social pressure had been undertaken at this point, there is a possibility that the injury would not have occurred. In the low-risk group, injuries (a minor burn and a metacarpal fracture) thought to have occurred because of negligence both involved children over two years of age. These children were well into the accident-prone toddler years, whereas injuries in the high-risk groups occurred at younger ages.

There was also an increased incidence of failure to thrive in the high-risk groups. Early identification and effective intervention in one case of failure to thrive in the HRI group was therapeutic for that child; this baby was promptly hospitalized at five weeks of age when failure to thrive was discovered. The weight gain was reestablished in the hospital, and failure to thrive completely resolved by four months of age. On the two year follow-up the child had normal growth parameters.

Therefore it appears that modest intervention in the HRI group precluded any injuries severe enough to require hospitalization for treatment and any injury that resulted in prolonged disability. The less serious injuries and the failure-to-thrive baby in the HRI group were promptly reported and effective community intervention established, which may have prevented subsequent, more serious problems.

The concept of early preventive pediatric and community intervention will, it is hoped, lead to progress in prevention of the harmful effects of child abuse and neglect. Families identified as being in need of extra services must have access to intensive, continuous intervention that is both positive and supportive. It makes little sense to provide excellent prenatal, obstetric, and neonatal pediatric care in our hospitals only to abandon the most needy young families at the hospital door and leave to chance, or to parent motivation, the needed access to helping professionals.

CONCLUSIONS

A high-risk group was successfully identified by the use of perinatal screening procedures; tbese children had encountered significantly different parenting practices than had the low-risk "control" group. Five children in the "high-risk nonintervene" group required hospitalization for serious injuries thought to be secondary to abnormal parenting practices, as contrasted to no such hospitalizations in the "high-risk intervene" and "low-risk" control groups.

Labor-delivery observations and nursery interviews and observations provided the most accurate predictive information; prenatal interviews and questionnaires did not add significantly.

It seems clear that perinatal assessment and simple intervention with families at high risk for abnormal parenting practices significantly improves the infants' chances for escaping physical injury.

REFERENCES

1. Klaus MH, Jerauld R, Kreger NC, et al.: Maternal attachment: Importance of the first postpartum day. N Engl J Med 286:460–463, 1972
2. Schneider C, Helfer RE, Pollock C: The predictive questionnaire: A preliminary report, in Kempe CH, Helfer RE (Eds): Helping the Battered Child and His Family. Philadelphia, Lippincott, 1972
3. Steele B, Pollock C: A psychiatric study of parents who abuse infants and small children, in Helfer R, Kempe CH (Eds): The Battered Child. Chicago, University of Chicago, 1968
4. Pollock C: Early case findings as a means of prevention of child abuse, in Helfer R, Kempe CH (Eds): The Battered Child. Chicago, University of Chicago, 1968
5. Riser S: The fourth stage of labor: Family integration. Am J Nurs 74:870–874, 1974
6. Kempe CH: Approaches to preventing child abuse: The health visitor concept. Am J Dis Child 130:941–947, 1976
7. Schmitt BD, Kempe CH: The pediatrician's role in child abuse and neglect, in Current Problems in Pediatrics. Chicago, Yearbook Medical Publishers, 1975
8. Kastenbaum MA: A note on the additive partitioning of chi square in contingency tables. Biometrics 16:416–422, 1960
9. Frankenburg WK, Dodds JB, Fandel AW: The Denver Developmental Screening Test. Denver, LADOCA Project and Publishing Foundation, 1970
10. Martin H, Beezley P, Conway EF, et al.: The development of abused children, in Schulman I (Ed): Advances in Pediatrics (vol. 21). Chicago, Year Book Medical, p 974
11. Martin H (Ed): The Abused Child: Multidisciplinary Approach to Developmental Issues and Treatment. Cambridge, Mass., Ballinger, 1976
12. Helfer RE, Kempe CH: Child Abuse and Neglect. The Family and the Community. Cambridge, Mass., Ballinger, 1976

Susan O'Connor, Peter M. Vietze,

Howard M. Sandler, Kathryn B. Sherrod,

and William A. Altemeier, III,

17

Quality of Parenting and the Mother–Infant Relationship Following Rooming-in

Strange as it may seem there are people who do not believe in rooming-in, people who think that we are making much ado about very little. These people concede that rooming-in may very well help the mother to learn how to change a baby's diaper, and that it may allow the proud father to see his offspring oftener in the flesh. "But what of it," they say, "won't all this happen when the family takes the baby home from the hospital? Why go to all this fuss to change our accepted present-day nursery care?" I believe that such people have a right to ask these questions, to feel the way they do. It is squarely up to us to answer them, to prove to sceptics that rooming-in means more than what they call "nothing but an eight-day hospital stay," that rooming-in has a life-time significance.

—Richard W. Olmsted (1947)[1]

Author's note: Thirty-three years after Dr. Olmsted issued this challenge, the question of any lifelong significance of rooming-in remains justifiably debatable.

DEVELOPMENT OF THE OBSTETRIC NURSERY

Sometime during the first half of the 20th century, separation of normal newborns from their parents following delivery became a routine and noncontroversial component of American culture. It is not entirely clear when and why this circumstance developed, but the

349

origin of premature nurseries has been better documented than that of nurseries for healthy neonates. Although it would be reasonable to expect that the former developed first as a means of increasing survival of premature infants and the latter was a byproduct of intensive care nurseries, it appears that the two actually originated concurrently. In his biography of one of the world's first neonatologists. Silverman[2] reviews the early history of the technological revolution which made it possible to preserve the health of infants born prematurely. In 1878, E. S. Tarnier, a Parisian obstetrician, persuaded a Paris zookeeper to adapt his warming chamber for the rearing of poultry into warm-air incubators for premature infants. Dr. Tarnier introduced this device, called a "couveuse," in the Paris Maternity Hospital in 1880. One of Tarnier's students, Pierre Budin, established the world's first center for the care of premature infants in Paris in the late 1890s. Budin devised the gavage feeding system used today for nourishing these "weaklings" by introducing milk through a tube extending from the mouth into the stomach. In 1896, one of Budin's students, Martin Couney, was sent to the World Exposition in Berlin to exhibit the Tarnier incubator. Couney borrowed premature infants from the Berlin Charity Hospital and reared them in incubators. The exhibit, named the "Kinderbrutanstalt" or "child hatchery," was placed in the amusement section adjacent to the Congo Village and the Tyrolean Yodlers and was immensely popular; none of the babies died. The following summer, Couney traveled to the Victorian Era Exhibition in London only to find that English physicians would not lend him their premature infants for his incubators. Couney therefore returned to Paris, gathered three wicker baskets of prematures from Budin's nursery, and transported them across the Channel for his London exhibit. They attracted such crowds that certain unscrupulous entrepreneurs were prompted to obtain premature infants deviously to show in incubators for profit without adequate concern for their care. This led Couney to publish a warning about these imposters in the September 18, 1897, issue of *Lancet*.

From London, Couney went on to the Trans-Mississippi Exposition in Omaha in the summer of 1898, an event for which he claimed to have borrowed Chicago prematures. Couney then exhibited at the World Exposition in Paris in 1900 and at the Pan-American Exposition in Buffalo in 1901. He finally settled in 1903 at Coney Island, where he exhibited every summer for the next 40 years and apparently created a solid reputation in the medical community as a specialist in the care of premature infants. Couney was acknowledged in 1922 and again in 1928 in texts concerning the feeding and care of premature infants written by the leading American expert on these subjects at that time. He was honored in 1937 by the New York Medical Society and cooperated in the research of Arnold Gesell in 1939 and 1940 that led to *The Embryology of Behavior* published in 1945. Couney retired when the first premature infant unit opened in New York City at Cornell's New York Hospital. In 1970, 20 years after his death, a bronze plaque was placed on the boardwalk in Atlantic City to mark the site of some of his exhibitions, noting that "Dr. Couney was the first person in the United States to offer specialized care for premature infants." Martin Couney voiced one complaint during his work which in retrospect forecasted a current problem of neonatal intensive care units. Occasionally parents resisted reassuming responsibility for babies who had been reared away from them. While there is no record of the kind of parenting these children received upon returning to their families, Couney probably was observing parental detachment from premature offspring that is now a recognized complication of preterm delivery. Current estimates are that four percent of babies discharged from neonatal intensive care units are subsequently mistreated by their parents.[3]

Silverman's review provides historical insight about the development of premature nurseries, but similar documentation of the beginnings of the normal newborn nursery is scant. In their history of the origin of obstetric nurseries, Clifford and Davison[4] suggest that the practice of sequestering newborn infants into separate nurseries may have been an American innovation. They base their opinion upon a 1930 survey that found almost all older European obstetrical institutions to be without nurseries while hospital nurseries were opening in the United States around the turn of the century. Since American nurseries therefore appear to have preceded others, they reason that obstetric nurseries for healthy neonates probably were American contributions. They did find evidence of nurseries in London at the end of the 17th century, but these were established by a retired sea captain for wayward girls and their offspring, and probably were foundling homes rather than the equivalent of current newborn nurseries. Clifford and Davison trace the development of normal newborn nurseries in the United States back to the New York Lying-in Hospital. Founded in 1799, this was the first obstetrical hospital in the country and was quartered in the old Hamilton Fish House between 1894 and 1899. Initially newborns were suspended at the foot of their mothers' beds in elliptical cradles that hung on davits like lifeboats on ocean liners. In 1898 J. Pierpont Morgan commissioned a physician to study newer hospital designs which might be incorporated into plans for a reconstruction of the New York Lying-in Hospital. This opened in 1902 and contained new-born nurseries. The Boston

Lying-in Hospital, founded in 1832, did not have a nursery until 1898 when a "night nursery" was established for infants. This probably resulted from their mission to provide perinatal care for destitute and homeless women who were often too weak or ill to care for their newborns, particularly at night. Once established, the night nursery soon became the shelter where infants requiring special care were kept while other babies continued to stay with their mothers around the clock. Gradually hospital staff became increasingly concerned about neonatal diphtheria and streptococcal infections transmitted from mothers; as economically advantaged women began to have more of their babies in hospitals, maintenance of quiet and orderly wards became a priority. As a result, the concept of the night nursery expanded until it became a barrier partitioning parents from their newborns for most of the lying-in period.

THE ROOMING-IN MOVEMENT

Over the decades since Martin Couney's pioneering work in this country, the science of neonatal intensive care progressed at a remarkable pace; in comparison the normal newborn and his parents appear to have been relatively overlooked. Generations of physicians have had the impression that healthy full-term newborns are rather dull and something of a problem since they must be fed, cleaned, and kept free of infection until their mothers are ready to leave the hospital with them; and there are so many of them! An efficient and orderly nursery policy therefore should mandate that the well babies be kept in a central area where hospital staff have convenient and immediate access to them. Any regrets that parents might have about this arrangement have no validity since they will have the rest of their lives to be with their children once they leave the hospital. This approach to handling neonates and parents in the lying-in period has recently come under vehement attack, and there is a general impression that the roots of the rooming-in movement lie in the 1970s. In fact, it can be traced back at least into the early 1940s. In 1947 The Josiah Macy, Jr., Foundation sponsored a two day conference in New York City devoted largely to "The Rooming-in Movement."[5] Much of the impetus for this movement appears to have come from the Grace-New Haven Hospital, now the Yale-New Haven Medical Center. It was there in the early 1940s that Gesell and Ilg[6] coined the term "rooming-in" when they were at the Yale Clinic of Child Development; they may have been inspired by the term "lying-in." Edith Jackson,

then a Child Psychiatrist in the Department of Pediatrics at Yale,
took up the concept with vigor and enlisted the support of the Chiefs
of Pediatrics and Obstetrics at the Grace-New Haven Hospital. They
persuaded the administration to remodel the maternity unit to accommodate a new program of rooming-in. Dr. Jackson invested personal
funds into the project, and Mead Johnson provided some financial
support. The first rooming-in mother cared for in that hospital was
Mrs. Joan Erikson, wife of Erik Erikson; that baby became Professor
Kai Erikson, a sociologist at Yale.[7] Dr. Jackson trained pediatric
fellows in her rooming-in unit, one of whom was Richard Olmsted,[8]
the current editor for Behavioral Pediatrics of *The Journal of Pediatrics* and medical Director of the Children's Hospital in Denver. Edith
Jackson originated her rooming-in unit because she believed that
experience would encourage flexibility in childrearing. Experts on
parenting at the time tended to advise rigid caretaking policies, and
Dr. Jackson understood the result of this to be parenting difficulties
and behavioral disturbances in children.[9]

Further understanding of the origin of this enthusiasm for rooming-in comes from an article entitled "Rooming-in the newborn with
its lying-in mother."[10] Published in 1949 by Dr. Robert A. Strong, it
describes early nursery errors that created doubt about the wisdom of
centralized neonate care. These included confusing the family identity
of babies, mistaking boric acid for powdered dextrose, aniline poisoning from inks used to stamp diapers, and epidemics of infectious
diarrhea or impetigo spreading through nurseries. This latter problem
had a profound effect at Duke Hospital; in 1947 compulsory rooming-
in was begun following newspaper accounts of a Pennsylvania nursery
epidemic of diarrhea in which many babies died. In 1951, Dr. Angus
McBryde[11] published a report of this change at Duke and concluded:
"It is hoped that hospitals in the future will be built without nurseries
for normal newborn infants who are born of healthy mothers." Mc-
Bryde suggested that early closeness in the parent–infant relationship
provided by rooming-in may be "the first step in forming the proper
close family relationship."

In his 1949 paper, Strong indicated an organization known as The
Cornelian Corner was instrumental in promoting the rooming-in
movement. This group of psychiatrists, psychologists, and pediatricians met for the first time in the Detroit Athletic Club in November
1942 to advocate revision of methods for rearing children. They were
opposed to artificial separation of the newborn from his parents,
allowing children to "cry it out," bottle-feeding on a strict schedule,
and regimentation or rigid disciplinary methods.[12] The organization
was named in part after Cornelia, the daughter of Scipio Africanus,

the Elder and mother of the Gracchi. After the death of her husband, Cornelia refused multiple marriage proposals to devote herself to the education of her children. When asked to exhibit her jewels, she presented her sons. The second word in the name came from an old custom; in days when the kitchen was used by all of the family as a living room, a nursing mother would face a corner of the room to shelter the baby from disturbance.

Strong's statements about the rooming-in movement, made 30 years ago, could be mistaken as current. He said the goal of the movement was to more satisfactorily fulfill "the psychologic requirements of the human infant so that its mental growth will be normal and it will be safeguarded from the genesis of factors which may result in behavior disturbances in childhood or mental illness in later life." Strong believed that "the rooming-in of the newborn with its lying-in mother is the most progressive step in mental hygiene in the first half of the 20th century." He described the movement as a recent enlightened campaign led by pediatricians and psychologists who had generated "a rather large number of papers, reports, and discussions" with the result that "it will not be long before many more hospitals will have to provide rooming-in facilities to meet demands which will be made."[10]

In spite of Dr. Strong's optimism, the historical trail becomes faint after 1950. It appears that enthusiasm for rooming-in faltered until this decade when several interrelated factors rekindled the campaign to abolish separation of parents and infants during the lying-in period. The first was a remarkable explosion of interest and knowledge about the behavioral competence of normal neonates and their relationship with parents. This surge of scientific activity refuted the notion that newborns are passive individuals who have little or no impact upon their environment and introduced investigators of normal newborns into the hospital territory of physicians. The best example of the latter is the legion of psychologists utilizing the Brazelton Neonatal Behavioral Assessment Scales; they have brought the expanding knowledge base about babies and the parent–infant relationship to the doorstep of physicians, who in turn have become increasingly concerned about hospital policies which prevent parents from experiencing the capabilities of their newborns.

The second factor influencing hospital and physician policy has been a consumer's movement of young parents who have become convinced that they have a right to their own preferences about childbirth and contact with their babies after delivery. One segment of this movement advocates home birth, and physicians alarmed about the well-being of children born at home without facilities to meet complications have begun reforming hospital childbirth to lessen interest in home birth. The third major influence in favor of rooming-in has been the work and public appearances of two pediatricians, John Kennell and Marshall Klaus, of Case Western Reserve University. These men have revived the scientific question of the impact early mother–infant contact might have upon the long-term bond between the two. They also have advocated changes in hospital policies to permit flexibility for normal childbirth. The results of their research have been summarized in earlier chapters.

THE NASHVILLE STUDY OF ADEQUACY OF PARENTING FOLLOWING ROOMING-IN

The studies of Klaus and Kennell and associates[13,14] suggest that early and extended postpartum contact enhance the attachment of mother to infant. Their findings led to a simple hypothesis. If Kennell and Klaus were correct, then perhaps extra parent–infant postpartum contact also would influence parenting adequacy. We were in an ideal position to test that hypothesis. Nursery policy at the time in our hospital separated newborns from their mothers until at least 12 hours after delivery, and there was no parental contact with the baby during the first hour following birth. After the first 12 hours, babies were with their mothers only every four hours for feeding. The hospital served a low-income population and delivered about 1400 babies each year, and we estimated eight to ten percent of these infants experienced significant parenting inadequacy. We therefore randomly assigned children born at Nashville General Hospital over a 22-month period to rooming-in and control groups. Hospital staff and patients were not informed about the hypothesis of the study. When obtaining informed consent in prenatal clinic, study mothers were told that the hospital was evaluating some new services and that the purpose of the investigation was to determine what "makes some mothers and babies get along so well with so few problems while other mothers and babies seem to have a lot of problems" and "to learn more about what leads happy mother–child relationships to break down."

Mothers in the control group experienced the existing hospital routine mentioned above. The rooming-in mothers followed this same routine until at least seven hours after delivery and then had their newborns with them for up to eight hours daily prior to discharge. After bed assignment, mothers were not forced to room-in, and seven preferred not to have it. These were retained in the rooming-in group for data analysis, since failure to do so might bias results in favor of the hypothesis. A rooming-in mother could be visited by the baby's father or maternal grandmother any time the baby was in her room; control mothers received visitors only during regularly scheduled hospital visiting hours, when babies were in the nursery. All chart and record reviews were done without knowledge of rooming-in or control status. The first occurred shortly after each baby was sent home, but before outcome data were collected, to eliminate subjects who had perinatal complications. By predefined criteria, only healthy primigravidous mothers who delivered normal, single, term infants vaginally and who planned to keep the babies were included. If either mother or baby developed a condition which precluded mother–infant contact, whether rooming-in or control, they were dropped from the study. Four additional families were dropped from each group when they moved out of our area immediately after delivery.

Although the full study occurred over a 22-month period, results are available so far only for the first nine months of deliveries.[15] During this time, 143 rooming-in and 158 control mothers and their babies met criteria for inclusion in the study. Over the first 48 hours postpartum, the control mothers averaged 2.15 hours with their newborns during the daytime, while mothers who participated in rooming-in averaged 11.44 hours. In order to examine the hypothesis, outcome data were gathered when the children averaged 17 months old and ranged from 12 to 21 months. Outcome information came from review of each child's hospital medical record and all reports of abuse or neglect in Tennessee, noting any episodes of physical or sexual abuse, nonorganic failure-to-thrive, voluntary surrender of major caretaking responsibility for the child, abandonment, medical or physical neglect, or hospital admission for any other pathology in the mother–infant relationship. Inadequacy in parenting was considered substantial if growth was affected, more than one hospitalization resulted, investigation by Protective Services confirmed maltreatment, abnormal development resulted, the parents voluntarily or involuntarily relinquished their responsibility for the child, or if the child was physically abused by the parent or with the parent's knowledge and consent. Episodes of parenting inadequacy not meeting one or more of these criteria were classified as minor. This study did not offer any form of intervention after discharge, and the parents decided themselves where to take their babies for medical care. Subject children who returned to the study hospital were cared for by staff practitioners who were either unaware of the study or unaware of which patients were in the study. Statistical comparisons of outcome were made using Fisher's Exact Test.

Rooming-in and control groups were compared for a variety of independent variables, and no differences were found for infant birth-weight, Apgar score, or sex. Mothers in the two groups were compa-rable in age, marital status, race, plans for breastfeeding, years of formal education, time spent with hospital nurses on the ward, employment or welfare status, and familiarity with the concept of rooming-in before delivery. About half of the babies were male, 60 percent of the mothers were married, the ratio of white to black was 1.7 to 1, and one-third were employed or had a family member who was employed. The mothers were young; both mean and median age was 18 years. Nine (six percent) rooming-in and 15 (nine percent) control families were completely lost to follow-up. The remaining 134 rooming-in and 143 control children constitute the base upon which all comparisons of outcome were made and did not differ in frequency of visits to the study hospital's emergency room or clinics nor in probability of being diagnosed as "well baby."

Parenting inadequacy occurred in ten control and two rooming-in families (p < 0.05). One rooming-in and nine control families had a substantial breakdown in parenting as defined earlier (p < 0.02). One rooming-in and eight control children were hospitalized at least once because of parenting inadequacy alone or in combination with an illness (p < 0.05). One rooming-in family and five control families were referred to Protective Services. Five control children but none of the rooming-in children were exclusively or primarily in the caretak-ing custody of adults other than their parents at the time of data analysis (p < 0.05), and the altered living arrangement appeared to be permanent for four of these control children. It is of interest that one of the two rooming-in mothers with evidence of parenting inade-quacy was one of the seven who preferred not to room-in with their newborns.

These results are generally consistent with other studies that have associated longer duration of breastfeedings,[16] more affectionate and self-confident mothering,[11,13,14,17-20] and less infant crying[19] with extra mother–infant postpartum contact. While the findings are in-teresting, there are, however, problems with the study that should be considered before conclusions are made. The first is a theoretical issue. Rooming-in mothers were permitted expanded visiting privileges in the hospital. The control mothers not only were restricted to regular hospital visiting hours but also were not allowed to have their babies with them to share with visitors. It is therefore conceivable that the improved parenting resulted in part from solidification of the family unit, rather than from the extra parent–infant contact alone. These expanded visiting privileges confound theoretical interpretation of the findings. On the other hand, the visitation issue is not a practical problem since introduction of family members into rooming-in is natural and seems intuitively desirable. The second problem with the study is that a relatively small number of parenting difficulties were available for statistical analysis, and the range of difficulties extended from the common phenomenon of nonorganic failure-to-thrive (six percent of babies born at the study hospital develop this problem during infancy) to subdural hematomas inflicted by a mother. Until the outcome of infants born during the remaining 13 months of this 22-month study is available, it seems prudent to withhold conclusions about the value of rooming-in to primary prevention of parenting difficulties.

MECHANISM OF EFFECT OF ROOMING-IN

The mechanism by which a few extra hours of mother–infant contact during the lying-in period could influence subsequent behavior has yet to be elucidated. Review of the literature provides a few clues, however. Investigations of certain animal species have determined the existence of a sensitive postparturition period for maternal acceptance of her offspring. Goat, sheep, and rat mothers, separated from their young for very brief intervals immediately after delivery, often fail to establish normal caretaking patterns.[21–24] Because this sensitive period involves several lower animal species and appears to be mediated by hormones which also are present in human females,[25] others have suggested the phenomenon may have some correlates in man.[26] Partly based on this hypothesis, Klaus and Kennell conducted the prototypic study of extra mother–infant postpartum contact in the early 1970s. They compared a control group of mothers with 14 low-income primiparous mothers who received an hour of skin-to-skin contact with their newborns during the first three hours after delivery and rooming-in for five hours daily during the first three postpartum days. The former had no early contact and were with their infants only for feeding every four hours. Differences were noted between the two groups as long as two years after delivery.[13,14,27] Because treatment mothers received both early contact and rooming-in, it was not clear that contact during a "sensitive period" immediately following delivery explained the findings. Several other investigators have completed studies with results at least compatible with this hypothesis, however. For example, deChateau and his colleagues[18,19,28] allowed an experimental group of 22 primiparous women and their infants skin-to-skin contact for less than 30 minutes during the first postpartum hour. Thereafter, this and the control groups experienced equivalent contact with their infants. Differences between the extra contact and control groups were found at 36 hours, three months, and one year postpartum. Hales et al.[17] studied three groups. The first had contact with their nude infants while on the delivery table and for the first 45 minutes in the recovery room; the second had the same experience but not until 12 hours after delivery; the third had no contact until 12 hours after delivery when *clothed* infants were brought to them. Subsequently, all three groups were with their newborns during waking hours for two days until discharge. Observations of mother–infant interaction made when the babies were 36 hours old identified differences in maternal affectionate behaviors between the groups. Carlsson and associates[29,30] found that mothers who had early contact with their infants during the first postpartum hour differed in frequency of contact behaviors with their newborns when compared with mothers experiencing no early contact. The effect was observed during the first week following delivery but could not be demonstrated five weeks later.

Some investigations have failed to substantiate the sensitive period hypothesis, but methodological differences may explain conflicting results. Taylor and his colleagues[31–33] compared no-early-contact mothers versus those with their infants for an hour beginning 30 minutes after delivery; a variety of outcome measures extending to 12 months postpartum were examined and virtually no differences were found. The design of this study differed from those of deChateau, Hales, and Carlsson in that the early contact was not nude, skin-to-skin, suggesting that mode of early contact may have a crucial influence upon subsequent behavior. This possibility has been examined by a comparison of nude versus swaddled early mother–infant contact.[34] Mode of early contact had no effect upon infant scores on the Brazelton Neonatal Behavioral Assessment Scales nor on infant behavior during observed mother–infant interaction at 2 and 28 days postpartum. Mothers receiving nude contact, however, demonstrated a higher level of facial expressiveness directed to their infants, while swaddled contact mothers talked to their infants more than skin-to-skin contact mothers. Interpretation of these results is somewhat difficult, however, because there was no control group that lacked early contact.

The weight of evidence resulting from these studies tends to support the sensitive period hypothesis, providing that early contact is skin-to-skin. Furthermore, human infants do seem to be uniquely prepared for contact with their parents soon after birth. During the first postpartum hour, normal term newborns tend to be more alert than during the subsequent 12 hours[35,36]; they will turn to a human voice and seem to prefer the higher pitch of a female.[37] The human face configuration appears to be of greater interest than a scrambled face to the newborn in the delivery room, as evidenced by visual fixation and head turning to follow the former.[38] In turn, human mothers place great emphasis upon eye contact with their infants during initial encounters.[39] Therefore, human mothers and neonates seem particularly primed for acquaintance during the first few hours after delivery. In our rooming-in study, however, mother–infant contact did not begin until seven hours after birth at the earliest. It appears that any increase in mother–infant contact during the postpartum hospitalization, regardless of its timing, may influence subsequent interaction. The model of a sensitive period, derived from studies of very early mother–infant postpartum contact, therefore may not explain our observation of increased parenting adequacy following rooming-in. Furthermore, while it is true that a sensitive postpartum period in man might extend over days rather than hours, this hypothesis still does not reveal insight into the mechanism of effect. For these reasons, a second study was done to examine the process by which rooming-in might enhance the bond between mother and infant.

The design was identical to that of the first study except: mothers of any parity were included as subjects, risk status for subsequent child maltreatment was estimated for each mother prenatally, and outcome data were collected using various psychological techniques rather than parenting adequacy. Maternal risk status during pregnancy was determined using an experimental interview described elsewhere[40]; it was developed to determine whether prenatal clinic patients at risk for subsequent child maltreatment could be identified during pregnancy. In a separate study, this instrument concentrated 60 percent of families who were later reported for abuse or delivered infants who failed to grow for nonorganic reasons, and half of those reported for neglect into the 20 percent predicted to be high risk.[41] The interview was used in this rooming-in study to examine the possibility that the randomization process had failed to equally distribute high-risk families between the treatment and control groups. Outcome data pertaining to rooming-in were collected using Brazelton's Neonatal Behavioral Assessment Scales[42] at 48 hours postpartum, The Bayley Scales of Infant Development at nine months of age, and direct observations of mother–infant interaction at 48 hours and at one, three, six, and twelve months following delivery.[43] The Neonatal Behavioral Assessment Scales consist of 27 behavioral and 20 neurological items which quantitate sensory, motor, and neurologic integrity of the infant. The 27 behavior items are clustered into four factors of social and motor control, state control, and response to stress. Initial and predominant states of the infant are also monitored on a six-point scale from one (quiet sleep) to four (quiet alert) to six (crying). Observations of mother–infant interaction were made by trained assistants using Electro General Datamyte Recorders. Predetermined codes relating to the type of caretaker setting, infant state, mother–infant proximity, and mother and infant behaviors were entered, while the time in seconds from the beginning of the observation was inserted automatically. Each tape was transmitted to a PDP 11/40 computer, edited, and made available for data reduction and retrieval. The codes for mother and infant each consisted of nine mutually exclusive combinations of four basic behavior categories and one code to represent none of the others. The four basic maternal behaviors were visual attention, vocalization, smile, and tactile play. Those for the infant were visual· attention, smile, vocalization, and crying.

The 90 control and 62 rooming-in dyads of the second study did not differ in initial independent descriptive variables (listed on page 357) and were similar to the subjects of the first study except for being slightly older (mean age at delivery 21 years), probably because multiparous women were included. About 17 percent of mothers in both groups were estimated during pregnancy to be at high risk for subsequent child maltreatment. The data that follow suggest to us that rooming-in influenced the parent–child relationship by facilitating reciprocal contingent responses that mutually reinforce synchronous interaction. All differences presented below are significant at less than 0.05 unless otherwise noted, and the results of the second study are summarized in Table 17-1.

At 48 hours, mean scores for first and second most predominant states during the Brazelton Neonatal Behavioral Assessment revealed that the rooming-in babies maintained a higher state of alertness: 4.44 versus 3.96 for the most prevalent state and 4.61 versus 3.97 for the next most frequent state. Infants in the two groups did not differ in their four cluster scores from these Scales. Mother–infant interaction observation at 48 hours found control infants more often alert while the rooming-in babies slept more, and rooming-in mothers spoke more softly to their babies. An interesting observation from the 48-hour data is that the rooming-in mothers were doing more non-

Table 17-1

Summary of Differences Between Rooming-in and Control Groups Over The
First Year

AT 48 HOURS

  First and second most predominant BNBAS* states higher for rooming-in
  During observation:
   Rooming-in babies more often asleep
   Control babies more often alert
   Rooming-in mothers speak to babies more softly and engage in
    more non-feeding-related caretaking

AT ONE MONTH

  Rooming-in children more often drowsy
  Control infants cry more
  Control mothers doing more non-feeding-related caretaking
  Control homes noisier

AT THREE MONTHS

  Rooming-in mothers exhibit more negative emotion physically toward
   children

AT SIX MONTHS

  Rooming-in mothers look at infants more and more rapidly respond to
   distress
  Control babies more often drowsy
  Rooming-in children tend to more alertness
  Control children tend to more crying

AT NINE MONTHS

  Rooming-in children more advanced in motor development

AT TWELVE MONTHS

  Rooming-in mothers smile at children more
  Tendency for rooming-in mothers to look at and speak to children more
  Rooming-in children more often drowsy but interact more with mothers

---

 *Brazelton Newborn Behavioral Assessment Scales

feeding-related caretaking of their infants. A possible explanation for
this is that the control mother perceived her task during the brief
contact with her baby to be relief of hunger, while the rooming-in
mother had time to do other things with her infant. This suggests
that rooming-in allowed the mothers to begin recognizing and responding to the cues of their infants.

When the infants were one month old, the rooming-in children
spent more time drowsy, while control infants cried more. Both groups
spent about the same amount of time fussing, but rooming-in pairs
were able to lower infant state to calmer levels while control pairs
were more likely to proceed to infant crying. Control mothers were
engaged in more non-feeding-related caretaking and their children

were experiencing more noise in their homes. This pattern at one month suggests that the rooming-in pairs had established their reciprocal interaction smoothly but control dyads were still negotiating synchrony.

The three-month data revealed nothing that significantly differentiated the two groups except one subjective rating scale which suggested that the rooming-in mothers expressed more negative emotion physically toward their babies. We have considered several ways of interpreting this difference. On the surface, it seems to contradict our hypothesis. However, possible scores on this scale range from a desirable score of one to a disturbing score of five. Since the mean score for the control group was 1.00 while the mean for the rooming-in group was 1.08, the difference although statistically significant was extremely small and may not have much real meaning. On the other hand, the differences could be meaningful and reflect different cycles of evolving relationship for the control and rooming-in mother–infant dyads. The period around three months postpartum is often a transition point when the infant's blossoming behavioral repertoire is accentuating maternal affection for her baby. It may be that the rooming-in mothers preceded the control mothers in intensification of affection; if so, the difference could have resulted from the control mothers just entering a transition in their relationships with their babies which the rooming-in mothers had already passed. Alternatively, the rooming-in mothers may have experienced a greater need to establish some independence at three months due to the preceding weeks of engrossment with their infants.

When the babies were six months old, rooming-in mothers looked at them more than did control mothers, and controls responded to infant distress less rapidly. Control babies were in the drowsy state more often, and the rooming-in children tended (p < 0.10) to be in the alert state more while the control babies tended (p < 0.10) to cry more. At twelve months, rooming-in mothers smiled at their babies more and tended (p < 0.10) to look at and talk to them more. Although rooming-in babies spent more time in a drowsy state, the control babies interacted less with their mothers. Scores on the Bayley Scales at nine months indicated rooming-in infants surpassed control babies in motor development; mean scores were 112 versus 102.

These findings over the first twelve months following delivery suggested that the rooming-in mothers and babies were engaged in interchanges which were more rewarding than those of controls. We gained a picture of a cascading effect following rooming-in: increased opportunity for positive reinforcement by reciprocal interchange encouraged subsequent interactions between mother and baby which in turn were mutually rewarding and so forth in a self-perpetuating cycle of synchronous maternal and infant behaviors. It appeared that the rooming-in mothers and babies accumulated more experience with contingent responses and mutual gratification during the immediate postnatal period. This served as a base upon which their relationship was to grow and provided more potential for building upon subsequent interchanges with one another. The results of the five-year follow-up of Klaus and Kennell's original Case Western Reserve study are also consistent with this theory of the rooming-in mechanism. They found that the manner in which extra-contact mothers spoke to their two-year-old children correlated with the performance of the children on standardized testing when they were five.[44] This correlation was not observed for control subjects, suggesting that extra contact pairs had been more capable of capitalizing upon their verbal exchanges while the controls lacked comparable potential in their relationships.

Although Sander et al.[45,46] employed a study design that differed from other investigations of early or extended mother–infant postpartum contact, their work also seems to reinforce our interpretation of the above data. They randomly assigned infants who were to be placed for adoption to either continuous rooming-in with a single nonparent caretaker or a nursery with multiple caretakers for the first ten days after birth. As might be expected, the nursery infants received caretaking asynchronous with distress signaling; their crying increased and by ten days occurred mostly at night. In contrast, caretaking in the rooming-in setting achieved synchrony with infant distress within the first few days. The infants cried less, and by the end of ten days did most of their crying during daytime hours. On the 11th day, nursery infants were placed in continuous rooming-in with one nurse, a situation analogous to discharge of the baby from the newborn nursery to parental care at home. Infant distress gradually decreased as caretaking synchrony was established, but only after several days of episodic distraught infant behavior requiring frequent caretaking intervention. The nursery infants differed from the rooming-in babies until the end of the study at two months in that they failed to achieve the same degree of stability from week to week in crying, sleeping, and time spent looking at the human face.[47] These findings suggest that rooming-in permits early adaptation between infant and caretaker with a minimum of stress to either. The alternative arrangement of nursery caretaking delays this adaptation and renders it more difficult because of increased and inconveniently timed infant crying plus less stability in infant behavior to which the caretaker must adapt.

Any proposed mechanism for the affects of rooming-in must account for the observation that most parents who lack extra postpartum contact with their infants do not have recognizable problems rearing their children. For example, over 90 percent of the control group in our first study suffered no visible adverse consequence from a lack of increased contact. It is possible, however, that rooming-in exerts the greatest positive effect upon parents who are already predisposed to maltreatment when their child is born. If the parent is one whose past experience and current stress create potential for difficulties in parenting, rooming-in might ease adaptation into early parenthood and thereby avoid initiation of a behavior cycle with the child that could lead to child maltreatment. For such parents, rooming-in may reduce subsequent parenting inadequacy by locking parent and infant into reciprocal regulation from the beginning. On the other hand, parents equipped with psychological strength or economic means may adapt to early separation from their infants with relatively few problems. This could also explain why some investigators[29–33,48–50] find only transient or no differences between extra contact and control groups when studying middle class families.

CONCLUSION

This field of inquiry into human behavior is relatively new, and many questions remain unanswered. The duration of the sensitive period for postpartum contact, if one exists, is unknown. The relative importance of immediate contact versus delayed rooming-in and of skin-to-skin versus clothed parent–infant contact are unclear. There is little agreement about the mechanism and duration of effects of extra contact, and it is not established whether some parents are affected differently than others by such experience. Nevertheless, the notion that placing mother and baby in early and prolonged physical intimacy so that the mother will be more strongly attached to her baby is commonly perceived as established in efficacy and of proven importance. There are now clinicians who speak of mothers and babies whom they have "bonded" as if it were a technical achievement. In fact, it is not yet totally clear that any such phenomenon actually exists for human mothers and their offspring.[51] However, there is sufficient evidence that expanded contact may have a beneficial influence on the mother–infant relationship to warrant further research.

REFERENCES

1. Olmsted RW: Rooming-in as a family experience at the Grace-New Haven Community Hospital (University Service), in Senn MJE (Ed): Problems Of Early Infancy. Transactions of First Conference. New York, The Josiah Macy, Jr., Foundation, 1948
2. Silverman WA: Incubator-baby side shows. Pediatrics 64:127–141, 1979
3. Hunter RS, Kilstrom N, Kraybill EN, et al.: Antecedents of child abuse and neglect in premature infants: A prospective study in a newborn intensive care unit. Pediatrics 61:629–635, 1978
4. Clifford SH, Davison WC: The origin of obstetric nurseries. J Pediatr 44:205–212, 1954
5. Senn MJE (Ed): Problems Of Early Infancy. Transactions of First Conference. New York, The Josiah Macy, Jr., Foundation, 1948
6. Gesell A, Ilg F, Learned J, et al.: Infant and Child in the Culture of Today. New York, Harper and Bros., 1943
7. Senn MJE: Personal communication (Southbury, Ct., 1979)
8. Olmsted RW: Personal communication (The Children's Hospital, Denver,1979)
9. Jackson EB: The initiation of a rooming-in project at the Grace-New Haven Community Hospital, in Senn MJE (Ed): Problems of Early Infancy. Transactions of First Conference. New York, The Josiah Macy, Jr., Foundation, 1948
10. Strong RA: Rooming-in the newborn with its lying-in mother. Diplomate 21:301–309, 1949
11. McBryde A: Compulsory rooming-in in the ward and private newborn service at Duke Hospital. JAMA 145:625–627, 1951
12. Moloney JC: The Cornelian Corner and its rationale, in Senn MJE (Ed): Problems of Early Infancy. Transactions of First Conference. New York, The Josiah Macy, Jr., Foundation, 1948
13. Klaus MH, Jerauld R, Kreger NC, et al.: Maternal attachment: Importance of the first postpartum days, N Engl J Med 286:460–463, 1972
14. Kennell JH, Jerauld R, Wolfe H, et al.: Maternal behavior one year after early and extended postpartum contact. Dev Med Child Neurol 16:172–179, 1974
15. O'Connor S. Vietze PM, Sherrod KB, et al.: Reduced incidence of parenting inadequacy following rooming-in. Pediatrics (in press)
16. Kennell JH, Trause MA, Klaus MH: Evidence for a sensitive period in the human mother. Ciba Found Symp 33:87–101, 1975
17. Hales DJ, Lozoff B, Sosa R, et al.: Defining the limits of the maternal sensitive period. Dev Med Child Neurol 19:454–461, 1977
18. deChateau P, Wiberg B: Long-term effect on mother–infant behavior of extra contact during the first hour postpartum. I. First observations at 36 hours. Acta Paediatr Scand 66:137–144, 1977
19. deChateau P, Wiberg B: Long-term effect on mother-infant behavior of extra contact during the first hour postpartum. II. Follow-up at three months. Acta Paediatr Scand 66:145–151, 1977
20. Greenberg M, Rosenberg I, Lind J: First mothers rooming-in with their newborns: Its impact on the mother. Am J Orthopsychiatr 43:783–788, 1973
21. Klopfer P: Mother love: What turns it on? Am Sci 59:404–407, 1971
22. Herscher L, Moore AU, Richmond JB: Effect of postpartum separation of mother and kid on maternal care in the domestic goat. Science 128:1342–1343, 1958
23. Herscher L, Richmond JB, Moore AU: Maternal behavior in sheep and goats, in Rheingold HL (Ed): Maternal Behavior in Mammals. New York, Wiley, 1963

24. Rosenblatt JS: The basis of synchrony in the behavioral interaction between the mother and her offspring in the laboratory rat, in Foss BM (Ed): Determinants of Infant Behavior (vol. 3). London, Methuen, 1965, pp 17–32

25. Siegel HI, Rosenblatt JS: Estrogen-induced maternal behavior in hysterectomized-ovariectomized virgin rats. Physiol Behav 14:465–471, 1975

26. Klaus MH, Kennell JH: Human maternal and paternal behavior, in Klaus MH, Kennell JH (Ed): Maternal–Infant Bonding. St. Louis, The CV Mosby Company, 1976, pp 38–98

27. Ringler NM, Kennell JH, Jarvelle R, et al.: Mother to child speech at two years. Effect of early postnatal contact. J. Pediatr 86:141–144, 1975

28. deChateau P: Effects of hospital practices on synchrony in the development of the infant–parent relationship, in Taylor PM (ed): Parent–Infant Relationships. New York, Grune & Stratton, 1980, p 137.

29. Carlsson SG, Fagerberg H, Horneman G, et al.: Effects of amount of contact between mother and child on the mother's nursing behavior. Developmental Psychology 11:143–150, 1978

30. Carlsson SG, Fagerberg H, Horneman G, et al.: Effects of various amounts of contact between mother and child on the mother's nursing behavior: A follow-up study. Infant Behav Dev 2:209–214, 1979

31. Taylor PM, Taylor FH, Broussard ER, et al.: Effects of extra contact on early maternal attitudes, perceptions, and behaviors. Presented at the biennial meeting of the Society for Research in Child Development. San Francisco, 1979 (unpublished)

32. Campbell SG, Maloni J, Dickey D: Early contact and maternal perceptions of infant temperament. Presented at biennial meeting of the Society for Research in Child Development. San Francisco, 1979 (unpublished)

33. Ottaviano C, Campbell SG, Taylor PM: Early contact and infant–mother attachment at one year. Presented at biennial meeting of the Society for Research in Child Development. San Francisco, 1979 (unpublished)

34. Gewirtz JL, Sebris SL: Maternal "attachment" outcomes and infant performance at 2 and 28 days as assessed by the Brazelton Neonatal Scale and by the mother. Biennial meeting of the Society for Research in Child Development. San Francisco, March, 1979

35. Desmond MM, Rudolph AJ, Phitaksphraiwan P: The transitional care nursery; A mechanism for preventive medicine in the newborn. Pediatr Clin North Am 13:651–668, 1966

36. Emde RN, Swedberg J, Suzuki B: Human wakefulness and biological rhythms after birth. Arch Gen Psychiatr 32:780–786, 1975

37. Eisenberg RB, Griffin EJ, Coursin DB, et al.: Auditory behavior in the human neonate: A preliminary report. J Speech Hear Res 7:245–269, 1964

38. Goren CC, Sarty M, Wu P: Visual following and pattern discrimination of face-like stimuli by newborn infants. Pediatrics 56:544–548, 1975

39. Klaus MH, Kennell JH, Plumb N, et al.: Human maternal behavior at the first contact with her young. Pediatrics 46:187–192, 1970

40. Altemeier WA, Vietze PM, Sherrod KB, et al.: Prediction of child maltreatment in pregnancy. J Am Acad Child Psych 18:205–218, 1979

41. Altemeier WA, Vietze PM, Sandler H, et al.: Prediction of child maltreatment in pregnancy. International Workshop on the "at risk" Infant. Tel Aviv, 1979 (in press)

42. Brazelton TB: Neonatal behavioral assessment scale, in: Clinics in Developmental Medicine (No. 50). London, Spastics International Medical, 1973

43. Anderson B, Vietze PM, Faulstich G, et al.: Observation Manual For Assessment of Behavior Sequences Between Infant and Mother: Newborn to 24 Months. JSAS Catalog of Selected Documents. *8*, 31, 1978

44. Ringler N, Trause MA, Klaus M, et al.: The effects of extra postpartum contact and maternal speech patterns on children's IQs, speech, and language comprehension at five. Child Development 49:862–865, 1978

45. Sander LW, Stechler G, Julia H, et al.: Early mother–infant interaction and 24-hour patterns of activity and sleep. J Am Acad Child Psych 9:103–123, 1970

46. Burns P, Sander LW, Stechler G, et al.: Distress in feeding: Short-term effects of caretaker environment of the first 10 days. J Am Acad Child Psych 11:427–439, 1972

47. Sander LW: Infant and caretaking environment: Investigation and conceptualization of adaptive behavior in a system of increasing complexity, in Anthony EJ (Ed): Explorations in Child Psychiatry. New York, Plenum Press, 1975, pp 129–166

48. Barnett DR, Leiderman PH, Grobstein R, et al.: Neonatal separation: The maternal side of interactional deprivation. Pediatrics 45:197–205, 1970

49. Leifer A, Leiderman P. Barnett C, et al.: Effects of mother–infant separation on maternal attachment behavior. Child Dev 43:1203–1218, 1972

50. Leiderman P, Leifer A, Seashore M, et al.: Mother–infant interaction: Effects of early deprivation, prior experience and sex on infant. Research Publications for Research in Nervous and Mental Disease 51:154–175, 1973

51. Vietze PM, O'Connor S: Mother-to-infant bonding: A review, in Kretchmer N, Brasel J (Eds): The Biology of Child Development. New York, Masson Publishing (in press)

Index

a
b
c
d
e
f
g
0 h
1 i
8 2 j